American

GOVERNMENT

Using 'The Force' to Defend a 'Galaxy' Near You

LISA DAVIS

Kendall Hunt
publishing company

www.kendallhunt.com
Send all inquiries to:
4050 Westmark Drive
Dubuque, IA 52004-1840

ISBN 978-1-4652-4702-5

Printed in the United States of America
10 9 8 7 6 5 4 3 2 1

CONTENTS

ACKNOWLEDGEMENTS

I dedicate this epic saga to the following people:
First, to my family – my mom, Linda, my dad, Keith, and my brother, Chris
It was you three who taught me to keep my eyes on the stars

Second, to the many wise professors who taught me the ways of the Force
And how to harness its power
From St. Charles Community College
Westminster College
And the University of Missouri-Columbia
The Force is strong with you all!!

Third, to the many amazing employers, friends, and colleagues
I have had the pleasure to encounter, befriend, and learn from over the years
There are frankly too many of you to list, but you know who you are
Never underestimate your power!

Lastly, and most importantly
To my former students – it was you who taught me to reflect
My current students – it is you who encourage me to hope
The students of tomorrow, both near and far – it is you who dare me to dream
And you, the fortunate few, who possess the power to shape America's future

Ignite your lightsabers, my friends, and let the 'Force' flow through your veins.
Learn the ways of the 'Jedi' and aid me in defending the freedoms our Founders fought for
By daring to make a difference in a democracy near you.

PROLOGUE

An Introduction from the Kingdom of Far, Far Away...

"Once there was a princess, but she had an enchantment upon her of a fearful sort which could only be broken by love's first kiss. She was locked away in a castle guarded by a terrible fire-breathing dragon. Many brave knights had tried to free her from this dreadful prison, but none prevailed. She waited in the dragon's keep in the highest room in the tallest tower for her true love and true love's first kiss."......."Yeah, like that's ever gonna happen. What a load of (flushing sound)...." (Myers).

Shrek is an Ogre but turns out to be the hero of this fairy tale gone wrong.

This is the opening dialogue in the groundbreaking animated film, *Shrek*. It tells the story of an Ogre going on a Quest to rescue his home in a swamp which is overrun by fairy tale creatures that have been displaced by the diminutive Lord Farquaad. For those of you who have seen the film, you know that on the Quest, Shrek encounters and rescues Princess Fiona, the damsel in distress described in the tale above, but she turns out to be far different and much more important than anyone could possibly imagine (Adamson and Jensen). This book is very similar to the storyline in *Shrek*. This goal of this book, put simply, is to restore power in America to its rightful owners just as Shrek tries (and succeeds) to get his swamp back.

One of the biggest problems in this country is that the powers that be seem to discourage people from talking about government and politics. We are told at a young age that discussing government in public is inappropriate, because it almost always leads to someone being mad at someone else. We are told that discussions about government are boring and often unintelligible. When one thinks of politics or government, an image of a stuffy professor or political talking head is speaking like the teacher in the *Peanuts* comic strip, "Wah wah wah wah wah." Actively participating in discussions about government is difficult because so many people are under-informed or, most unfortunately, they believe the 'truth' aired by the media (from both sides of the political spectrum) is unbiased, Absolute Truth. In all honesty, many believe that government is boring because they don't care or don't feel that their voice carries any weight in the big scheme of things.

I have been an American government professor for nearly five years now, and I remember the first day I walked into the classroom. The students – all of them – had blank stares on their faces. Many had their heads on their desks. Clearly, they expected American Government class to be a boring, sleepy affair. I swore that day that my classes would never be boring; they would engage students, encourage participation, and (hopefully) spur political activism. The first topic I tackled was, according to my students, the worst topic in government – the United States Constitution. Instead of approaching it like most professors do – quizzing students about a document most of them have never read or given any thought to, I compared the important elements of the document to another pastime in America – Major League Baseball. For every important element in the Constitution, I connect it to some rule or common occurrence in or during a baseball game that the students could refer back to in order to better understand and retain information associated with the Constitution. Being a professor in St. Louis right after the miraculous World Series comeback win by the Cardinals in 2011, baseball was a topic I was sure would resonate with the young members of Cardinal Nation sitting in my classroom. It did – a lot.

I got rave-reviews about the baseball lesson and decided to gradually shift all of my course lectures in a similar direction. For every topic in government, I found a comparison in pop culture, sports, or the world of enter-

Busch Stadium – St. Louis' field of dreams

tainment, and the addition of new 'analogy' lectures only increased the demand and popularity of my course. And so, that is how this book is written. For every topic relevant to American Government, I have devised a comparison for it from the stuff our media and government says is more important than the self-governance that is indicative of a properly functioning government.

We, the People, are told that video games, movies, sports, and music are where our attention should lie; it has been like that for years, and the media continues to encourage those sentiments today. In that vein, using the media and government's own tools against them, I attempt to demonstrate that the worlds of entertainment, sports, and pop culture can be compared to and help you better understand the same government that you have the power to interact in, shape, and (if necessary) remake through the democratic process. Similar to the plotline in the film *Shrek*, we're going on a Quest to understand, preserve, and protect our homeland by embarking on an adventure which will take us to the Kingdom of Far, Far Away and beyond. Let the adventure begin!

Username: TakingAmericaBack
Password: KingdomOfFarFarAway

Works Cited

Shrek. Dir. Andrew Adamson and Vicky Jenson. Perf. Mike Myers, Eddie Murphy, and Cameron Diaz. Dreamworks Studios. 2001.

CHAPTER 1

Facebook Friend Request: Government as a 'Social Network'

How many of you have a Facebook account? I would imagine that probably 95% of you do. Facebook has become the most popular method of online communication of the day. People post their favorite songs, root on their favorite teams, play games, post statuses about life events – the list goes endlessly on. Facebook has taken America and the world by storm, and it is a phenomenon most are familiar with, some to the point of silliness – especially you Candy Crush players. In this chapter, I will compare this cyber phenomenon to the fabric that protects humanity from its animalistic self – government.

Social Networks

Facebook, at its barest roots, is – as a film defined it in 2010 – a 'social network'. For the purposes of this book, let us define a **social network** as an arena where people congregate, interact, and communicate in and about the world around them. Social networks on Facebook range from colleges to churches, workplaces, sports teams, political parties, and so on. The types of social networks existing on Facebook are seemingly endless, so it is easy for an individual to find something on Facebook that applies to him or herself and enables that person to engage in the world in which he or she lives. Social networks are 'social' in that they invite individuals to become part of a congregational whole. They offer opportunities to escape the hermit-like lifestyle that this world of technology seems to encourage – especially among the younger generations. When you can talk online, why bother to call someone on the phone and talk in person? Why call and talk when a text is quicker and allows one to get to the point in a more efficient way? I am sure that some folks out there would argue that our society is being discouraged from social contact, for without such interactions, there can be no social upheaval. I, however, would contend that social contact has not diminished in any way, but rather, it has evolved to meet the technological advances of our time. Whether it has caused societal evolution or the breakdown of social interaction, Facebook has brought individuals together into a global network that, twenty years ago, would not have been thought possible.

Government, like Facebook, is also a social network. It attracts and encourages individuals to become part of the political process. **Government** is the social network that encourages individuals to make rational choices about how they want society to function, what should be legal and what should be considered intolerable, where we are as a nation, where we ought to be, and how to get from here to there. A government's job is to protect its people from themselves and from outsiders who may seek, through force, to acquire their land, resources, technology, and so on. Generally speaking, governments exist because the people have agreed, either through spoken or unspoken word, that survival in an incredibly harsh, cruel world like ours is not likely on one's own. People tend to organize in groups under the rule of governments because it is far easier to establish, protect, and preserve a large group than it is to defend oneself and the principles that the individual seeks to preserve alone.

While governments, especially in ancient times, were founded predominantly for protection and self-preservation, governments of the modern era are, more often than not, organized around ideological principles. Modern governments tend to be made up of individuals who have similar empirical and normative views. An **empirical** view is one's interpretation of how the world actually *does* work. One's **normative** view is one's interpretation of how things *should* be. In general, it is far easier to get people to agree on empirics, but far more difficult to get people to concur on the normative possibilities that could potentially play out; however, even within a government, there are often heated disputes that try to identify what problems exist and how best to address them. So, even within governments built on the same principles, we end up with factions that disagree on what the problems actually are and also how to get from the empirical to the normative – or from "the **real** to the **ideal**," as one of my political philosophy professors, John Langton, put it. All of these things are the stuff that governments, our political 'social networks', must consider carefully and address as they see fit.

'Friends'

On Facebook, to interact in the social network, you must first acquire 'Facebook Friends'; these are the people one actively chooses to interact with on this cyber social network. Finding 'friends' on Facebook is not as straightforward as it sounds. Individu-

Facebook Friend Request

als can search for people they know by using the 'search for Friends' function. Users can search the 'People You May Know' app that Facebook provides that assesses your 'friends list' and attempts to identify people you may have something in common with by considering the people you have already 'friended' and also the interests that you and your 'friends' share in common. People can be 'friend requested' by other people on the social network. The list goes on and on. The method for 'adding' friends and 'accepting' friend requests is many and varied. You will rarely find a Facebook user, however, who has failed to connect with other users in the social network through the "Facebook Friend Request."

Just as 'friends' are the users that an individual interacts with on Facebook, the individuals that intermingle together in a government – our political social network – are known as **citizens**. These are people who are guaranteed rights that noncitizens are denied and have the power to either directly or indirectly affect policy. Citizens have modes of communication by which they can express their opinions to the government of which they are a part. Citizens exert the power to prop a government up or, in extreme cases, tear it down and remake it to better serve their interests and reflect the principles espoused by the people.

One can become 'friends' with Facebook users in many ways. Similarly, there are multiple ways to become an American citizen. The first and most common method is *being born on American soil.* For example: Imagine an expecting couple from Germany was vacationing in Florida, and the woman gave birth to her child while she was there. By our laws, that child, even though the parents are German, is entitled to all the rights due any American citizen simply because the child was born here on U.S. soil. Another way one can become a citizen is if one is *born to parents who are citizens.* For instance: imagine that your parents are citizens of the United States, but your family has chosen to stay in a foreign country, say, to study at a prestigious university in Europe, and your mother gives birth to you in the country in which the university she is attending is located. Even though you were not born on American soil, you are guaranteed the rights and responsibilities of citizenship because your parents are also endowed with those privileges. The final method of acquiring citizenship, unlike the first two, can only occur once a person becomes an adult, and it is known as becoming *naturalized.* The naturalization process, once your application is accepted, takes five years to complete. Interested parties must enroll and pass either an American history or an American government course, become proficient in the English language, pass a citizenship test, and pay a fee (and it's not cheap).

Some argue that the naturalization process is unnecessarily difficult – especially those who come from countries where English is not the 'first' or predominant language. Others contend that newcomers need to assimilate or become 'American' and leave their old life behind if they really want to stay and truly fit in. It's certainly a touchy topic and one that is not likely to be agreed upon by everybody anytime soon. Those immigrating to the United States

Aliens! Most come in peace....with documentation.

want to maintain a sense of identity while also desiring to be accepted and welcomed into American culture; Americans don't want to be insensitive to those coming here but also don't feel the need to change their cultural norms to accommodate immigrants coming from foreign lands. It's a problem that America has dealt with since the inception of this country, and it's a quandary that is not likely to be resolved in the near future.

Non-'Friends'

On Facebook, millions and millions of people access and use the social network on a daily basis, but by no means are all of them your 'friends' – in some cases, far from it. Most of the people you are not friends with are simply that – not your friends or, at least, people that you are unfamiliar with. Most people consider the people they're not friends with to be harmless and completely safe, but there are users on Facebook – at times – with less than savory intentions – the hackers. Oftentimes, these individuals will hack into or replicate the Facebook account of one of your 'friends', will send you a message with a picture or video in it and tell you to click on it. Well, speaking from past experience, these pictures or videos sent through messages by hackers are bad news. Clicking on them can open your computer itself to being hacked and your information store on it stolen, or the pictures themselves can give your computer viruses which, in some cases, require professional removal. Hackers are, by far, the most unfriendly individuals intermingling on Facebook.

Our government, like Facebook, also addresses the concerns of non-citizens or 'aliens' as well – and I'm not talking about the little green guys. Aliens are individuals who interact with the government but have no say in government via the tools available to citizens. Unfortunately, there are two types of aliens – legal and illegal.

Legal aliens have permission from the government to live and work here. Sometimes, aliens are granted permission to stay permanently and in other instances, their permission to live and work here is only temporary. Legal aliens have social security numbers, have a **visa** or **green card** – physical identification that denotes their permission to live and work here, are required to pay income taxes, and are expected to follow the laws dictated by the government. Illegal aliens, however, are not guaranteed these rights nor held to these responsibilities. Simply put, illegal aliens do not have the government's permission to be here. Oftentimes, these individuals are seeking asylum from an oppressive government or are seeking work that might enable them to provide for their families back home. Like non-

'friends' and the less than savory hackers using Facebook, there are plenty of people living here who do not share the rights and privileges of citizens; some of these folks are here with permission, and some of them are not.

Action

Now, those of you who have Facebook – all of you – have at least one 'friend' on your list that uses Facebook to the point of stupidity. They let you know what's going on roughly every second of every day by constantly changing their 'Facebook status', they most annoyingly invite you – sometimes many times a day – to play games like Farmville or Candy Crush. They have automatic posts from news sites or groups they find important which are set up to appear on your 'news feed' – a function that updates you on your friends' activity. To put it simply, we all know an 'active' Facebook user. We also know of people who essentially have Facebook to say that they have it – to look 'cool'. They rarely, if ever, check their Facebook account. They are the ones that take six months to respond to your wish of 'happy birthday,' an event very nearly as bad as leaving your Christmas lights up until June. Just as there are active Facebook users, there are inactive or 'passive' Facebook users.

Similarly, there are **active citizens** and **passive citizens.** Active citizens are exactly how they sound – active. They participate in and with their government in varied ways. They might write their state representative, senator, or governor. They might sign a petition. An active citizen would most certainly be registered to vote and would partake of that activity at every opportunity. Active citizens keep up with current events. They don't believe everything the media tells them; they trust…but verify the information provided by the notoriously biased media outlets out there. Active citizens participate because they believe that their voice matters and plays a key role in policy formulation and implementation.

Passive citizens are less motivated and are more…passive. They tend to avoid government interaction, because they believe that their voice isn't the loudest and is therefore insignificant; they are convinced that their efforts won't matter, that they aren't informed enough to make rational policy decisions, or that they simply don't care about politics. In my personal experience, I would say that the

Making things happen – one citizen at a time

most common reason for passivity among citizens is that people simply don't care about what goes on in the political realm.

We live in a country populated by nearly 300 million people. Where is your voice in that concert of noise? Many would argue that nobody could hear them, and, in general, I concur. Most voices that are small and quiet remain unheard by the rest of the chorus. However, one person shouting in a room of whisperers, which we Americans arguably are, can make a huge difference. Being courageous and speaking thoughts that others – perhaps many others – have thought encourage quieter voices to become louder and bolder. With enough voices singing the same tune, the government has been and can be compelled to listen and respond to the people's song. In this country echoing with millions of voices, your voice could well be heard if it's humming the right melody at the right time. Only history and circumstance have the power to determine whether or not your opinion and voice is worthy of political relevance. You won't ever know unless you try.

Some choose not to participate in government, because they don't feel informed enough to make good decisions in regard to policy. In this regard, I support the decision of those individuals, but I will not enable their endeavors to remain uninformed. In this world of instant answers that technology equips us with, there is no reason why individuals can't access and digest the information available out there regarding current events, government, and the political process. In most cases, I would call their lack of information 'user error' – meaning that people errantly choose to be uninformed rather than attempt to understand the information provided to them. Clearly, there are some in society not mentally capable (because of illness) of registering what's going on, but the rest of us, in my opinion, have no excuses. When all the information you need is accessible from tapping your phone or surfing the internet, there is no reason to be uninformed. You can even do it while relaxing in your recliner and can keep your pajama pants and t-shirt on. You have my permission. One of my former professors once said that there are three kinds of people in this world: the kind that make things happen, the kind that watch things happen, and the kind that wonder what happened. Citizens need to employ the first strategy, making things happen, and to avoid the other two.

As I said in the brief introduction to this book, I think that the media (and perhaps the government) has convinced most Americans that politics are boring and far less interesting than the newest film or the hottest sports team. Some argue that political suppression by the media is unintentional, and yet others believe the opposite. With so much money necessary to promote and maintain the popularity of certain media venues, I find it hard to believe that the wealthy in government haven't used the monetary need of the media to their own ends. Compare, say, Fox News Channel and MSNBC. Fox News is known for having a conservative bias, and MSNBC is known for its liberal slant. Is it simply ratings that drive these networks to espouse the ideological tendencies they do? I think not. Nothing in life, given my experience, is ever that simple, and coincidences in the world of politics almost always prove to be purposed and not accidental. I can see why things are the way they are – why people have such a dislike and disinterest in government and the political process, but that doesn't mean that's how it should be.

I find it extremely ironic how most active citizens feel that their voice and efforts matter, while most passive citizens argue the opposite. Perhaps if more of the passive citizens became interested and involved, they would see the harvest of the seeds they sow. Maybe they would hear more people echoing their views, because they themselves were bold enough to utter them. If more people were active, there would be less people feeling a weak connection to the government which, by definition, is theirs to rule. One cannot feel powerful if one refuses to use the power he or she possesses. In the realm of political participation, more is always better than less.

Forms of Government

Early in the chapter, I said that governments are social networks. The vastness of history and the resonance of reality indicate that there are various forms of government in existence. This is also true of social networks. Twitter, MySpace, and LinkedIn are only a few examples of the numerous social networking tools available to today's society. Similarly, there are many forms of government that one should be aware of. When considering the different forms of government we need to consider two things: **(1) how many people rule?** and **(2) how does the ruling actually get done?**

How Many People Rule?

This consideration of the various forms of government is the simplest and most straightforward. The number of people involved in the ruling process says a great deal about how a government functions. The fewer the people involved in the ruling process, the quicker (or more **efficient**) that decisions are made.

When Nobody Rules

When there is NO ruler – no government at all – that is defined as **anarchy**. There is no method of protecting oneself from whatever dangers might be waiting outside your front door. Anarchy allows men to embrace their animalistic tendencies and embrace what Aristotle – an ancient Greek philosopher – would call "the state of nature" (Aristotle Book I). At our most basic disposition, humans are just like any other animal. We do what we have to in order to, as my former professor John Langton put it, "survive and thrive." If we have to steal, kill, pillage, rape, and otherwise do horrific things to ensure our success or our survival, so be it. In an anarchical system, anything goes.

You either win or you die.

When One Person Rules

When only one person is involved in the policy process and only one person is making the decisions, that is known as an **autocracy** – *auto* being the prefix for 'one'. This form of government tends to be very absolutist. From the point of view of the autocrat, what he or she says is absolute law and absolute truth. These folks generally rule by dividing their area of governance into smaller parts and assigning those areas to cronies whom they trust; the regional lords are answerable only to the autocrat himself. This provides the autocrat with a method of indirect governance; if a region of his territory finds itself in financial or material distress, the autocrat can hold the regional lord responsible and still appear to be concerned with his or her subjects without actually having to lift a finger.

Often autocracies are painted as oppressive regimes as they leave little, if any, room for policy debates, individual liberties, disagreements regarding how the territory is governed, violation of the law, and so on. From the autocrat's point of view, he or she rules with an iron fist because appearing to be weak or indecisive could potentially open the door for a usurper aspiring to remove the ineffective autocrat and, in the former autocrat's place, take over as the new boss in town. I would argue that the rule of law in an autocracy is strict and punishments are severe, because the lack of control only encourages those bold enough to take steps to shift the power structure.

When Many Rule

When considering how many people do the ruling, the last form of government to explore is when many people rule. We know this form of government as a **democracy.** The word *democracy* comes from two Greek words – *demos* (rule) and *kratia* (the many). So, democracy is, according to the Greeks, the rule of the many. The first true democracy, incidentally, emerged in ancient Athens, a *polis* or township (and incidentally, where we derive the word 'politics' from) – now the capital of Greece. The roots of American democracy can be traced as far back as this first true democracy where the citizens of Athens ruled the polis by embracing the self-governance typical in most modern democracies.

How the Ruling Gets Done

Exploring forms of government through the number of people ruling only provides part of the picture as to how governments work. One must also consider how these people do their ruling. As there is *no* system of rule in anarchy, this section will therefore consider only the different types of autocracies and democracies.

Autocracies

There are many variations of the autocratic form of government – where only one person does the ruling. Some autocracies you will probably recognize while others may not be as familiar. I will provide both real-life and fictional examples so that you can picture what these governments – in general – look like.

The most well-known and nastiest form of autocracy is a **dictatorship.** Dictators get their power through *force*. In general, the dictator will find some way to oust or kill the current ruler, set himself up as ruler, and imprison or kill anyone who is unhappy with that venture. Dictatorships are often oppressive, tyrannical, and (most of the time) very brutal regimes. A recent dictator most of you are probably familiar with would be Adolph Hitler – the chancellor and dictator of Nazi Germany shortly before and during World War II. Hitler, while widely acclaimed for the rebuilding of the German manufacturing system and economy, was responsible for the outrageous atrocities of the Holocaust. A fictional dictator would be Scar from Disney's *The Lion King*. Scar was the king's brother who became jealous when King Mufasa and his wife had a son, Simba. Until Simba's birth, Scar was next in line for the throne, but with Simba's birth, he was all but assured that he would be denied the throne and the power that came along with it. Unable to contain his jealousy and suppress his lust for power, Scar arranged to have his brother assassinated, banished Simba under pain of death, and anointed himself king. Both Hitler and Scar gained their power and maintained it through force – the trademark of a dictatorial regime.

The next most familiar form of autocracy is probably a **monarchy,** a government ruled by either a king or queen who acquires his or her power through *lineage* – or royal birth. The kings of England, France, Spain, and Portugal in Europe are all monarchies. The throne in each kingdom passed from the current monarch to the next of kin when the sitting king or queen died. Some of these realms allowed for female rulers – others did not. Realms that only allow for male monarchs are known as **patriarchies.** A **matriarchy**, conversely, is a territory that allows and, oftentimes, encourages female rulers. Queen Elizabeth in the United Kingdom is a good example of a modern-day monarch. She gained her throne when her predecessor – her father, King George VI – died. She has been queen for quite some time now (over 60 years), and the people of the United Kingdom revere her. She is expected to sign royal decrees and participate in ceremonial events. The United Kingdom's seat of government, however, is not with the queen but with the houses of Parliament – a phenomenon I will explore shortly. A fictional monarch that many of you are likely familiar with is Robert Baratheon, the sitting king of the Seven Kingdoms in J.R.R. Martin's *A Game of Thrones*. In the book, King Robert ends up dying, and the throne passes to his supposed son, Joffrey. Exceedingly cruel and arrogant, Joffrey makes many enemies early in his young reign (he is 14 when he assumes the throne), and doesn't live past his wedding day.

Monarchs have the propensity to rule their subjects well, but some of these autocrats fail in that endeavor. Many kings and queens of the past have allowed the singular power they wield to go to their heads and, almost always, this poor leadership style has resulted in exceedingly short reigns and almost always notably bloody ends to the affairs. Mediocrity among monarchs isn't discussed as much because, understandably, history tends to remember both the particularly benevolent and also the notably oppressive monarchs that have governed over time.

The final type of autocracy to be discussed here is a **theocracy**. In this form of autocracy, the ruler is appointed by a religion or church, so the theocrat is not only a religious cleric but also head of government. The most recognizable theocracy is Vatican City, the seat of the Roman Catholic Church where the current pope serves as head of government as well as head of the Roman Catholic faith. Theocracies are relatively rare, because most modern governments embrace some variation of the **separation of church and state** principle – the idea that religious expression and political discourse should remain separate. Despite this, however, more people across the globe claim to follow the pope's lead than there are American citizens to follow their own president.

Autocracies, though brutal and oppressive, are known for being **the most effective form of government.** By **an effective** government, I mean a government that makes policy decisions quickly. Autocracies are known for getting their agendas completed faster than any other form of government, and that can be attributed to the number of rulers involved in making those decisions – one. When only one person has a say in policy formulation, the length of time it takes to approve policy proposals is minimal. Autocracies, far more than any other form of government, has the upper hand in effectiveness.

Democracies

Just as there are many variations of autocracies, there are many different forms of democracies as well. The first democratic government, as stated earlier, existed in ancient Athens, a polis in Greece. It was what we know as a **true democracy** or a **direct democracy.** With this form of government, each person's vote *directly affects policy*. Each person's political opinion significantly matters, as one vote can and has approved policy and also caused policy proposals to fail. An **indirect democracy** or **representative democracy** exists where, instead of every citizen having a direct impact on policy, the citizens elect representatives to vote in their stead to represent their interests from a political, economic, and social standpoint. Indirect democracies tend to occur in countries with larger populations where the functionality of a true democracy would be in doubt because of the population size.

The representatives that govern in indirect democracies have two leadership styles at their disposal. The first style is known as the **delegate model.** In this model, the representatives' votes reflect the will of the people – even if the politician believes that the will of the people is against their own interests. The other leadership style – the **trustee model** – dictates that the politician do what he or she thinks is in his constituents' best interest, even if it seems contrary to the people's will.

In general, I think most of us would like to be represented by a delegate. Such representation suggests that the views of individual citizens matter, that one's opinions are worthy of serious consideration, and that one's representative won't ever write you off in the attempt to secure political advancement. Conversely, however, some also contend that there are definitely some positives to be had from the trustee model. This model, at least indirectly, implies that representatives can and have considered multiple outcomes to every decision and are ever aware that decisions, however popular, can have catastrophic consequences.

Unlike autocracies, democracies aren't very effective at all. With all of the voices that have input in the political process, it takes a very long time for those voices to agree on anything, pass something, and get it approved and implemented as law. They are, however, very efficient. **Efficient** governments, rather than getting things done quickly, are able to successfully do things better, approve better legislation, and better meet the needs and wants of their constituencies.

Often we, as citizens in an ineffective democracy, become frustrated with how slow the policymaking process progresses. We should be glad, however, that things operate the way they do, because the time our politicians take to consider the laws they propose and implement enables them to propose policy situations in a troubled world that are far more likely to positively pan out than an autocracy would. The old fable 'The Tortoise and the Hare' declares that 'the slow and steady win the race'. For democracies, far more than for autocracies, the fable adage is true.

Hybrid Governments

Not every government fits neatly into one of the two classifications previously mentioned. Some governments can be classified one way numerically, but then functionally operate on a different level. To conclude our discussion on forms of government, we consider governments that are more…complicated.

We the People…as defined by this.

The first hybrid we explore here is an **oligarchy.** Oligarchies are governed by a small group of people – often a political party or high-ranking members of the military. According to 'how many rule', oligarchies qualify as a democracy, but according to 'how the ruling gets done', these governments function more like dictatorships. The rulers in oligarchical states gain their power, like in a dictatorship, through force, and though a small group rules, they rule with one voice rather than the many varied opinions associated with modern democracies.

Next, we consider **republics.** A republic is a representative democracy where the majority rules ONLY – meaning the minority party has virtually no say in policy formulation. For instance, imagine that America is a republic. Imagine 60% of the seats in Congress went to the Republicans and 40% went to the Democrats. During that congressional session, the Democrats would have to sit back and watch the Republicans write, pass, and implement policy without their input or help. In a true republic, minority parties are pretty helpless which leaves their constituents in a bad place – one without any real say in the political landscape. This form of government, like an oligarchy, functions more like an autocracy, a regime with one voice, even though, numerically, a republic classifies as a democracy.

Another hybrid government is a **constitutional monarchy.** Earlier, we said that the United Kingdom's monarch – Queen Elizabeth II – functions as *head of state* while the houses of parliament function as the real seat of political power and the prime minister functions as *head of government.* In a constitutional republic, the monarch serves only as a ceremonial leader while the prime minister and parliament lead the charge in policymaking. So, according to 'how many rule', a constitutional monarchy is complicated. Technically, the monarch rules; however, functionally, a constitutional republic's constitution dictates that representatives in parliament have the real power and moreover functions as a democracy.

The final hybrid to be considered here is the one that we as Americans identify with – a **constitutional republic.** Like a republic, the representative democracy protects the majority; however, the country's constitution mandates guaranteed protection for specified groups in society. The United States Constitution, when it was ratified, only protected rich, white, male property owners. Through the Amendment process, the Constitution has expanded protection and political power to other groups across the nation – African Americans, women, Native Americans, young people, and so on. Without the piece of paper that is the United States Constitution, almost no one you know would have any political power. Having constitutional protection makes one important and powerful.

Just as there are many different social networking venues, the different forms of government are scattered, embraced, and maintained across the globe. Some are becoming ever more popular while others, gradually, are losing their flare. Some instill fear and insecurity among citizens while others encourage the public to become more engaged, more involved, and more concerned with the events going on around them.

Jeff Foxworthy: "You might be a democracy if..."

'You Might Be a Democracy If…"

One of the Blue Collar Comedy Tour's most famous characters is Jeff Foxworthy, a comedian who is famous for his 'redneck' heckling, but Foxworthy brings up a notable point that most people pass over. Some things you recognize by sight. There are many heralded websites online that identify the differences between 'Walmart shoppers' and the rest of civilized society – you know Walmart shoppers when you see them. Would you know a democracy by seeing it?

What, in your opinion, does a democracy look like? What qualities does a government have to possess for it to be worthy of the title 'democracy'? Some argue that a booming economy is necessary for democracy to take hold and flourish; a political scientist, Sam Huntington, made that very argument (68-80). Others – Ronald Inglehart and Christian Welzel – argue that political institutions and a culture espousing individualism are other 'democratic' attributes (15-47). From my own perspective, I think that high voter turnout, informed citizens, and a responsive legislature are 'democratic' by nature, but not every democracy displays all of these requisites. In fact, many governments are classified as 'democratic' though culture that meshes with that form of rule is struggling to adapt to such challenges. What is a democracy? What does a government have to do to 'make the team'? Even political science has been slow to say. Perhaps that's the wisest path; oftentimes, things are not always as they seem.

When most of you close this book, you will head off to your computer and log onto Facebook or some other social networking site. As you do that, remember how comparable that social network is to the government which depends on you – the 'user' – to interact with it to enable it to remain relevant. Getting involved in the political social network can be as simple and instantaneous as logging onto your social network of choice – minus all of the annoying game invites! Don't be afraid to get involved or to become informed; the information you need, quite literally, is only a few clicks away.

Food for Thought

At the end of each chapter, this little section is designed to encourage critical thinking about the meat and potatoes (if you will) of the lesson from the previous pages. Open-ended questions will challenge you to form your own opinions about government, politics, and the world in which you live. So grab your plate, and fill it. There's plenty of 'food' for everybody.

Government

Why do we, as humans, need government (or, at least, seem to embrace it)? Does government exist because it helps us feel safe? Do we need government because it ensures that second chances – if we fail – are possible? What about our social nature? Does government exist because we, as humans, function better working together as opposed to combatting the world's challenges on our own? Does the ability to reason draw people together or do our animalistic, survivalist instincts do that? What do you think?

Democracy is...

Citizenship

In the United States, most people are born into citizenship just as monarchs, princes, and other royalty are born into their inheritance. Should we be guaranteed citizenship through birth? Conventional wisdom suggests that roughly 35% of Americans are active citizens; that means that roughly 65% of citizens either are less active or entirely passive when it comes to utilizing their rights and exercising their responsibilities as citizens. Should citizens have more privileges than noncitizens? In a country succumbing to the effects of **globalization** – the spread of national cultures, food, and other trends across the planet – should we expect visitors to be okay with being treated differently than citizens? Should the government have the power to strip individuals of their citizenship? If so, under what pretenses should this be permissible?

Activism

Should citizens be more active in the political process than they are? Why might noncitizens (or aliens) be more active in politics than citizens? Do you think, as a citizen, that your voice matters? Why are people so uncomfortable discussing politics with friends, family, or other acquaintances? Is your action or inaction a product of a lack of interest, discouragement perpetuated by the government and the media, or a little of both? What can be done to encourage political activism? Do you think that democracy and active citizenship go hand in hand? Americans believe our regime is democratic, but do we function as a democracy?

Forms of Government

Why are people so afraid of anarchy? Which do you think is the stronger feeling – the desire to survive (fear of death) or the desire to be included (fear of being alone)? If humans are so inclined to societal development, why do people shun certain groups in society? Why is it easier to subject yourself to the governance of one person, like a king or queen? What are the drawbacks to autocratic rule? Are all autocrats tyrants? Are all dictators 'evil'? Do all democracies represent their citizenries well? Can democracies be tyrannical? Which model of representation do you prefer – the delegate or trustee model and why? Which form of government do you feel would exact justice the best and the worst? Do you believe constitutions are fluid and eligible for change or rigid and unalterable?

Governance

We are an indirect democracy, but does it work 'well'? Do you feel as if an autocratic system would function better or worse than our representative democracy does? How do kings and queens differ from our president? How do dictators govern differently than our executive? Would we be better off with a weaker national government or a stronger one? Some argue that we would best function as a theocracy since so many people in America subscribe to a religion; do you agree or disagree? Is it possible for a person to separate their religious views and their political beliefs? Do you feel as if the democratic process is efficient enough? What steps could be taken to make the system more efficient?

Democratization

What, in your opinion, constitutes a fully developed democracy? If you could draw a picture of what the ideal democracy should look like, what would you capture in your drawing? Do you think that democracies require universal representation? What is a 'political institution'? Why might an individualist culture be important to the democratization process? Do you think globalization encourages the spread of one form of government over others? Is democracy the 'best' form of government and why do you feel that way?

Facebook Friends...

Win the Wand, Use the Stone, Wear the Cloak
"Together, they make the Deathly Hallows
Together, they make one Master of Death"

Xenophilius Lovegood

Works Cited

Aristotle. *Politics*. Chicago: Chicago University Press, 2013.

Huntington, Samuel. *The Clash of Civilizations and the Remaking of World Order.* New York: Simon and Schuster, 1996.

Ingelhart, Ronald and Christian Welzel. *Modernization, Cultural Change, and Democracy: The Human Development Sequence.* Cambridge: Cambridge University Press, 2005.

CHAPTER 2

Harry Potter and the Deathly Branches of Government

If there is one problem common among America's youth, it's that they are not book readers. They are not encouraged to imagine, create, or believe in the impossible. One of my favorite quotes comes from Tim Burton's *Alice in Wonderland* – "Gentlemen, the only way to achieve the impossible is to believe that it *is* possible." What a telling statement, and how relevant it is to our discussion here. So many young people are shooed away from 'make-believe' and are thrust into reality before they've even had a chance to enjoy being a child. Childhood provides the foundation on which society is built – that *innovation* requires a strong *imagination.*

In this chapter, we delve into the magical world of Harry Potter – a young Wizard who happens across three magical objects described in a Wizarding fable, "The Tale of Three Brothers." These three items, once united, are believed to make the possessor invulnerable, invincible, and undefeatable. Once we understand these three items, where they came from, and who possesses them, I compare each magical object to a corresponding branch of American government. Finally, the general parallels that will be elaborated on later in much greater detail will be discussed and analyzed.

Harry Potter and the Deathly Hallows

The Harry Potter series, written by J.K. Rowling, is a seven-part saga that tells of

Hermione Granger (Emma Watson), Harry Potter (Daniel Radcliffe), and Ron Weasley (Rupert Grint)

the adventures of Harry Potter and his two best friends, Ronald Weasley and Hermione Granger. Harry is no ordinary boy; at age one, his parents were killed by the most evil Dark Wizard of the age, Lord Voldemort (also known as the Dark Lord, You Know Who, and He-Who-Must-Not-Be-Named). The seven-part saga by Rowling investigates Harry's attempts to rid the world of the Dark Lord and restore peace and justice to the Wizarding world.

In the seventh and final book, *Harry Potter and the Deathly Hallows*, Harry and his friends attempt to destroy objects (Horcruxes), which bind Lord Voldemort to the living world. Before their search begins, however, they attend Ron's brother's wedding. At the celebration, they notice their friend, Luna Lovegood, and her father, Xenophilius. Luna's dad is wearing a strange necklace – one that seemingly depicts an eye inside of a triangle. The three heroes (Harry, Ron, and Hermione) find the pendant odd – just as most people believed Luna and her father to be 'different', but they lacked the nerve to say anything. Later on, however, the symbol is seen twice more – once on a gravestone next to the final resting place of Harry's parents and second (and most importantly) on the title page of a children's tale in the book *The Tales of Beedle the Bard.* Now thoroughly curious, the three protagonists seek out Luna's father in hopes of unraveling the mystery of the odd symbol (Rowling DH, 394-396).

Luna's father informs them that the glyph is a symbol of three items united – the Deathly Hallows. He describes the three items as they are discussed in "The Tale of Three Brothers." Essentially, three brothers evade Death and, as a trick, he awards each of the brothers a 'prize' for having been clever enough to outsmart him. The oldest brother acquires a powerful weapon – the Elder Wand. The second brother acquires a pebble that has the ability to bring back the dead – the Resurrection Stone. The third brother, not trusting Death, asked for something he could use to escape Death's clutches – the Cloak of Invisibility. Luna's father concludes the tale and argues that, if united, the Deathly Hallows would make one 'Master of Death'. He argues that uniting the Deathly Hallows has the propensity to make one immortal and invincible. The Deathly Hallows, argues Luna's father, are powerful tools when used separately, but concludes that, when united, they hold unique abilities and inexhaustible power (Rowling DH, 407-410).

The Deathly Branches of Government

While powerful individually, they make one invincible when united. That sounds a lot like how the Founding Fathers saw the three branches of government; three individual bodies set up to do different things, but each body dependent on the other two. How like the Deathly Hallows our three branches of government are! Let us take a closer look at each item of the Deathly Hallows as well as their corresponding branch of government.

The Elder Wand and the Executive Branch

Antioch, the oldest brother in the story, wanted "the most powerful wand ever made – a weapon that would always win duels for its owner, a wand worthy of one who had beaten Death" (Rowling BB, 408). And so, he received the Elder Wand. Two things of note are mentioned here – that the Elder Wand is exceptionally *powerful* and that the Wand was intended to be used as a *weapon* – indeed, the most powerful weapon in existence as, according to the story, unbeatable.

The issue of power is one that carries through the rest of the book; in the end, Harry Potter acquires the Elder Wand by defeating Lord Voldemort who was, at the time, the current possessor of the Wand. According to Rowling's work, Harry was the only person 'worthy' of possessing the Wand because he intended to use its power judiciously to benefit others (Rowling DH, 720). This thought process is starkly different from that of Voldemort who sought to possess the Wand in order to kill Harry and thus remove the only real threat to his power.

The Wand was also referred to as a formidable weapon. Luna's father argues that, unlike the other two items comprising the Deathly Hallows, that "Wizarding history was stained with the blood shed by the Elder Wand" (Rowling DH, 412). According to legend, the Wand had passed from owner to owner – usually (but not exclusively) through murder. Again, Harry is seen as the only person capable of obtaining the Wand through nonlethal means and possessing it with no intentions of domination, tyranny, or oppression – again, starkly different from Voldemort.

I argue that the Elder Ward is comparable to the Executive Branch of government – the president, the vice president, his advisers, and the people who ensure that the laws he (or she) signs are implemented appropriately. Just as the Elder Wand provides one with seemingly inexhaustible power and a formidable weapon, the Executive Branch is perceived as a possessor of power and the wielder of a powerful weapon as well.

Power – something many aspire toward, few attain, and even fewer use selflessly, yet power is something that every American president is granted. Though the Electoral College technically elects the president, the electoral votes from each state almost always reflect the outcome of the popular vote in each respective state. If the vote margin between the two presidential nominees is large enough, the

The Elder Wand – the most powerful wand ever made

Presidential power

winner is said to have won a **public mandate** – wide-reaching public support for the president-to-be and his agenda. A public mandate arguably gives a president an exorbitant amount of power. It gives the executive officer leverage over other branches of government – typically Congress – and allows the president the ability to think and act virtually without impunity – so long as he (or she) stays within the constitutional limits – which are more complicated than one would initially think (a topic to be discussed later).

Presidents, arguably, wield more power than any other individual in the world. The president's ability to shape American political policy, the agenda of his own political party, the functionality of America's massive **bureaucracy** – the body of people who enforce and implement laws – makes the president a powerful person indeed. Using this power judiciously, however, is a whole other ballgame. It is true that some presidents have tested the limit of their powers. Abraham Lincoln did so by declaring the South's secession from the Union to be illegal and unconstitutional. Franklin Delano Roosevelt did it by attempting to force the Supreme Court to rule favorably on his New Deal policies. Both of these instances created a new **precedent** – or standard – regarding the power presidents have and the power these individuals claim for themselves.

Like the possessor of the Elder Wand, presidents have the power to affect the world around them, and this power is not limited to U.S. borders. As the head of government of the world's **superpower,** or 'boss country', the president's agenda often ends up making the global to-do list. For example: President Obama has been – and is – concerned with the effects of global warming (or climate change). By working with the international community and pushing for tougher environmental restrictions, President Obama has encouraged other nations to pitch in environmentally to reduce the effects of climate change and make our world a more beautiful, healthier place to live – one which future generations will be able to enjoy because of the efforts of governments across the globe.

Both on a national and international scale, the president has powers that other leaders lack and that other heads of government can only hope to attain. With great power, however, also comes a huge amount of responsibility. If a president, from the public's perspective, uses his power recklessly or poorly, he can and will be held accountable. Power is not without burden; one must use it in such a way that it augments one's persona as opposed to diminishing it.

Like the Elder Wand, the executive branch is one that embraces, utilizes, and (in some cases) extends its power. "The Tale of Three Brothers" describes the Elder Wand not only as immensely powerful but also as a formidable – perhaps even unbeatable – weapon. Something similar can also be said about the executive branch. The president's military powers – his role as Commander-in-Chief – leave him with the might of the most dangerous and deadly weapon in the world at his disposal – the United States military. Considered to be far more technologically advanced than its opponents, the United States Armed Forces can and have ended wars with one, swift, decisive blow.

The president's military powers aren't his only weapons. As the head of government of the world's only superpower, our head of government is often perceived as the executor of international treaties and trade agreements, an important voice in international disputes, and one of the five leaders in the world who have automatic veto power in the only international governmental organization in existence – the United Nations. The president's power is vast and is used, mostly, to make America the country of legend – a place where, if you try hard enough, success can be yours. The president's power over the Armed Forces makes him a force to be reckoned with – one that most other countries would rather not disturb. The president's ability to send military forces anywhere, in some cases without detection, instantaneously while, at the same time, possessing the ability to affect international relations and the global marketplace with diplomatic prowess encourages people, both near and far, to perceive the president in the same light as the Elder Wand – powerful, dangerous, and possibly invulnerable.

The Resurrection Stone and the Judicial Branch

The second brother in the story, Cadmus, an *arrogant* man, asked for the ability to *bring people back from the dead.* Death selected a stone from the riverbank, gave it to the second brother, and claimed that the Stone would give the second brother the ability to do just that. Using the Stone, the second brother, Cadmus, brings back to life his previously deceased sweetheart, but she was "sad and cold and separated by him as if by a veil, and did not truly belong in this world" (Rowling DH, 409). All three of these points, the arrogance

The United States Armed Forces – the wand as a powerful weapon

A gift from Death to bring back the dead

of the second brother, the ability to resurrect the dead, and the imitation of life rather than true 'lively' life are key comparisons I make to the judicial branch.

What a power to bring back the dead!! How many of us have said this of lost loved ones: "If only I could ask them…." or "if I only could have told them…"? I think most of us have second-guessed ourselves at some point in life and have desired to consult those who have gone before us. Human life is plagued with sorrow and regret, and all too often, we contend that some of that pain could have been avoided if we had the ability to seek out the knowledge and experience of those who have died – those people we identify as both stronger and wiser than ourselves.

The judicial system is uncannily similar. Judges are expected to read and interpret the Constitution and rule on cases when laws are controversial or ambiguous (vague). Don't you think justices often wish they could consult those Americans who, being older and wiser, wrote the documents by which these modern-day justices base their judicial decisions? I am sure they do, and fortunately, such a venture is possible. Not only did our Founding Fathers leave behind the Declaration of Independence, the Articles of Confederation (our first constitution – epic fail), and the United States Constitution (our current constitution); they also left behind countless writings – some being correspondence between each other and others being notes written back to state legislatures explaining what was going into the Constitution and why such measures were being taken. So, if our justices regularly consider the intentions of the Founding Fathers as they make judicial rulings, from a certain perspective, they 'bring back the dead' every time they consult the wisdom of these revered men – the men of the Revolution and the young America.

The story indicated that the second brother was arrogant and that, beyond the oldest brother's act of demanding the uninhibited power of the Elder Wand, the second brother wanted to "humiliate death," and so he asked for the possession of a power often attributed exclusively to one with supernatural powers – bringing the dead back to life (Rowling DH, 408). Arrogance ends up being the second brother's undoing, however, as he got more than he bargained for out of his agreement with death. His now-resurrected sweetheart was "sad and cold"; moreover, he was denied the ability of truly sharing what the couple experienced prior to her untimely death. The second brother was driven mad by her grief

Bringing 'the dead' back to life through constitutional interpretation

and his desire for things to be the way they were, and he ends up taking his own life in an effort to make things right – for both of them (Rowling DH, 409).

The courts, too, are often accused of unparalleled arrogance. With no real **checks,** or oversight over the court system, judges can essentially do whatever they want. It is exceedingly rare for a judge to be removed from office, because, simply, the power to do so is almost nonexistent. This arrogance and the lack of restrictions can and has enabled justices to make decisions – arguably – based on their own political agendas rather than on the constitutionality or lack thereof in specific cases. For example: in 2010, a case – *Citizens United v. Federal Election Committee* – disputed whether or not corporations – like people – could make donations to political campaigns or candidates without restriction. The Supreme Court at the time was dominated by justices who sympathized with the Republican Party – the party, generally speaking, of the wealthy. The Court ruled that, yes, corporations can be viewed as people and should have the same campaign donation capacities as any individual. Some legal scholars argue that the decision was made with total disregard for the Constitution and sought only to give the generally perceived party of the wealthy – the Republicans – a significant monetary advantage in future elections by opening the fiscal floodgates of Corporate America. Others contended that corporations are made up of people and thus should be given the same rights and privileges that individuals possess.

In this case, as well as many others, the Court has been accused on playing politics rather than interpreting the Constitution. It has been rumored – but not confirmed – that justices have accepted bribes to make one decision regarding a case instead of another. It has been noted that, in controversial cases, justices almost always rule along political party lines – either Republican or Democrat. Some contend that, rather than bringing back the dead through the written wisdom of the Founding Fathers, many justices espouse the arrogance of the second brother and consider the opinions of people which they consider to be more pertinent and relevant to America's current situation – the opinions they hold themselves.

"Sad and cold as if separated by a veil" is how Rowling describes the sweetheart that the second brother brought back from the dead (Rowling DH, 409). So alive, yet so lifeless she became! How much like life is the sweetheart? We work toward goals, we aspire for greatness, we dream of glory and respect, and yet when those dreams and aspirations come to fruition, oftentimes, the glory of the feat is less than we expected. Falling short – that is the moral of the story with the second brother and his beloved.

How different is exacting justice? What is 'justice' anyway? Is it making sure that punishments fit the crimes committed? It is protecting the defenseless? Is it innocence to the highest bidder? I think most of us have ideas as to what justice is – or, at least, what justice means in terms of us and our personal rights. However, I think if put in a position where we relied on justice to protect us, like in the attainment of major milestones, reality falls short of the idealized perception of what could and should be.

What is good for me (or you) oftentimes is harmful to others. In my opinion, justice is an absolute term; something is either just or it's not. It is not and should not be relative – changing from one person to the next. Governments should attempt to identify and exact justice and attempt to squash injustice wherever it exists. Success shouldn't be handed to individuals, but it should be possible for each individual; in our society, the way the current power structure protects the current perception of justice, it is not. The second brother thought that bringing his beloved back from the dead would make him happier, but instead it drove him mad. Do our perceptions of justice, what should be done in this instance or other, end up hurting many people in our society? Are we like the second brother in that what we think is best for us ends up being the very thing that destroys us?

In *The Deathly Hallows*, Harry ends up using the Resurrection Stone not to bring back his family and friends to keep them in this world as slaves, but rather to help him carry through with his own self-sacrifice which, in the end, enables Harry to defeat the Dark Lord, Voldemort (Rowling DH, 698-704). Justice, as viewed by many, is very relative; people perceive the concept as one defining self-protection rather than societal safeguards for all. Perhaps our perception of justice should be more reaching than it is at present. Maybe an important thing to remember is that personal decisions affect not only oneself but also the world around you as well as the many people in it.

The Cloak of Invisibility and the Legislative Branch

The third and final item that comprises the Deathly Hallows is the Cloak of Invisibility. The third brother, Ignotus, acquired the Cloak because "he did not *trust* death," and he wanted to be free of Death's searching clutches (Rowling DH, 408). The Cloak's most obvious feature is that it makes one *invisible* or *transparent*. Harry, before he realized what it was, used the Cloak through the Harry Potter series to *avoid detection when he was acting mischievously* or *to conceal his absurd fascination with breaking rules.*

The Cloak of Invisibility – escaping Death's clutches

What a powerful and useful tool invisibility would be! We would be privy to private conversations without those involved being any the wiser. It would allow us to do and see things that cannot be done as (perceptibly) whole, solid beings. Invisibility could provide individuals with a front-row seat to see things that the NSA (National Security Agency) could only hope to be in the 'know' about.

The Cloak of Invisibility, as stated before, encourages *transparency*. The ability to 'see through' otherwise solid impenetrable things is a gift that the Cloak allows. As active citizens, we want and expect Congress to be transparent. We want to know what Congress is doing for us, what they're doing to feather their own pockets, what shady activities they're involved in, and what they've done that goes against the reasons that we, the People, elected them in the first place. Generally speaking, Congress *is* very transparent and very accessible.

The procedures by which Congress operates are no secret and are, on a regular basis, available for viewing by the public. Many people travel to the Capitol building in Washington, D.C., every year, and most of them choose to sit in on a session of Congress. The votes held by Congress are done in the general assembly room and are open to the public and are also aired on CSPAN – a cable network that exclusively covers the goings on in the House of Representatives and the U.S. Senate. The operations of Congress – the debates and the votes – are *transparent* and available for the public to attend, view, and scrutinize.

Operations in both Houses are, again, accessible to the general public and are also well documented. The House of Representatives (the lower house) is run under the strict principles of 'parliamentary procedure.' This style of governance is very formal, respect-

Members of Congress: the Wearers of the Cloak

ful, and (many argue) deathly boring. The House is rigidly controlled by the Speaker of the House – its boss, the leadership of the political parties, and the party policemen (the whips). If one House operates according to the precepts your mom taught you – all the 'pleases' and 'thank yous', it is the House of Representatives.

The Senate is governed in an entirely different manner. People, on a regular basis, yell at each other, call each other names, interrupt each other, speak endlessly to prevent a vote (filibustering), and so on. The Senate, compared to the House, has fewer leadership positions which only encourage the madness. Compared to the House, the Senate is, by its very nature, exceptionally anarchical; to be fair though, it probably is the more interesting and fun legislative House to view as a citizen and also to occupy as a politician.

Congress' record, contrary to popular belief, is also available to the public (except the classified information revealed in certain closed committee meetings). A person can subscribe to receive the daily transcript from one (or both) Houses, they can view and print the Congressional Record off of each respective House's website, or they can view and print specific hearings or debates of interest. Congress is very open in terms of its procedures and its records of action (or inaction). The public merely needs to make the effort to access these resources.

Another thing that makes Congress transparent is the role of political parties in both Houses. In general, political parties are relatively static; they don't change their **platform** or **ideology** – their political values and the issues they care about – very often at all. Party politics make members of Congress (in general) predictable. When you vote for the guy with the 'R' next to his name, you can be pretty sure (in general) what his political values are and what solutions for current problems that he will push for in Congress – simply because you know that he identifies as a Republican. The same goes for the folks with a 'D' next to their name. These members of Congress typically uphold the values and the agenda of the Democrats. The political parties ascribed to by the members of Congress provide us with a lot of information in regard to their values and agenda without even knowing their name or where they came from.

Congressional procedures, its record, and its partisan way of doing things all make the legislative branch *transparent* just as the Cloak of Invisibility made the third brother invisible. Another quality of the Cloak, as mentioned before, is that it enabled Harry Potter to move about while exploring and doing things that might have – in solid, visible form – gotten him into trouble. So too do members of Congress attempt to *'conceal' their failures* and *'expose' their triumphs or noteworthy actions.*

A notable political scientist, David Mayhew, argues that the most important thing to a politician is getting elected and reelected (Mayhew, 46-48). To do this, the politician employs three tactics: "advertising, credit claiming, and position-taking" (73). All three of these tools build a recognizable and attractive political persona which encourages the public to support and (re)elect this individual.

Advertising is the art of making one's name memorable (Mayhew, 46-52). Politicians often utilize political campaign ads – on television, over the radio airwaves, and in newspapers – to get their names 'stuck' in people's heads. One of my favorite ads of all time is a John F. Kennedy ad where the ad sung Kennedy's name and why he was a valid presidential contender. At the time, the Kennedy family name was not as recognizant as it is today, so Kennedy's campaign team produced a catchy ad that was designed to get stuck in people's heads. Even sixty-some years later,

Hiding failures, exposing successes, winning elections

I will hum the tune from the ad as I'm shopping and some senior citizen will stop and ask if the tune was from the Kennedy ad. The tune clearly did its job, and so do all good political advertisements.

Credit claiming is public self-acknowledgment of political successes (Mayhew, 52-61). This is something members of Congress do a lot. For example: imagine that you submitted the proposal for a particularly popular piece of legislation – both in Congress itself and also at home with your constituents. Politicians are quick to jump on those kinds of opportunities. Another example: Imagine that a controversial piece of legislation is being debated; you don't like the proposal at all, but someone promises needed money or resources to your state. Many politicians use their votes as leverage to acquire things that their state or congressional district desperately needs. Claire McCaskill, a senator from Missouri, voted to pass the Affordable Care Act (i.e., Obamacare). Not only did she support the legislation, but her vote also ensured that the funding for the completion of a new highway would be covered – money that the state of Missouri did not have. Most people outside the boundaries of Washington, D.C., will tell you that they don't like 'pork' – extra stuff (like the highway funding) added onto unrelated legislation. I bet, however, if they knew what the 'pork' actually was, they'd be quicker to pick up their knife and fork and support it.

Lastly, members of Congress attempt to assure themselves re-election by engaging in **position-taking** – openly expressing one's opinions regarding a political value or issue (Mayhew, 61-73). Position-taking, understandably, is far more common when the issues are *not* controversial. For example: imagine that Missouri's highways are the forty-seventh worst in the country (okay, we're not imagining). Do you think fixing those roads would be popular or not so much? I guarantee you that – even if it costs a substantial amount of money – most people would support repairing the highways. Conversely, other issues are more complicated and far more controversial. Abortion, same-sex marriage, the current tax rate, nationalized health care, and education – all of these issues are highly controversial, and supporting one side or the other of these arguments has the potential to cost political candidates votes.

In regard to these controversial issues, instead of taking a position on them, candidates often choose not to respond with their opinion. If you had a sheet of paper with all of the pressing issues and candidates involved listed, most candidates would respond 'NR' (no response). In an effort to produce the highest and most positive **voter turnout** – the number of people who show up at the voting polls – politicians often choose not to reveal their opinions on issues that are known to be politically divisive.

The last notable thing in regard to the Cloak of Invisibility is that the third brother asked for it because he did not *trust* Death. Trust is something that we as citizens find hard to place in our government. Most people perceive the people in Congress as greedy heathens whose goal is to feather their own pocket with our hard earned tax dollars. Despite the predictability that the partisan nature of congressional

Wand, Stone, Cloak : Executive, Judicial, Legislative – becoming "Master of Death" and the greatest democracy in the world

leadership provides and the information that **incumbents** – politicians that are reelected over and over – possess because of their years of experience, we the People tend to trust them less than any other branch of government. Consistently, congressional approval ratings are FAR lower than the approval ratings of the U.S. president or the judicial system.

Invincible Combination

As stated before, Harry's friend's father indicated that although the items that comprise the Deathly Hallows – Wand, Stone, and Cloak – were immensely powerful in and of themselves individually, he contends that, if a person were to possess all three Hallows and use them, doing so would make that person invincible and undefeatable. All three items are powerful separately, but are invincible together.

The same can be said of the branches of government. In and of themselves, each branch of government is immensely powerful. Congress wields the power of the People as both Houses are elected by **popular vote** – election by citizens. The president has the ability to sign laws, reject or **veto** laws, choose what laws are implemented, and determine how strictly they are enforced. The judiciary can, through judicial opinion writing, deem laws approved both by Congress and the president as unconstitutional. The Court has the final say as to what the Constitution – the document that protects us all – says and doesn't say, who it protects and who it doesn't, what is legal and what is not.

Each branch of government operates alone but, at the same time, with the aid (or prohibition) of the other two. Power alone, but more powerful together. Our system of government has this built-in independent dependence that we know as **checks and balances.** Our attempt at this form of government was the first of its kind. It was, as Monty Python would argue, "something completely different," and it is the model on which most modern democracies are built. Just as the three brothers sought to gain power and invulnerability, so too have governments around the world struggled to find a form of government that would best enable them and their citizenries to thrive.

And in the Real World, There's This…

So, we've compared the items of the Deathly Hallows to the three branches of government, and we have explored the art of uniting three to make a more perfect whole in both the Wizarding world of Harry Potter as well as our own. Now, granted, Rowling is an English writer and likely her story has no intended connection to our government insofar as she is concerned. However, the symbol of the Deathly Hallows is very similar to a symbol a good number of Americans are familiar with – the masonic All-Seeing Eye. It appears on the back left-hand side of the U.S. dollar bill atop a pyramid. Who would have thought that a symbol similar to another that sets atop a children's tale in the Wizarding world of Harry Potter is on the American dollar? Abracadabra. No pun intended!

Food For Thought

The Three Brothers

Two of the brothers sought to cheat, outsmart, or defy death. Do you think most of humanity is more like these brothers or the youngest brother who accepted death as a part of life and sought only to be unafraid of Death? Why are so many people afraid of Death? Is it the thought of leaving everything behind that we love here on Earth or is it fear of the unknown? Death is something that happens to everyone. Is it natural to run from Death or accept it as a part of life?

The Deathly Branches of Government: the currency connection

The Deathly Branches of Government

Are any weapons truly unbeatable? The legends surrounding the Elder Wand indicate that invulnerability is the Wand's main trait; is it accurate? If the Wand isn't all-powerful, can we compare the power paradox to the president? The first brother let his power go to his head. Do you think presidents are the same way? The first brother was killed and claimed by Death because he bragged about his new power in front of someone that had bad intentions. How does that loose-tongued problem relate to the president and his political career and future?

Just as the Stone brings back the dead, the judicial system attempts to do the same thing. Is the judicial branch successful in 'bringing back' the true intentions of our Founding Fathers, or do you see their actions as a political press for power? After being brought back from the dead, the second brother's beloved is identified as superficial, "sad and cold" – not the real thing. Would you say that the judiciary does a good job 'bringing back the dead' or is the justice exacted by the Courts more like the second brother's sweetheart? What, in your opinion, is justice? How far from your own personal ideal do you see our country? What, from your perspective, can be done to get us from where we are to where we ought to be?

The Cloak allows one to become invisible or transparent, and I argued that the legislative branch is very transparent. Why is it that most people believe that Congress is inaccessible and very solid? Is it because most people – as discussed earlier – are passive citizens who haven't taken the time to find out how transparent Congress really is, or do you believe that it is legitimately difficult to access information about Congress, the decisions it makes, and why? Do you think members of Congress are too worried about (re)election, and not worried enough about doing their job? Is there a difference in these two questions: "Do you trust your own members of Congress?" and "Do you trust Congress?" Is it easier to trust someone you have the power to remove from office? Is it simpler to mistrust people you don't know? Do you think political parties, given the way they affect the goings on in Congress, are too weak or too strong?

Checks and Balances

Do you think that our government would run differently if one branch of government were significantly more powerful than the other two? Why do you think the Founding Fathers were so concerned with implementing a system of checks and balances in (at the time) the young democracy they were creating? Is power a tool that can be restricted or reined in? If you had to identify the most powerful branch of government, which would you choose and why?

While the branches of government are separately powerful, like the Deathly Hallows, united they are powerful as a united whole. Tell me why that is. Could any of these branches of government exist on their own without the aid of the other two? How are the branches of government 'better together'? Do you think our government is 'invincible' as the possessor of the Deathly Hallows is considered to be? If not, why not? Is anything, insofar as government is concerned, indelible? Is it possible for our government to endure for eternity? If not, is it possible to preserve it through gradual change, or is drastic change necessary?

Together, they make the Deathly Hallows...
Together, they made a man Master of Death...

A long time ago
in a galaxy far, far away...

Works Cited

Mayhew, David. *Congress: The Electoral Connection.* New York: Yale University Press, 1974.

Rowling, J. K. *Harry Potter and the Deathly Hallows.* New York: Arthur A. Levine Books, 2007. *Modernization, Cultural Change, and Democracy: The Human Development Sequence.* Cambridge: Cambridge University Press, 2005.

CHAPTER 3

The Saga Begins: The Star Wars Prequel Films and American Political Philosophy

A long time ago in a galaxy far, far away…” (Lucas). This is how all of the films in the *Star Wars* saga begin. The prequel films tell the tale of the young slave child, Anakin Skywalker, his journeys as a Jedi Warrior, and ultimately his turn toward the Dark Side of the Force. The *Star Wars* films, though also indicative of our own journeys between Light and Dark, provide a perspective from which to view the political world in which we live. First though, let's get a little background in regard to *Star Wars* as compared to the nuts and bolts of political philosophy.

"The Force" and the Power of the Human Intellect

In the *Star Wars* saga, there are two groups of people that move the plot along: the Jedi Knights and the Dark Lords of the Sith. Both of these mysterious groups use a power known as 'the Force'. According to the films, the Force is an energy field that flows through all living things, and only the Jedi and the Sith have the ability to use and manipulate it (Lucas I). Rumor has it that the Jedi use the Force for selfless reasons in an effort to promote peace and justice in the Galactic Republic – the democracy in which they live. The Jedi, therefore, are always referred to as the group who uses the 'Light Side' of the Force. The Sith, on the other hand, are known for using the "Dark Side" of the Force for selfish reasons with hopes of destroying the Republic, the Jedi, and everything else good and worthwhile (Lucas I).

Just as the Jedi and the Sith have the ability to manipulate the Force where no other beings can do so, so too can we as humans use our own unique gift – the power of our *intellect.* Our intellect enables us to reason things out and make calculated decisions. Science has argued that our intellect, like the use of the Force by the Jedi and the Sith, make humans unique, self-empowered creatures.

Our intellect provides us with the mental tools to make contributions to the world in which we live. We can either, like the Jedi, use our intellect for altruistic, selfless reasons to help others, or we can embrace the mentality of the Sith and use our intellect to get us the farthest in life, regardless of how our ascent to power affects other people, places, and things around us. The Force flows through humanity through our ability to use our intellect.

In this chapter, we are going to cover the three main philosophical debates that the Founding Fathers considered when shaping our government. I compare the philosophers engaged in these debates to Jedi Knights from the *Star Wars* saga. Before I delve into the philosophical debates, however, I provide a brief summary of the three prequel films for those of you who are unfamiliar with the *Star Wars* movies, so that you may not only become more familiar with the *Star Wars* saga but also so that you can understand the parallels that I pose later in the chapter.

Star Wars Episode I: The Phantom Menace

In this, the first installment of the *Star Wars* prequel trilogy, we meet two Jedi warriors – Qui-Gon Jinn (played by Liam Nelson) and Obi-Wan Kenobi (played by Ewan McGregor). Qui-Gon and Obi-Wan are being attacked by the Trade Federation – a group in the Galactic Republic that is attempting to disturb the tranquility and stability of the democracy of the Republic. After barely escaping, the two Jedi find themselves with a spaceship in need of repairs and land on the sand-covered planet of Tatooine (Lucas I).

Upon arriving there, they meet Watto, the owner of an auto-parts store, and young Anakin Skywalker, a young slave child (played by Jake Lloyd). Watto wants more for the necessary parts than the Jedi can afford, but Anakin formulates a plan. In secret, Anakin had been building a pod-racer – much like a race car in our world. He offers to enter the biggest pod race of the year which was to be held in two days. Watto reluctantly permits Anakin, his slave, to enter. If Anakin wins, the Jedi get the parts they need for free and secure Anakin's freedom. If Anakin loses, the Jedi give Watto their ship. Anakin wins the pod race, the parts for the Jedi, and his freedom (Lucas I).

Ewan McGregor (Obi-Wan Kenobi)

After Qui-Gon completes an examination of Anakin, he discovers that Anakin's *midichlorians count* – much like red or white blood cells to us, but particles than enable one to manipulate the Force – is higher than anyone ever. Qui-Gon is convinced that Anakin is 'the Chosen One' – one spoken of in Jedi prophecy that is to bring balance to the Force and destroy the Dark Lords of the Sith. With this conviction, Qui-Gon convinces Anakin to travel with him to Coruscant – the capitol of the Republic and also the location of the Jedi Council headquarters (Lucas I).

Qui-Gon presents Anakin to the Council and makes his case as to why Anakin should be trained as a Jedi. No doubt, the Jedi Council was impressed, but the oldest, wisest, and most respected of the Jedi Masters was not convinced – Jedi Master Yoda (voice performed by Frank Oz).

Yoda

Yoda argued that Anakin's upbringing as a slave child had taught him to be constantly afraid to such an extent that fear became a defining element of his character. The old Jedi Master argued that upon deciding to train him, Anakin would be forever dominated by the fear impressed upon him for so long, and Yoda argued that this fear would ultimately be Anakin's undoing. The Jedi Council, because of Yoda's very valid point, was divided on the issue of Anakin's training, but Qui-Gon asserted that – with or without their permission – he would train Anakin anyway, and so the apprenticeship of Anakin to Qui-Gon began. It ended fairly quickly as Qui-Gon was killed by the Sith Lord, Darth Maul, late in the film. Upon Qui-Gon's death, Obi-Wan Kenobi, Qui-Gon's other apprentice, was made a Jedi Master and was set the task of completing Anakin's training (Lucas I).

Star Wars Episode II: The Attack of the Clones

The second film of the prequel trilogy is dominated by wars fought between the Galactic Republic and the Separatists – a group aided by the Trade Federation and an unknown Sith Lord in their efforts of destabilizing the Republic. The war, however, is the least important event in the film for the purposes for this text (Lucas II).

In this film, we see Anakin growing into manhood and being granted more and more responsibilities as he climbs in the Jedi Order.

One of his missions is to protect Padme Amidala (played by Natalie Portman) – the senator from the jungle-covered planet of Naboo. Over the course of the film, Anakin and Padme fall in love. This is problematic to the extreme, because Jedi Warriors take an oath to remain single and celibate. Anakin and Padme can't seem to help themselves, although Padme tries – for the longest time – to deny her feelings for Anakin in hopes of protecting him from the wrath of the Jedi. At the end of the film, in an effort to hide their love from the Jedi Council and the bureaucrats of the Republic on Coruscant, Anakin and Padme are married in secret on Naboo (Lucas II).

Anakin's first real test in his Jedi training comes about when he begins to have dream-visions of his mother, Shmi, in terrible pain. The dreams reoccur and they disturb Anakin deeply, so much that he and Padme set out for Tatooine to find and rescue her. Upon arriving at the settlement where his mother had been living, he discovered the worst. Tusken Raiders (rascally, fiendish inhabitants of the uninhabited lands of Tatooine) had raided the moisture farm on which Shmi lived, and in the raid, Shmi was captured. Anakin set out to find her, and he found her in enough time for her to die in his arms. Filled with rage, Anakin killed the Tusken Raiders – not just the men but also the women and children. He told Padme that he couldn't help himself; it was the only thing that removed the pain of his mother's death – at least, for a little while (Lucas II).

Another occurrence in the film is Anakin's befriending of Chancellor Palpatine (played by Ian McDiarmid). Anakin knew of and was protected by Palpatine when he arrived on Coruscant as a child, but now Anakin and the Chancellor's friendship became deeper. Anakin, arguably, saw Palpatine as more of a father figure than a political figurehead – the view held by the rest of the Jedi Council. He told Palpatine of his massacre of the Tusken Raiders, and the Chancellor, rather than judging Anakin's actions, praised him for standing up for what he believes in. While Anakin felt comfortable telling Padme and Palpatine about this mishap, he hides his massacre of the Tuskens from his colleagues on the Jedi Council. Near the end of the film, the Chancellor is kidnapped by high-ranking members of the Separatist army. Anakin and Obi-Wan set off to rescue him (Lucas II).

Star Wars Episode III: The Revenge of the Sith

The war rages on while Anakin and Obi-Wan attempt to rescue Chancellor Palpatine from the Separatists and their leader, an alien clone, General Grievous, and a Sith Lord, Count Dooku (played by Christopher Lee). Anakin, at the behest of the Chancellor, kills Dooku, but General Grievous escapes before he can be destroyed. The rescue mission, however, is successful. Anakin and Obi-Wan deliver the Chancellor back to the Senate on Coruscant and Anakin is left to bask in the praise of the politicians from planets across the galaxy (Lucas III).

Padme, hiding in a corner, finds Anakin and informs him that she is pregnant with their child. Knowing that he will be expelled from the Jedi Order (and likely killed) if the truth is discovered, he keeps the news of his unborn child a secret. Closeted alone, Padme and Anakin discuss their excitement and their angst over the possibilities of being parents. That night, Anakin has another dream-vision – this one of Padme dying in childbirth. Feeling that he could have saved his mother if he had acted on his dream-visions from the past, Anakin seeks the advice of the Jedi through indirect hints. He seeks out Master Yoda who tells him to "train himself to let go of everything you fear to lose" (Lucas III).

Anakin finds this to be an irrational and unsatisfactory answer and seeks the advice of Chancellor Palpatine – who reveals that they are now privy to the location of General Grievous. Palpatine tells Anakin the Sith legend of Darth Plagueis the Wise. The Chancellor suggests that Plagueis has the ability to use the midichlorians in his blood to create and protect life; he further implies that Plagueis could keep the ones he cared about from dying. Anakin was beyond interested, but Palpatine informs him that no Jedi can teach him to use the power Plagueis possessed (Lucas III).

Not long after the encounter with the Chancellor, Anakin begins to doubt himself and the Jedi Order. He desires to remain loyal to the Jedi but cannot accept that Padme might die if he chooses not to act. Palpatine reveals to Anakin that he is Darth Sidious – the Sith Lord that the Jedi have been looking for and also the apprentice of Darth Plagueis. He tells Anakin that, although his Jedi instincts were to turn Sidious over to the Jedi, only he could aid Anakin in saving Padme's life. After a number of the Jedi Council members attempt to arrest the Chancellor and Jedi Master Mace Windu (played by Samuel L. Jackson) nearly assassinates him, Anakin slices off Windu's hand with his lightsaber, allows the Chancellor (Sidious) to kill Windu, and makes his pledge to Sidious and the ways of the Dark Lords of the Sith. Anakin Skywalker becomes the most feared and renowned villain in fantasy lore – Darth Vader.

Darth Vader

Sidious sends Anakin to kill all the Jedi on Coruscant while the Chancellor orders his generals to complete Order 66 – an executive order to kill all of the Jedi. Only Yoda and Obi-Wan Kenobi survive. After his attack on the Jedi Temple is complete, Anakin briefly visits Padme but then departs for the volcanic planet of Mustafar to destroy the rest of the Separatist leaders and end the war (Lucas III).

The two remaining Jedi return to Coruscant and discover the massacre that had occurred in the Jedi Temple. Yoda deduces that only a Jedi could have committed such an act, because all of the fallen had been murdered by a lightsaber – a weapon only carried by Jedi Knights. Obi-Wan and Yoda look at a security recording and discover that Anakin – now Vader – was responsible for the massacre. Yoda orders Obi-Wan to find and kill his former apprentice while he – Yoda – confronts and destroys Palpatine (Lucas III).

Obi-Wan seeks out Padme and reveals that Anakin has turned to the Dark Side. Padme denies it, unable to accept the truth of what had happened. Disturbed by what Obi-Wan had told her, Padme climbs aboard her own ship and departs for Mustafar to talk to Anakin and attempt to discover the truth. Before Padme's ship leaves Coruscant, Obi-Wan sneaks on board the ship and hides in a secret compartment, unnoticed (Lucas III).

On Coruscant, Chancellor Palpatine convenes a special session of Congress and alleges that the Jedi had attempted to overthrow the Republic. He assures the Senate that all the Jedi have been successfully defeated but declares that to protect the integrity of the Republic and ensure its security, that it will be reorganized into the Galactic Empire and sets himself up as Emperor (Lucas III).

Padme arrives on Mustafar and confronts Anakin about Obi-Wan's tale regarding the security recording – which shows Anakin murdering Jedi Padawans – children. Anakin then reveals his true nature and suggests the new powers granted him by his training as a Sith would make the both of them invincible. Padme admonishes Anakin and tells him that she only wants his love, not power or invulnerability. Anakin rebukes her and declares his dark intentions – to overthrow the Emperor and to remake the governments of the former Republic into a shape more pleasing to him. Realizing she has lost the man she knew, Padme tells Anakin that she can't follow him down this dark path. At this point, Obi-Wan reveals himself and Anakin, in his anger at Padme's supposed betrayal, attempts to choke her to death. Obi-Wan saves her, fights Anakin in an epic lightsaber duel, and successfully defeats his former apprentice by slicing off his remaining limbs (Lucas III).

Yoda is not so lucky in his battle with the Emperor. Instead of defeating Sidious, Yoda and the Sith Lord end up in a stalemate and Yoda is forced to flee. He seeks the aid of a sympathetic senator, Bail Organa (played by Jimmy Smits). Yoda suggests that the Jedi must go into exile until the time is right to reemerge (Lucas III).

After the fight on Mustafar, Obi-Wan returns with Padme to the Republic and is granted asylum on Organa's planet of Alderaan. By this time, Padme had gone into labor. She gives birth to twins – a boy, Luke, and a girl, Leia. Shortly after the children are born, Padme dies – not from the pain of childbirth as Anakin had foreseen but from the pain of a broken heart. The children are separated to protect them from the Sith; Bail Organa and his wife adopt Leia while Obi-Wan takes Luke to his aunt and uncle on Tatooine. The Jedi, Yoda and Obi-Wan, go into exile to await the time when Luke is old enough to be trained as both a Jedi Warrior and the last hope for the preservation of the ideals of the Galactic Republic (Lucas III).

American Political Philosophy

In the realm of philosophy, there were a number of great thinkers whose theories held a great deal of sway over the Founding Fathers when they designed how our country would look through the Constitution. The three areas of political philosophy considered by the Founder Fathers were *the nature of humanity*, *the separation of powers question*, and the *social contract dilemma.* These philosophical discussions shaped how our Founding Fathers designed the country in the Constitution, altered the way they perceived that the new government would operate, and set up certain boundaries to allow but also limit the power of those in government.

The Nature of Humanity

As we said earlier, in the first prequel film, *The Phantom Menace*, Jedi Masters Qui-Gon Jinn and Obi-Wan Kenobi found Anakin and his ridiculous midichlorian count on Tatooine and decided to bring him before the Jedi Council to determine whether or not he would be trained as a Jedi. At Council, Qui-Gon made the argument that *Anakin was good as all children are good, and because of his high midichlorian count, is destined for greatness. Anakin, Qui-Gon implied, may be the 'Chosen One' from the ancient Jedi prophecy who was destined to bring balance to the Force and destroy the Lords of the Sith* (Lucas I).

Jedi Master Yoda disagreed. He argued that *Anakin's history as a slave-child had taught him to constantly be afraid, and he argued that the fear had become an innate part of his character and personality. Yoda argued that, if trained as a Jedi, Anakin's destiny would forever be dominated by that fear, and he was predisposed to betray the Jedi and become a Sith Lord – a being the Jedi's first duty was to destroy* (Lucas I). And indeed, Yoda proved to be right. Anakin was unable to fight the fear of losing his wife, Padme, turned to the Dark Side of the Force, and became a Sith as well as the greatest villain of all time, Darth Vader (Lucas III).

In ancient Greece, there were two toga-wearing sages who shared the philosophies of Qui-Gon Jinn and Yoda, and both had different philosophies on *human nature* just as the two Jedi had theories about *Anakin's nature.* The two philosophers were Plato – the author of *The Republic* – and his student, Aristotle. Both men were citizens of ancient Athens – the first 'true' or 'direct' democracy, and their perception of human nature invariably shaped the government of Athens and also affected how it operated.

Plato was the eternal optimist. He always "looked on the bright side of life" – as Monty Python, a British comedy troupe, would say. Plato argued that *humans are inherently good and, because of their ability to reason and use their intellect, are destined for great things – power, glory, honor, and respect. He argued that the evil in the world came from humans growing up in a world dominated by fear, jealousy, and hate* (Plato 32-59). For Plato, humans were good to begin with but were corrupted by their environment.

Aristotle felt differently. This philosopher lived during troubled times in Athens and saw the darker side of humanity. Aristotle contended that *while humans have their intellect and therefore have the capacity to make rational, thought-out decisions, humans are – first and foremost – animals, and it is in the nature of any animal to do whatever it has to in order to survive. Because of our animalistic nature, humans are innately prone to doing unspeakable things to each other in the name of surviving and succeeding in the world* (Aristotle 30-44).

To put it lightly, the debate over human nature is an epic battle of Light and Dark. The Jedi disputed Anakin's nature and destiny just as these two ancient Athenians debated the nature and destiny of humanity. If humanity really *is* good by nature, would there really be a need for government? Couldn't the good, selfless humans take care of themselves without having to be told what one can and cannot do? If humans *are* innately self-interested, self-preserving animals, what restrictions

Plato, Greek philosopher

Aristotle, Greek philosopher

should a government put on humanity to encourage them to embrace their better nature? How far should the restrictions go before they become intrusive into the privacy and everyday lives of a government's citizenry?

Most philosophers concur that Aristotle was correct – that we humans are animals by instinct, and that we will do, if permitted, whatever we have to in order to make it in the world. In fact, most philosophers argue that Plato was exactly wrong – that it isn't culture that corrupts, but rather, it is culture that instills values, morals, and a sense of right and wrong. We can look at our world today and see places where this positive reinforcement takes place: churches, food pantries, places of education, hospitals, and so on. There are so many venues in society that encourage humans to work *with* each other instead of *against* each other, but were these institutions absent, it is likely that humans would give in to their baser tendencies – the desire to have, to take, to dominate, to control, and to prevent others from threatening one's place in the world – wherever that is.

The debate over human nature is one that is not easily resolved. Many people argue that humans cannot be evil, self-interested animals. Some concur with Plato simply because they are incapable of conceptualizing themselves as animals by nature. Others hold this belief because of all the good they see in the world. There are many optimists out there, and that's all to the good; our society needs more of them, but our society also the people who operate in the realm of reality.

Aristotle's supporters fall more into this category. Understanding the reason behind laws and government enables humans to get a glimpse of their nature. If humans were indeed good, selfless creatures, there would be no need for laws against murder, rape, assault, or other such atrocities. The truth is that humans are complicated creatures with unique abilities, which makes our nature difficult to pinpoint. We have, however, through philosophical discourse, come closer to understanding more about our instinctive selves.

The Separation of Powers Question

In the Galactic Republic, there were three bastions of power. The first and most noticeable was the Senate – the legislative arm of the Republic. Both Padme Amidala and Bail Organa serve as senators until the birth of the Empire. The executive arm of the Republic was controlled by Chancellor Palpatine (i.e., Darth Sidious). He used his power and influence to shape the war in which the galaxy was immersed to the point where he convinced Anakin and the Senate that the Jedi Council hoped to overthrow the Republic and take the power for themselves. The judicial element of the Republic was the Jedi Knights and the Council that governed them. It was the duty of the Jedi to defend and protect the various systems in the galaxy from injustice as well as to balance the power between the Senate, the legislators, and the Chancellor (the executive officer). The Republic's three-part governance system worked well together until the Chancellor began using his power against everyone else and encouraging strife between the other two that was previously absent (Lucas I, II, and III).

America also has a three-part system designed to separate and balance the power between them, and this idea was first proposed by a Frenchman – Baron de Montesquieu. Montesquieu believed that giving power to one man or to even two different bodies set society up for unnecessary power struggles. He argued that a certain level of power struggle was necessary to ensure that well-thought-out legislation was written that would have real benefits for society; however, he argued that the more you split up the power, the less likely it would be that one power structure would try to dominate the other two (Montesquieu 21-30).

The Galactic Republic's three-part governance structure is similar to ours except for the Republic's apparent lack of checks and balances. **Checks and balances** is the method by which the power of one government body is limited by the oversight of the other two bodies. For example, if things had worked properly, the Senate and the Jedi Council should have been able to keep Chancellor Palpatine – the executive – in check. They failed in that attempt because instead of working together to limit the power of the Chancellor, Palpatine had the other two government bodies at odds with each other. In a properly functioning three-part system, each body checks the power of the other two. So far, this has been modestly successful in most modern democracies.

In the *Star Wars* saga, it is noticeable that the Jedi Council followed its own mind a lot and did its own thing regardless as to what the Senate or the Chancellor said about it. The decision as to who the Jedi trained, which systems they aided, and what laws they enforced were decisions the Jedi Council made independent of the influence of the Senate or the Chancellor. The Jedi Council was, from a certain sense, the most powerful government body, because there was fewer checks on its power than the other two bodies – the Galactic Senate or the Chancellor.

Montesquieu argued that a strong and relatively independent judicial branch was an important facet to a three-part system. He argued that politics, by nature, will become political and that it would be inevitable for the three bodies of government to compete for greater power. He argued, however, that it only makes sense that one body be, at least partially, independent of political influence. No elections should tap these citizens into office and no term limits should restrain them. Montesquieu argued that this body should be the entity of justice – the judiciary, for putting justice in the hands of people with apparent agendas, he argued, was dangerous and could be disastrous for the system as a whole (Montesquieu 21-30).

So, as the most independent body, the Jedi Council exacted justice across the galaxy as it saw fit just as the judiciary dispenses justice as it sees fit – free of political jargoning. As sage-like leaders, the Jedi used their philosophical prowess to exact true justice across the galaxy insofar as they could. The same can be said of the judicial bodies that exist in modern democracies that embrace this three-part governance structure; power, without political pressure, to exact their interpretation of justice is the power held by the judiciary – in this case, the Jedi Council.

The Social Contract Dilemma

The human nature and separation of powers discussions are fascinating, but the social contract debate is the discourse that probably influenced the Founding Fathers the most. First, before we discuss both sides of the argument, let us define what a social contract actually is. A **social contract** is an agreement made between a government and its citizens. The government agrees to protect its people and also to provide basic needs – food, shelter, and so on. The people agree to adhere to the laws implemented by the government and to follow its lead if the government is threatened from outside by foreign powers. Social contracts, sometimes, are unwritten declarations of the people and their government's unique accord. Other social contracts are actually written on paper.

In the third and final prequel movie, *The Revenge of the Sith*, the man Anakin turns to the Dark Side of the Force, becomes Darth Vader, and becomes the key defender of Chancellor (soon to be Emperor) Palpatine. Anakin becomes an *agent of the Galactic Empire*. Instead of supporting his Jedi colleagues and attempting to preserve the democratically governed Galactic Republic, Anakin betrays his friends and props up Palpatine and his evil Empire. Obi-Wan Kenobi, Anakin's Jedi mentor, opposes Anakin, Palpatine, and the Empire. As a sworn protector of the Galactic Republic and democracy, Obi-Wan – albeit reluctantly – seeks out, pleads with, and ultimately attempts to destroy Anakin (Lucas III).

Anakin Skywalker, played by Hayden Christiansen

Two British philosophers discussed the ability of citizenries to dissolve their social contracts with their governments or not. The first of these philosophers is Thomas Hobbes. Hobbes, like Aristotle, believed in the dark side of human nature and argued that governments are created to keep humanity's baser nature in check. People, he argued, entered into social contracts with governments – even tyrannical ones – because the safety government provided was far better than going it alone in a very brutal and dangerous world. Hobbes argued that once the two parties – government and citizenry – had entered into a social contract, that the *social contract could not be broken.* He argued that the severing of social contracts allowed for the possibility of anarchical existence – so, the state of nature taking hold. He argued that the evil nature of humanity, the desire for power, and humanity's unfettered greed would make things far worse than anything a tyrannical king or warlord could do. So, like Anakin, Hobbes is the philosopher who would support propping up governments and their control – even if those governments cease in fulfilling their end of the social contract. Anarchy, according to Hobbes, is always worse than the dictatorial alternative (Hobbes 341-343).

His counterpart, John Locke, disagrees. He contends that government can become so tyrannical and oppressive that the governments themselves can be worse than the temporal anarchy that might exist between regimes. Locke argues that *if a government becomes tyrannical, oppressive, or ceases in fulfilling its end of the social contract, then social contracts can and should be broken.* Locke believes that governments should do their job, and that the citizens are the only people who can and should have the ability to rein in a government's power and also to ensure that the government is adhering to the social contract. To Locke, a bad government is worse than no government at all, for the absence of government provides the opportunity for the creation of something new, different, and better (Locke 1-3 and 101-108).

John Locke, British political philosopher

Hobbes, like Anakin (Darth Vader), believed in clinging to a decadent, oppressive regime whereas Locke and Obi-Wan Kenobi believed in fighting and defeating governments who had ceased to keep their end of the social contract. To put it simply, Hobbes opposed altering the status quo whereas Locke believed that altering the status quo is not only tolerable but, in specific circumstances, an effort that should be encouraged.

The Revenge of the Sith and America's 'Deal-Breaker'

The final prequel film, *The Revenge of the Sith*, tells the story of Anakin's path to the Dark Side – the path to Darth Vader. At the beginning of the film, however, the possibility of Anakin abandoning the Jedi seems ridiculous. The film begins with Anakin and his teacher, Obi-Wan Kenobi working together and interacting as if they were brothers in an effort to rescue Chancellor Palpatine. In fact, Anakin rescues Obi-Wan even though Palpatine pressures Anakin to abandon him (Lucas III).

Things begin to change when Anakin attempts to find a reasonable solution to the possibility of Padme dying in childbirth. The Jedi offer no solution other than forgetting about her – something Anakin is unwilling, and perhaps unable, to do. Instead, he seeks out Palpatine who provides him with the answer he seeks – a way to save Padme. Ultimately, we know that Anakin succumbs to the allure of the power of the Sith Lord, Darth Sidious (Palpatine), and turns to the Dark Side. Anakin was then sent to the Jedi Temple to kill all the Jedi dwelling there. Soon after, Obi-Wan and Yoda view a security hologram that provides them with intimate details of the massacre (Lucas III).

Obi-Wan Kenobi is dismayed by what he sees, but he still believes that his friendship with Anakin can be salvaged. He confronts Anakin on the volcanic planet of Mustafar in an attempt to reason with him and to attempt to bring him back to the Light Side of the Force – a feat no one had ever achieved. It is not to be; Anakin is too far gone, and Obi-Wan then does what his duty calls him to do – he confronts Anakin in an all-out, epic lightsaber duel.

The lightsaber duel on Mustafar – the end of a friendship

As fighters, Obi-Wan and Anakin are equally matched, and so, ultimately, there is a break in the action where Obi-Wan tries again to bring Anakin back to his former self. Again, the attempt fails, and Obi-Wan resigns himself to the reality that Anakin is irredeemable and the only solution to the problem – as all Jedi are instructed – is to remove the new Sith Lord from the picture. Obi-Wan then finishes the duel by slicing Anakin's remaining limbs off in a single stroke; he leaves Anakin for dead on the edge of a fiery lava pit. The once beautiful and deep friendship of Anakin Skywalker and Obi-Wan Kenobi was no more (Lucas III).

How like these two friends were Great Britain and their colonies in America! In the beginning, England and its colonies had a great relationship. In fact – even in the midst of the American Revolution, most citizens of the colonies identified themselves as British, not American. The relationship began to change after 1763 when Great Britain's French and Indian War concluded. Britain was deep in debt, and its solution was to begin taxing the American colonies – something that has not been done. The taxes themselves were not what disquieted the colonies; it was the fact that these same taxes weren't being imposed in England. On top of that, the houses of Parliament, England's legislature, refused to allow the appointment of colonial representatives. The all too famous cry of, "No taxation without representation," became commonplace. At this point, the colonies had expressed their displeasure through word of mouth, but things became more militant quickly (Brinkley 100-112).

England imposed another slew of taxes, the Townshend Acts and the Tea Act – most of them geared to tax what the colonists perceived to be random things – paper, tea, coffee, and other everyday wares. The colonists responded radically and engaged in the famous Boston Tea Party, dumping carton after carton of tea into Boston Harbor. After the Tea Party, England attempted to restore order and silence rebels by issuing the Intolerable Acts, which closed Boston Harbor for business, stationed troops in Boston, allowed for the quartering of soldiers in colonial homes, and so on. Many of the colonists were furious, and it was the stationing of troops in Boston that prompted the colonies to remember the ideas of John Locke: if a government ceased to fulfill its end of the social contract, the people had the right to nullify

The Jedi and the American colonies: combatting the Empire

the social contract and start over as they saw fit. The colonists began to stockpile weapons at Lexington and Concord, and that is where the American Revolution began soon after (Brinkley 110-118).

Even after Lexington and Concord, the colonists hoped to avoid a war by making a final appeal to the king of England, George III. The plea went unanswered, and the colonies gave up. The next piece of paper the king received from the colonies was their formal end to their social contract with England – the Declaration of Independence. The colonists then began the battle to secure their independence from England – a country that not so long ago had been one that these same men would have died to defend, preserve, and protect (Brinkley 117-118).

Anakin's path to the Dark Side and the end of his relationship with Obi-Wan Kenobi is eerily similar to the path that Great Britain and the colonies tread. Like Anakin – who propped up the might of Chancellor Palpatine and the Galactic Empire, Great Britain attempted to assert its control – as Empire – over its colonies. Like Obi-Wan, the American colonies eventually came to the conclusion that some friendships, some agreements, are impossible to maintain when the other party fails to keep their end of the bargain. Just as Obi-Wan severed the limbs from Darth Vader's body, the colonies severed themselves from the body that was the empire of Great Britain. Both of these adventures – the tale of Anakin and the story of America – were only just beginning (Lucas III).

Food for Thought

Human Nature

In your opinion, are humans innately good and selfless like the Jedi or evil and self-interested like the Lords of the Sith? Do you think the 'nature' side of humanity is stronger than the 'rational' side and why? Palpatine argues that 'good' and 'evil' are points of view. Do you agree or disagree and why? Can a 'bad' person become 'good' again? Why do 'good' people do bad things? Can a person's perception of 'good' and 'evil' change as they age and why do you think that? Do people set double standards – meaning they believe something to be wrong for others but not themselves?

Separation of Powers

Do you believe that any of the three branches of government is more powerful than the others? If so, which one and why? Are all branches of government beholden to someone or is there a branch that has no checks to restrain it? Are all branches of government influenced by politics? In *The Revenge of the Sith*, Palpatine first had to take out the Jedi Council – the arm of justice – before he could erect his empire. Could the same be said for anyone wishing to destroy this country? Is our government invulnerable to such attempts? If so, why do you feel that way; if not, why not? Are there benefits in limiting executive power? How should executive power be limited? Should the branches of government work mostly as independent bodies or mostly as bodies dependent on the others?

Social Contracts

Should social contracts be general or specific in what the government promises that it will do and what the people should do? Should social contracts be revisable? Should citizens be able to break the social contract that they made with their government? Should the government have the ability to break the social contract that it forged with its people? Should social contracts be written down, or are most of the tenets of such documents what most would consider to be common sense? Does the breaking of social contracts always result in violence and revolution, or can peaceful replacements of social contracts be forged without conflict? Are some differences irreconcilable in terms of government?

Do you feel sorry for Anakin and understand why he did what he did? If you were Anakin, would letting Padme die be a better course of action than trying to save her? Once Anakin assumes the persona of Darth Vader, the extension of his power begins to overshadow his desire to save Padme. Do you think that Anakin made the right choice for the wrong reasons, or do you think that he made the wrong choice for the right reasons? Do you think Obi-Wan was right in ending his friendship with Anakin?

Do you think that the American colonies were right in breaking their social contract with England, or did the colonies hold unreasonable expectations of the British government? Were the American colonies treated any different than any other British colonial network? Why was England so unwilling to meet the colonists' demands to lower or limit its taxation? Was the Boston Tea Party a catalyst to the violence that was to follow? How is the Declaration of Independence a 'Lockean' document? Do you think Locke would have joined the colonists in their fight for independence or the British in their fight to maintain order and stability in the colonies?

The Revenge of the Sith

In your opinion, are our political leaders more like the selfless Jedi Knights, the selfish Sith Lords, or something more like Anakin – a person who starts off as a selfless person but is corrupted by greed and a lust for power? Do you think people get into politics for personal gain or because they really want to try and aid their constituents? Name a few examples of selfless policies that people in government have enacted for the people. Conversely, give some examples of selfish policies that people in government have signed into law that benefit only themselves. Why is corruption such a problem in politics? Is power a gift or a curse? What about control – gift or curse?

The Force will be with you…always…
Just ask the St. Louis Cardinals…

Works Cited

Aristotle. *Politics.* Chicago: University of Chicago Press, 1984.

Brinkley, Alan. *American History: A Survey. Volume 1: To 1877.* Eleventh Edition. New York: McGraw Hill Higher Education, 1977.

Hobbes, Thomas. *Leviathan.* New York: Penguin Books, 1968.

Locke, John. *Second Treatise of Government.* New York: CreateSpace Publishing Platform, 2013.

Montesquieu, Baron de. *The Spirit of the Laws.* Cambridge: Cambridge University Press, 1989.

Plato. *Republic.* Indianapolis: Hackett Publishing Company, 1992.

Star Wars Episode I: The Phantom Menace. Dir. George Lucas. Perf. Liam Nelson, Ewan McGregor, Jake Lloyd, Ian McDiarmid, and Frank Oz (voice). Twentieth Century Fox, 1999. Film.

Star Wars Episode II: Attack of the Clones. Dir. George Lucas. Perf. Hayden Christiansen, Natalie Portman, Ewan McGregor, Ian McDiarmid, and Frank Oz (voice). Twentieth Century Fox, 2002. Film.

Star Wars Episode III: The Revenge of the Sith. Dir. George Lucas. Perf. Hayden Christiansen, Natalie Portman, Ewan McGregor, Ian McDiarmid, Samuel L. Jackson, Jimmy Smits, and Frank Oz (voice). Twentieth Century Fox, 2005. Film.

Major League Baseball and the U.S. Constitution – America's Two Pastimes

There once was an automobile commercial that advertised the following items as truly 'American' (and you can hum along if you want) – "baseball, hot dogs, apple pie, and Chevrolet." The commercial first hit the airwaves in the 1970s but was remade and aired during the 2011 baseball season – one that is especially memorable for me as a St. Louis Cardinals fan. I can still see Prince Fielder, the former first baseman for the rival Milwaukee Brewers, humming the clever, catchy tune. Baseball is America's sport – we created it (well, ol' Abner Doubleday did anyway), we refined it, and man, can we play it! Baseball is truly one of America's greatest traditions.

Insofar as politics are concerned, we have another, far more significant tradition to uphold and defend. Unlike baseball, the defense of this tradition stirs immediate and incessant debate. This tradition is the United States Constitution. This document has served as the foundation for American government since the time it was ratified into law by nine of the thirteen colonies-made-states – the two-thirds support necessary for any law adoption on a federal level. Interestingly enough, that tradition has held up to this day. By virtue of the Amendment process and **judicial precedent** – legal standards set by judicial decision making – the Constitution has been changed and interpreted to preserve this first and best of American traditions – our government. Before we delve into the actual document, let us first consider the fundamentals of baseball so that the comparisons made later make sense to those of you who are less familiar with baseball than tradition might indicate.

Written long ago but relevant today

Baseball is played on a diamond-shaped field. On this diamond, there are a number of places that prove to be important. First, in the middle of the diamond, a mound is raised a bit higher off the ground than the rest of the field; this serves as the pitcher's mound. The pitcher throws the ball in a straight to downward motion toward our next point of interest – home plate. At home plate (which is roughly 60 feet from the pitcher's mound and 17 inches across) is the batter, the catcher, and the umpire (or referee). The batter (or hitter) uses a bat (a 30-40 inch long, round stick) to hit the ball thrown by the pitcher. The catcher works with the pitcher in an effort to get the batter to either (1) miss with his swings or (2) fail to swing at good pitches, or strikes, as defined by the home plate umpire. The difference between a 'strike' and a 'ball' is defined by the 'strike zone'.

The Strike Zone

The strike zone is as wide as home plate (17 inches), as high as the letters on the batter's jersey, and as low as his kneecaps. Any ball thrown in this area is designated a 'strike'. All other pitch locations are designated non-strikes, or 'balls'. Players often mishit balls so they fail to end up within the parameters of the field. For example: a batter may hit the ball so that it lands in the area behind the catcher and umpire. If it lands, this is known as a 'foul ball' and counts as a strike in the batter's count (number of balls and strikes against the batter). Three strikes thrown in an 'at-bat' or turn at the plate constitutes the batter as 'out' or a failed attempt. One cannot strike out on a foul ball unless the batter is attempting to 'bunt' or deaden the ball right in front of home plate. Four balls constitute a 'walk' or a free trip to first base – a batter's first offensive stop around the baseball diamond.

Some argue that the strike zone is subjective – a zone that is different from umpire to umpire, but in general, the strike zone varies very little from game to game. In fact, Major League umpires have to train a great deal before they are permitted to call a Major League game. Emphasis on strike-zone accuracy is paramount here, so erroneous calls are limited by lots of practice and post-game scrutiny. The bottom line here is three strikes constitute a batter being called 'out' or finished with the at-bat.

The Infield

If a batter draws a walk or gets a hit, he heads to first base – the first of three bases in the 'infield' or the area inside or near the baseball diamond. There are also second and third bases. From home plate, first base is 90 feet diagonally to home plate's right side. When standing on first base, second base is 90 feet diagonally right from first base. Third base is the same, and from third, the base runner can then run the final 90 feet back to home plate and score a point or 'run'. Defending the infield are six players: the pitcher and catcher (already mentioned), the first baseman, the second baseman, the shortstop (who plays between second and third base), and the third baseman. All of these players are responsible for defending against balls that are hit within or shortly outside of the baseball diamond.

The Outfield

Three other players play deep outside the diamond but in front of the fence, the end of the playing area; this space is known as the 'outfield'. There is a right fielder who plays along the first baseline (the first baseline stretches from first base to the end of right field). Anything hit to the left of the first baseline is considered a 'fair ball' and permits batters to run to the base they can get to before being thrown out. Anything to the right of the first baseline, if it lands, constitutes a 'foul ball' and counts as a strike in the batter's count. The center fielder plays in the outfield behind second base. The left fielder defends the third baseline; anything that lands to the right of it is 'fair' while anything that lands to the left of it is 'foul'.

The job of the outfielders is to catch 'fly balls' – or balls that fly through the air. Generally speaking, balls that outfielders play on the ground will give batters a 'base hit' which allows them to advance from home plate to first base. Balls that are missed in the outfield (depending on the speed of the runner and the accuracy and speed of the relaying throw from the outfielder) constitute either a 'double', the batter reaching second base, or a 'triple', the batter reaching third base. Triples are fairly rare. Any ball hit over the fence in the outfield is known as a 'home run'. The batter gets to round the bases and score a run for his team. Any players on base when a home run is hit also round the bases and score their respective runs. A home run hit with the bases loaded (all three bases occupied by previous batters) is known as a 'grand slam'. It scores four runs (one for each successful batter).

Innings and Outs

We said earlier that a player could 'strike out' by hitting a ball into foul territory or by missing the ball when he swings at it. An 'out' constitutes one of three opportunities that the offense (hitting team) gets each period or 'inning'. Each team gets the chance to hit in each inning. The visiting team always bats in the first half or 'top' of the inning, and the home teams always bats in the second half or

Baseball scoreboard: innings, outs, balls, strikes, and other important stuff

'bottom' of the inning. A complete, regular game is nine innings long, but a tie game is broken by playing as many innings as is necessary for one team to score more runs than the other. So in general, the winning team (in a regular game) has to get 27 batters from the other team out to win (3 batters for each of the 9 innings).

Major League Baseball and the United States Constitution

Now that we have a better understanding in regard to how baseball is played, let's take a look at the game in greater depth as it compares to elements in the Constitution that are worthy of note. This bit of the chapter is separated into five sections: (1) Beginnings, (2) The Fielders and the Legislative Branch, (3) the Pitcher and the Executive Branch, (4) the Umpire and the Judicial Branch, and (5) Other Interesting Comparisons.

General Information

How do all baseball games begin? The first pitch? The handing of the lineup cards to the home plate umpire? No. Every ballgame begins with the teams – home and visiting – standing along their respective baseline; the home team on the first baseline and the visiting team along the third baseline. Once everybody is in their specified location, a pre-specified person or group sings the National Anthem – that is, "The Star Spangled Banner." Sometimes, the anthem is sung by a school choir, and other times it is sung or performed by a nationally recognized entity; but regardless, this is how every baseball game begins – with a tribute to America.

Similarly, the U.S. Constitution begins with a declaration of what the goals of the county and the bodies that govern it will seek to achieve. This declaration is known as the Preamble. Promoting justice, securing liberty, providing for the common defense, and ensuring the welfare of its people are all items included and deemed important by the Framers of the Constitution by including this powerful declaration we know as the Preamble (United States, 90).

Baseball and the Constitution: different ways to view "the game"

Interestingly enough, both the National Anthem and Preamble are also comparable in that they are widely recognized as dictates of American government. The National Anthem is known as a hymn that describes the victory of the Continental Army in the American Revolution. The Preamble is, for all intents and purposes, a summary of what the Founders sought to achieve once the American Revolution was won and national independence from Great Britain was attained.

Baseball's grandest stage – the 'end game' if you will, is the World Series – the championship of baseball, and like the rest of the matchups that present themselves during the course of the season, this contest between two teams extends longer than just one game and is, in fact, several games long – at the bare minimum, four. In its finest form, however, the World Series can span for seven games full of nail biting, hair pulling drama. Just ask any Cardinal fan who saw their team down to their final strike – twice – in 2011 but yet saw the team advance to and win an epic Game 7 in the 2011 World Series. The World Series, simply put, is a best-of-seven series. The first team with four victories wins the World Series and earns the title of being the best in baseball – well, at least until the next year's champs are crowned.

The Constitution, as well, is 'best with seven'. The document has seven or sections. Each section delineates what each branch of government's responsibilities are, the role of the federal government, the process by which the Constitution can be amended, the role of state governments and their relationship with the federal government, and so on. The Founding Fathers found seven major concepts worthy of inclusion in the social contract it sought to present to its citizenry; thus, we have seven articles to the Constitution. Just as the World Series victor is determined by a (potentially) seven-game matchup, the Constitution was deemed perfect with its seven sections (United States, 90-100).

Anyone who has been to a Major League baseball game will tell you that it's an opportunity that everyone should experience at least once in their lifetime. There is nothing like smelling ballpark hotdogs five blocks away from the stadium or hearing the roar of the crowd when your heavy hitter belts a home run. What else compares to seeing your team's

Baseball and the Constitution: matters of perspective

mascot – in my case, Redbird Fredbird, doing the Gangnam Style dance in a Jedi robe on Star Wars night at the ballpark? That's right – nothing compares to being at the game in person. It is a special experience – one that is quite different from the experience that fans at home can only hope to capture on their respective couches.

At home, surely, the price of watching the game is smaller by a wide margin. There is no $20 parking fee, $9 beers, or $8 hotdogs. There is no smell of the grass, no roar of the crowd, no intimate connection with the home team when you sit and watch at home. Conversely, however, most fans have a better view from their televisions than anyone at the ballpark does. The cameras and technology of today bring the games home to fans in such a way that the game is almost more viewable from the couch than it is in the stands. Another positive feature one gains from watching the game at home is the leisure of getting up and being able to pause the game and resume later it if one needs a break. If you have to get up at the ballpark, the game moves on – whether you're watching it or not.

The same differences in perspectives are distinguishable in the way people read the Constitution as well. There are many people out there who see the Constitution as a static, unchangeable, perfect document. They read the Constitution – word for word. Issues like abortion, gay marriage, and the Keystone pipeline (to name a few) are untouchable according to this crowd; if these issues (or problems like them) were for the government to decide, these literal readers contend that the Founding Fathers would have included addendums in the Constitution that would have dealt with these current events that stir controversy (Strauss, 1).

Other readers of the Constitution argue that it is a document. The Founding Fathers included an addendum for **amending**, or changing, the Constitution. With that provision set there, readers who believe in constitutional change argue that issues like abortion, gay marriage, and other issues facing the present generation of readers can be resolved by either (1) considering the first ten amendments to the Constitution (the Bill of Rights) or (2) utilizing the amendment process to permanently alter the Constitution by adding new provisions. For example: when the Constitution was ratified, women did not have the right to vote. The

The Constitution: a literal or living document?

country decided in due course that women should have that right, and so the federal government with the states utilized the amendment process that made women eligible to vote. The Constitution can be viewed on paper – the literal document – or can be viewed from the lens of whatever time period you are living – the living document (Strauss, 1-3).

Now that we've set the stage, let us now take a deeper look into the branches of government as they are defined and given power by the Constitution; we will compare these rules and specifications that are dictated therein to the ins and outs of Major League Baseball. Here, I compare the fielders or defense to Congress, the Legislative Branch. I then compare the pitcher to the U.S. president, the Executive Branch. Finally, I compare the umpires to the Judicial Branch.

The Branches of Government on the Field of Dreams

In baseball, I discuss three entities that are comparable to the branches of government as described in the Constitution. These entities always play a major role in how the games turn out. The fielders, if successful, keep the opposing team from scoring runs and prevent them for winning the game. The pitcher is the central figure of the defense and has the ability, through his skill and accuracy, to control the ability of the opposition to get hits and accrue runs. The umpires can affect the game in many ways. First, the umpire at home plate calls balls and strikes. If his strike zone is wider or narrower than normal, that can affect the confidence and performance of the pitcher. The umpires stationed at the bases (first, second, and third) are there to make calls in regards to the running game. Players can be thrown out, picked off (if they stray too far from their base), be caught in a rundown (when an opponent's ally hits a ball and is caught before the runner has time to get back to his base), and so on. The umpire has the say-so in all of those close plays and more. These three entities are extremely important, and the same can be said for the three branches of government that correspond with them.

The Fielders and Congress

Top and Bottom

The fielders who defend against balls that are hit in the infield, the outfield, behind the catcher at the backstop, or in foul territory are comparable to the legislative bodies that we know as Congress. First, we said that each team has the ability to defend against runs but also the ability to score runs by virtue of having a top and bottom of each inning. The legislative branch is divided into two respective Houses. The upper House, the United States Senate, is considered to be the most prestigious of the two; the form of governance in this House, however, is known to be much more anarchical than the rule in the lower House, the United States House of Representatives.

The number of representatives that each state has in the House and in the Senate differs.

Top and bottom of inning = upper and lower Houses in Congress

Representation in the House is based on population; each state gains a representative for every (roughly) 300,000 citizens in their state. For example: Missouri has ten congressional districts, so Missouri houses (roughly) 3 million citizens that must be represented. In the Senate, however, representation for each state is equal; each state has two senators representing it (United States, 90).

The Numbers 6 and 2

In baseball, there are six (6) infielders: the first baseman, the second baseman, the shortstop, the third baseman, the pitcher, and the catcher. All six of these boys are tasked with defending the infield and a bit of the area shortly behind the infield diamond. Two (2) of these players have more responsibilities than the other four. The pitcher and catcher are responsible for controlling the defensive strategies of the game; the pitcher throws the ball and the catcher provides pitch suggestions as well as prevents runners from stealing (or advancing to the next closest base when the pitcher begins his motions). Because the pitcher and catcher have more responsibilities, it is often said that they are the 'representatives' of the team.

Similarly, the terms (or time in office) of persons in Congress correspond with those two respective numbers. Six – the number of infielders – corresponds with the six-year term for a U.S. senator. Conversely, the number 2, which represents the pitcher and catcher – the 'representatives' of the team – represents the two-year term of elected persons in the U.S. House. Ironically like the pitcher and catcher, the persons responsible for governance in the House are known as representatives (United States, 90-91).

Necessity

On the field, the defense is expected to do whatever is necessary and proper to prevent the opposing team from getting hits and scoring runs. For example: on regular occasion, the second baseman or shortstop will have to dive to field the ball in an attempt to prevent the ball from scooting to the outfield and assuring the batter a base hit. Another example: suppose as a pitch is thrown, a runner on first base takes off for second base. The catcher, after having caught the ball, attempts to get the ball to the second baseman to tag the runner before the runner touches second base. That play is known as a pickoff or a failed steal-attempt.

Within the Constitution is a phrase known as the "Necessary and Proper Clause." The clause states that Congress has the power to do whatever is necessary and proper to best protect, preserve, and defend the people of the United States. Through this clause, the creation of a national bank (now known as the Federal Reserve), the imposition of Franklin Roosevelt's New Deal policies, the limitation of farmers' ability to grow crops, and so on, has been deemed an application of the Necessary and Proper Clause. Congress, in short, has the power to do whatever it feels is in America's best interests (United States, 94).

Duties and Responsibilities

In baseball, all the fielders have their own specific responsibilities that they are supposed to take care of. The pitcher pitches, the catcher catches and controls the running game, the first baseman defends the first baseline and prevents runners from advancing to second by communicating with the catcher, and the players in the outfield defend against fly balls and often leap to rob batters of home runs, and so on. Each player on the field has a list of duties and responsibilities that he must successfully accomplish it he wants to keep his team in the game.

Each House has a set of responsibilities that it is supposed to carry out as well. Many of the duties discussed in the Constitution, however, have been delegated to other branches of government (most especially, the Executive Branch, or president) over time by virtue of tradition. The House, because of its more

He got 'em!! Doing what is necessary to help the team win.

rigid governance style, was originally given more duties than the Senate, which makes sense; if, by nature, the governing body is more organized, it is then more capable of successfully completing more tasks (United States, 93-94).

The Constitution mandates that the House complete a long list of duties. Some of these include proposing new laws, declaring war, ratifying treaties, coining money, keeping track of the government's finances and budget, impeaching the president (if necessary), and so on. All of these tasks are difficult ones – especially keeping track of the stupid amounts of money that our government spends on a daily basis. Easily, our government spends more money in one day that you can ever hope to earn in your lifetime – billions of dollars. To most people, the money spent by our government is not and cannot be a concrete reality, because they simply cannot fathom how much purchasing power that amount of money holds (United States, 93).

Although the Constitution mandates that the House do certain things, some of these powers assigned to the House have been passed on or delegated to another branch of government – namely, the Executive Branch. For example: up until 1945, declaring war was a job that the House was responsible for. Since then, declaring war has become essentially obsolete. Instead of the House (a congressional body) declaring war, the president, the executive, sends troops into 'military conflicts' and can keep these troops in action for 90 days before being required to seek congressional approval for the continuation of the conflict. Another power the House has delegated to the president is the power to ratify treaties. Treaties, like declarations of war, are peace documents that have essentially gone out of style and have been replaced by **executive agreements** – resolutions to end conflicts or maintain peace that are negotiated and agreed upon by national executives. In our case, the national executive is the president; in England, the prime minister is the national executive, and so on. So while the House has certain duties it must attend to per constitutional mandate, tradition now dictates that some of these constitutional powers now belong to another branch of government.

The Senate, being the more anarchical body, is assigned fewer tasks. The Senate is responsible for considering laws proposed by the House, confirming presidential appointees, approving the appointment of federal judges, and convicting the president if he (or she) is impeached by the House. Most of these tasks occur on a rare basis which helps business move forward in the Senate, but even these deliberations can be put on hold by the anarchical, chaotic nature of this legislative body (United States, 93-94).

Different Ways to 'Play the Game'

Earlier, we said that fielders in the infield and in the outfield play the ball differently. The infielders generally play balls that are hit right at them (line drives) or play the ball as it bounces to them on the ground. They then throw the ball to a base where securing one (or two) of the necessary outs is possible. On very rare occasions, triple plays can and have been turned or successfully carried out. Outfielders, conversely, play the ball as it flies through the air. If an outfielder catches the ball before it hits the ground, it counts as one of the three outs necessary to retire the opposing team in that inning. Outfielders sometimes don't make it to the ball before it lands. If this occurs, the fielder nearest the ball is expected to throw it into the base where an out is most likely to take place. Typically, this is either second base (where the batter is running) or to home plate (where a previous batter is attempting to score a run).

Just as both areas of the field require different tactics to succeed, both Houses of Congress function very differently. The House of Representatives is rules-oriented, highly structured, ultra-formal, and very reserved. The form of governance that exists in the House is a European tradition known as **parliamentary procedure.** This governance style requires likely speakers to ask permission from the leader of the legislative body – in this case, the Speaker of the House. The Speaker dictates the amount of time (if any) that speakers will be given, and they are not permitted to deviate from the time limit that is specified. The speakers' opponents are given a specified time limit for rebuttal; no deviation is permitted here either. The Speaker specifies when an item is to come up for a vote (if it is allowed to at all), and a time limit for the voting process is delineated by and enforced by the Speaker. Put simply, the House is structure on steroids.

The governance style in the Senate, however, is much different. Although touches of parliamentary procedure exist in the Senate, this

Different ways to field and different ways to govern

legislative body is much more prone to heated, oftentimes offensive debates. Name calling, interruptions, and partisan blasting are everyday occurrences in the Senate whereas in the House of Representatives, these tactics are strictly forbidden insofar as polite speech can prevent them. Senators have a tactic at their disposal that can prevent legislation from coming up for a vote. This tactic is known as a **filibuster.** A filibuster allows a senator to ramble on endlessly as long as he or she sees fit in the effort of preventing a vote. Senators have been known to read out of phone books, novels, newspapers, talk about the weather, or perform some other action during their filibusters. The longest filibuster went for over two days with the speaker not taking any breaks – no meals, no trips to the restroom, no sleep. Clearly, such people are opposed to whatever legislation is up for vote. The Senate, unlike the House, has the ability to stall votes because of the chaotic nature of that legislative body.

Checks on Power

The fielders defending against the hitting team do their best to prevent the other team from getting hits and scoring runs. Many of these fielders leave the ballpark with grass stains on their pants they received when they dived for, caught, and fielded a particularly pesky ground ball. Other players, like St. Louis Cardinals right fielder Allen Craig, ran into the wall and injured his ankle in the effort to catch a fly ball. Fielders play the game (most of the time) to the best of their ability, but their ability to keep the game in hand is limited by the pitcher's skill and the fairness and accuracy of the umpires. Imagine that you are a fielder and your pitcher throws home-run ball after home-run ball. All of those home runs add runs to the other team's tally, and there is nothing a fielder can do but watch and grimace as the score gets more and more out of hand. Similarly, imagine that a batter hits the ball to the second baseman. He fields it and throws to the first baseman, and the ball lands in the first baseman's glove just as the batter's foot touches first base. It is then up to the umpire who gets the call – the speedy runner or the second baseman and his throw to first. In short, the fielders' ability to succeed is limited by the skill of the pitcher and the fairness and accuracy of the umpires.

Congress is limited in a similar fashion. Its most important duty is to pass legislation. Doing that in today's world is a real job; party politics have gotten so nasty that it is rare for a controversial piece of legislation to make it through both Houses unscathed. If it does, however, the bill (or piece of legislation) is left at the mercy of the president and the courts. The president could **veto** the bill – or refuse to support it. The courts could deem the legislation **unconstitutional** – or something not in accordance with the rules, regulations, and liberties established by the Constitution (United States, 94-95).

Here is an example. In 2009, the House and Senate were attempting to pass a health care reform bill. It took great pains to get the House and Senate to find enough votes to get the bill approved. President Obama could have vetoed the bill, but he did not. He signed the bill into law, but even today, the Affordable Care Act is being challenged in federal court in respect to its constitutionality. The efforts of Congress could be, if the Court rules against the legislation, for naught. The power of Congress to do its job is limited by the president's veto power and the Court's power to make rulings based on their interpretation of the Constitution.

Removal

In baseball, nine fielders start each game, but they can be removed and replaced by other players. A fielder might be removed if he performs poorly or if he does something illegal. A poor play might be dropping the ball, missing an easy catch, failing to tag a base runner, mis-throwing the ball to an intended target, and so on. Any of these errors can lead to a player's removal from the game. A player can also be removed if he does something illegal. A fielder cannot throw the ball directly at a runner. Fielders are not permitted to throw equipment at opposing players (like their glove). Fighting with opposing players is illegal, and so on. Any of these actions can result in a player being ejected (removed) from the game.

Members of Congress can also be removed from office. The most common method of removal occurs due to poor performance; in the next election, the public can opt to support a new, better candidate over the poorly performing one currently serving in the congressional district or representing the state in the Senate. In general, once a politician has been successfully elected in at least two elections, his chances of re-election in the future become astronomically high. This advantage for repeatedly elected officials is known as the **incumbency bias.** Generally speaking, it is more common for relatively new members of Congress to be voted out and less common for incumbents (repeatedly elected officials) to be ousted through the electoral process (United States, 91).

The other two methods of congressional removal are much less common. The first – **impeachment** – occurs when a member of Congress does something Lying under oath, selling one's votes on a certain piece of legislation for money or other favors, bodily harming another person in relation to some congressional issue, and so on are all grounds for impeachment. The impeachment proceedings occur in the House. If a member of Congress is impeached by the House, the case then heads to the Senate to decide whether or not the party in question should be convicted and face jail time. Impeachment is rare but not unheard of.

The final method of congressional removal occurs when a member of Congress does something This kind of behavior merits a **censure** or public disgracing rather than the process of impeachment. If a member of Congress, say, was caught saying something universally offensive like publically criticizing an opponent based on race, gender, or background or was caught in some sort of unethical act like accepting gifts from major campaign donors, that member of Congress would have committed an act that could be deemed grounds for censure. Censuring is not outright removal from office, but public disgrace of the guilty party which often leads to the guilty party's resignation. For this reason, being censured is classified here as a means of congressional removal (United States, 91).

The fielders in a baseball game undergo the same sort of scenarios and are held to the same standards as members of Congress are. They have similar duties and responsibilities, they share the same consequences of poor performance, and they operate under the same conditions of necessity and duty. Next, we consider how the pitcher – the guy who throws the baseball and runs the game – compares to our guy who controls and runs our 'game' (arguably) – the president.

The Pitcher and the President

The pitcher is the fielder who is in charge of and held responsible for the outcome of the games in which he pitches. The catcher typically makes suggestions to the pitcher as to what pitch to throw, but ultimately it is the pitcher's choice; and it is his responsibility if he unsuccessfully throws a pitch in a certain location or if he selects the wrong pitch and the batter hits it. The pitcher is the player on the field whose statistics hold him accountable for success and failure; this statistic is known as his win-loss record. No other player on the field is held responsible for game outcomes like the pitcher is. The catcher is there to make suggestions and also to back up the pitcher if he makes an errant pitch or if some scenario arises where aid is needed, such as a foul ball being hit behind the catcher that remains in play.

The president, much like the pitcher, is considered to be 'the boss'. He is expected to present an agenda to Congress, sell it to the American people, and operate within the bounds of the Constitution. If he succeeds, he is hailed as a great president; if not, he will likely be voted out in the next election and replaced with someone whom the Electoral College (and by extension, the American People) feels is more fitting for the job. The vice president, like the catcher, is there to back the president up if something goes wrong; in this instance, the vice president is second in line in the presidential succession. So, if the president dies while in office or is assassinated, the vice president is then sworn in as the next president (United States, 96).

Like the pitcher, the president is held responsible for

Pitcher and catcher – president and the vice president

the goings-on in American national politics, even though sometimes the things that go wrong are outside of the president's control. Just as the fielders and umpires can cause the game to go awry and leave the pitcher with a poor win-loss record, Congress and the courts can contribute to political upheaval and watch as the blame is laid on the president rather than the parties that are actually guilty of causing the problem. In general, the American public seems to find it easier to hold the president – one man – responsible for the failings of many people. It is easier to remove one man from the scene than the 535 members of Congress who are constantly berated by the public.

Each pitcher is different and has his own unique abilities. Some pitchers are known for getting opponents out by getting them to strike out. Other pitchers are good at getting hitters to hit balls on the ground to infielders who throw them out. Yet other pitchers are known as 'contact pitchers' – these pitchers induce batters into hitting fly balls which are caught by one of the three outfielders. Each pitcher uses his unique skills to shape the game in such a way that he has the greatest propensity to win and improve his win-loss record.

Presidents have done the same thing, and their ability to do so exists because of the Executive Clause in the Constitution. The Executive Clause essentially says that the president has the power to execute the laws. There are no details included in this clause – only this simple statement. The Clause is recognized to be extremely vague, and presidents have used this vagueness to their own advantage. Presidents have used the lack of detail in the Executive Clause to presidential power. So, over time, presidential power has steadily as presidents have broadened the expanse of the Executive Clause (United States, 95-96).

For example: Franklin Roosevelt was trying to get his New Deal policies through Congress and signed into law in 1938. He wanted to do what he could to help end the Great Depression – the worst economic crisis in American history. Congress was more than willing to go along with the president, but the Supreme Court was not. They found every piece of New Deal legislation unconstitutional, much to the annoyance of Roosevelt. To counter the Court's attempt to suppress his policies, Roosevelt alleged that the members of the Court were, in general, too old to cope with the work assigned to them; six of the nine Justices at the time were over the age of 60. Roosevelt proposed adding a new Justice for every sitting Justice that was 60 years old or older. That would have added six new Justices to the Court, and as Congress was willing to do essentially whatever Roosevelt wanted, he could have stacked the Court with Justices that would be sympathetic with his New Deal policies. Of course, the Court found this proposal to be unconstitutional, but it also scared the Court. The president's attempt to meddle with the Court was enough to encourage them to, for the rest of his tenure in office, support the president's endeavors. Thus, the New Deal policies, after having been revised, were signed into law, and the Court permitted these policies to be enacted. The Constitution allows for checks and balances, but this was the first time the Court's power was ever challenged. In this tussle, the president won, and many attribute this victory to the president's use of the Executive Clause. Roosevelt did what he had to, for a certain point of view, to execute the laws that he had signed – even if it meant challenging another branch of government for power.

In the game of baseball, the pitcher is considered to be the key defender; it is he who ultimately throws the ball to the batters and his skill that ultimately determines the overall outcome of the game. He works with the catcher, the infielders, and the outfielders to set a game plan that is the most likely to produce success. He will often call certain fielders to the pitcher's mound to discuss certain options available with particular batters and base runners. The pitcher, ultimately, is the guy who has to execute these plays. Any miscue on his part or any poor communication with his fielders can result in blown plays and poor outcomes.

The president can also be categorized as our 'key defender'. The Constitution designates the president as the Commander-in-Chief and provides the president with control of the full might of the United States Armed Forces. He can and has sent troops into battle in the name of national security, democracy, and human rights. This power is one that allows the president to protect us in times of danger and international upheaval (United States, 96).

The president – our key defender as Commander-in-Chief

After the southern states seceded from the Union, President Abraham Lincoln dispatched the full might of America's Armed Forces against the armies of the Jefferson Davis Confederacy. Lincoln instituted a draft that mandated young men participate in the war effort, he helped organize and plan attacks with Ulysses Grant and other Union generals, and would have aided in peace negotiations if he had survived the Civil War. A president, although always a civilian, plays a direct role in the ordering and operation of the United States military through his power as Commander-in-Chief.

In a game, there are four tools a pitcher can use to best aid his team in the prevention of the opposition scoring runs. He can strike batters out, entice them to hit balls on the ground to infielders, encourage batters to hit the ball in the air to one of the outfielders, or intentionally walk a batter. Intentional walks are rare events that are utilized primarily when there are runners on base and the pitcher is facing a notably good hitter. These four tools – strikeouts, groundouts, fly outs, and intentional walks – enable a pitcher to manage the game in such a way that he gives his team the best chance to win.

The president, similarly has four years to do whatever it is that he promises to accomplish when he campaigns for the presidency. In other words, the president serves a four-year term (United States, 95). If he is successful (at least in part) at keeping his campaign promises, he is more likely to be reelected and entrusted with another four years to complete his agenda. Presidents are only permitted to serve two terms. This tradition exists because of two standards.

The first standard was set by our first president – George Washington. He felt that two terms was enough for any executive. Most of the Founders designed the presidency in such a way that it was in direct contrast with the king of Great Britain, George III, who was set to reign for life. Washington, along with the other Founders, desperately wanted our executive officer to function in a way starkly different than the despised British king, and so limiting a president's tenure in office seemed only rational.

The second tradition was set at the beginning of the Cold War. Our enemy – the Soviet Union – had an executive who, like a king, was set to serve for life. Wanting to differentiate ourselves from our opponents, our government made a president's two terms official as opposed to mere tradition by ratifying the 22nd Amendment which officially limits a president's tenure in office to two terms. One presidential term is four years long, but he can serve up to two terms in office.

In a game of baseball, the pitcher does his best to keep the game in hand, but sometimes things don't work out the way he had it all planned out. Fielders – both in the infield and also in the outfield – make errors that lead to 'unearned' base runners and subsequent runs. The pitcher, despite his efforts, may run across a home plate umpire who has an entirely different conception of the strike zone than the pitcher does; that can make for a really long night for any pitcher. Sometimes, it seems as if the strike zone varies from team to team; some pitchers will have their pitches called as strikes when they land on the edge of the strike zone, and other pitchers won't. So, sometimes, the fairness of the umpires comes into question. In short, the pitcher is limited by the other entities present in the game. Because the pitcher does not have absolute power, the pitcher is innately vulnerable to the blunders of his teammates as well as the skill and fairness of the umpires.

The same is true for the president. He is in charge of signing bills into law and seeing to it that they are implemented and enforced. His ability to do so is limited by two things. The first is the willingness of Congress to work with and adhere to the president's agenda. In general, if the president belongs to one political party while Congress is dominated by his party's opposition, very little – if anything – will be accomplished during the president's tenure in office. Conversely, if the political party of the president and Congress are akin, it is likely that the president will be very successful in achieving the goals he campaigned on (United States, 95-96).

The president is also limited by the Court's decision to uphold or strike down the laws the president signs. If the Court feels that the laws approved by Congress and signed by the president are unconstitutional, the Court can strike down the law and prevent it from being implemented and enforced. If, however, the Court deems the law stays within the bounds of what the Constitution allows, they will uphold the law and allow its implementation and enforcement to begin. Just as the pitcher is limited by his fellow fielders and the umpires, the president is limited by the willingness of Congress to work with him as well as the Court's discretion regarding the constitutionality of laws that are passed in Congress and approved by the president (United States, 97-98).

Pitchers can be removed from the game if they perform poorly or if they do something illegal. Especially later in games, a pitcher's ability to throw accurately in the strike zone with the same velocity wanes; if this becomes evident, oftentimes, the pitcher is removed from the game and replaced by a fresh pitcher or 'reliever'. If, near the end of the game, the pitcher's team is winning by three runs or less, oftentimes, the

A baseball that is 'high and tight' can quickly end a pitcher's night

'closer' will be brought in to 'save' or protect his team's lead in the game; typically the closer pitches only in the ninth and final inning, but sometimes the closer is asked to pitch the eighth and ninth innings, respectively.

A pitcher can also be removed from the game for doing something illegal. Pitching a ball at a batter's head or 'beaning' a batter is illegal and often results in the pitcher being ejected from the game. Sometimes, pitchers are allowed to remain in the game even after a batter is hit in the head if the umpire determines that the plunk was due to a lack of pitching command (a missed pitch location) rather than malicious intent. Pitchers are not allowed to spit on the ball to give them a better grip either. That is also illegal and grounds for ejection.

The president can be voted out of office and denied a second term if he performs poorly. Oftentimes, poor performance is associated with a failure to keep his campaign promises, a financial collapse, a military conflict gone horribly wrong, and so on. Many of the things blamed on presidents, by and large, are out of their control; however, as we noted earlier, the American people often find it easier to blame and punish one man than hold more than 500 people responsible.

Presidents can also be impeached if they do something illegal. President Bill Clinton was impeached while in office for committing perjury – lying under oath. He, a Democrat, was impeached by the Republican-dominated House, but the Democratically controlled Senate failed to convict him of that charge. Impeachment is a rare event; only two presidents – Bill Clinton and Andrew Johnson – have been impeached. As of yet, however, no president has been convicted of his impeachment charges. Pitchers share many similarities with our executive officer – the president. The umpires in a baseball game, similarly, share much in common with the final branch of government, the Judicial Branch – the courts (United States, 97).

Umpires and the Courts

In a typical game, umpires (a kind of referee) are expected to do a number of things. First, the home plate umpire is expected to call balls and strikes. The umpires for each of the bases – first, second, and third – are expected to make the final decisions in relation to close plays made in their line of sight. A regular

Nine innings in a ballgame – nine Justices on the Supreme Court

game is typically nine innings long, and so the umpires are expected to do their respective job during those nine innings of play.

Umpires and federal judges – making close calls for life

Our Supreme Court is made up of nine Justices who are responsible for making decisions regarding the constitutionality of laws. The initial size of the Court was six – a number mandated by Congress (United States, 93-94) – but the number was later increased to nine as the population of the country began to grow. As stated before, Franklin Roosevelt threatened to increase the size of the Court in 1938 but failed to do so. The current number of Justices on the court, therefore, remains at nine.

Umpires who appear in Major League games took a long, difficult road to get to their current position. After years of intensive training in MLB-approved umpiring schools and umpiring at the Minor League level, they are assessed and approved by Major League Baseball. For every 300 students who attend the MLB-approved umpiring schools, only 30-35 of them will succeed in becoming an umpire in the Major Leagues.

Becoming a Supreme Court Justice isn't as difficult. There is no constitutional mandate for specific training. All that the Constitution requires is that Justices be appointed by the president and approved by the Senate. As is the case with controversial bills, if the president belongs to one political party but the Senate is governed by the opposition, garnering approval for the judicial candidate can be a painstaking process (United States, 96).

Something else associated with judicial selection is **senatorial courtesy.** When a Justice dies or retires, it is considered senatorial courtesy for the president first to consult with the senators from the state in which the dead or retired Justice came from to seek potential candidates for the vacant spot on the Court. The president does not have to choose a candidate from the senators' lists, but it is considered courteous to consider their list of candidates first before consulting with anyone else.

Now that we have considered how the branches of government compare to entities on the baseball field, we now will consider some final points of comparison necessarily relevant because of the final three articles of the Constitution. They deal with the rights of the federal government, the rights of states, and the processes by which the Constitution can be amended.

Tying Up Some Loose Ends

Advantages

The argument can definitely be made that the home team has advantages over the away or visiting team. The home team practices and plays in the stadium that they're the most familiar with. Their families and friends are nearby and ready to spend time with them when the baseball life permits. If necessary, the home team bats last in the ninth inning and if unnecessary, the home team doesn't have to bat if they're winning after the opposing team. The home team's space is also bigger and, in some cases, much newer and well kept. Some parks are known for having clubhouses (areas where the team hangs out before and after the game) not much bigger than a closet. The home team definitely has numerous advantages over the away team.

Just like the home team has the upper hand in numerous ways over the visiting team, the federal government has numerous advantages over state governments by virtue of the Supremacy Clause. The most important advantage that the Supremacy Clause dictates is that federal law always supersedes state laws. For example: one of the things that Lincoln used

Home field advantage and the Supremacy Clause

to justify the Civil War was that the states, because of the Missouri Compromise, had no right to dictate whether or not they would be a slave state. Many southern states disagreed with the Compromise and set about imposing slavery. The choice of states to ignore federal law is known as **nullification,** and it is illegal. For this reason, among others, Lincoln argued that the Union's quarrel with the Confederacy was just and thus, the Civil War was waged and won by Lincoln's Union. Another different, yet similar, element to the Supremacy Clause is that federal courts have the ability to consider, uphold, or strike down cases and their decisions that were initially made at the state level. The federal government, the 'home team', has distinct advantages over state governments, the 'visiting team' (United States, 99).

Change

Baseball is not a static game; it has changed over time. Players used to wear wool trousers and high socks during every game. Now, the pants are designed to be cooler and high socks are no longer required. The baseball teams in the United States split into two 'leagues' in the 1960s – the National League and the American League. The most notable difference between them is that in American League ballparks, the pitcher is not required to bat. Instead a designated hitter (DH) bats in place of the pitcher. In National League parks the pitcher is still expected to bat. The height of the pitching mound used to be much higher than it is now but it has been lowered to give hitters a better chance at beating the pitcher. Put simply, baseball is a game that has changed over time.

The Constitution also has been subjected to numerous changes. Initially, the Constitution included the original document with seven Articles, but not enough votes for ratification existed. The Founders were encouraged to write a Bill of Rights that delineated the rights, liberties, and responsibilities of citizens – an issue we will cover in the next chapter. After including the Bill of Rights, the Founders succeeded in acquiring the necessary number of votes required for the ratification of the Constitution – nine. Since ratification, the Constitution has been amended a number of times (United States, 98-99).

The Number 27

In a regular, nine-inning baseball game, the winning team has to get 27 of the opposing team's players out. Three outs induced or incurred by batters or runners per inning through nine innings of play is 27. The way the outs are garnered is unimportant. All that matters is that they are secured within the nine innings of regular play.

The Constitution, including the Bill of Rights, has 27 Amendments that provide rights to citizens of the United States. Individual freedoms, judicial protection, citizenship specifications, voting rights, and government interference in our lives are only a few of these changes that both the federal government and the states thought necessary to add to the Constitution. To amend the Constitution, the Amendment must be passed by both the House and Senate, signed by the president, and then ratified by at least two thirds of the states' legislatures. Failure to do so will cause the proposed amendment to die.

The Number 17

Home plate – the site of baseball's toughest and closest calls and plays – is 17 inches across. A rather odd-shaped 'dish', home plate serves as the starting place and the finish line around the bases. Home plate, from a certain point of view then, serves as a beginning and ending for anything of import on the baseball field. Pitches must cross home plate to be considered strikes. Base runners must touch home plate for a run to be tallied for their team. Home plate is the focal point during most of a baseball game.

Major League Baseball and the United States Constitution – America's two pastimes

The Amendments to the Constitution are also often considered to be the central focus of the Constitution as the Amendments are the only part of the document that directly affects us – America's citizenry. Since the ratification of the Constitution, there have been 17 Amendments added to the document. The end of slavery, the approval of women's suffrage (voting rights), the inclusion of Native Americans as citizens, the imposition of the federal income tax, the limiting of presidents to two terms, and so on, are all Amendments that have been added since constitutional ratification. These Amendments likely affect either you directly or someone that you know. These Amendments are the parts of the Constitution that hit closest to home as they have the potential to directly affect our lives. The great game of baseball as played in the Major Leagues is uncannily comparable to America's other pastime – the United States Constitution – a document that serves as the social contract between 'we, the People' and our government.

Food for Thought

General Information

The Preamble is often considered to be a summary of the contents of the Constitution. Do you think so, and if so, why? If so, why isn't the Preamble used more often in judicial decisions because of its interpretive power? Why have people interpreted the Constitution over time instead of reading and taking it word for word? Is this a good thing or bad? What are the advantages and disadvantages for both readings – 'literal' and 'living'?

The Fielders and Congress

Why is the Senate considered the Upper House when the House of Representatives has more responsibilities and functions 'better'? What is the difference between desire and necessity? When utilizing the Necessary and Proper Clause, what constitutes real need? Should Congress have to defend its use of this Clause or is this congressional power inherent and non-negotiable? Compared to the other two branches of government, how powerful is Congress? How dependent is Congress on the other two branches of government to use their power effectively?

The Pitcher and the President

The president is 'the boss' since the Constitution designates him (or her) as the executive officer, but how much power does the president really have to shape policy? Does the president have the power to write legislation or only to sign it? What powers does the president have – constitutionally – that would enable him (or her) to deal with the economy, international affairs, social problems, and so on? Are all – or any – of these within the president's sphere of influence, or do other branches of government have a larger say on these issues than the president does? The Executive Clause, we said, is vague. How far, in your opinion, can and should the Executive Clause be stretched to increase presidential power? How far is too far? When you think of a 'great' president, who do you think of and why? What qualities should a good president have?

Umpires and the Courts

Why are there nine Justices on the Supreme Court from a population perspective? Wasn't six enough? Why or why not? Would fewer Justices on the Court make for less corruption? Justices on the Court are not elected but are appointed. Is it good that one branch of government exists, at least theoretically, outside the realm of political squabbles? Can Justices be politically biased in their decision making? If so, how? When interpreting the Constitution, does a strict interpretation indirectly indicate a Justice's Republican leanings? What about a loose interpretation of the Constitution – does that indicate that the Justice is likely Democrat? Should politics play a role in judicial decision making and is it possible to keep politics out of the justice system? Why is it that the Supreme Court tends to hear and rule upon controversial cases?

Tying Up Some Loose Ends

Does the federal government have too much power? What should the role of the states be in engaging with the federal government? Should nullification, in some circumstances, be legal? Some people are clearly opposed to change. It is true that while the Constitution has been amended, many of these changes took generations to take hold and be culturally accepted. Look at the Amendments and see how many of these you feel that way about. Should laws be made that are counter to cultural norms? Are such laws harder to enforce and why?

Extending the Comparisons

There are persons on or near the baseball field whose roles I have not addressed. Similarly, there are entities that exist in American politics that are not mentioned in the Constitution itself. Using entities OTHER THAN THE ONES ALREADY USED HERE, where do you think a baseball team's manager fits in? What about the batter? The fans? From a political perspective, where do political parties, lobbying firms and interest groups, and the American people fit in? What baseball entity has the greatest propensity to change the game? What does that say about that entity's government comparison's power to affect American politics?

What is the rally cry of the baseball fans in Pittsburgh?

LET'S GO PIRATES!!

Works Cited

Strauss, David A. *The Living Constitution* New York: Oxford University Press, 2010.

United States. *The United States Constitution* New York: Dover Publications, Inc., 2009.

CHAPTER 5

Here Be Pirates!!
The Pirate Code and the Bill of Rights

Arrrrgh!! The Disney film series *Pirates of the Caribbean* tells the story of Captain Jack Sparrow and his exploits as a pirate in the Caribbean during the time of British occupation. The pirates of the time, or so the films depict, lived according to a certain set of rules known as the "Pirate Code." It is noted, however, by Captain Barbossa, the captain who 'stole' Sparrow's ship *The Black Pearl*, that the code is "more like guidelines than actual rules" (Verbinski, film). The code, from the perspective of the scurvy scoundrels we know as Caribbean pirates, was subject to interpretation, incidence, and scrutiny.

Some argue that the same can be said of the first ten Amendments to the Constitution, a compilation that is commonly known as the Bill of Rights. The first ten Amendments protect the rights and individual freedoms that some citizens hold dear but that many Americans take for granted. The scope of these Amendments, however, has changed over time because of the interpretive power the Judicial Branch possesses to shape and reshape how these Amendments are read and applied. Here, we will explore the Bill of Rights – Amendment by Amendment – as we consider what is meant by each of them, and ponder how each constitutional addition applies to today's world.

Amendment 1: Rights of the Individual to Personal Liberty

The First Amendment guarantees individual citizens the freedom of religion, speech, press, and assembly. The scope of these freedoms in some cases is far-reaching; in others, it is much less so. The times we live in and the events that occur around us are constantly affecting these individual liberties. Some of them, many argue, are being thrown by the wayside in the name of keeping everybody happy. Others contend that the happiness of everyone is impossible to guarantee in a democracy like ours – a form of government where differences in opinion, belief, and culture are not only permitted but encouraged (United States, 183).

Religion

When people typically think of their freedoms relating to religion, they usually ponder one of two things. The first is known as the individual's freedom to practice whatever religion they want to – or not. This right is addressed in the **Establishment Clause** which prohibits the government from establishing a national religion. The government cannot force anyone to embrace Christianity, Judaism, Islam, or any other organized religion or moral code. Other modern democracies aren't as willing to allot such freedoms. The United Kingdom's (England) national religion is Anglicanism, better known as the Church of England which was established by King Henry VIII. Each citizen is expected to give 10% of their income to the Anglican Church. We don't do that here (United States, 183).

In America, you have the right to choose whether or not you will practice any religion and also what religion (or not) you will ascribe to. Your First Amendment right to individual choice regarding religious practice (or not) is delineated in the **Free Exercise Clause**. For example: I, as an individual, can choose to be Catholic, Protestant, Jewish, Muslim, Hindu, an agnostic, or an atheist. The Free Exercise Clause protects my right to make my own decisions in regards to my religious practices. The only exception the First Amendment denotes is religions that either espouses human or animal sacrifice or any behavior that is deemed a 'clear and present danger' are prohibited (United States, 183).

Another concept that is often associated with but **not included** in the First Amendment is the **separation of church and state** – the idea that religious values and political dictates should not mix. While the concept is not included in the Constitution, it was discussed in detail amongst the Founding Fathers. One of the most outspoken Founders regarding this issue was Thomas Jefferson. In a letter he wrote in 1802 to the Danbury Baptists residing in the state of Connecticut, he denoted how strongly he opposed the mixing of religion and government. He argued that mixing the two would only encourage political and religious strife in the new country – something most of the initial American settlers fled Europe from in the first place (United States, 183).

Modern Dilemmas

There are many issues facing America today that revolve around the First Amendment's

The freedom to worship who you want however you want...within reason

religious element. The first of these has to do with the place of religion in public-funded areas. For example: should it be permissible to display, say, a manger scene on the grounds of City Hall? Should the Ten Commandments be on display in a courthouse? Should we be permitted, in a public setting such as a department store, to advertise 'Christmas' and all of its trimmings and espouse its traditional greeting 'Merry Christmas' – or, out of respect for non-Christians, should retailers and other public domains celebrate 'the holidays'? All of these scenarios are hotly contested among the American public.

The 'Christian majority' (or so they are called) argue that, in a democracy, the majority rules, and that the will of the majority supports Christian traditions like Christmas. They further contend that it is impossible in a **melting pot** – a racial, ethnic, cultural, and religious hodge-podge of people – to please everyone or ensure that someone isn't offended, so it only makes sense to make the most people happy that is possible.

The opponents of this view contend that, as a constitutional republic, that all views – Christian and otherwise – should be represented in the public sphere and rather than catering to the interests and agenda of one group (in this case, Christianity), we should instead try to be more inclusive rather than exclusive. These citizens argue that we should be trying to minimize potentially offensive situations and moving toward a more accepting, welcoming social sphere.

Another religious debate that is ongoing across America today is that discussing the existence and toleration of religious radicalism. Exactly how radical of a religion are we, as Americans, willing to legally tolerate? One of the newest churches on the block is the Westboro Baptist Church. The church is known for being staunchly anti-military and anti-gay to the point where the church protests at military funerals, sporting events, government rallies, and so on, and suggests that the military and gay people are evil (Drain, 4-8). In the Supreme Court case *Snyder v. Phelps*, Snyder, the surviving spouse of Matthew Snyder – a Marine lance corporal – sued the Church who protested at Matthew Snyder's funeral. His wife contended that the protest disturbed the mourning process and funeral activities of the family and that the protest was a violation of the family's right to privacy. The Court ruled against Snyder and decided that, despite the horrific circumstances and actions of the Church, their right to protest the funeral was guaranteed by the First Amendment. Some argue that the Church's activities constitute a 'radical' church – one that should not be protected by the dictates of the Constitution; according to the Court's ruling, the judiciary has decided otherwise (United States Supreme Court, 1).

Speech

Another freedom guaranteed by the First Amendment is the right to free speech and expression. In general, you can say anything you want to whoever you want whenever you want. This freedom was predominantly meant to guarantee citizens the right to talk about, and perhaps disagree with, the government without fear of future punishment for whatever it was they might have said. In a country such as ours – one that considers itself correctly to be a representative democracy – there inevitably will be differing opinions that will vie for adherence by society. Some voices are louder than others, and it is those voices that tend to get the attention of both the media and the politicians in Washington and elsewhere (United States, 183).

Your freedom of speech, however, is limited in a number of ways. You cannot say things that might endanger people in an enclosed or crowded area. For example: you cannot yell "Fire!" in a movie theatre. Hate speech is highly regulated, and racial slurs are not tolerated. The lines that are drawn for what is and what isn't 'hate speech' are blurred at best. For some folks, racial slurs themselves are what constitute as 'hate speech'. Other people include threatening the president (which is not protected by the First Amendment) and condemning racial, ethnic, or social groups as well. The Supreme Court has made many decisions regarding free speech, and we are at the point now where it is unclear what it is and isn't okay to say (Shapiro, 46-71).

Political correctness (PC) is the act of saying things in such a way that what you say is less likely to be perceived as offensive. For example: instead of identifying short people as 'short', they are now, according to PC, 'vertically challenged'. People with mental handicaps are known as 'mentally challenged', and so on. Encouraging respect of others in society by implementing a politically correct manner of speaking has been perceived by some as a move in the right direction. Others contend that necessarily in a democracy, people will be upset with stuff other people say no matter how much we try to regulate the right of free speech. How far should this regulation go?

Modern Dilemmas

In terms of current events, there are a number of things that have happened recently that call into question how far the reach of free speech actually goes. Earlier, we noted how the Westboro Baptist Church protests at military funerals and declaims those who have served in the military as heathen-like degenerates. According to the First Amendment, these pronouncements – although untrue – are protected by one's right to free speech. However, the Ku Klux Klan can't go running around racially slurring African Americans or any other minority.

What about the 'war on Christmas'? Is a person's right to wish someone a 'Merry Christmas' protected by free speech or is it solely a religious freedom issue? Clearly, a person wishing someone a 'Merry Christmas' is not a gesture of ill-will. It is meant to be a kind, friendly deed. Others argue, however, that the expression "Merry Christmas" is offensive because it is perceived to force people to acknowledge the Christian holiday which commemorates the birth of Jesus. How far do we go in catering to the people who are 'offended' by every little thing? Is the 'Christmas' thing a small issue or one of greater significance?

Another ongoing debate regarding free speech is the legality of burning the American flag in protest of something or other. The Supreme Court in the case *U.S. vs. Eichman* allowed for the burning of the American flag and argued that the First Amendment protected such an act as one of *symbolic speech*. Other decisions by the Court since then, however, have limited the time and place of such demonstrations. Burning the flag is also permitted to ceremonially burn it when it is worn out or touches the ground. All of these examples are current debates gravitating around free speech and the limitations therein.

Press

Another right guaranteed by the First Amendment is the right to free press. This allows for a free, open, and uncensored (most of the time) media. This liberty protects both written and spoken media. **Media** is anything used to communicate ideas from one person to another. Fox News, a notably conservative media outlet, caters to an audience that is, by and large, proponents of the conservative ideology. Similarly, the cable news outlet MSNBC is known for its liberal bias. Both of these outlets have the right, according to the First Amendment, to pick and choose what they show on TV, even if their coverage is notably biased (United States, 183).

There are some things, however, that the media cannot do. The authors of written media are prohibited from espousing **libel** or writing something about someone or something that is intentionally malicious and false. Similarly, talk show hosts, news anchors, and others who produce spoken media are forbidden from employing **slander** – speaking about someone or something in an intentionally false, damaging way. By and large, it appears to be much harder to convict someone of slander than libel. When you speak about something to an audience, you have the opportunity to defend the positions you take, no matter how objectively false and malicious they may be. From the speaker's point of view, he or she may be entirely accurate in the assessment of the subject, but objectively be inaccurate. These kinds of cases almost always are thrown out of court. Libel, however, is easier to prove. A writer's only recourse is what he or she has expressed in written word. Unless the writer defends their assessment in writing, the subjectivity of the writer's speech diminishes and the objectivity increases. If it can be proved that the author's assessment is objectively malicious and false, this person can likely be convicted of libel. The important thing to remember here is that explanation of one's pronouncements is salvation whereas blanket statements that are malicious and false are more prone to legal action (Shapiro, 157).

Modern Dilemmas

In recent history, one of the most well-known instances of a person's freedom of press being challenged was Rush Limbaugh and his 'slut' comment. In 2012, Limbaugh discussed the comments of Sandra Fluke, a Georgetown University law student's supportive comments about the Affordable Care Act's coverage of contraception – namely, 'the pill' and the morning-after pill. As an opponent of contraceptive coverage in the ACA, Limbaugh labeled Fluke as a "slut" and a "prostitute" and essentially argued that only sluts and prostitutes had any need for contraceptives to be cheaper and more widely available. In response to Limbaugh's comment, he lost a slew of sponsors to his show which prompted Limbaugh to apologize for his comment and cited how it may have been a bit excessive (Ashtari, 1-2).

Limbaugh's accusation of Fluke, in terms of slander, could qualify from a certain standpoint. While Limbaugh may view Fluke in a poor light, it is impossible to factually prove that she fits either of the labels that Limbaugh attached to her. Because of his explanations of his comments, however, he defended adequately (at least from his perspective) his own subjective perception of Fluke. So you see, it is incredibly hard to be convicted of slander as it is virtually impossible to disprove an individual's personal opinions or subjective assessments.

Amendment 2: The Right to Bear Arms

Lock 'n load!! This Second Amendment protects an individual's right to own, carry, and use guns. It also protects the rights of individual states to form militias in the case of war or disaster. This right goes back, once again, to the ideas of John Locke (i.e., Obi-Wan Kenobi). Locke argues that, in the presence of political tyranny exacted by one's own government, citizens have the right to sever the social contract with said government and start over in the hopes of forging a more lasting social contract with another center of power; in other words, one can only hope that, once the old social contract is thrown away, that the new one that is forged between a citizenry and the new government will last longer and will be honored by both parties. In some cases, one has to assume that severing a social contract with one's government will lead to war. If this indeed occurs, it is then necessary for the citizens to both be able to defend themselves and fight for their cause. For this reason, the allowance for weaponry was deemed necessary by our Founders and included in the form of the Second Amendment (United States, 183).

The right to bear arms – the right to protect ourselves from our government

Modern Dilemmas

While for some this Amendment seems very straightforward, it is much more complicated to others. Some argue that gun ownership should be regulated while others contend that restriction to such possession limits a citizenry's ability to combat its own government should it become oppressive and tyrannical. Some argue that a blanket ban of guns is necessary in today's society while others contend that *guns* are not the problem – *people* are.

One of the first tragedies that comes to mind when considering gun violence is the shooting at Columbine High School in 1999. A couple of students who attended Columbine killed over a dozen of their peers and a number of their teachers (Ferner, 1-3). Another school shooting that occurred more recently happened at Sandy Hook Elementary in Newtown, Connecticut. In this case, a single shooter killed his mother – one of the kindergarten teachers – as well as numerous others (Vogel, Horowitz, and Fahrenthold, 1-3).

Other instances of gun violence that have occurred in the recent past took place in numerous spots across the country. One such massacre happened in an Aurora, Colorado, movie theatre on opening night of *The Dark Knight Rises* (Pearson, 1-3). Another occurred at a constitutional meeting in Tucson, Arizona, which saw U.S. Representative Gabrielle Giffords targeted among over twenty others. The events at Sandy Hook, Aurora, and Tucson have all happened within the last six years. What is contributing to all of these mass shootings?

Gun and Ammo Availability

Opponents of gun ownership tend to argue that the wide availability of weapons and also the lack of depth in background checks have made it easier for unstable individuals to get and use guns against other people. Still others contend that the failure to regulate ammunition sales is another contributing factor to our country's high rate of gun violence. Proponents of gun ownership argue the opposite – that it isn't the guns or the ammo that is problematic; rather, it is the people using these weapons for their own evil designs. These folks argue that since it is not the gun's fault that a shooter uses it for malevolent deeds, it is not necessary to regulate guns as they have not been proven to be the root of the problem.

Mental Health Concerns

Some supporters of gun control contend that the ability for people to buy and own guns sets society up for failure, because inevitably, someone not mentally capable of all of the requirements and responsibilities of gun ownership will end up with a weapon and do something stupid with it. Another problem closely related presents itself when parents who own guns leave them unattended, accessible, and fully loaded in the presence of their children.

How can a government restrict gun ownership in terms of citizens who have mental disabilities? Should their Second Amendment rights be challenged if they are not found to be dangerous – only unstable? Where is the line in the sand, if any, that the government should draw between what is and what isn't considered to be a mental handicap? How, with the current restrictions on the release of doctor-patient confidentiality, can the authorities force these potential gun owners to demonstrate their mental capacity to own a gun? All of these are valid points and ones that should be considered in depth before any binding decisions are made to restrict a group's ability to exercise their Second Amendment right.

People and Responsibility

A wide array of gun owners contend that *guns* are not the real problem, but the *people* who use them poorly are. These folks argue that the irresponsibility of both gun owners and those who supply them with their weapons have led to the increase in gun violence. The shooter at Sandy Hook used guns that his mother allowed him to shoot; the guns did not legally belong to the shooter, and yet a massacre involving guns occurred all the same through the use of guns that were, at one time, obtained legally by the shooter's mother. The same thing goes for the shooter in Aurora, Colorado. Both of these massacres involved weapons and ammunition that was bought and purchased in the method that the law prescribes; one involved an illegal use of weapons (Sandy Hook) where the other (Aurora) did not.

Another notable point is that there are those who obtain their guns illegally without going through the necessary checks by buying their weapons on the black market. These individuals – regardless of gun regulation – will always find a way to get a gun since they don't follow the legal avenues to gun ownership in the first place. One cannot say that all gun violence is a result of the black market, nor can we say that only guns obtained legally are the source of gun violence, either. We can say, however, that gun violence is a problem and a societal malady that is likely to stick around for some time.

What are we to do about the problem of gun violence without unduly restricting our right to protect ourselves from our government? Should background checks be more stringent? Should potential gun owners have to subject themselves to a mental exam before obtaining a weapon? Should there be a national gun registry so that local authorities will have access to the knowledge as to who owns guns and how many they possess? Should we require universal background checks – even in transactions from person to person? Should gun violence strip the guilty party in these crimes from their Second Amendment right? Should parents of children who are involved in gun violence be punished to the same degree as their kids? Is the enforcement of the laws we have on the books enough to prevent gun violence, or are new laws necessary? It is widely accepted that gun violence is a problem, but the root cause and also the potential solutions for this problem are hotly contested.

Amendment 3: Restrictions on the Quartering of Soldiers

The Third Amendment to the Constitution puts restrictions on the quartering, or housing, of soldiers. During wartime, quartering of soldiers is only permissible if the resident gives consent, but is totally forbidden in times of peace. This Amendment was included because of numerous Quartering Acts issued by Great Britain in the months preceding the breakout of the American Revolution. The colonists despised these Acts for a number of reasons, and it wasn't simply because their houses had more guests than normal (United States, 183).

The issuing of the Quartering Acts gave British soldiers access to private residences. This was problematic for a number of reasons. First, a household had to provide food and shelter for whatever soldiers demanded such services of them, and many families were likely struggling with putting enough food on the table for the family living in the residence itself. Second, all of this occurred in a time when men were the sole breadwinners and women were expected to stay home and maintain the house. While their menfolk were away working, the British soldiers were free to use the womenfolk however they saw fit; one can infer that rape was probably a big problem in a time when refusing to house British soldiers constituted treason and severe punishment.

Our Founders sought to spare us all of this unnecessary drama and restricted the quartering of soldiers during wartime to be expressly dependent on the willingness of individual residences to house and feed soldiers. The Founders further prohibited the quartering of soldiers during peacetime; it was seen as unnecessary and an undue stress on the relations between civilians and military personnel. This is the only Amendment that has not been challenged at the Supreme Court level and is often seen as the least controversial Amendments in the Bill of Rights. Some ponder, however, when the quartering of soldiers might be necessary today or whether this Amendment has become obsolete.

Imagine you live in California, an earthquake-prone region, or in Missouri, a state prone to the devastating effects of tornadoes. What if a major disaster were to devastate 'a city near you', and the National Guard was called in to help with disaster relief? What if one of your family members was trapped in the rubble and Guardsmen promised that,

The redcoats are coming....in. And camping out.

after spending the night, they would help extract your loved one from the debris? I bet there aren't many among you who would ask these folks to sleep someplace else. In general, you probably would want to give your loved one the best chance possible of survival, and so you would – through your Third Amendment right – consent to quartering these soldiers in the hopes of saving your beloved. Maybe the Third Amendment isn't obsolete after all. I bet if you asked victims of Superstorm Sandy, Hurricane Katrina, or the Joplin, Missouri, tornado how they felt about this issue, they would support the consensual quartering of soldiers and thus, the enforcement of the Third Amendment.

Amendment 4: Prohibition of Unreasonable Search and Seizure

The Fourth Amendment prevents the government from invading on your privacy when your criminal background is not in question; in other words, if you are not suspected of a crime, the government doesn't have the right to search you, your car, or your house. If the government *does* have a reason to suspect you of a crime, however, it is within their rights to search and seize anything that might be construed as criminal (United States, 183).

The ability of government authorities to search and seize is dependent on one of two things – probable cause or a search warrant. **Probable cause** exists when the authority in question either suspects or has personally witnessed some sort of criminal wrongdoing. A **search warrant** is a court order issued by a judge when criminal activities or a criminal past is suspected; typically speaking, probable cause is required in order for local authorities to get a search warrant. Probable cause alone, however, can and has been used for grounds for searches and seizures.

Let's use an example most of you are probably familiar with. On the television show COPS, the same scenario occurs in virtually every episode. First, a police officer will pull over someone who either (a) is driving a car with a license plate that doesn't match the car's make and model or (b) is recklessly driving or speeding. The cop, after having obtained the driver's license and proof of insurance, will either smell marijuana smoke or the scent of alcohol and will use it as grounds to search the car. This *does* constitute as probable cause and does give the police officer the right to search the suspect's car and seize anything in it that he or she deems to have a criminal nature.

Another COPS scenario involves a police officer being called to address a domestic (home) disturbance. The officer is usually sent on such calls because of a complaint call from a disgruntled neighbor. The call itself typically qualifies as probable cause, but the rules of search and seizure are different for homes than they are for cars. Without a search warrant, a police officer can only view what is visible from standing in the doorway of the home; thus the officer only has access and can only criminally accuse the inhabitants of anything that is in *plain sight.* A search warrant grants the police more sweeping access to the house; the officer with a warrant can enter the house and can thoroughly search it and arrest the inhabitants for anything found to be criminal in nature. The 'in plain sight' rule is what makes search and seizure in private residences different from the application of the Fourth Amendment when applied to motor vehicles.

Modern Dilemmas

An extension of the Amendment, as stated before, protects an individual's right to privacy. Without proper proof or evidence of criminal activity, the authorities are prohibited from interfering in an individual's personal life. Some members of the lesbian, gay, bisexual, transgender (LGBT) community argue that the Fourth Amendment protects the right of individuals to love and have sexual relations with whoever they want. They argue that the absence of criminal activity denies authorities with the probable cause or a warrant necessary to interfere with such relationships. Oppositions to the LGBT community contend that since many states have sodomy laws on the books, probable cause of such behavior does indeed merit the intervention of local authorities. As homosexual behavior becomes more accepted (or tolerated) in society, this line of thinking seems to be becoming less prevalent. Either way, there have been and still are people who seek to interpret the extent to which the Fourth Amendment protects people from the interference of the government in their private lives.

Whatcha gonna do when they come for you?

Amendment 5: Rights of the Accused

The Fifth Amendment predominantly deals with the rights of individuals who have been accused of crimes. The Amendment addresses a number of topics including necessary indictments for capital crimes, double jeopardy (not the game), the right to silence in one's own defense, and one's Miranda rights. Less related to individual rights is the right of the government to exact **eminent domain** – claiming a private residence for public use. Each of these issues merits a deeper discussion as to what is meant and who is applicable in each instance (United States, 183).

Necessary Indictments

The first element of the Fifth Amendment asserts that a person cannot be convicted of a capital crime or a **crime of infamy**, an offense that requires a strict or severe punishment, without first being indicted and formally tried for such an offense. Before such conviction occurs, the suspect must first be indicted by a **grand jury** or a jury of one's peers. The case then proceeds to trial and the will of the jury serving on that respective case will determine the guilt or innocence of the accused person. This is known as **due process** or the procedure by which justice is carried out. The **Due Process Clause** in the Fifth Amendment guarantees that a person's guilt or innocence will be determined through an established process and not through the (potentially biased) opinion of a specific individual (United States, 183).

Double Jeopardy

Double jeopardy is the attempt to legally try a suspect for the same crime twice. According to the Fifth Amendment, double jeopardy is illegal. Let us consider O.J. Simpson. Back in the 1990s, Simpson was acquitted in the case surrounding the murder of his girlfriend. Legally, it is not possible for Simpson to be tried for that crime again in criminal court. He could be, and was, tried for a slightly lesser charge in civil (noncriminal) court. The Amendment protects an individual from being repeatedly tried for the same crime (United States, 183).

'Pleading the Fifth'

The Fifth Amendment protects individuals from **self-incrimination** or implicating oneself in a crime. In criminal trials, defendants cannot be forced to testify against themselves if what they say has the potential to implicate them for the crime they're being tried for. In civil cases (noncriminal), this right also applies but the choice to 'plead the Fifth' in civil cases can and has resulted in a guilty verdict and restitution to be assigned to the defendant (United States, 183).

The protection of the individual against implicating oneself in a crime is included in one's Miranda rights – namely, in a person's "right to remain silent." In this way, individuals are advised of their Fifth Amendment rights before they might accidentally incriminate themselves. Of course, individuals can choose to waive their right to silence in the hopes of being convicted of a lesser charge through a deal with the prosecutor or a **plea bargain.** If one's guilt is in serious question, however, most lawyers advise their clients to employ their Fifth Amendment right to keep their mouths shut.

Eminent Domain

The less-criminal element to the Fifth Amendment deals with the allowance for **eminent domain** or the seizure of private lands for public use. This right of the government on both a federal and state level is limited by the last line of the Fifth Amendment – the **Takings Clause** – which mandates that individuals who own private property that the government wants to seize are justly compensated. Typically, this compensation is the cash value of the land and properties in question plus extra as a courtesy (United States, 184).

The utilization of eminent domain is typically unpopular. In general, people spend a lot of time building and maintaining their property and are less than thrilled when the government – whether federal or state – seeks to claim these properties as their own. Even with the payment required by the Takings Clause, many property owners feel themselves ill-used. For example: along the Missouri River near St. Louis, the floodplains used to be farmland used to grow soybeans and corn. In the late 1990s and early 2000s, the state of Missouri claimed the farmlands by eminent domain. Court cases were filed and heard, and the state of Missouri prevailed. Now, the floodplains are dominated by industrial parks and commercial properties – all the result of eminent domain. Through eminent domain, this industrial park has sparked an economic surge in St. Charles County (Holyoke, 1-2).

Amendment 6: Rights to a Speedy Trial and to Legal Counsel

Right to a Speedy Trial

The Sixth Amendment guarantees both the defendants subject to legal litigation and also the victims of crime a speedy trial. The need for and guarantee of 'speed' is one that ensures that legal action regarding individual crimes does not unduly drag on. In other countries, legal action can and does drag on for long periods of time. This is particularly true in autocratic governments. The Sixth Amendment guarantees that this will not occur (United States, 184).

Speed, however, is a relative term; it is entirely different from one legal jurisdiction to another. Some time is necessary for the legal proceedings to occur in their due course. Both the defense and prosecution need time to appropriately prepare their materials that enable them to defend their client. One of the ways this time is distributed is through **continuances** or postponements in the case granted by a judge to give either the defense or prosecuting attorneys more time to find and prepare evidence for trial. The issuance of continuances is relatively common and thus, the speed of trials is not necessarily as speedy as one would initially think (Cole and Smith, 377-392).

Right to Legal Counsel

Defendants are also guaranteed the right to legal counsel – a lawyer to advise a defendant

The right to a speedy trial – but slow enough to exact justice

of his or her rights and the best way to proceed which would be most likely to encourage the jury to acquit the defendant. There are an abundance of lawyers in this country, and not all lawyers are 'the same' per se. For example, there are divorce lawyers, family lawyers, corporate lawyers, labor lawyers, lawyers trained to represent the federal government, and so on. For each type of legal dispute, it seems as if there are lawyers specifically trained to address those concerns (United States, 184).

Unfortunately, however, lawyers don't usually come cheap. The better the lawyer is, generally speaking, the higher his or her service fees are. Some of the best lawyers in the country charge thousands and thousands of dollars for their services, and I think it is safe to say that individuals amassing small incomes will find lawyers of that caliber out of their reach. Indeed, there are individuals who can't afford a lawyer at all, and the Sixth Amendment guarantees these individuals legal counsel as well. This counsel comes in the form of a public defender (Cole and Smith, 428-430).

A **public defender** is a lawyer employed by the state to represent low-income individuals. Generally speaking, these lawyers are freshly out of law school and were unable to find a law firm that wants them. Like any new job hunter, many (but not all) lawyers start off serving as public defenders. It is widely known that public defenders are highly overbooked and have little time to set aside for each individual case. A friend of mine was assigned a public defender, and when the lawyer showed up, he asked my friend what he was being accused of. Clearly, the public defender had no knowledge of my friend's case and had a limited capacity to defend her as the lawyer had not had time to research the matter as other lawyers do as a standard part of their services.

Something to ponder here is whether or not low-income citizens, by way of public defenders, garner the same quality of 'justice' as individuals who have the money to pay for the better lawyers. I think we as a society would have to conclude that no, justice – in a lot of cases – is determined by the lawyer you can afford; it is not necessarily about defining an absolute 'right' or 'wrong'. This is , in my opinion, a travesty. In a society as advanced and 'civilized' as ours, anyone who stands in the court of law should expect to receive the same consideration and the same degree of justice no matter their **socioeconomic status** or their place in the economic social structure.

Amendment 7: Right to a Jury of Your Peers

The Seventh Amendment guarantees you the right to a jury of your peers. This description of how a jury should look is intriguing. What *is* a jury of your peers? What should it look like? Who should and shouldn't be on it? When most people think of 'their peers', they consider people they know – their friends, co-workers, fellow church members, and the like. In general, most people see 'their peers' as someone like them. Based on the information we have regarding the makeup of juries across the country, a jury of 'your peers' doesn't exactly meet those criteria as much as most of us would think (United States, 184).

Modern Dilemmas

Take this story for instance. My dad was once selected to serve on a jury in a federal trial. The 'victim' was the driver of a tractor trailer who hauled logs from the various logging sites to the nearest sawmill. In order to tighten the logs down on the trailer, the driver employs a number of tools to make the load sufficiently tight, and one of the tools the victim used was a long, grey-blue galvanized pipe known as a 'cheater bar'. The cheater bar, unfortunately, broke and the victim had his eye poked out (Davis, 1).

My dad grew up on a farm, and most farmers own at least one cheater bar. Interestingly enough, says my dad, cheater bars specifically state on them that they are not to be used for tightening loads onto trailers. Apparently, there had been a court case before the one in question that mandated such a warning be printed on these cheater bars. Well, after my dad told all of this to the attorneys selecting jurors, they told him that he need not serve on the jury and was excused. A point worth mentioning is as soon as my dad was excused, both lawyers held a brief meeting, and the victim agreed to drop the case (Davis, 1).

A jury of one's peers decides the fate of the accused.

Here is a valid question: why, in a venue where we are supposed to be trying to exact justice, would someone like my dad – who had factual knowledge to render in this case – be dismissed while less knowledgeable people were allowed to sit on the jury before the attorneys made their deal? Does the justice system really want to provide justice or rather, justice according to whichever lawyer presents a more convincing case? Is it advantageous to exclude knowledgeable people like my dad away from judicial proceedings, or is the exclusion of such jurors a miscarriage of justice?

Let's consider another more recent trial – the George Zimmerman case. In this case, George Zimmerman, a neighborhood watchman, suspected the young African American, Trayvon Martin, of wrongdoing in his neighborhood, and Zimmerman pursued him. Most evidence suggests that there was a physical altercation between the two men, and Zimmerman pulled out his gun and shot Martin. This case received all kinds of media coverage, as the case was portrayed by the media to be a racially charged attack despite the fact that Zimmerman was of Latino rather than Caucasian descent (Hanna, 1-3).

There are some interesting things to note about the jury in the Zimmerman case. First, all six jurors in the case were women while both Zimmerman and Martin were males. Why not include a male juror so as to better represent the reactions and emotions a male may have experienced in a situation like the one Zimmerman and Martin were a part of? Another oddity in this case was that although the victim, Trayvon Martin, was African American, this racial group was not represented by any member of the jury. There was a lot of outcry from the African American community in this regard; how can we be sure that justice was done when the perspective of race was not represented in the 'jury of peers'?

I think there are a number of things we can garner from these two stories. First, a 'jury of our peers' is not necessarily a group of people who share the same interests or life experiences as we do, nor do these people necessarily represent us racially, economically, religiously, and so on. Simply put, a jury of one's peers could be – at its simplest state – a group of people who happen to live in the same judicial jurisdiction as you whom both the defense and prosecuting attorneys approve of. Such a group doesn't ensure that the people who might decide your fate are intelligent, nor does it guarantee that they share anything in common with you. A 'jury of one's peers' by experience is not what most would consider to be a 'jury of one's peers' by the definition that most of us hold.

Amendment 8: Protection Against Excessive Bail, Fines, and Cruel and Unusual Punishment

The Eighth Amendment protects individuals from a number of things. First, the Amendment protects individuals from excessive fines that might cause the accused parties in crimes to be imprisoned indefinitely. This is considered to be a violation of the 'innocent until proven guilty' principle; removing an individual's ability to escape prison before a guilty verdict has been reached was, according to the Founders, a miscarriage of justice. The second thing the Eighth Amendment protects against is excessive fines from wrongdoing. One cannot be fined, for example, for the value of one's house for speeding, nor can a person be sentenced to life in prison for a misdemeanor (or minor) charge. This addendum to the Amendment props up the idea that 'the punishment should fit the crime', but the last and most well-known element of this Amendment, at least in some cases, limits the scope of punishments that are available for use against convicted criminals by the prohibition of 'cruel and unusual punishment' (United States, 184).

Modern Dilemmas

In today's world, there is a lot of controversy surrounding the Eighth Amendment, and most of this contention gravitates around the use of capital punishment (the death penalty) and the use of torture against terrorists and other serial criminals. These issues are not simple; there are many points on both sides that continue to garner support. Capital punishment is becoming less popular over time as is the use of torture; however, both are current events worth mentioning and delving into.

Capital Punishment

The use of the death penalty has become one of the most societally dividing practices still employed widely across the country. There are lots of folks out there who oppose the death penalty while there are others who contend that the use of capital punishment is the only reasonable method for removing the imminent and clear threat posed by career criminals. The death penalty's supporters and opponents approach the issues from a variety of angles – some based on a type of moral high ground, some based on practicality, others based on the financial aspect of the issues, and still others focus on the role of the government to protect and defend citizens.

The most common defense for the death penalty is that the punishment fits the crime; in other words, the death penalty does and should remain an option in crimes where a victim or victims are killed. Supporters of capital punishment often argue that the death penalty guarantees the families of victims closure and justice; these individuals support the 'reap what you sow' and the 'let the punishment fit the crime' mentality. Opponents of this standpoint contend that two wrongs don't make a right – no matter how heinous the crime was. These folks argue that fighting fire with fire still leaves something burning. One cannot justify death with death, or so some opponents of the death penalty contend. Employing the death penalty doesn't bring the victims back to life; it's sad, but true. Essentially, the opponents of this death penalty argument assert that two wrongs don't and won't ever make a right. Another problem with the 'justice' argument is that oftentimes, our justice system lends itself to the rich, white, male majority. In general, you see far more individuals who are low-income earners or members of minorities convicted of capital crimes than any other socioeconomic groups. One could argue that our justice system caters to those who have the ability to buy their way out of trouble. For this reason, some argue, the death penalty should be avoided if not entirely scrapped.

Some supporters of the death penalty argue that prison's intent is to rehabilitate people, but there are some criminals where such an outcome is not possible. Take, for example, Charles Manson and his little group of followers. Under Manson's instruction, his followers mercilessly killed several people (Bugliosi and Gentry 24-26). Some would argue that rehabilitation for serial killers is not possible, so thus the employment of the death penalty in those cases makes more sense that paying to rehabilitate those beyond hope of such an end result. Opponents of this perspective allege that rehabilitation and/or salvation is always possible and should therefore, at the very least, be attempted. Not offering those who commit these crimes is a disservice to the criminals who, according to these folks, be offered the opportunity to accept and pursue positive change in their lives.

From a financial perspective, supporters of the death penalty argue that capital punishment is far cheaper and cost effective than housing a career criminal in jail for the rest of his or her life. Some prisons enable 'lifers' to go to college, to acquire jobs – sometimes even off-premises, and so on. Many contend that lifers shouldn't be given these luxuries that other criminals who are incarcerated are denied. Opponents of this perspective argue that if these people are going to sit in prison, they might as well do something useful and productive with their time. Also, life sentences provide the ability to acquit innocent people, as some convicts who have been executed have been later exonerated due to DNA testing and other new technologies.

Torture

Torture is a questionable application of the Eighth Amendment. Since the late 1800s, however, the Supreme Court has seemed to indicate that torture is prohibited by this Amendment. The question, however, is what the United States can do in regard to non-citizens. Particularly since September 11, 2001, the question of torturing terrorists for information has become more widely debated. One of the most famous centers of terrorist torture is the infamous Guantanamo Bay military prison (Cucullu, 89-118). Similarly, one of the most famous fictional, albeit realistic, depictions of torturing terrorists occur in the TV hit series *24*, where counterterrorism agent, Jack Bauer, occasionally utilizes different methods of torture to force terrorists to

Jack Bauer, counterterrorism agent, a reluctant but dutiful user of torture during the interrogation of terrorists

divulge information that ends up saving lives (Weed, Davis, and Weed, 91-104).

Those who contend that torture is an appropriate interrogation method argue that the information gained from such methods can and does save the lives of countless citizens. Numerous terrorist plots have been foiled through the information that interrogators have garnered from employing methods of torture. Others, however, contend that the use of torture is not necessary to gain the information that is needed; these folks contend that alternative methods of interrogation can and have been used to garner similar results. The debate over the effectiveness of torture as an interrogation method is likely to continue for some time.

The brutality of torture is another area in this discussion that is hotly contested. Those who advocate the use of torture argue that only through such brutal tactics can the information they want be obtained. Many interrogators argue that the methods short of torture are ineffective in gaining the information that they and the government are seeking. Other interrogators assert that as other countries – particularly the ones where most of these terrorists are from – employ methods of torture in their interrogations, it only makes sense that those tools be available to American interrogators as well. Opponents of torture argue that the methods employed are too brutal and inhumane. Others assert that, as a leader in the global community, the United States should not be willing to stoop to the level of countries that are typically associated with human rights violations and a general lack of interest in the adherence to international law. The opponents of torture essentially argue that America is too civilized a country to use such archaic methods to gain the information they seek. The humanity of such methods is another area of the debate that will also be one talked about for years to come.

Amendment 9: The Exclusionary Rule

The Ninth Amendment is one of the most straightforward of the ten Amendments that comprise the Bill of Rights. This Amendment assures individuals that rights exist that are not discussed explicitly in the Constitution. This is the Amendment that most current events are applied to in order to determine their constitutionality. Issues like abortion rights and same-sex marriage are issues not explicitly discussed in either the Constitution or the Bill of Rights. This Amendment gives the people facing these modern issues the hope that the rights that they seek are protected via the courts and the establishment of legal precedent (United States, 184).

It is important to mention here that this Amendment was initially designed to apply only to the federal (or national) government. It was designed to empower the federal government to expand the rights of individuals, NOT to expand the power of the federal government itself. This is an important difference that is worthwhile to understand. For example: say, a majority of people want to expand federal rights for same-sex couples or for women who seek to employ their right to choose to have an abortion. These fall within the bounds of the Ninth Amendment because both of these issues deal with the rights of *individuals*, not the expansion of the power of the federal government. An example of this would be, say, giving the courts the ability to override a presidential veto without constitutional defense behind it. Another example might be for the Executive Branch to claim the right to write legislation while the Constitution clearly states that the formulation of legislation is a job assigned to Congress.

The most well-known method of federal expansion of individual rights is through the Amendment process, so some folks argue that the Ninth Amendment indirectly asserts the Founders' intent that the Constitution can and should be both changed and interpreted in whatever time the current readers live – not necessarily from the mindset and circumstances that faced the Founders at the time of the actual adoption of the Constitution. To amend the Constitution, the Amendment has to go through Congress, be signed by the president, and be approved by two thirds of the state legislatures. Since the adoption of the Constitution and the Bill of Rights, the Constitution has only been amended seventeen times; this should demonstrate how rare and difficult constitutional change can be and has been.

Constitutional change because of the Exclusionary Rule: making America better together

Amendment 10: The Rights of the Federal Government and of the States

The Tenth Amendment was one that was written to protect the individual sovereignty of the states while, at the same time, preserving the overarching power of the federal government. The Amendment mandates that the powers not explicitly discussed in the Constitution to be the responsibility of the states respectively and also the people. States therefore have the ability to make laws regarding issues that are not explicitly dealt with in the Constitution insofar as these laws do not step into the bounds of the powers enumerated to the federal government. Also, legal **precedent** or the interpretation of the Constitution should be considered in this discussion as oftentimes, the decisions handed down by the Court dictate the federal application of constitutional interpretation (United States, 184-185).

Modern Dilemmas

An issue that often comes up when discussing the Tenth Amendment is the problem of **nullification** – the attempt of a state to make laws that directly negate federal law. A more antiquated example is the spread of slavery after the Missouri Compromise. This agreement made the deal that future states that entered the Union (the United States) would be labeled a free state or a slave state. Every other state after the Compromise would be a free state while every other state would be a slave state. Some states, particularly the ones who widely used slavery, weren't happy with this agreement and many sought to enter the Union as slave states; others entered the Union as free states but continued to condone slavery. The issue of nullification rather than the issue of slavery was the main contributor to the election of Lincoln and thereafter, the breakout of the Civil War.

A more recent example of nullification – one that will probably not end as violently as the issue of slavery did – occurred during the 2012 election season. Both Colorado and Washington legalized the recreational use of

Nullification - one of the catalysts of the Civil War

marijuana. Long ago, the federal government deemed marijuana as an illegal substance and possession and trafficking of this drug was deemed a prosecutable offense. The legalization of marijuana, some claim, is Colorado and Washington state's attempt to 'nullify' or override the federal law prohibiting the purchase and sale of the drug. Some contend that, inevitably, the legalization of this drug will be struck down as unconstitutional by the Supreme Court, because the legalization of the drug is, in effect, nullification and therefore, illegal. Only time will tell.

The Pirate Code and the Bill of Rights

At the beginning of the chapter, I argued that the Bill of Rights is akin to the Pirate Code from the *Pirates of the Caribbean* films as the pirates themselves argue the code to be 'more like guidelines than actual rules.' With the very lengthy exploration of each Amendment, its intent, and its modern-day application to real-world situations, I think most of you will probably agree that tradition dictates that we, like the Caribbean pirates, should keep to the "Code."

The Bill of Rights and the Pirate Code: more like guidelines than actual rules

Food for Thought

Amendment 1

How far should the freedom of religion go? How much freedom should religions have to promote their interests with the public? Have we as a society gone overboard with political correctness, or do you think that making many people feel safe and comfortable is okay even if it infringes on the rights of others? Are there some forms of protest that should be prohibited? Is the burning of the American flag in protest, in your opinion, wrong or unpatriotic? Why do you think libel and slander are so hard to prove in court? Do lawyers have the ability to rationalize most anything, or is it hard to define what objective or subjective truth exactly is?

Amendment 2

I argued that this Amendment was designed, in the mindset of John Locke, to protect us from our government. With all the regulation on gun ownership, does the Amendment still serve this purpose; would we stand a chance against our government if we were to break our social contract? In your opinion, do guns kill people, or do people kill people? Are current laws enough to curb gun violence? Do we have a gun problem or a violence problem? What has society done to encourage people to believe that using guns to solve quarrels or disputes is okay? If you believe gun laws need to be changed, what needs to be changed? Should there be some way to require mental health testing to prevent people who are mentally incapable of owning guns from do so? Should we regulate the number of guns or ammunition people can buy? Should we have a national gun registry that denotes all the gun carriers? Should guns be banned when we know that criminals will always find a way to get a gun, even if they're illegal?

Amendment 3

Do you think the threats present during the Revolution in regard to the quartering of soldiers are rational threats today? Is this Amendment obsolete? In the event of a disaster, should the public be able to quarter soldiers as the Constitution permits, or is there something valuable in separating military and civilian (normal citizens) life? Should there, if permitted, be restrictions on who can be quartered and should the willing families be compensated by the government for the services these families choose to render to these servicemen and women?

Amendment 4

What constitutes probable cause? How does one know if a police officer is feigning probable cause just to make an excuse to search one's vehicle or home? Why is the 'plain sight' principle important when considering probable cause in the instance of a home search? Should this Amendment be interpreted to protect the right to privacy? If so, how far should the protection of a person's privacy go? Would the government reading your emails or text messages (like the NSA has done recently) be a violation of your privacy, or are those acts an attempt to protect national security?

Amendment 5

Why is due process an important standard that is upheld by our justice system? Why is it important to prevent double jeopardy? Should double jeopardy apply to criminal and civil law or only exclusively to criminal law. Why? Why is eminent domain a right guaranteed to the federal government? Should the federal government have the right to take your property and put it to public use? Would monetary compensation plus a bonus make up for having to move, find a new home, and so on, or does eminent domain put undue pressure on private homeowners?

Amendment 6

Should the trial process take less time than your average trial typically does, or does the length of the trial process make the carriage of justice more successful? Should there be a limit on the time the prosecution and defense attorneys have to prepare their materials, or should they have unlimited time so as to best represent their clients? This Amendment guarantees individuals the right to legal counsel; should everyone have access to a good lawyer regardless of one's ability to pay? What can we do to make public defenders more effective representatives of their clients? Do you believe the justice system is biased in favor of certain groups in society, and, if so, which groups?

Amendment 7

In your opinion, what is 'a jury of your peers'? Does the Seventh Amendment's application in the trial system support or negate your perception of said jury? Do you think the justice system would rather see informed individuals sitting on juries or ignorant people with no knowledge of the subject matter of the trial? Are some juries set up to convict or acquit the defendant on purpose? What do you think the prosecuting and defense attorneys look for in a 'good' juror? What qualities would lead a juror to be dismissed from serving? What does that tell you about the way jury trials are run?

Amendment 8

Do you think excessive bail gives the impression that a person is guilty until proven innocent instead of the other way around? What is your opinion on the death penalty? Should it be allowed, banned, or are you somewhere in the middle? Why? What, in your opinion, constitutes a crime worthy of the death penalty? Should there be forensic evidence provided that ensures that a guilty conviction and execution are merited, or can the prosecution prove guilt beyond reasonable doubt without forensic evidence? How do you feel about the use of torture as an interrogation technique? Are there lines in regard to this issue that you would be unwilling to cross? Since torture is prohibited according to international law, should it be a tool that the United States, a global exemplar, employs or not?

Amendment 9

Do you believe constitutional interpretation is okay, or should the Constitution be read and taken word for word? Can one argue that the Constitution protects certain rights without directly addressing them? If not, should the amendment process be more straightforward? Are there advantages to the drawn-out process by which the Constitution is amended? Are the requirements to amend the Constitution too stringent or not? Do you think states have the right to make and enforce laws that directly negate federal law; in other words, do you support nullification?

Amendment 10

How much power should the federal government have in relation to the states? What about the other way around – how much power should states have when considering their relationship and interconnectedness with the federal government? Which do you think should have more power – the individual states or the federal government? Why? Given the fact that the failure of the Articles of Confederation essentially proved that a weak federal government with powerful states didn't work, where is the balance between federal and state power? How powerful is too powerful? What safeguards should be set up so that one bastion of power doesn't overstep it? Would said safeguards be effective and enforceable?

First, filling the Dead Man's Chest

Next, obtaining the Master Sword and restoring peace to Hyrule

Works Cited

Ashtari, Shadee. "Rush Limbaugh, Sandra Fluke." *The Huffington Post. http://www.huffingtonpost.com/news/rush-limbaugh-sandra-fluke* . Posted on 11/06/2013.

Bugliosi, Vincent and Curt Gentry. *Helter Skelter: The True Story of the Manson Murders.* New York: W. W. Norton & Company, 2001.

Cole, George F. and Christopher E. Smith. *The American System of Criminal Justice.* Belmont: Wadsworth Publishing Company, 2010.

Cucullu, Gordon. *Inside Gitmo LP: The True Story Behind the Myths of Guantanamo Bay.* New York: Harper Luxe Publishers, 2009.

Davis, Armin. Personal interview. October 10, 2010.

Drain, Lauren. *Banished: Surviving My Years in the Westboro Baptist Church.* New York: Grand Central Publishing Company, 1995.

Ferner, Matt. "Columbine High School Massacre." *The Huffington Post. http://www.huffingtonpost.com/news/columbine-high-school-massacre* . Posted on 06/13/2013.

Hanna, Jason. "This Just In: Zimmermann Charged With Second-Degree Murder." *CNN News. http://news.blogs.cnn.com/2012/04/11/prosecutor-to-announce-decision-on-zimmerman/* . Posted on 04/11/2012.

Holyoke, Larry. "370 Corridor Drives Boom in St. Charles." *St. Louis Business Journal. http://www.bizjournals.com/stlouis/stories/1998/12/28/focus2.html* . Posted on 12/27/1998. Article.

Pearson, Michael. "Gunman Turns 'Batman' Screening Into a Real-Life Horror Film." *CNN. http://www.cnn.com/2012/07/20/us/colorado-theater-shooting/index.html* . Posted on 07/20/2012.

Pirates of the Caribbean: The Curse of the Black Pearl. Dir. Gore Verbinski. Perf. Johnny Depp (Captain Jack Sparrow) and Geoffrey Rush (Captain Barbossa). Walt Disney Pictures, 2003.

Shapiro, Martin. *Freedom of Speech: The Supreme Court and Judicial Review.* New Orleans: Quid Pro, LLC., 1966.

United States Supreme Court. *Snyder v. Phelps Assenting Opinion. http://www.supremecourt.gov/opinions/10pdf/09-751.pdf* . 2010.

United States. *The United States Constitution: The Full Text With Supplementary Materials.* New York: Dover Publications Inc., 2009.

Vogel, Steve, Sari Horowitz, and David A. Fahrenthold. "Sandy Hook Elementary Shooting Leaves 28 Dead, Law Enforcement Officials Say." *The Washington Post. http://articles.washingtonpost.com/2012-12-14/politics/35846598_1_schools-administrator-gunman-public-shootings* . Posted on 12/14/2012.

Weed, Jennifer Hart, Richard Brian Davis, and Ronald Weed. *24 and Philosophy: The World According to Jack.* New York: Blackwell Publishing, 2007.

CHAPTER 6

The Legend of Zelda: A Link to the Past and American Federalism

One of the most well-known video games of all time is *The Legend of Zelda: A Link to the Past.* By far, this video game is the most played and the most widely sold of all time. It invites the gamer to travel along the path trodden by the hero, Link, in his Quest to restore peace to the land of Hyrule. The game encourages the player to solve puzzles, find treasures and tools, and defeat Ganon (the villain) and his minions which stand between Link and the peace that Hyrule so desperately desires. While this game is buried deep in fantasy innuendo, I believe it is comparable to an interesting phenomenon in our world today – that of American federalism.

Link: the Hero – the one destined to obtain the Master Sword, defeat Ganon, and restore peace to the Kingdom of Hyrule

The Bill of Rights mandates that while the federal government is granted certain powers, the states are allotted authority over certain matters as well. Over time, the powers of both of these entities – the federal and state governments – have become blurry and distorted. The powers of the federal and state governments in the United States encompass American federalism – a system where both state governments and the federal government have some sort of control over individual lives and also a responsibility to the citizens whom they govern. I contend that the powers of the federal and state governments have blended together just as the Light World and Dark World in *The Legend of Zelda* have been bridged – both by Ganon's connection to Hyrule Castle and by the Magic Mirror obtained by Link in the game. Before I elaborate on the comparisons, however, let me first give you a summary of the game's backstory and plotline so the connections I make later are more helpful.

The Legend of Zelda: A Link to the Past

A Link to the Past takes place in the mythical Kingdom of Hyrule, a beautiful land full of waterways, mountains, and forests. For generations, the land has been ruled by a line of kings who had taken the advice from seven wise sages and their ancestors. Long before the plotline in the game begins, however, other important events of note took place, and perhaps the most important of these is the creation and hiding of the Triforce (also known as the Golden Power).

The Triforce: Wishing the World Away

The 'creators of the world' created a mysterious magical object known as the Triforce (Nintendo, 12). The Triforce looks like three golden triangles stacked in a pyramid. The Triforce grants the individual that touches it whatever wish he may desire, no matter how large or small, complicated or simple. The Triforce was placed in the Golden Land, a kind of parallel universe, by the creators of the world, but the Triforce, as a magical object, seems to 'call' people to it so as to grant their wishes (Nintendo, 12). The entrance to the Golden Land was kept secret so as to prevent people with evil hearts from finding the Triforce and making wishes that would be a detriment to the people of Hyrule. The makers of the Triforce, like the people of today, believed that humanity could not be trusted; they insinuated, through the hiding of the Triforce and the entrance to the Golden Land, that men tend to make decisions that are self-centered and are unconcerned with their decisions' consequences for the rest of humanity.

The Triforce: changing the world one wish at a time

The Rise of Ganon – the King of Thieves

For a time, the Triforce remained unsullied in the Golden Land, but Ganon, the King of Thieves, accidentally stumbled upon the secret entrance to the Golden Land, the place protecting the Triforce from evil-hearted men. Ganon obtained the Triforce and wished for absolute power and dominion over all things. So it happened – partially. Ganon's minions spread across the Golden Land and destroyed it, and in Hyrule, the Golden Land became known as the Dark World (Nintendo, 13).

The King of Hyrule discovered Ganon's capture of the Triforce and quickly sought out the seven wise-men – sages with astounding magical powers – and commissioned them to reseal the entrance to the Golden Land (or Dark World) in order to trap Ganon and his evil creatures there and prevent Hyrule (the Light World) from being overrun and destroyed through Ganon's evil doings. Initially, the seven wise-men's magic was successful and they impeded Ganon's entry into the Light World, but the power of their seal was not to last. Eventually, Ganon succeeded in breaking the seven wise-men's seal and his minions poured into Hyrule. Many of Hyrule's bravest and most valiant Knights were killed; only a few of these men with the Hero's blood running through their veins survived (Nintendo, 13).

It was at this time that the Master Sword, a blade with the strength to deflect the evil powers Ganon possessed, was forged. It was hidden in the depths of the Lost Woods where, one day, the True Hero who had captured the Pendants of Courage, Power, and Wisdom would be able to extract the Sword which had been thrust into the heart of a stone plinth in the depths of the Forest (Nintendo, 151). The Master Sword, unlike other blades, possessed the ability to channel an individual's inner power while also deflecting evil magic utilized by enemies. Until the True Hero surfaced, however, the Master Sword slept in the depths of the Lost Woods, shrouded in a mysterious fog (Nintendo, 13).

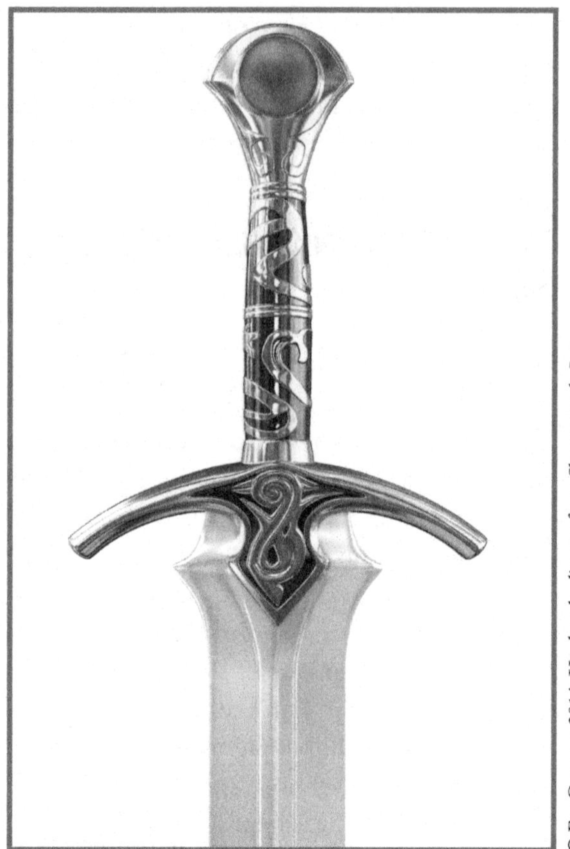

The Master Sword: Evil's Bane and the weapon to defeat Ganon

Aghanim, Ganon's Agent and Means to Power in the Light World

The seven wise-men, through tremendous effort, were once again able to trap Ganon and his evil creatures back in the Dark World and Hyrule entered into a period of peace. Years went by and the people of Hyrule forgot the threat of Ganon, the power of the Triforce, and the story of the Master Sword and how the legendary Hero was to obtain it. The Kingdom of Hyrule was immersed in a golden age of peace, but it was not to last. Hyrule began to face disasters of all sorts – earthquakes, torrential rains, and other such calamities. The age of peace that had settled over Hyrule was over, and the kingdom plunged into turmoil (Nintendo, 14).

The King of Hyrule was at a loss in terms of what to do until a mysterious wizard, Aghanim, surfaced and offered to free Hyrule from the plagues and disasters that were devastating the kingdom. The King assented, the disasters ended, and Aghanim became one of the King's most trusted advisors. What the King didn't know was that Aghanim was an agent of Ganon; Aghanim bided his time and gradually amassed power and respect among the King's court. This era of tranquility and political stability in Hyrule was not to last, for while the people of Hyrule were idle, Aghanim and Ganon certainly were not (Nintendo, 14).

The Seal of the Seven Wise-Men

As Hyrule slept, Ganon and Aghanim spent their time seeking the ancestors of the seven wise-men – the mages who had sealed the gateway to the Golden Land (or Dark World). Ganon hoped that by uniting these ancestors, he could reopen the gateway between Worlds and would be able to allow his wish to dominate the Kingdom of Hyrule to come completely true. With the Triforce as his ally, only a Hero would be able to stop him and prevent his wish of universal conquest and dominion from becoming realized (Nintendo, 14-15).

Gradually, Aghanim began to abuse his power. The wizard deposed and imprisoned the King. More importantly, he sought far and wide for seven maidens – the seven ancestors of the wise men who had created the seal between the Light and Dark Worlds. As time passed, Aghanim found and captured all seven of them, the last being the daughter of the King, Princess Zelda. Through telepathy, Zelda cries out to anyone who might hear, and her pleas for freedom are heard in a dream by the youth, Link. His uncle ventures out into a raging thunderstorm and leaves Link at home to ponder his uncle's sudden departure. Link pursues the message of the dream and travels to Hyrule Castle. He is contacted again by Zelda and informed that she is imprisoned in the castle's dungeon. Upon entering through a secret doorway, Link finds his uncle, injured, in a damp tunnel. His uncle charges him to save the Princess. Link leaves his uncle, takes his sword and shield, and promises to return after having rescued Zelda (Nintendo, 16).

The Game Begins: Rescuing Zelda and Obtaining the Master Sword

Link successfully rescues Zelda and takes her to the Sanctuary, a chapel of sorts, where the Sage vows to protect and hide her from

Link: the legendary Hero arises to save Hyrule from Ganon's clutches

Aghanim. Link is sent to a wise man, Sahashrala, who tells him the tale of the Master Sword. He tells Link that to obtain it and to have any chance of defeating Aghanim, Link must enter three dungeons overrun by Aghanim's monsters and obtain the Pendants of Courage, Power, and Wisdom and take them to the location of the Master Sword – a stone plinth hidden within the depths of the Lost Woods. Link succeeds and acquires the legendary Sword, but is instantly contacted by Zelda through telepathy as she is captured by Aghanim's soldiers. Link then travels to Hyrule Castle and confronts Aghanim. Link arrives just as Aghanim causes Princess Zelda to vanish, and the evil wizard is able to partially open the gateway between both Worlds. The battle that ensues between the Hero and Villain becomes a stalemate; rather than admitting defeat, Aghanim draws Link into the Dark World through the gateway that now existed at the gate to Hyrule Castle (Nintendo, 66-68).

Saving the Seven Ancestors and Defeating Ganon

Once Link arrives in the Dark World, he is contacted telepathically by Sahashrala. Ganon's use of Aghanim as a pawn is revealed, and Link is told that Ganon had trapped the seven maidens – the ancestors of the seven wise men – in crystal cocoons and hidden them in dungeons spread throughout the Dark World. In order to save Hyrule from Ganon's evil dominion, Link must find and rescue the maidens so they can break the seal to the entrance of Ganon's Tower so that then, Link can confront and defeat Ganon, capture the Triforce, and restore peace to the Kingdom of Hyrule (Nintendo, 66-67 and 105).

American Federalism and *The Legend of Zelda: A Link to the Past*

Just as Link makes his way through the Light and Dark Worlds seeking the pendants, the Master Sword, and the descendants of the seven wise men, America has created and employs a new form of government, one not seen by the

Trapped in seven crystals, the ancestors of the seven wise-men wait to be released by Link as he embarks upon the Quest of defeating Ganon and restoring peace to Hyrule

world before – federalism – and has watched it evolve over time. **Federalism** is a system of governance in which two separate government entities exist – the national government and state governments. While independent of each other for the most part, some of the power claimed by each governing body overlaps the authority asserted by the other.

The Light World and Dark World: Worlds and Governments Apart

In the game, Link travels across the land of Hyrule seeking the Pendants of Courage, Power, and Wisdom so as to gain the legendary Master Sword. In the Dark World (formerly the Golden Land), Link is charged with finding and rescuing the descendants of the seven wise men who are locked deep within numerous dungeons scattered across the space of land that had once protected the Triforce. Both of these Worlds exist independently, but Link must traverse interchangeably between them to complete his Quest. His ability to combat Ganon is dependent on his obtaining the Master Sword. Link's successful location and rescue of the seven wise men's descendants enable him to embark upon a final confrontation with Ganon, destroy him, and restore peace to Hyrule. While Link must accomplish independent goals in each World, success in one World is often dependent on Link's knowledge and success in overcoming various obstacles in the other.

The American **federal system** is very similar. As stated before, a federal system employs both a national government and state government which, while having a significant amount of individual and independent power on their own, have responsibilities that overlap and create a significant amount of confusion as to who has what powers and why. America's federal system is unique in that both the federal and state governments have real power and much of these responsibilities are protected from infringement.

Pendants from the Light World to obtain the Master Sword to defeat Ganon once and for all in the Dark World. Government power can be independently claimed or shared.

This is different from what we started with upon our nation's founding. When the colonies won their independence from Great Britain, we employed a **confederal system.** A confederal system's power rests primarily in the hands of individual state governments while the federal government is assigned only basic tasks of governance like national defense

– although each state had its own standing army or **militia**. The confederal system of early America is much like the European Union of today. Each state is allowed to have its own currency, governing bodies (legislatures, executive officers, and judicial systems), and elections. The national government exists only to resolve interstate or international disputes and to protect its citizens from outside threats.

The Articles of Confederation, our country's first attempt at a constitution, arguably provided individual states with too much power and deprived the federal government of the authority necessary to keep the whole thing together. Indeed, the Constitutional Convention, some claim, was called because disputes across the country, like Shay's Rebellion, were threatening national stability, and the Founding Fathers felt a revision of the Constitution was necessary to prevent the young United States from falling apart (Brinkley, 149-167). The Founders concluded that too much power and responsibility had been assigned to the independent state governments and that the balance of power between the federal and state governments should be far more equal than it was under the Articles of Confederation. Thus, our Founders established the federal system we recognize and adhere to today in our new and standing social contract, the United States Constitution.

Our federal system, unlike most European democracies, has distributed the power between the national and state governments relatively equally – at least on paper. In most European democracies, the national government is absolutely supreme while the local governments are subservient to the national government. This kind of system is known as a **unitary system.** For example: Great Britain created the colonies and allowed them to govern their own affairs but ultimately they were controlled and were answerable to the British Crown. The colonies were allowed to regulate many things that affected individuals – travel, business, transportation, and the like – but taxation, military intervention, and other major governmental functions were left to the British government.

In *A Link to the Past*, both the Light and the Dark Worlds exist as independent lands, and Link is expected to complete certain tasks in each respective World. America's system of government is also divided into two worlds, if you will – the realm of the national government and the influence of the state governments. Each has independent responsibilities and each is protected from the infringement of the other's interference – to a point.

Unique and Shared Powers: Worlds Divided and United

In *A Link to the Past*, Link has challenges that he has to overcome in both the Light and Dark Worlds. In the Light World, Link's first task is to rescue Princess Zelda from the depths of Hyrule Castle. After Sahashrala tells Link the tale of the Master Sword, he is instructed to seek and find the three pendants hidden in the Eastern Palace, the Desert of Mystery, and on Death Mountain. Once Link secures these magical artifacts, he must go deep within the Lost Woods to obtain the

Link's Magic Mirror and his link between both Worlds – like the concurrent powers that national and state governments share

legendary Master Sword. Once Zelda is captured by Aghanim's soldiers, Link must return to Hyrule Castle to confront him.

While Link follows this main plotline, Link must also seek out objects that can only be found in the Light World. Some of these objects include the Magic Mirror which allows Link to warp between Light and Dark Worlds, the Magic Cape which makes Link invisible and impervious to attacks, the Book of Mudora which allows Link to translate the ancient texts of Hyrule, and so on.

In the Dark World, Link's main objective is one relayed to him telepathically by Sahashrala. He must find the maiden descendants of the seven wise men who are trapped within crystals in seven dungeons spread across the Dark World. Once he obtains the seven crystals imprisoning the descendants of the seven wise men, Link must take them to Ganon's Tower so their combined powers can break the seal protecting Aghanim within it. He then must make his way through the dungeon itself so as to confront Aghanim for the final time. Once Link defeats the wizard Aghanim, Ganon rises from his dead body and carries Link toward a pyramid in the center of the Dark World as a bat. Link must then fight and defeat Ganon so he can take possession of the Triforce and reverse the evil that Ganon had done, restore peace to Hyrule, and remake the Golden Land into the place of watchful serenity it had once been.

While there are duties that Link can only achieve in one World or the other, there are some things that Link can do in both Worlds. Link can buy magic potion, find pieces of heart (life), earning Rupees (the currency of Hyrule), and so on. All of these things can be achieved in both Worlds. One of the items Link has to find is the Magic Flute. To obtain the Flute, Link has to dig it up in a grove of trees slightly to the west of his own house. However, the shovel used to dig it up can only be obtained in the Dark World. So, for some adventures, Link has to travel between Worlds to achieve them. The same thing is true for one of the magic potion storage bottles Link obtains in his travels. He finds a treasure chest and must warp into the Light World and carry it to a locksmith near the Desert of Mystery to have it opened. Some tasks, unlike the finding of the Master Sword and the release of the seven maidens, takes place in both Worlds as opposed to only one of them.

In terms of America's federal system, the same is true of federal and state governments. Some powers are reserved exclusively to the federal government while other powers are reserved for the states. The federal government is responsible for coining money, national taxation, national defense, promoting the general welfare, and so on. State governments are allotted many electoral powers as well as local and police powers. Some of the electoral powers allotted to the states are the direct election of senators, the election of the representatives for each state's congressional districts, and the allocation of each state's electoral votes in presidential elections. Other powers of the states enable each to aid their citizens in everyday life. Keeping birth and death records, providing marriage licenses, and so on are just a few examples of the power of the states to aid their citizens. The final power that states possess is their **police powers** – the ability of states and local municipalities to protect and preserve the peace. This means making laws that keep a state's citizenry safe through police enforcement, fire and rescue, disaster plans, and so on. Each state is granted these powers whereas the national government is denied these powers. There are powers, however, that are denied the states; states cannot enter into treaties with foreign countries or coin money. These powers are reserved for the national government alone.

While state and national governments have independent powers, there are some that they share. These are known as **concurrent powers.** Any power that is considered to be powers inherent to any government falls under this classification. Some examples of concurrent powers are the power to tax, to pass laws, to create courts to exact justice, to establish a police force to keep the peace, and so on. Concurrent powers, as stated before, are inherent powers granted to all levels of government; this includes governments at the national, state, and local levels. While the number of powers allotted specifically to the national and state governments far outstrip the concurrent powers common at all levels of government, it is important to know that these universal powers of government exist.

An important point to make here is that each state government, while acting independently from the national government at times, can choose to work side by side with other state governments to achieve common goals. This is known as **horizontal federalism.** An example would be the states of Missouri and Illinois working together to maintain the Mississippi River as a waterway that can be utilized to move trade goods as well as create an environment that encourages boating and interstate tourism. Many states can and do engage in horizontal federalism regularly. Just as Link accomplishes some of his tasks exclusively in the Light or Dark World while others require visiting both Worlds, the powers allotted to the government can be specifically granted to national or state government or can be shared at all levels of government.

Bringing Peace to the Light World and More Power to the National Government

Link's adventures in both Light and Dark Worlds are such where many objectives are fulfilled. The Master Sword is found and won. The descendants of the seven wise men are found and freed from their crystals. Ganon is destroyed and removed from power. The Triforce is touched by Link, a person with a good heart. Finally, and most importantly, Link restores peace to the land of Hyrule, that is, the Light World. All of Link's journeys culminate in the completion of this final objective. Once Link does so, the gamer who controls Link and his exploits wins the game.

The powers mentioned above – both national and state – are known as **enumerated powers**. These are powers granted the federal and state governments by the United States Constitution. Some of these powers are directly mentioned while others are broadly discussed and have been further elaborated on over time through judicial review. It is the **implied powers** that the federal government claims which have changed the dynamic of our federal system over time. In the Constitution, two clauses were included by the Founding Fathers which the national gov-

Restoring peace to the Light World of Hyrule: Increasing the power of the American national government

ernment has used over time to increase the breadth of its power. These two clauses are the Necessary and Proper Clause and the Supremacy Clause.

The Necessary and Proper Clause gives Congress the power to do whatever is considered to be necessary and proper to protect and defend the needs and wants of the citizens of the United States. The national government has used this Clause over time to increase its power. The first application of the Clause occurred when Alexander Hamilton and his cohort wanted to establish a national bank. Anti-Federalists (a political party) were strictly opposed to the creation of a national bank, because they believed that such an act would encourage the national government to take additional powers that were, at the time, reserved exclusively for the states. Supreme Court Justice John Marshall disagreed and cited that the Necessary and Proper Clause protected the national government's right to do such things as it was necessary in providing national economic stability (Brinkley, 169-170). A more recent application of the Necessary and Proper Clause was in reference to the Patient Protection and Affordable Care Act (i.e., Obamacare). The Supreme Court used the Commerce Clause in tandem with the Necessary and Proper Clause to prop up the 'individual mandate' element of the law – the part that requires everyone to procure health insurance.

The Supremacy Clause, put simply, declares that laws made by America's national government in Washington, D.C., are the supreme law of the land and cannot be negated by the states (nullification). The national government under Lincoln denied southern states the right to enter the Union as a slave state after the Missouri Compromise of 1820. This decision ultimately encouraged the southern states to secede from the Union in 1861. Soon after, the newly formed Confederate States of America (the South) attacked Fort Sumter and instigated the beginning of the American Civil War. Ultimately, the war was fought over the attempt of states to deny the national government its right to make sweeping laws regarding the rights of the states to regulate business (i.e., the slave trade). To make a long story short, the states lost and have lost in many other instances. While, by definition, we operate under a system of dual sovereignty (national and state government powers are relatively independent), some contend that we are headed toward a unitary system of federalism where the national government is supreme in most decisions while the states have the right to make laws regarding menial things not dictated by the national government – like marriage licenses and trash pickup. Just as Link seeks to restore the Light World of Hyrule to its former glory, the argument can be made that through the application of the Necessary and Proper Clause and the Supremacy Clause, the national government's power precedes and supersedes that of the individual state governments.

The Evolution of American Federalism: The Backstory Before *A Link to the Past*

Before the events of *The Legend of Zelda: A Link to the Past*, much occurred both in Hyrule and in the Golden Land before Link's part in the story began. Similarly, American federalism was not always as it is now. It has evolved over time and has been influenced both by historical pressures and by the politicians in power who were responsible for the changes that occurred. Let us consider the evolutionary process of American federalism as it compares to the development of the *Zelda* backstory and activities that occur within *A Link to the Past.*

The Beginning: Two Sovereign Governments, Two Separate Worlds

The beginning of the story starts describing Hyrule, a beautiful land full of waterways, forests, mountains, and glens. In a seemingly parallel world exists the Golden Land – the home of the Triforce, a mysterious, magical object which grants the wishes of the next person who touches it. While the gate to the Golden Land was open, it was hidden by powerful magic. Both Worlds exist simultaneously and operate independently. On the one hand, the seat of power in Hyrule, the Light World, was the King and his Knights. On the other hand, the Golden Land's power rested in the Triforce which preserved the tranquility that rested there.

America's federal system started off as one of **dual federalism**, and it continued roughly until the presidency of Franklin Delano Roosevelt – the president serving for most of the duration of the Great Depression. The national government in Washington had a set of responsibilities while the individual state governments had theirs. While the state and national governments cooperated on a variety of issues, most objectives were addressed independently, either solely by the national government or exclusively by the individual states. As I mentioned before, the national government instituted a national bank and printed American currency. State governments across the country were responsible for their enumerated powers, most especially their electoral powers, police powers, and powers to make, implement, and enforce statewide laws (Purchell Jr., 178-181).

Turmoil and Cooperation: The Gates to the Golden Land Open

For ages, the land of Hyrule and the Golden Land existed as separate entities. Each was independent of the other, but that was not to last. Unexpectedly, Ganon stumbled upon the gateway to the Golden Land, the home of the Triforce. He captures the magical object, wishes for dominion and conquest, and the gateway between Worlds is opened so that anyone can traverse between both Worlds. Ganon opened the gateway so that his minions that he had amassed in the Golden Land, through his wish, could enter, inundate, and conquer the land of Hyrule. Many valiant Knights died but ultimately, the seven wise

Many heroic Knights died to thwart Ganon; the national and state governments struggled together to find a resolution to the Great Depression.

men were able to reseal the gateway between Worlds and trap Ganon in the Golden Land (now known as the Dark World).

The second era of federalism, like the second part of the *Zelda* plotline, occurs during a time of political turmoil – the Great Depression and World War II; in fact, this system of federalism lasted till the middle of the 1960s. During this era, the government was trying anything to attempt to alleviate the American public from the horrific effects of the national economic meltdown. To make things easier, the state governments surrendered some of their powers so as to make it easier for the national government's attempts at fixing the economy more smooth. This era is known for its public works projects which occurred across the country. The building of man-made lakes, dams, the planting of forests, and various other undertakings were employed by the government as an effort to get people back to work. State governments allowed the national government to go forward with these plans without protest as these acts did have a positive impact in jumpstarting America's economy (Brinkley II, 704, 718). Because states and the federal government worked together during this era to achieve a common good, ending the Depression, we know this era as one of **cooperative federalism** (Purchell Jr., 178-181).

The Rule of the King, Aghanim, and the Dominion of the National Government

Once the seven wise men had sealed the gateway to the Golden Land, trapped Ganon, and forged the Master Sword, peace rested over Hyrule for years beyond count – so long that the people of Hyrule forgot the threat of Ganon and the legend of the Master Sword. Only the descendants of the seven wise men and the historians in Hyrule kept these things close to their hearts. Soon enough, however, calamities of all kinds began to manifest themselves in Hyrule – torrential rains, earthquakes, and other such disasters rattled the people of Hyrule and their King. The King of Hyrule sought a solution to these problems and was thus approached by the evil wizard and pawn of Ganon, Aghanim. He, through magical arts, ended the disasters and became one of the King's most trusted advisors. During this time, however, Aghanim sought the descendants of the seven wise men so as to break the seal which trapped Ganon in the Golden Land.

The new age of federalism that emerged after the era of cooperative federalism was realized primarily under the presidency of Lyndon Johnson – the mid to late 1960s. It is known as **centralized federalism** – a system of federalism where the national government imposes its will onto state governments. The implementation of the Civil Rights Act of 1965 was one of the directives implemented and enforced by the national government on the states, some of them being unwilling participants – especially in the South. The national government imposed its will on the state governments by placing conditions on the lending of money to state governments. To receive funds, the state governments had to adhere to some statue imposed by the national government. These are known as **grant-in-aid programs** (Brinkley II, 833-835). To acquire monies controlled by the national governments, states had to do something to appease the national government in return for the monetary transfer to occur. This age of federalism was extremely short-lived and was replaced with the current form of federalism employed in the United States, **conflicted or 'new' federalism.**

Partially Opening the Gateway: Conflicted Federalism

The plotline of the actual game, *The Legend of Zelda: A Link to the Past,* follows Link as he combats Aghanim and Ganon. After having obtained the legendary Master Sword, Link seeks out Aghanim and finds him as he is trapping Princess Zelda in a crystal and is

Aghanim traps Princess Zelda inside a crystal, breaks the seal of the seven wise-men, and partially opens the gateway between the Light and Dark Worlds; American federalism – a conflicted mess of dual, cooperative, and centralized federalism.

successful in partially opening the gateway between the Light World of Hyrule and the Dark World. Unlike the era of the Knight Heroes, the gateway is only partially opened near Hyrule Castle, so Ganon is still unable to make his wish upon the Triforce come completely true. While Ganon seeks to open the gateway entirely, Link travels around the Dark World and frees the descendants of the seven wise men from their crystals so as to lead him to confront and defeat Ganon once and for all.

The final evolutionary stop in our trip down Federalism Lane drops us off in an arena of uncertainty. Since the presidency of Lyndon Johnson, presidents have attempted to partially decentralize the power accrued by the national government and reallocate some of these responsibilities into the hands of the states. Since this has gone on, however, both the national government and state governments have become unsure of what powers are theirs to use and which are not. For this reason, this era is known as that of **conflicted federalism.** This type of federalism is a confusing compilation of the previous three – dual, cooperative, and centralized federalism. On some occasions, the national and state governments operate independently. In others, the two levels of government work together to get things done. Yet in others, the national government seeks to assert its power over state governments. To be frank, the federalism we see today is a complicated mess that is difficult to comprehend, both for citizens and the public officials that are expected to function within the parameters of America's federal framework (Ryan, 98-104). Recent presidents like Richard Nixon and Ronald Reagan, however, have espoused the return of more powers to the states. Some consider this an attempt to reverse the historical evolution of federalism; we define this as **devolution.** Devolution is a popular idea across the board – both with Republicans and Democrats. The problem both sides have, however, is coming to a consensus in terms of what powers should be returned to the states and which should remain in the hands of the national government. Until both sides can come to a consensus, however, the Supreme Court will be the final voice in terms of what powers the national and state governments will be granted (Ryan, 324-326).

As it stands now, we appear to be evolving backwards to the era where the sovereignty of the national and state governments are independent as both bodies perform different but necessary tasks and thus require the power to complete them. However, we can definitely say that the national government is far more powerful now that it was during the early days of the country. Some attribute this to the assertion of the national government's implied powers granted them through the Necessary and Proper Clause and also the Supremacy Clause. In the recent past, the courts seem to side with the national government in terms of the allocation of power, so we can probably conclude that a return to true dual sovereignty is unlikely whereas a tempered centralized federalism – one that allows states *more* power but not *equal* power seems far more reasonable.

The Legend of Zelda: A Link to the Past tells the story of the Kingdom of Hyrule and its re-

The Master Sword sleeps again...forever! Similarly, American federalism is a permanent fixture in the realm of American politics.

lation to the Golden Land, the home of the magical Triforce. The story indicates that the evil Ganon, through various attempts, tries to use the Triforce to gain dominion over both the Light and Dark Worlds. American federalism too is much like the game. Rather than being stagnant, American federalism is fluid and constantly in a state of change. From dual sovereignty to cooperation, from centralized control to devolution, America, like Hyrule, is trying to re-allocate power between two worlds; in America's case, we are trying to restore independent power to the states through devolution so as to make the power between the national and state governments more balanced. Unfortunately for the United States, it will likely take a bit more than a piece of legendary steel and a handful of crystals to make significant progress toward that ultimate goal.

Food For Thought

Federalism vs. Other Means of Power Allocation

Federalism allots power to not only a national government but also to state and local governments. Are there any pros and cons to such a system? Why might the Founding Fathers have been wary of a unitary system like Great Britain has? The United States, before the Constitutional Convention, operated under a confederal system; why did it fail? Which government body, in your opinion, should have more power: the national government or state governments? Which powers should be the realm of the national government's influence and which should be the responsibility of state governments? In a unitary system, how powerless do you think local and state governments are in relation to the national government? Is that problematic? In a confederal system, how much power does the national government have in relation to the amount of power held by the states? Is that problematic? Do you think the Founding Fathers sought a 'happy medium' between national and state power by creating American federalism?

Powers of State and National Governments

Why are some powers reserved for either the national or state governments while other powers are shared? Do you think the national government has too much power? Are the state governments too weak? Do you think the powers each level of government holds make sense? Should the national government have any powers that it currently does not? What about state governments? Should the national and state governments collaborate more on policy? Would it be easier to implement and enforce policy or would it be more difficult?

Powers: Enumerated and Implied

Many of the powers claimed by the national and state governments are explicitly outlined in the Constitution. Do you think the Founding Fathers left any important powers out? Do you think they allotted too much power in any one area (either national or state)? Implied powers for the national government have been asserted through the application of the Necessary and Proper Clause and the Supremacy Clause. Do you think these two clauses of the Constitution are overused and over-applied, or do you think that the Founders intended the national government to be more powerful than the state governments? Are there some powers that you think the national government could claim by using either of these clauses that they have not yet attempted to gain? If so, what? The Supreme Court, over time, seems to support the increasing power of the national government as it has used these two clauses to validate the national government's power in a number of instances. Do you think the Supreme Court's application of these clauses is correct or has the application of these clauses exceeded the original intention of the Founding Fathers?

Dual Federalism

Dual federalism has dominated the larger part of America's history. What caused this era of federalism to end? Did it end for a good reason or was dual federalism worth maintaining? Is it philosophically possible for the powers of national and state governments to be entirely independent, or will there necessarily be some infringement of power by one government body or the other? Is dual federalism employed even if national and state governments compromise on some things, or does that qualify it as a new form of federalism?

Cooperative Federalism

Cooperative federalism emerged in an era of political and economic turmoil; why does it seem that government bodies compromise and cooperate more during times like these while in times of peace and prosperity, government bodies tend to compete with other government bodies and inhibit forward progress? Do you think the cooperativeness of the national and state governments during this era was in response to the willingness of the American people to compromise with each other so as to potentially end the Great Depression? How bad do things have to get before the government bodies of today will cooperate? Are some powers – either state or national – worth fighting over? If so, which ones?

Centralized Federalism

During the 1960s, Lyndon Johnson's presidency became one that was known for its centralized federalism where the national government asserted its dominance, indirectly, over state governments; would you say that, at this time, we were moving toward a unitary system as opposed to a federal system? Are there some advantages of the national government gaining more power? Are there drawbacks in the states losing power? Do you think that everyday citizens would notice if state powers gradually decreased and the power of the national government increased?

Conflicted Federalism

We are, some argue, in a real mess. We don't know what kind of federal system we are anymore. We're a mix of dual, cooperative, and centralized federalism. What elements of each do you see in existence? Should we change it? Arguably, we're in a state of devolution; we're moving backwards and moving toward dual federalism again. Do you think that the national government should be more powerful than the states? Should the national government have significant control over the states or should, in a typical scenario, both national and state government operate with separate, independent powers and only interact in special cases? Should the states be significantly more powerful than they are right now or would that inhibit the ability of the national government to fulfill its obligations as a governing body?

Now that Link has obtained the Master Sword, rescued the seven maidens, and defeated Ganon,

Middle Earth has to keep Sauron from recapturing the One Ring – the Ring of Doom.

Another dangerous adventure with a legendary Hero…

What are we waiting for??!!??

Works Cited

Brinkley, Alan. *American History: A Survey. Volume 1: To 1877.* New York: McGraw Hill, 2003.

Brinkley, Alan. (II). *American History: A Survey. Volume 2: Since 1865.* New York: McGraw Hill, 2003.

Nintendo. *The Legend of Zelda: A Link to the Past Nintendo Player's Guide.* Redmond: Nintendo of America Inc., 1992.

Purchell Jr., Edward A. *Originalism, Federalism, and the American Constitutional Enterprise: A Historical Inquiry.* New Haven: Yale University Press, 2007.

Ryan, Erin. *Federalism and the Tug of War Within.* New York: Oxford University Press, 2011.

"Supreme Court Upholds Individual Mandate, Obamacare Survives." Fox News: Politics. http://www.foxnews.com/politics/2012/06/28/supreme-court-upholds-individual-mandate-obamacare-survives/. Posted on 06/28/2012.

CHAPTER 7

The Council of Elrond and the Fate of the Ring of Doom: Political Values, Ideologies, and Public Opinion

"Three rings for the elven kings under the sky
Seven for the dwarf lords in their halls of stone.
Nine for the Mortal Men, doomed to die
But one for the Dark Lord on his dark throne
In the land of Mordor where the shadows lie.
One Ring to rule them all.
One Ring to find them
One Ring to bring them all
And in the darkness, bind them."
(Tolkien, 49)

In the fantasy world of Middle Earth, J.R.R. Tolkien creates a grand adventure which has captivated generations of readers. This is the tale of Frodo, a hobbit, who carries and seeks to destroy the Ring of Doom – a magical ring created by the Dark Lord, Sauron, who sought to use its power to enslave the inhabitants of Middle Earth. Before Frodo begins his journey, however, the Wise of Middle Earth must decide what to do with the Ring, and the issue proves to be extremely divisive. I contend that the controversy surrounding the Ring and its fate at the Council of Elrond – the meeting of the Wise in Tolkien's tale – is not unlike the debates that occur in America due to ideological differences. Before those comparisons are made, however, let us first consider Tolkien's tale – the forging of the Ring, its history, and the debate surrounding its fate – the Council of Elrond.

The Creation of the Rings of Power and the Deception of Sauron

In the *Lord of the Rings* saga, J.R.R. Tolkien depicts the creation of the Rings of Power by the Elves of the plain-lands of Eregion in Middle Earth. The three that belonged to the Elves were made in secret while the seven possessed by the dwarves and the nine possessed by men were not. The creation of these was known to Sauron, the Dark Lord of Mordor. Also in secret, Sauron forged a Ring that was designed to dominate the rest, so that his will might stretch across Tolkien's mythical world of Middle Earth (Tolkien, 236).

The Fall of Sauron and the Passing of the Ring to Men

At the height of his power, however, Sauron loses his ring and it is taken by Isildur, a mighty son of great kings beyond the Sea. Isildur, instead of destroying the ring as he was counseled to do, keeps it and treasures it; the Ring, having power of its own through Sauron, betrays him to his death. For centuries thereafter, the Ring was lost to the living world. Though many sought for it – Sauron, the heirs of Isildur, and Wizards – it seemed to be lost forever (Tolkien, 247-238).

Then, a chance encounter that took place near the location where Isildur lost the Ring and was killed, the creature Sméagol found it and took to cherish it. The Ring corrupted him, however, and soon he was shunned by his own people and viewed as a thief and murderer. He went into exile and lived within the deep caverns of the Misty Mountains, and his bitterness because of his misfortunes and the corruption of the Ring turned him into a vile, evil creature. The Ring lingered with Sméagol (now called Gollum because of the horrid noise he made in his throat when he coughed), but the Ring of Power – the One Ring – was growing restless (Tolkien, 243-244).

Odd things began to happen in Middle Earth. Sauron, having been removed from his ancient stronghold of Mordor, returns and re-asserts his power and reconvenes his wars with the realm of Gondor – the land of Isildur and the last stronghold of mankind. Evil things crept out from the mountains. Forests became shrouded in mist and evil things multiplied and dwelled there. The Ring perceived the turmoil astir in Middle Earth, and it made its move.

The Finding of the Ring

The Ring betrayed Gollum, but then the Ring was obtained by someone no one could have foreseen – Bilbo Baggins, a hobbit (a short human with hairy feet) of the northern Shire – much akin to the likes of Ireland or Scotland. Bilbo took the Ring and treasured it and used its unique powers, by wearing it, to become invisible when in the presence of an unwelcome or annoying guest. Upon the guest's departure, however, Bilbo would take off the Ring. The Ring gifted Bilbo with unnatural longevity so he ceased to age upon finding the Ring; his family and friends thought it queer, but most hobbits thought Bilbo strange to begin with (Tolkien, 244).

The Fate of the Ring Debated

Through much research and effort, Gandalf the Wizard discovered that Bilbo's ring was indeed the One Ring made and possessed by

Hobbiton – the home of Bilbo Baggins, the newest Ring-bearer

the Dark Lord, Sauron; it was the One Ring that the Dark Lord was now seeking and issuing all of his strength to retrieve. Gandalf convinces Bilbo to bequeath the Ring to his nephew and heir, Frodo. Gandalf then sends Frodo and his most trusted friend and willing servant, Samwise (Sam) Gamgee on a dangerous journey to the Elven city of Rivendell (known by the Elves as Imladris). Gandalf believed that Elrond, the Elven lord of Rivendell, would know what to do with the One Ring that had been found.

Elrond asserts that the might of the Elves could not protect the Ring from Sauron's clutches if the decision was make for the Ring to remain in Rivendell. Little trust existed between the Elves and the Dwarves, so Elrond was reluctant to send the Ring to their realms hidden within the mountains of Middle Earth. The decision was finally made to call a Council – the Council of Elrond – that would gather all of the races (Elves, Dwarves, Men, and Hobbits) together to decide the fate of the Ring – indeed, perhaps the fate of Middle Earth itself.

The Council of Elrond

At this meeting, a lot of strange tales were told that brought everyone in attendance up to speed on the losing and finding of the Ring as well as Sauron's attempts to recover it. The first part of the Council was dedicated to describing the Last Alliance – the battle where Sauron lost the ring when Isildur cut it from his hand with the shards of his father's (Elendil) blade, Narsil.

The Losing and Finding of the Ring

Elrond, the lord of the Elves, told this part of the tale, for he alone among the Council members was alive at this time, for Elves are granted the gift of immortality. Three thousand years ago, he saw the Ring cut from Sauron's hand. The lord of Rivendell had counseled Isildur to destroy the Ring in the fires of Mount Doom, a volcano in the heart of Mordor where Sauron forged the One Ring; Elrond implied that it was only there that the Ring could be unmade and its threat removed forever. Instead, Isildur kept the Ring, and over time, it corrupted and betrayed him to his death. He was slain by evil creatures, and for a time, the Ring disappeared from the wide world (Tolkien, 236-238).

Gandalf, a bearded Wizard dressed all in grey, tells the next part of the tale. The hobbit-like creature Sméagol finds the Ring in the river Anduin near the site where Isildur had been slain. The Ring, as a corruptible object, enticed Smeagol to thieve, spy, and scheme to the point where his people banished him. He fled his home and cursed the people who spoke against him and hoped to one day gain his vengeance. He traveled into the Misty Mountains and dwelled for 500 years on the wrongs done him by those he had once loved and called family. The Ring's power granted him the immortality only common in the Elven folk, but the trinket also corrupted him and turned him into a slimy, evil thing. It was in this state that Bilbo, a very respectable hobbit from the Shire, finds him and his Ring (Tolkien, 246-248).

Bilbo had been coaxed into an 'adventure' by Gandalf amid his protests of "never having any adventures or doing anything unexpected" (Tolkien). He was labeled a "burglar" and was brought to aid twelve Dwarves, led by the great Thorin Oakenshield, to reclaim the "Lonely Mountain" that was currently under the watchful eye of the dangerous dragon, Smaug. On the way, however, Bilbo gets lost and ends up meeting Smeagol (now called Gollum). Gollum finds Bilbo appetizing (the vile creature that he was, and decides to eat him. Bilbo, being a clever hobbit, challenges Gollum to a game of riddles which Bilbo wins (arguably by trickery). He leaves Gollum's lair with the One Ring in his possession and keeps it safe for over fifty years (Tolkien II, 68-90).

The Ringwraiths, Sauron's minions, pursue Frodo in an attempt to recapture the Ring and kill the one who carries it.

Gandalf, upon learning of Sauron's moves to reassert his power in Mordor, encourages Bilbo to pass the Ring onto his heir, Frodo. Bilbo finds this proposition hard to bear, but ends up taking Gandalf's advice. Frodo is sent out of the Shire in search of Rivendell by Gandalf, for he believes that Sauron's minions – the dreaded Black Riders (wraith-like creatures cloaked in black) have been sent to find the Ring and kill the current owner. Frodo does indeed meet and escape them on a number of occasions, but is injured in one of the capture attempts. As Frodo reaches Rivendell and is rescued by one of Elrond's people, Frodo begins to succumb to the pain and damage of the wound inflicted on him. He arrived just in time, however, for Elrond to save him (Tolkien, 68-209).

The One Ring passed through many hands and in no case had it failed to corrupt its owner. Sauron was evil from the start but the Ring only augmented his power. Isildur, a mortal man, was corrupted and betrayed by the Ring to his death. Smeagol/Gollum let the Ring corrupt him and lost everything he had once held dear. Bilbo even felt the effects of the Ring as did his heir, Frodo – particularly in the presence of anyone who wanted to see or handle the thing. The Ring, argued many on the Council, was altogether evil and capable of doing great harm to anyone who possessed it.

Sauron's Attempts to Reclaim the One Ring

Another discussion which occurred during the Council of Elrond focused on the tales told by the Dwarves and by Gandalf of Sauron's attempts to regain the Ring. The Dwarves' representative, Gloin, tells the story of how Sauron sent an emissary to Balin, one of Gloin's relatives, who resided in Khazad-dum (known most commonly as Moria). Sauron, claimed the emissary, knew that Bilbo had, at one time, been among the Dwarves and had acquired a Ring that Sauron wanted back. The Dark Lord offered the Dwarves other rings of power that Dwarf lords of old had possessed in return for information regarding the whereabouts of Bilbo or the Ring that Bilbo, at that time, possessed (Tolkien, 234-235).

Gandalf too brought a sobering tale about his superior, Saruman. Long ago, the Wise (the Elves and Wizards in Middle Earth) had discussed what would be done if the One Ring were to be found. Gandalf suggested the Ring be sent over the sea or destroyed while Saruman refused to put forth an opinion and indicated that the Ring was beyond lost and its finding was little hoped for. However, Gandalf learned through lesser Wizards that Saruman had gone to the last city of Men, Minas Tirith, and studied long the words of Isildur concerning the Ring. Saruman had traced the Ring to the site of Isildur's death – the river Anduin, and it was there, or so Saruman believed, that the Ring had floated down the river and into the Sea (Tolkien, 250-255).

Upon Frodo's finding of the Ring, Gandalf sends him toward Rivendell while he himself sought of Saruman in his stronghold of Isengard. He tells Saruman all he knows and assumes that, like him, Saruman still seeks to keep the Ring out of Sauron's grasp. He quickly learns, however, that an alliance had been formed between Saruman and Sauron and that Saruman was greedily seeking the One Ring in Sauron's name. Gandalf, through a stroke of luck, escapes Isengard and flees to Rivendell just in time to see Frodo being healed by Elrond of his hurts. So it was that Gandalf discovered the evil intentions of Sauron and Saruman – the joint agreement to find the Ring and mutually dominate Middle Earth and its inhabitants (Tolkien, 250-255).

The Debate of the One Ring's Fate

After the tales of the Ring's loss and discovery were told in full and the evil intentions of Sauron and Saruman were laid bare, the last thing left to debate in the Council was what should be done with the Ring now that it was evident that this Ring that Frodo carried to Rivendell was indeed the One Ring that Sauron was so eagerly searching for. This debate proved to be a very divisive one. Two perspectives emerged in the Council deliberations. The first was presented by Boromir, son of Denethor – the ruler of Gondor, the dominion of men and also the ancient realm once ruled by Elendil, Isildur, and their heirs.

Boromir's Plan

The line of kings long ago was broken and the heirs of the kingship of Gondor went into exile to escape the evils that befell their ancient realm. Boromir and his father had long memories and had long held grudges with most of the other peoples in Middle Earth. They believed them to be cowards or too lazy to deal with the might of the Dark Lord, Sauron, and his minions. The Elves had long hidden in their secret lands and offered little help to the Men of Gondor. The Dwarves were seldom seen and were perceived to be more interested in their mining and delving in the mountains to care enough to enter into Gondor's service.

Most of the major races weren't even aware of the hobbits living in the Shire. So, Boromir perceived the Men of Gondor to be entirely alone – the last hope of Middle Earth should Sauron rise to prominence again and attempt to recapture the Ring and enslave the inhabitants of Middle Earth (Tolkien, 239-241).

Boromir, with all this in mind, proposed that the Ring should be sent to his city of Minas Tirith, the capital of Gondor, and given to his people to be used in their wars against Sauron. He believed that the bloodshed incurred by the Gondorian people was reason enough to trust its people to fight and defeat Sauron through the use of Sauron's own weapon. It is not outwardly spoken of in the books, but it is hinted at that Boromir also seeks to acquire the Ring to secure power and respect for himself as the next Steward of Gondor – the ruler governing in place of the exiled king. Boromir is refuted, however, by another Man named Aragorn who is revealed to be Isildur's long lost heir; immediately, Boromir perceives Aragorn as a political threat to his inheritance as Gondor's ruler and instantly rejects his claim. Boromir continues to insist that the Ring should be given to Gondor and indirectly implies that the Ring would be wielded by none other than himself (Tolkien, 260-261).

The White Tree: the symbol of the Men of Gondor and the sigil of the Gondorian kings

Elrond's Plan

The words of Boromir trouble Elrond greatly. As the sole member of the Council who had lived during the days when Sauron first lost the Ring and its power passed to Isildur, Elrond remembered his counsel to Isildur that the Ring be destroyed and also how Isildur refused to listen to his advice. Shortly afterwards, Isildur was betrayed by the Ring and was killed by arrows. The Ring passed on and on, and whoever possessed it soon became enamored with it and the Ring began to corrupt them. As the Ring had consistently proved to be an object that spawned evil – both in the wide world and also in the lives of those who had possessed the Ring, Elrond counseled that no one should use the Ring, because the One Ring only seemed to lead to evil outcomes (Tolkien, 261).

Instead, Elrond presented two options. The first, which the Dwarves opposed, was sending the Ring over the Sea to the distant land of the Elves who had fled Middle Earth after the wars of Sauron had ended. The Dwarves had, for a long time, been unsure of the Elves' intentions and perceived that maybe the Elves sought to obtain the Ring to augment their power over all of the other races in Middle Earth; this is essentially what Gloin said to Elrond in response to this first proposition. The enmity between both races was made even more evident when an Elven prince, Legolas, backed Elrond and shunned the argument of the Dwarf as childish and irrational (Tolkien, 262-263).

In any case, Gandalf the Wizard also opposed this path and contended that the Elven roads to the Sea were watched closely by the minions of Sauron. He contended that following that path was too predictable as the Elves had fled that way in times of trouble before. Gloin, at this point, attempts to use his battle axe to cut the Ring apart and fails. Most of the Council is stunned and horrified, for the failure to destroy the Ring with such a mighty weapon suggested to them that the Ring was protected either by some evil magic or by Sauron's own black will which appeared to be somehow connected with the Ring (Tolkien, 262).

Elrond finally suggested that the only choice the Council had that could lead to a real solution to the problem but would not set one race above the others would be to destroy the Ring once and for all. He noted here, as he did to Isildur so many years ago, that the Ring was forged in the volcanic fires of Mount Doom in the heart of Mordor and only there could it be destroyed. He argued that a member of the Council should be chosen to possess and carry the Ring on a journey deep inside the

Mount Doom: the place where the Ring was forged – the one place it can be destroyed

bowels of Sauron's dark realm in an attempt to destroy it (Tolkien, 263).

Again, the Council appeared to be divided on the issue. Instantly, the Elves and Dwarves began to quarrel about who would and wouldn't be permitted to carry it; the strife between these two races went back for many generations, and neither was willing to take the risk of allowing the Ring to fall into the other race's possession. Frodo Baggins, Bilbo's heir, ended up volunteering to carry the Ring to Mordor, and to this bearer and path, Elrond assented. Elrond appointed a number of companions to travel with Frodo as far as they were willing to go or as far as fortune allowed. This band of travelers is known as the Fellowship of the Ring (Tolkien, 264 and 268-269).

The Political Parallel

There are many comparisons that can be made by considering the histories and interactions of the characters that participated in the Council of Elrond. From a historical perspective, we see that what happened in the past can and does influence decisions in the present. We also notice that the views of each character exist, because each character adheres to certain beliefs and attitudes regarding the issues pressing the Council. Third, these beliefs and attitudes affect how each character interacts with the others and responds to their proposals. Fourth, we garner that the members of the Council agree, in general, on what the actual problem is – that the Ring had been found and must be dealt with. The controversy arises when two characters – Elrond and Boromir – propose opposing solutions regarding the fate of the Ring.

Political Values

Elrond and Boromir have strong opinions about what the fate of the Ring should be. Boromir believes that the Ring should be used, because has faith in the strength and fidelity of Men. He also clearly believes that he himself has enough inner strength to wrench the power of the Ring to his will so that he might defeat Sauron and become victorious. Elrond, having personally witnessed the inability of Men to destroy the Ring long ago, is reluctant to see the Ring fall into the hands of Men again; the Elf lord sees this possibility as folly since his trust in Men had proved fruitless numerous times before. The Dwarves and Elves mistrusted each other, because their histories were filled with conflict.

All of these characters' beliefs and attitudes shape the way they interact at the Council. A person's beliefs and attitudes about politics or political issues is known as their **political values.** Political values are developed through the interaction with other people, through experience, and through education. By far, human interaction is the largest shaper of political values. We will consider a number of sources of political values and identify why these sources are so influential.

Family

The group that affects a person's political values the most is one's family. The easiest way to explain this is perhaps to simply assume that a person is around their family more than anyone else. Particularly during a person's childhood, parents and siblings have enormous power play an enormous role in shaping an individual's political values. Those separate histories and experiences affect the interaction had between family members and thus the past experiences of individual family members shape other members of the familial group (Lewis-Beck et al., 138-141).

Friends

Aside from an individual's family, people tend to spend the majority of their time with their friends – particularly from a person's youth through middle age. People tend to associate themselves with people who are similar to them, so the political values of an individual are augmented and reinforced by the association with and the experiences one incurs with one's friends. In general, friends share opinions and have conversations that other less bonding relationships typically prohibit, and so political beliefs and attitudes tend to be affected more when in contact with people you share more in common with (Lewis-Beck et al., 231-234).

Religion

Another entity that tends to shape a person's political values is one's religion or moral code. Individuals who belong to a religion are taught to hold a certain conception of what is right and wrong. Naturally, those moral attitudes shape the way a person approaches certain political issues. Some religions are more overt in their encouragement of certain political attitudes than others; however, it cannot be denied that a person's moral belief system affects the way he or she approaches politics and the issues involved in that realm (Lewis-Beck et al., 136-137).

Another point worth making is that some people's moral codes can and do exist outside the realm of any formal religious influence. Many agnostics and atheists have moral codes that they live by as well. These moral codes tend to be shaped by experiences as well as a person's intellectual investigations. A person's ability to reason is a tool that is used to shape many moral codes. To assume that agnostics and atheists are amoral (lacking moral backbone) is unacceptable; it is unreasonable to assume that individuals who aren't sure about or don't believe in a god espouse or utilize no moral code at all. An individual's religious background or moral code plays a substantial role in the development of that individual's political values.

The Workplace

Another venue which shapes people's political values is an individual's place(s) of employment. Many factors in the workplace have the potential to affect one's political values. First, many employers are unionized. In these workplaces, workers are protected and defended by labor unions in situations where employers attempt to lower pay, decrease benefits, lay off people, and so on. Unions exist to prevent workers from being treated unfairly. Union membership can and dues influence individual political values in a notable way (Lewis-Beck et al.,, 136-138).

Another element within one's workplace that influences individuals are co-workers. The people that we work with can and do change who we are, how we perceive life, and how we approach the world. Their reach stretches into the political sphere as well. Our co-workers' experiences indirectly alter what we perceive to be right and wrong from a political standpoint, what is important and what is insignificant politically, and what kinds of things should be done to get America's political situation from where we are now to where we ought to be.

Education

Lastly, but perhaps most importantly, an important venue where individuals learn about political issues is during the years of their education – from their childhood all the way through college and beyond if that be their choice. Throughout their education, individuals are expected and encouraged to encounter and explore various viewpoints and issues in order to develop educated opinions based on critical thinking over time. The information that individuals gain from a formal education that enables them to develop their political values is, of course, shaped both inside the classroom and outside in the real world. Education, from a certain standpoint, does not end when they receive their desired college degree. It continues until life's end as they continue to learn through experiences and the curve balls that life throws at them (Lewis-Beck et al., 336).

I think it's fair to point out here that many teachers – particularly in college – seek to

Political values: individual beliefs and attitudes regarding politics or current events

push (if not force) students to espouse political beliefs and attitudes that are similar to their own. This, in my opinion, is NOT education; this is indoctrination and is totally unacceptable. Again, in my own opinion, I think that, although it is especially hard for one educated in politics to be neutral, I believe it behooves educators to at least attempt to maintain neutrality. To present only one side of an argument to students denies them the information, attitudes, and values espoused by other individuals and thus prohibits students from forming educated opinions and making informed decisions about the world around them. In my opinion, there is no 'right' or 'wrong' views – they are merely different. Each individual's life experiences lead them to espouse one view over all the others, and that is okay.

Political Ideologies

We know that the characters involved in the Council of Elrond had good reasons for espousing their own views of the world around them. They all agreed on the problem that was plaguing Middle Earth – the Ring. What differs, however, are their opinions on what to do about it. A person's political values are not singular; typically, individuals have differing opinions on a variety of issues, and this is also true of the Council members. A person's political values often incline them to espouse certain ways of dealing with problems over others. In other words, one's political values often encourage a specific plan of action. Individuals identify what problems exist, but political values dictate how one addresses that problem.

As individuals grow up and become educated, they develop political values. They then consider how these values can be applied to solve real problems. This compilation of political beliefs and a corresponding plan of action is known as a **political ideology.** Although each individual's political ideology is slightly different from everyone else's due to life experiences, many people's beliefs and plans of action overlap. In the Council of Elrond, two ideologies emerge; one encourages the use of the One Ring while the other incites its destruction. In America, two ideological frameworks have emerged – **conservatism** and **liberalism.** While each espouses their own set of political values, there is a notable amount of philosophical overlap. First, we will investigate the political values that are embraced by each ideology. Then, we will take a look at

Liberals (left-wingers) and Conservatives (right-wingers)

a few current political issues from the eyes of both ideologies. Again, neither is better than the other – only different, and variety is one of the things that makes America great and enables our democracy to function the way that the Founding Fathers intended.

Conservatism

Conservatism as an ideology functions a lot like the name suggests. Conservatives like to conserve and preserve things that are already here. They believe in saving money and being financially responsible. They believe in hard work and thus removing the need (or most of the need) for government assistance programs which put our country into debt. Conservatives like tradition in nearly every sense. They accept the Constitution as a literal (as opposed to an interpretive) document. They believe in the importance of family and religious fervor. Conservatives generally dislike 'big' government that seeks to interfere in the lives of individuals. They believe freedom is great but that it doesn't come cheap; for this reason, they tend to be very strong supporters of the military and bolstering national defense. A major attribute of conservatives is their dislike for change. As the ideology of tradition and what is, it makes sense that these folks are reluctant to embrace change and alter the status quo.

Common Criticisms

Conservatives are often criticized for a number of these political values. First, conservatism is often associated as the ideology of Judeo-Christian values. As such, many proprietors of this ideology tend to be discriminatory of other religions in terms of their proposed political policies. Some find this problematic because of the Establishment Clause contained in the First Amendment which protects against the setting of one religion above all others. This has been interpreted by many conservatives, however, as an attempt to limit the individual's right to religious freedom and the right to conscience. This is one of those debates that is not likely to be resolved anytime soon (Eilperin, 1-3).

Second, conservatives are often accused of being the ideology that supports racist policies. Throughout American history, conservatives have been known as the ideology that fought against equal rights for African Americans, women, homosexuals, and others. Their instinct to cling to tradition makes this more understandable – even if it may not be acceptable from some people's point of view. Issues like immigration reform, same-sex marriage, and welfare reform are all issues that their proponents contend that conservatives shirk because of their potential racial implications (Blow, 1-3).

Third, conservatives are typically labeled as the ideology which supports unrestrained free-market capitalism; in other words, conservatives believe that the government should stay out of business affairs and mind their own business. The problem with this ideological stance, some argue, is that the lack of government interference puts the safety and well-being of the working class in jeopardy, because many business owners will, if allowed, pay as

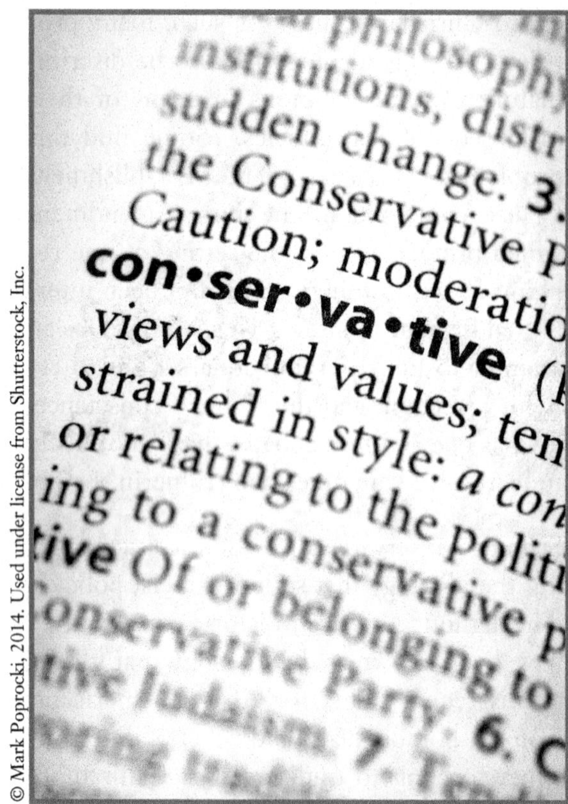

Conservatism: tradition, opportunity, individual initiative

little as possible and force employees to work as hard as possible without proper compensation or job security (Sargeant, 1-2).

Finally, conservatives, as the ideology that espouses low taxes and saving money, oftentimes is willing to sacrifice programs and cut funding that help people who genuinely need assistance in the name of limiting the abuse of the system. While some programs definitely need to be significantly reformed, some contend that conservatives take this position too far and give the impression that they support the interests of businesses and corporations more than the needs of everyday average Joes – particularly those that they label as lazy freeloaders (Ungar, 1-3).

Liberalism

Just like conservatism, liberalism is an ideology that has its own set of political values and also has its own set of criticisms. Liberals tend to support big government, higher taxes, and more government regulations. They argue that with as large of a population and land mass as we have, it is necessary to have government institutions that are big and strong enough to appropriately meet the needs of the people. Liberals tend to be very inclusive; they are not typically considered to be racist or discriminatory – generally. They support the equal rights and treatment of women, minorities, homosexuals, and so on. Liberals are also known as the ideology of labor relations. Liberals are supported by labor unions which fight for the rights and dignity of many working-class Americans. Liberals are also often designated as the ideology of the poor. They tend to support the maintenance and expansion of government assistance program (welfare); these programs include Social Security, Medicare, Medicaid, WIC, and others. Liberalism is often identified as the ideology that espouses the expansion and availability of a quality education for all Americans. These folks work to make education through college accessible and affordable for all who wish to pursue such a path. These folks are also the ones who lobby for animal rights and environmental protection.

Common Criticisms

Like conservatives, liberals are often criticized for their political values. Liberals' support of big government is often criticized on a number of levels. First, some contend that government interference is nothing short of a curse; it throws anything it touches into chaos and makes it harder for average people to get what they wanted to begin with. Another criticism, some allege, is that the government takes over responsibilities that should belong to the individual. Many criticize liberals for their advocacy of higher taxes and argue that, in many cases, the government wastes money that individuals maybe would not have (Herman, 1-2).

The support liberals lend to minority groups (racial and social) is often criticized as well. Some contend that this preferential treatment (as some call it) only encourages these groups to demand more aid instead of empowering them. Some further contend that these groups make a show of themselves in the eyes of the media to get what they want, and the liberals, or so their opponents argue, are sometimes too quick to jump on the bandwagon. Opponents of the liberal view, instead of adapting to different people, argue that society shouldn't have to adapt to new types of people. People should adapt to placate the 'moral majority' (Wallstein, 1-4).

As the ideology of labor relations, the liberals are often accused of encouraging laziness and the lack of initiative – a view that is also often a criticism of the liberals' belief that government assistance programs should be expanded rather than reined in. The liberals' relationship with labor unions is well known, and some argue that labor unions are corrupt and even influenced by members of the mafia. Opponents of Big Labor sometimes pose the argument that government shouldn't willingly associate itself with groups that are known to be corrupt or to have a noted criminal past (Gross, 1-3).

Liberals are often criticized for their support of quality education as well. Many contend that liberals seek to indoctrinate the masses by getting them to attend college. Some contend that most college professors tend to teach with a liberal slant. Based on previous experience, I can attest that, in general, this is pretty accurate. However, not all professors teach in that way nor do they try to force their own views on their students; for sure, it definitely is a problem, but I don't believe that it is as big a problem as the opponents of higher education would have you believe (Mooney, 1-2).

A final criticism about liberals is their strong defense in protecting the environment. There are two critiques that are often posed. First, some contend that certain liberals care more about the environment than they care about people; they would rather protect the white wolf in Wyoming than use funding to create jobs and get people off of welfare. The second critique of environmental protection is that liberals claim that protection of the environment is necessary to prevent the effects of global warming or climate change from becoming worse. Many liberals allege that all of the massive storms, hurricanes, tornadoes, and intense heat are effects of climate change; opponents of this view argue that weather on

Earth is cyclical and that the planet is currently in a warming trend and not seeing the effects of climate change – a theory that many people question. Essentially, the opponents of climate change contend that many liberals are overreacting in terms of their fervor in protecting the environment (Liptak, 1-3). Some liberals believe that climate change could bring about the 'end of the world as we know it'; others don't and 'feel fine' (REM).

The Truth About Individual Ideologies

Okay, so now we understand the difference between liberalism and conservatism. In general, though, I don't want you all assuming that if someone identifies as a conservative or a liberal that this person ascribes to every view typically associated with that ideology. Generally speaking, there is a lot of gray area between the ideologies, and most Americans fit somewhere in the middle of the ideological spectrum. Some Americans are conservative when it comes to financial issues like taxes but are liberal when it comes to social issues like abortion and same-sex marriage. Similarly, it is entirely possible for a person to be socially conservative but fiscally (or financially) liberal. It all depends on an individual's political values and how that person seeks to put those values into action.

Another truth about an individual's ideology is that it tends to change as one grows older.

Political ideologies, like most things in life, are not nearly as simple as they seem.

Generally speaking, a person tends to begin their political life ascribing to one ideology, and that belief system tends to garner support from the individual until he or she enters college. Generally speaking, many individuals tend to become more liberal during their college years. Whether this is because they're exposed to so many new ideas at once or if it's true that professors push a liberal agenda, research shows that college tends to impress liberal values upon individuals (Lewis-Beck et al., 223, 425). Once an individual graduates college and enters the workforce again, however, most individuals' ideologies move in a more conservative direction. When someone begins paying the bills, naturally they're going to be pickier about where that money goes and how it is spent. The ideological shifts of life are just one way in which a person's political makeup changes over time.

Public Opinion

One might wonder how experts measure the political values and ideologies of individuals across America. The media attempts to do this every day through public opinion polls and surveys. Although some media outlets go to great pains to make sure that their results are unbiased, they very rarely succeed. In short, most public opinion polls and surveys *are biased.* There are a number of different ways that the results of these polls and surveys could be skewed. I will briefly discuss the ways these polls and surveys can be biased and give examples of each case.

Well, That's Random

Suppose you're watching Fox News, MSNBC, or any of the large cable news networks. Imagine they ask a question about President Obama's handling of the economy, and they report the survey results. Before they even began surveying folks, there was already a problem with their survey – their sample was not *random.* A **random sample** is one where one individual is just as likely to be surveyed as any other. It's like when you roll a six-sided, 'fair' dice. Each side has an equal shot of being the one that lands face-up. We cannot say that about the audiences of cable news networks. Generally speaking, liberals tend to watch MSNBC while conservatives tend to watch Fox News, so liberals are less likely to be surveyed by Fox while conservatives are less likely to be surveyed by MSNBC. Since there is an ideological slant to the viewership of these networks, the survey samples procured by these media outlets are unlikely to be random and are therefore, by statistical standards, biased.

Living Large

Another problem one often sees with surveys and polls is the size of the sample. Suppose I surveyed one of my classes about their political beliefs, but then I attempted to argue that my students' opinions were representative of college students across the country. Among other problems, my class size is nowhere near large enough to constitute a statistically sound sample size. There is no way that one can state that thirty people adequately represent millions. The sample size is simply too small. Statistically speaking, sample sizes need to be large enough to compensate for potential 'outliers' or folks who don't share the opinions, beliefs, or attitudes of the majority of the actual population size you're looking at. For a **population** – or the group of people a survey is trying to represent – to be adequately represented, the sample size of the survey or poll must be large enough to capture the big picture.

The larger the represented population is, the larger the sample size must be.

Watch the Way You Say Things

Yet another problem with public opinion surveys and polls is their tendency, by the wording of questions, to set the person being surveyed up into answering in a certain way. Consider the following questions.

1) Do you support, have no opinion, or oppose immigration reform?

2) Do you support, have no opinion, or oppose immigration reform even though we know that supporting such reforms will only give the Democrats more votes in future elections?

Which question do you think is 'fair' and which one is biased? The biased one is Question 2 – the one that suggests that immigration reform might have positive effects on elections for the Democrats in future elections. Most conservatives would, when posed this question, oppose immigration reform, because it might help the Democrats while liberals would likely support such a measure. Question 1, with no hints of any bias, is the 'fair' question; it is not set up to garner a particular answer from either side of the ideological spectrum.

Well, I Could Be Wrong...

When doing polls and surveys, statisticians understand that, as hard as they may try, their statistics have a certain propensity to be off a bit. The way to account for these potential discrepancies is by including a *margin of error* or the percentage by which your statistic could be wrong. For example, say your survey results indicated that 47% of people support President Obama's new health care law and your statistic has a 5% margin of error. What this means is that it's possible that as few as

42% of people support the law and as many as 52% of people support the law. A margin of error is a statistician's way of accepting that despite all the effort put into making a survey as accurate as possible, sometimes we just can't capture reality through statistical analysis and sometimes, statistical assertions of fact have been and can be, simply put, wrong.

Just as the members of the Council of Elrond came from different backgrounds and have endured different experiences which affected their political philosophy on what should be done with the One Ring, so too do the experiences and interactions individuals encounter develop and change their political values and political ideologies. The attempt of the media to capture public opinion, while a valiant attempt, is often unsuccessful; sometimes, the failure of these outlets is more purposeful while other attempts simply fall short from a statistical standpoint. To achieve truly unbiased data, one needs to look beyond venues that stand to gain from the results of their research.

Food For Thought

The Council of Elrond

J.R.R Tolkien defined the Ring as inherently evil; do you think Sauron, the creator of the Ring, shares this opinion? For everyone who believes some event or action is positive, is there always someone out there who disagrees? Do you think that there are numerous solutions to every problem? How do we, like the Council, learn to compromise and work together to solve problems without compromising our own principles? Out of all the great persons at the Council, Frodo – a seemingly unimportant hobbit – was chosen to carry the Ring to Mordor in an attempt to destroy it. What does that say about our role in a government that is becoming more powerful over time?

Political Values

Do you believe that family is the most influential shaper of an individual's political values? What entity, in your opinion, is the second most influential? How influential, in your opinion, is a person's religion or moral code in shaping an individual's political values? Is it possible to separate one's moral views from one's political views? Is that someone we should expect of American citizens, or should a person's religious/moral views play a designated role in an individual's political makeup? Another source of our political values is our peers (friends and co-workers). In general, do you think we tend to associate with people who are similar or different from us? Do you believe that labor unions are effective in shaping political values and ideologies in the places where they operate? For example: is the influence of labor unions stronger among auto workers (unionized) versus Walmart employees (nonunionized)?

Political Ideologies

Out of the two major ideologies discussed here, which are you closer to – liberalism or conservatism, and why? Are you strict in your ideological stance or do you, like many Americans, fall someplace between liberalism and conservatism? In your opinion, what is the main reason you identify with one ideology over the other? Do you believe that these ideologies have changed over time, or have they stayed relatively the same?

I said repeatedly in this chapter that no ideology is better than the other – only different. What is something that, while you disagree, the opposing ideology supports that you respect? Thinking your opponents are wrong is one thing, but thinking they're idiots is entirely different; such a perspective is counterproductive and a hindrance to compromise – something that our government sorely lacks. Choose one political stance held by the opposition that you feel is absurd; go research it, and find out why they feel the way they do. What did you learn, and is that political stance as awful-sounding now as it was before you did the research? I don't ask you to agree with the other side's stances. I don't even expect you to like their perspectives, but I DO want you to understand why they believe the way they do. Only through understanding one's opposition can we ever find common ground.

Public Opinion

I concluded that most public opinion polls and surveys are biased. If this is the case, why even pursue them? Is it possible to ensure that a survey sample is entirely random? How big is big enough in terms of a survey sample size? Is there a way to word a question in such a way in which it is unbiased? Is listing a survey or poll's margin of error really that important? Do you think some polls and surveys are done in a biased manner on purpose or is this merely coincidence? What can be done to ensure that polls and surveys done by cable news networks lack bias? Do we, as media consumers, like to hear biased results? If so, why?

One man to save them all
'The One' will rush to greet them
The Truth is what he'll teach to all
And from the Matrix, he will free them

Works Cited

Blow, Charles M. "Blacks, Conservatives, and Plantations." *The New York Times. http://www.nytimes.com/2013/05/23/opinion/blow-blacks-conservatives-and-plantations.html?_r=0.* Posted on 05/22/2013.

Eilperin, Juliet. "After Veto in Arizona, Conservatives Vow to Fight For Religious Liberties." *The Washington Post: Politics. http://www.washingtonpost.com/politics/after-veto-in-arizona-conservatives-vow-to-fight-for-religious-liberties/2014/02/27/4e0f877a-9fcb-11e3-b8d8-94577ff66b28_story.html.* 02/27/2014.

Gross, Daniel. "Latte Laborers Take on a Latte-Liberal Business." *The New*

York Times. http://www.nytimes.com/2007/04/08/weekinreview/08gross.html?_r=0. 04/08/2007.

Henneberger, Melinda. "Family Values Still Matter – When It's the Other Party's Indiscretions." *The Washington Post. http://www.washingtonpost.com/opinions/do-family-values-still-matter-in-politics-as-long-as-its-not-your-family/2012/01/26/gIQADoevVQ_story.html.* Posted on 01/27/2012.

Herman, Arthur. "Mr. Obama, It's Not the Software That's the Problem. It's Big Government Liberalism." *Fox News. http://www.foxnews.com/opinion/2013/10/24/mr-obama-it-not-software-that-problem-it-big-government-liberalism/.* Posted on 10/24/2013.

Lewis-Beck, Michael S., Helmut Norpoth, William A. Jacoby, and Herbert F. Weisberg. *The American Voter Revisited.* Ann Arbor: University of Michigan Press, 2011.

Liptak, Adam. "For the Supreme Court, A Case Poses a Puzzle on the EPA's Authority." *The New York Times. http://www.nytimes.com/2014/02/25/us/justices-weigh-conundrum-on-epa-authority.html.* Posted on 02/24/2014.

Mooney, Chris. "Does College Make You Liberal – Or Do Liberals Make Colleges?" *The Huffington Post: Science. http://www.huffingtonpost.com/chris-mooney/does-college-make-you-lib_b_1312889.html.* Posted on 03/01/2012.

Sargeant, Michael. "Impeding Jobs: The Bad Business of the GOP's Social Agenda." *The Huffington Post: Politics. http://www.huffingtonpost.com/michael-sargeant/the-bad-business-gop_b_4877092.html.* Posted on 03/03/2014.

Tolkien (I), J.R.R. *The Lord of the Rings.* New York: Houghton Mifflin Company, 1994.

Tolkien (II), J.R.R. *The Hobbit: There and Back Again.* New York: Ballantine Books, 1982.

Ungar, Rick. "The Minimum Wage Fight: Ground Zero in the Clash of Conservative vs. Progressive America." *Forbes Magazine. http://www.forbes.com/sites/rickungar/2013/02/16/the-minimum-wage-fight-ground-zero-in-the-clash-of-conservative-vs-progressive-america/.* Posted on 02/16/2013.

Wallstein, Peter. "Obama's 2012 Campaign 'Operation Vote' Focuses on Ethnic Minorities, Core Liberals." *The Washington Post. http://www.washingtonpost.com/politics/obama-2012-campaigns-operation-vote-focuses-on-ethnic-minorities-core-liberals/2011/09/23/gIQAlY7JuK_story.html.* Posted on 09/24/2011.

CHAPTER 8

Trapped Inside *The Matrix* by the American Media Machine

In 1999, the Wachowski brothers produced a groundbreaking, epic film which depicts humanity as a species trapped and controlled by a computer program known as "the Matrix" – a software program devised by intelligent machines which had turned on the humans who created them. The main character, Neo (portrayed by Keanu Reeves), is a computer programmer and underground hacker who, through the aid of a rebel named Morpheus (portrayed by Laurence Fishburne) and a fellow hacker known as Trinity, discovers the existence and purpose of the Matrix and attempt to free humanity from the Matrix's control and the clutches of the malevolent machines that had created it.

From a certain point of view, the media in the United States is a lot like the Matrix. Just as the Matrix subdues and controls humanity under the illusion that the computer program replicates 'true reality', some contend that the American media machine subdues and controls the American public by what it advertises, condones, and forbids. Through 'spin' or intended notable bias, the media convinces the masses, through propaganda, that their point of view is the correct one and that everyone else's opinion is ignorant, stupid, dated, or irrelevant. The media, in a large sense, determines what is 'real' for us just as the Matrix presents a portrait of reality to the billions of humans trapped within it. Both from a political and a cultural standpoint, this chapter contends that we – like humanity in the film – are trapped inside the Matrix, and that it is up to us – just as saving the masses is a task that falls to Neo – to forbid the media (or limit it) from influencing our life, our culture, and our government.

The Matrix: A Synopsis

Thomas Anderson is a computer programmer but also an underground hacker whose alias is Neo, the name I will use for this character throughout this chapter. Neo, like the vast majority of humanity, believes that the world he lives in is real – that is, until he comes across the term "the Matrix" in his hacking excursions. Another widely acclaimed hacker, Trinity (played by Carrie-Ann Moss), tells Neo that a man named Morpheus could explain the Matrix to him. Initially, Neo rejects meeting Morpheus and continues to live his double-life.

As Thomas Anderson, he goes to work the next morning but is contacted by Morpheus and Trinity while there and informed that someone is seeking him to punish him for his hacking crimes. At that moment, three agents – all in black – enter his office, Agents Smith, Brown, and Jones. Neo attempts to flee but is eventually captured by the Agents. They claim to have proof of Neo committing "virtually every cyber-crime that they have a law for." The Agents attempt to blackmail Neo into revealing the locations of Trinity and Morpheus, but Neo refuses as he is not privy to that information. The Agents implant a tracking device into Neo's navel and Neo passes out.

When he awakes, he is in his own bed and believes the encounter with the Agents was just a dream. Morpheus contacts him and reveals that Neo's importance in the grand scheme of things has been greatly underestimated. Trinity picks Neo up and takes him to Morpheus and is presented with two pills – a blue one and a red one. The blue pill will allow Neo to plunge back into the world of ignorance and continue 'life as he knows it' within the Matrix while also returning Neo to his bed so that he can resume his former life – without any interference from the Agents, or from Morpheus or Trinity. The red pill will allow Neo to absorb the knowledge Morpheus is willing to present him with. In hopes of discovering the true nature of the Matrix, Neo chooses the red pill and loses consciousness.

When Neo awakes, he finds himself naked and attached to an elaborate machine along with millions of other humans. Shortly thereafter, Morpheus arrives and rescues Neo. Morpheus tells Neo that the reality that most humans perceive to be the 'real world' is actually a computer program that the intelligent machines had created – the Matrix. Every human who Morpheus has not 'unplugged' (freed from the Matrix's control) lives, works, and dies assuming that the alternate world created by the Matrix is completely real. Through many demonstrations, Morpheus convinces Neo that he is correct – that the life he had lived since birth was no different from video games like *The Sims*, a game where the player creates humans, families, homes, neighborhoods, and communities while, at the same time, dictating what the humans in the game perceive as reality.

Once Neo accepts that the 'real world' actually *is* a computer program that replicates 'the real world', Morpheus shows Neo that the program's built-in boundaries provide an advantage to them as individuals who are free of the Matrix's control. They can do things that other beings still trapped in the Matrix cannot, because they are free of its power whereas the rest of humanity is restricted by the boundaries of the Matrix's technology which Morpheus, Neo, and the rest of the rebels had escaped. Neo and Morpheus, through a complicated series of events, discover that Neo is "the One" – the person who is meant to free humanity from the Matrix's control and end the conflict between humanity and the machines.

Which should Neo take: the blue pill of ignorance or the red pill of knowledge?

© Captblack76, 2014. Used under license from Shutterstock, Inc.

The agents in the Matrix are like antivirus software. They're designed to attack and destroy anything or anyone who threatens the continuity of the Matrix.

At the end of the film, Agents Smith, Brown, and Jones – the humanoid characters who function like antivirus software, through the efforts of Neo – are defeated, and Neo vows to eliminate the Matrix and return humanity to the realm of true reality, not one based on fabrication and pre-determined boundaries. The final shot of the movie shows a computer program crashing and Neo's voice tells humanity that, although change is hard, it offers them possibilities not possible within the Matrix's programming. What humanity does with their newfound freedom once the Matrix is destroyed, Neo argues, is up to each individual. Reality, according to Neo, should be defined and shaped by your choices – not by the Matrix or the machines that created it.

The Matrix and the American Media Machine

The parallels between the Matrix, the computer program that the malevolent machines use to control humanity, and the American media are uncanny. Between what the media's actual purpose is, what the media does to get their point across, how the media affects the cultural and political landscape, and other valid parallels only enhance the comparative

© Featureflash, 2014. Used under license from Shutterstock, Inc.

Neo vows to free humanity from the Matrix and make peace with the machines.

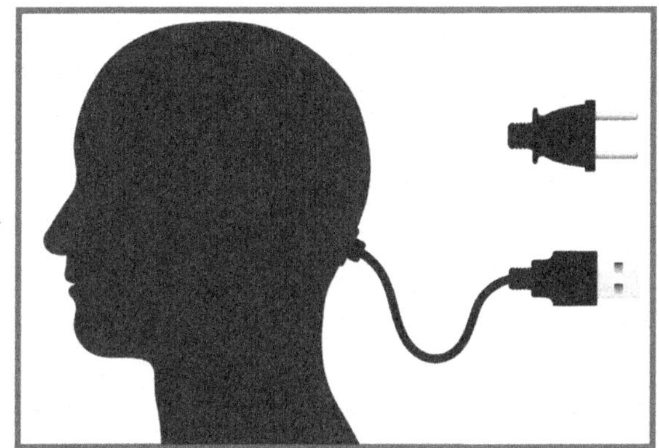

"Have you ever had a dream, Neo, that you were so sure was real? What if you were unable to wake from that dream? How would you know the difference between the Dream World and the Real World?" (Fishburne).

power between the Matrix and the American media machine.

The Matrix and the Media – Information Overload

In the film, Morpheus informs Neo that the Matrix is a computer program that is responsible for shaping humanity's perception of reality. The Matrix replicates humanity's five senses; their conscience; their sense of past, present, and future; and other things that humans utilize to perceive what is truly real. Morpheus reveals that all of this information is transmitted from a master computer to humankind through a plug-like tube which is inserted right behind the nape of a human's neckline. Through this wired connection, the machines that created and maintain the Matrix control humanity and use their bioenergy as a power source (Wachowski).

America's media machine is no different. **Media** is the passage of information from one entity to another. There are three types of media you should be aware of. The first is **print** media; print media is all the stuff that you can *read*. This type of media includes newspapers (like the *New York Times*), magazines (like *Time Magazine*), books (like the *Harry Potter* series), song lyrics (like The Beach Boys' "Surfin' USA"), and so on. The second type of media is **broadcast** media; this type of media is anything that you can *hear*. Forms of broadcast media include television airings (like the television show *24*), radio shows and presentations (like Rush Limbaugh's talk show), film (like the new *Star Trek* movie), and music (like classical, rock, rap, and so on). The final type of media I want you to recognize is the most recent – the **internet.** Forms of internet media are social networking sites, news sites, blogs, emails, and online advertisements. Most Americans encounter all three of these media types on a daily basis and are therefore subject to their influence.

What Is Really 'Real'?

In *The Matrix*, Morpheus reveals to Neo that the world in which he has lived – the world that everyone else lives in – is not real but an illusion created by a computer program, the Matrix. He shows Neo what is *really* real – that humanity all across the globe is wired to the computer on which the Matrix runs and thus is able to subdue and control them while using their biological heat for energy. The differences in reality from what Neo had known his whole 'life' and what Morpheus reveals to him are starkly different (Wachowski).

The same can be said in regards to what actually occurs in the world and what the media says goes on. All of the information that passes from the media to consumers, that is to say – us – is meant to convince individuals what is real and truly important. There are three tactics the media uses on regular occasion to achieve this goal: priming, framing, and agenda setting. **Priming** is an attempt by the media to bring attention to and shape the public's view of an issue before they gain much information about it. **Framing** is when the media describes an issue in a certain context so as to help the public better understand the issue; some also contend that framing occurs when the media twist a historical event intentionally so the public views it in a certain regard. **Agenda setting** is achieved when the media decides, either purposely or accidentally, which issues will get media coverage and which won't; by denying certain issues coverage, the media, at least indirectly, deems those issues less important than the ones that they decide to cover.

Here's an example of priming. Imagine that you get an advertisement from Kohl's a few weeks before Christmas and it urges you to shop "before it's too late." Some people would be enticed to shop because the ad suggests that the reality of the situation is that the holidays are close by and also that the stuff you might want to get people you're close to might be gone if you wait too long. Obviously, reality in 'our' world is much more 'real' that the reality created by the Matrix in the movie; however, reality can be clouded by bias, and anyone who denies that our media is biased is kidding themselves.

Let's use a couple of political examples of framing. First, on September 14, 2008, *Saturday Night Live* (or *SNL*), a comedy show, aired an opening scene depicting the virtually non-existent relationship between Sarah Palin, the former governor of Alaska, and Hillary Clinton, the former First Lady and former U.S. Secretary of State, who is married to Bill Clinton. The skit projects Sarah Palin to be a pretty bimbo and Clinton to be a "harpy, shrewd" woman bent on gaining greater political power. The skit became famous for pointing out such quotes made by the woman playing Palin, Tina Fey, "…and I can see Russia from my house," and, in reference to the Bush Doctrine, "…and I don't know what that is" (*Saturday Night Live*). Whether Palin is an idiot or not, this skit helped shape Palin's reputation as someone not fit for public office. Some argue that the skit significantly hurt the McCain/Palin ticket's chances of winning the presidency in 2008. Hillary Clinton, on the other hand, was portrayed as a bitter, snippy woman who liked to criticize Palin for her quick rise to fame. In fact, at one point in the skit, Clinton, portrayed by Amy Poehler, rips a piece of the podium off in her anger at the current situation.

So what, in this scenario, is reality? Is Sarah Palin really an idiot? Is Hillary Clinton a snippy, power-hungry, cranky old woman? I think we can say with assurance that neither of these women fits the skit's portrayal. Palin is definitely no idiot – at least, she is no worse than other politicians out there. She said a

Sarah Palin: former vice-presidential hopeful

couple unintelligent things, but so do most people serving in elected positions. Clinton definitely isn't as blood-lusty and power-hungry as the skit portrays either. There is a clear history of her desire for political power, but the skit exaggerated this character trait, some contend, to the point of foolishness. Simply stated, the TV portrayals of Clinton and Palin on *Saturday Night Live* are not accurate representations of their personalities. The skit, put simply, is like the Matrix – a fabricated (but widely accepted) projection of reality. It shaped or *framed* the public's perception of Palin's and Clinton's personalities.

Another political example comes from a song written by Green Day, a pop-punk rock band that has been popular since the late 1980s. The song they wrote was called "American Idiot"; it was also the title of the album on which the song debuted. The song is a political critique of George W. Bush's presidency, but most notably, Bush's pursuit of the War in Iraq. The song calls Bush's plans a 'redneck agenda' and criticizes Americans for being hoodwinked by a politician like Bush (Armstrong 1).

Was George W. Bush a redneck idiot? The media sure thought so, but some contend that the facts don't back up the media hype. From the band's point of view, Bush may have fit that description, and many other people certainly agreed with them. In the wide scheme of things, however, many others believe that Bush was a smart man and a memorable president. The band portrayed or *framed* Bush as an idiot, but that doesn't mean that he actually fit that bill.

Here is an example of the final media tool, agenda setting. On *CNN*, a cable news network, you see less and less political news and more and more news that gravitates around the world of entertainment. For example, *CNN* and *MSNBC*, another cable news network, spend less and less time focusing on politics and current events, and more time focusing on reality TV shows like *Survivor*, *The Voice*, and other forms of entertainment. The media appears to be shifting our attention away from the things that really matter and toward the things that are, in truth, insignificant and unimportant.

Issues that are legitimately important are known as **salient** issues. Good examples of salient issues would be elections, major pieces of legislation, natural disasters, current events (both national and local), and so on. Unfortunately, the media seem less interested in the important issues and more interested in making insignificant issues look important to the public. This is known as the **illusion of salience.** Unimportant issues the media has 'made' important are the winners of the MLB World Series, the newest greatest movies or video game consoles, the most recent Hollywood breakups, and so on. Unfortunately, that is what you see on TV, watch at the movies, read in the newspapers, and hear on the radio more often than not. Our culture is one that is dominated by a media bent on creating a culture that is more interested in entertainment and 'the good life' than being concerned with the events that might potentially affect it (Gallagher, 1). Some would even say that the media – and maybe the government – are trying to keep us distracted from the truly important things that are actually going on. I think you could definitely make a convincing case in that regard.

These examples depict the media's interpretation of reality or, if you will, life inside the Matrix. We, the media consumers, are left to ponder what the media presents and how they portray cultural and individual personalities. Media consumers should approach these outlets with caution, because just as humanity in *The Matrix* was duped into believing and accepting the alternate reality created by the Matrix, so too can we as media consumers be tricked into mistaking the bias in the media as actual Truth.

Parameters of the Matrix and 'Regulation' of the Media

After Neo accepts the truth regarding the existence of the Matrix and the fabrication of everything he has known to be 'real', Morpheus reveals to Neo that because they know the truth of the Matrix, they are also able to take advantage of its built-in limitations. Humans within the Matrix are limited to certain physical boundaries; conversely, 'free' humans like Neo, Trinity, himself, and the other rebels are capable of achieving things that humans still trapped inside the Matrix believe to be superhuman or impossible. The ability to operate outside the boundaries of the Matrix which had been set by the machines that had designed it gave Neo and his comrades the ability, in the end, to gain an initial victory over the machines and instill hope that life outside the Matrix is possible for the rest of humanity.

The Matrix, like the American media, operates under a certain set of rules and limitations.

The media, like the Matrix, is limited by its own set of regulations. One of the most widely recognized entities responsible for media regulation is the Federal Communications Commission (FCC). This group is notably responsible for ensuring that whatever is seen on television or heard on the radio is suitable for the audiences that might consume it. If the programming or music isn't suitable for all audiences, it is the FCC's job to ensure that potential viewers or listeners are aware of the potential problems with the programming whether it be explicit language, violence, sexual images, or whatever (FCC, 1).

The controversy surrounding media censorship is one that has gone on for decades and is not likely to conclude anytime soon. Specifically, people were initially concerned with the lack of censorship – particularly when movies and music became more vulgar and explicit (FCC II, 1). Since the censorship of films, TV shows, and music began, some of the artists of such media outlets became angry that their art was being altered in the name of being politically correct. The film *Warning: Parental Advisory* tells the story of Dee Snider and Frank Zappa, two music artists, and their protest of lyric labeling laws (Waters). They find the censorship of music to be an infringement of their First Amendment rights. In the film, Snider and Zappa are portrayed to be heroes as the film was produced and aired by VH1, a cable network that airs music videos from various genres and artists 24 hours a day.

Other regulations that limit the media's ability to air what they want exist as well. Many of these regulations exist so as to prevent the media from embracing any form of bias. Three of these regulations are the **equal time rule,** the **right of rebuttal,** and the **fairness doctrine.** The equal time rule is designed to ensure that all candidates in a political campaign should be given the same opportunity, in terms of time, to present themselves and their political positions as their opponents (Bennett, 1-2). For example: technically speaking, any media outlet hosting Mitt Romney and Barack Obama are required to allot equal time coverage for both candidates – except for Fox News Broadcasting, the Public Broadcasting Service (PBS), and Capital Cities/ABC which gained an exemption from the FCC in 1996 (Bennett, 1).

The right of rebuttal is the right of a political candidate to respond to any political attack posed by the opponent or the proposition of political endorsement by an outside party. This right, however, seems to be suspended (conveniently) before major elections. In 2000, the FCC suspended the right to rebuttal right before the presidential debates began (Associated Press, 1). The suspension of this rule poses a number of problems; most notable among these concerns is that candidates can (and do) say anything about their opponent with no guarantee that the accused party will be permitted to respond to the allegations posed by the opponent. The right to rebuttal, though a good idea, is one that tends to be set aside.

The last media regulation, and perhaps the most important, that we will investigate is the fairness doctrine. This regulation mandated that media outlets provide fair and balanced coverage in regard to political issues – particularly the ones surrounded by controversy (Mills, 42). For example: under the fairness doctrine, media outlets need to allow equal time for both anti-abortion and pro-choice advocates to make their case for their respective political stance. Media outlets, however, are notorious for ignoring the fairness doctrine and embracing only one side of specific political issues. Cable news networks are well-known for employing these methods. Fox News is noted for presenting conservative perspectives on issues while MSNBC, CNN, and CNBC tend to lend support to the liberal side of political issues. The regulation of the media is an activity that the government has pursued for quite some time with little success. Based on what I've seen going on in the world of politics insofar as the media is concerned, I think that it is unlikely that the government's efforts will prove any more fruitful in the near future.

Defending the Matrix – the Agents: Defending the Media – Limited Voices

In the film, Neo encounters, on numerous occasions, three Agents – Agent Smith, Agent Brown, and Agent Jones. While appearing to be entirely human, Neo is informed by Morpheus late in the film that these Agents are not men – they are the built-in defense mechanisms that are designed to protect the

The Agents – the defense mechanism that protects the Matrix from failing; limited perspective: the media's defense mechanism against change

integrity of the Matrix. They function much like the antivirus software that most people download onto their computers. These three Agents attempt to protect the Matrix from Neo, Morpheus, Trinity, and the other rebels' attempts to defy and destroy it. Through the efforts of these three (Agents Smith, Brown, and Jones), the Matrix is protected, defended, and maintained.

The American media machine also has a built-in protection, and that is the limited number of people who control it. By limiting the number of people who have direct power over the media, the number of opinions projected by the media is also restricted. Truthfully, we could probably count the people who control the media on two hands. The ability to limit competition and the variety of opinions expressed by the media enables those in power to remain there (Lutz, 1-4). With fewer people holding the power, the power structure built by the very limited number of media moguls is fortified simply by limiting the voices, opinions, and proposed changes to the millions of media outlets which make up the American media machine.

The Concept of Time in the Matrix and the Media's Influence on History and Culture

After Neo takes the red pill and is introduced to the truth about the Matrix, Morpheus informs Neo that although he thought he was living in the year 1999, that was not the case. Instead, it is nearer to 2099; the Matrix has programmed humanity to believe that it is 1999 and has been for an indefinite length of time. The way time is depicted in Neo's instance is a constant repetition of motions. His alarm goes off at the same time every day. He goes to work, comes home, hacks computers, and falls asleep at the keyboard only to wake up to his alarm clock as the normal time each day in exactly the same way. Through looking at newspapers and doing research, Morpheus, Trinity, and the other rebels had come as close as they could to pinpointing what year it actually was while the rest of humanity remained ignorant. The Matrix had hoodwinked humanity into believing that time essentially stood still while that is simply not the case (Wachowski).

The Matrix's portrayal of time in the film is very similar to the media's attempts to shape

The Matrix distorts humanity's conception of time and history. So does the American media machine.

how historical events and cultural change are perceived, interpreted, and remembered. Films and music during the 1940s attempted to persuade the American public to support World War II (Koppes and Black, 52, 55, and 56). Music (excluding the new, 'dangerous' rock 'n roll), television, and film depicted the economic boom of the 1950s as well as the establishment and maintenance of the 'moral majority ' (Quart and Auster, 53-54). The 1960s were depicted by the media initially to be a move from the Wild West (hello, John Wayne) (Quart and Auster, 56) toward the realm of space as depicted in *Star Trek* (Reagin, 1-3). The media portrayed the 1970s as decade of drugs, revolution, and rebellion (Quart and Auster, 110-116). The 1980s became known as the decade of economic prosperity and the period of time that brought about (but did not see) the end of communism. The 1990s are known for the political scandal of the Clinton presidency as well as the era where African Americans became lead actors in film (Quart and Auster, 171-175, 196-200). The most recent decades, the 2000s and 2010s, are known for their dystopian films like *The Hunger Games* (Arrow, 21-26).

In all of these instances, the media used whatever venue was available to shape the way the American public viewed the events occurring around them. Whether it was war, social change, political scandal, or times of peace, the media played a large part in shaping how both the people of the past and present view historical events. Only through careful scrutiny of the historical evidence can we as media consumers hope to siphon away the propaganda and the drama to find the actual facts that indicate what actually has happened in our past, what's going on today, and what is likely to happen in the future.

Recognizing the False Reality of the Matrix and the Bias and Power of the Media

Until Morpheus presented Neo with the red pill which enabled him to view (and later accept) the reality of the Matrix, Neo was unable and perhaps unwilling to accept that the world around him was actually fabricated. He believed his bed, computer, room, job, car, clothes, and everything else he dealt with on a regular basis was real. That, simply put, was not the case. Everything Neo had known his whole life was a massive fabrication presented to him by means of the computer program, the Matrix.

I would wager to say that it is far easier to notice the media's influence of the past than it is to see what the media is dabbling in at present. It is easy to see how the media affected individuals long ago, but most of us would be unwilling to admit (or are genuinely unaware) that the media affects us all on a very personal level. I argue that a lot of our personal preferences – what we wear, eat, read, watch, listen to, and other such things – are, at their barest, dictated, at least in part, by the media. For example: I am a big Mountain Dew drinker. Why? Because I like it? That is too simple an answer. To put it bluntly, I drink Mountain Dew because the media advertises that it both tastes good and gives you energy. Both of these two criteria are appealing to me, so I choose Mountain Dew over the plethora of other soft drinks out there – many of which, coincidentally, the media advertises heavily. Why do I wear what I do or watch the movies that I choose to? The media, either directly or indirectly through friends or family (who saw trailers or advertisements), suggest that these products or productions are worthy of my attention. Why do I shop at Kohl's and not at other retailers? Probably the most reasonable conclusion is that the advertisement of their sales and coupons makes shopping there appealing from both a fashion and a financial perspective. Why do I own a foreign car rather than an American-made car? The media tells me that foreign cars last longer and get better gas mileage. To make a very, very long story short, almost everything that you and I, at one time, considered to be individual decisions are not as independent as we all think. Most decisions that we make in terms of what we like, what we buy, or what we support are, at least in part, impacted by the media's advertising or propagandizing in the product's favor. To come to terms with this, I am sure Morpheus would argue, we need to open our eyes to see and truly understand the world around us. We need, as Neo did, to choose the red pill of knowledge as opposed to the blue pill of ignorance.

Now that we are aware that our own personal lives are affected by the media's influence, let us explore how the media itself is biased. Particularly in political terms, there are really two kinds of media outlets – conservative outlets and liberal ones. Generally speaking, no media outlet is completely unbiased. For the purposes of this book, we're going to call a media outlet with a notable bias a **spin zone.** Bill O'Reilly refers to his talk show on Fox News, *The O'Reilly Factor*, as a "no-spin zone" (O'Reilly). Most media outlets employ some sort of spin; some embrace a liberal slant while others lean toward conservatism. Fox News is known for being conservative (Wemple, 1-5) while MSNBC and CNN are known for being liberal (Stanley, 1-2).

The One, the Force of Change: Neo and You, the Media Consumer

In the film, Morpheus reveals to Neo that he is the One – the man who was prophesized to be destined to free humanity from the Matrix and also end the conflict between humanity and the machines that created the Matrix. Neo, therefore, decides to dedicate his life to those two goals. Neo, unlike the other rebels, has the ability not only to exist outside the Matrix but also to defy and potentially destroy it so as to restore true reality to humanity.

Just as Neo has the power to manipulate and defy the Matrix, we as media consumers have the power to control and influence the media. The power we have is granted us through our power of choice. We choose what media we consume and what we don't. Whatever we as a society support will be maintained by the media, but what we choose to ignore or decide that we don't like will be discarded. The media measures our likes and dislikes through **ratings** – an effort to measure how many people consume certain media and how often. For example: the O'Reilly Factor wouldn't get airtime on Fox News if the show had no viewership. Clearly, the ratings for the O'Reilly Factor are high enough to keep the show on the air. Another example: *The New York Times* is one of the most well-read newspapers in the world. In other words, its ratings are exceedingly high. There is little chance, if any, that *The New York Times* will ever go out of print; it is simply too popular. We determine what songs are played on the radio, what books are popular, what magazines are widely read, and what internet websites are visited the most. Our ability to influence the media is almost equal to the media's ability to influence us. While we are subjected to its propaganda and its intrusion in the decisions we make in daily life, the media is entirely beholden to the American public's interests, desires, likes, and dislikes. We, like Neo, have the power to exist outside, manipulate, and defy 'the Matrix.'

Just as Neo as 'the One' strives to crash the Matrix and free humanity, so too are we 'the Ones' who have the power to force the American media to report the news in an unbiased, honest way.

Living With, But Not In, the Matrix – Learning to Recognize and Mitigate Media Influence

Neo, a computer hacker, is enlightened by Morpheus, a rebel, about the reality of the Matrix. He is informed that only he, Neo, has the ability and the power to thwart the machines that are at war with humanity by defying the limits of and, in the end, destroying the Matrix. Neo goes through rigorous training which prepares him to enter into, combat, and exit the Matrix at will. His ability to do so makes him unique; as Morpheus alleges, Neo comes to believe that he is indeed "the One" – the man destined to destroy the Matrix, bring humanity back to the Real World, and to end the conflict between humanity and the machines.

We, despite our best efforts, are like Neo was before Morpheus showed him the truth. We are trapped inside the Matrix and are essentially helpless to defend ourselves against the propagandistic appeals posed by the American media machine. Only through self-evaluation can we see just how much the media has impacted our life in our past and present and also has the potential to further affect our life-story in our future. Only through individual initiative can we, as media consumers, seek to understand and alter what the media presents to us. Only through patronage and the ratings that reflect it can we hope to change a media that is far too interested in entertainment but almost entirely ignorant or uninterested in the important events going on in the world today. Only we, like Neo, can step out of the Matrix. Only we can free ourselves and the rest of humanity from the media's influence. What we do about our 'Matrix', as Neo put it, "is a choice I leave to you" (Wachowski).

Food For Thought

Information

The media's job is to pass information on to us. Do you think that's what they actually do? If not, what is the goal of the American media machine? Is it to inform us about what is important or to shift our attention from what really is important to what's not? How much valuable information does the news present? Do you, in your opinion, think that the media shares actual information or simply propaganda? Out of the three kinds of media (print, broadcast, and internet), which do you think is the best form? What is the most widely used form of media? Are newspapers going to lose relevance because of the internet? What about the radio?

Distorting Reality

The Matrix presents humanity with a completely false presentation of reality. Do you think the media does the same thing? How can we tell the difference between what is really real and what is fabricated? Give some examples of fabricated 'news' that you have heard of in the recent past. Give an example of a legitimately important issue that received less coverage than you thought it should have had. Do you think that the media distorts reality on purpose? Do you think the government encourages the media to distract the public during times of political turmoil? Do you think the media's focus on entertainment makes us less intelligent and therefore less likely to say anything about its distortion of reality?

Operating Within the Boundaries of the Matrix: Media Regulation

The Matrix forces humans to operate within its own boundaries; certain things just aren't possible inside the computer program because it has been designed that way. Neo, Morpheus, and the other rebels are able to defy these restrictions and do things that, to other humans within the Matrix, seem super-human. Do you think the media is like Neo in that respect – that they can ignore the regulations set up by the government and do as they please? Should the media be as regulated as it is? If so, why? If not, why not? The First Amendment protects the individual's right to the freedom of the press. Does this mean that not only does the press have the right to publish whatever they want but also that individuals have the right to the truth about the world in which they live?

The Agents and the Limited Voice in the American Media

If I were to count the number of people who have power and influence in the American media, I could count them on fewer than ten fingers. Is the limitation in perspective good or bad for America? In a democracy, should the media represent more or fewer opinions? Are there any advantages to having limited opinions in the media? We said earlier that, in general, there are two perspectives presented by the media – the liberal perspective and the conservative perspective. As we know from the previous chapter on political ideologies, we also know that most people are not exclusively conservative or liberal. How do individuals find a media outlet that fits their ideology when it seems that the media is so polarized? Do you think that the polarized media contributes to the polarization that exists in Congress and the Supreme Court? How could the media invite more voices into its fold? Would they do such a thing, or are those in power afraid to lose it?

Time Distorted Within the Matrix: The Media as Historical Interpreter and Shaper

As we know, life in the Matrix appears to be repetitive and redundant. Neo believes he lives in 1999 while Morpheus and his friends contend that the year is actually closer to 2099. Therefore, the Matrix has hoodwinked humanity into the perception that time essentially stands still. How has the American media shaped the American public's perception of historical events? Choose three things that have happened in America's recent past, and tell me how the media shaped the public's perception of those events. Do you think the media's portrayal of events in America's past has influenced how the public reacted to those events and acted in efforts to change the status quo; use World War II and the Vietnam War as two examples to consider. How did the media portray these events? Did the media portray them similarly or differently?

Recognizing the False Reality of the Matrix and Media Bias

Do you think that the media affects you on a personal level? Do you think individual decisions are, at least partially, influenced by outside sources – the media included? Name a few products that are widely advertised, and tell me (honestly) if you first started consuming these products because of the advertisements you saw. Do you think some advertisements are better than others? What is the advantage to jingle ads? Do the catchy tunes really encourage people to consider consuming the products they advertise?

We said that the media is extremely biased. Do you believe this to be true or to be untrue? Which media outlets, in your opinion, project the highest level of bias, and why do you say that? Do you think that people enjoy the bias projected by the media outlets that they tune into? Why or why not? Is media bias something that can easily be taken away, or are we, as citizens in a democracy, predisposed to express our opinions? Does our media take its bias too far sometimes? Can you name an unbiased media outlet? If you can, what is it? If you cannot, why do you think that media outlets – all of them – have some level of bias?

Neo as 'the One': The Power of Change Is Yours

In *The Matrix*, Morpheus argues – and Neo comes to believe – that Neo is 'the One' – a man destined to free humanity from the Matrix and end the conflict between humanity and the machines. Do you think that we have the same power and abilities as Neo? Can we help make others aware of the media's subtle attempts to influence our lives? How can we achieve this goal? Can we alert others to the bias in the media without sounding like we simply disagree with the ideology espoused by the media outlets we are criticizing? In order to discuss media bias, do we have to accept that all media possess a bias or not? Is it possible to prevent the media from shaping our personal tastes and attitudes or are we powerless to stop their influence like humanity, without Neo, is hopeless to prevent the Matrix from controlling and subduing them?

Neo's efforts inside the Matrix lead to humanity's 'power surge'

In the National Hockey League, penalties lead to 'power plays'

Works Cited

Arrow, V. *The Panem Comparison: An Unofficial Guide to Suzanne Collins' Hunger Games from Mellark Bakery to Mockingjays.* Dallas: BenBella Books, 2012.

Associated Press. "FCC Suspends On-Air Rebuttal Rule for 60 Days." First Amendment Center. . Posted on 10/05/2000.

Bennett, James. "FCC Eases Equal Time Rule for Three Networks." *The New York Times Online. http://www.nytimes.com/1996/08/22/us/fcc-eases-equal-time-rule-for-3-networks.html.* Posted on 08/22/1996.

Federal Communications Commission. "What We Do." FCC News. . Last updated 12/06/2013.

Federal Communications Commission (II). "Regulation of Obscenity, Vulgarity, and Profanity." FCC News. . Last updated 12/06/2013.

Gallagher, Nathaniel. "Media Should Focus More on News, Less on Entertainment." *The Breeze. http://m.breeze-jmu.org/opinion/columns/article_42b-440fc-15c2-11e3-8bb8-001a4bcf6878.html?mode=jqm.* Posted on 09/06/2013.

Green Day. *American Idiot.* Reprise Records, 2004. Audio CD.

Koppes, Clayton R. and Gregory D. Black. *Hollywood Goes to War: How Politics, Profits, and Propaganda Shaped World War II Movies.* New York: Tauris Parke Paperbacks, 2000.

Lutz, Ashley. "These 6 Corporations Control 90% of the Media in America." *Business Insider Online. http://www.businessinsider.com/these-6-corporations-control-90-of-the-media-in-america-2012-6.* Posted on 06/14/2012.

The Matrix. Dir. Andy and Lana Wachowski. Perf. Keanu Reeves (Neo), Laurence Fishburn (Morpheus), Carrie-Ann Moss (Trinity), Hugo Weaving (Agent Smith), Paul Goddard (Agent Brown), and Robert Taylor (Agent Jones).

Mills, Kay. *Changing Channels: The Civil Rights Case That Transformed Television.* Jackson: University Press of Mississippi, 2004.

O'Reilly, Bill. *The No Spin Zone: Confrontations with the Powerful and Famous in America.* New York: Three Rivers Press, 2003.

Quart, Leonard and Albert Auster. *American Films and Society Since 1945.* Santa Barbara: Praeger Books, 2011.

Reagin, Nancy. *Star Trek and History.* Hoboken: Wiley Publishers, 2013.

"Sarah Palin and Hilary Clinton Opener." *Saturday Night Live.* NBC. Atlanta, 2008.

Stanley, Alessandra. "How MSNBC Became Fox's Liberal Evil Twin." *The New York Times. http://www.nytimes.com/2012/08/31/us/politics/msnbc-as-foxs-liberal-evil-twin.html?_r=0.* Posted on 08/31/2012.

Warning: Parental Advisory. Dir. Mark Waters. Perf. Dee Snider (as himself) and Griffin Dunne (as Frank Zappa. Charter Films Inc. Houston, 2002.

Wemple, Erik. "Fox News All Day: Hard and Conservative." *The Washington Post. http://www.washingtonpost.com/blogs/erik-wemple/wp/2013/03/27/fox-news-all-day-hard-and-conservative/.* Posted on 03/27/2013.

CHAPTER 9

The Puck Drops Here: Political Parties and the National Hockey League

"And now, at center-ice, the ref drops the puck, and off they go." This is how every game of professional hockey begins. The National Hockey League (or NHL) has been in existence for over a hundred years and has brought joy to hockey fans all across the United States and Canada. Professional hockey teams from major cities compete against each other to win the Big Prize – the Stanley Cup. Some teams are engaged in epic rivalries while some struggle to stay afloat. Some teams have won the Cup numerous times while others, though in existence for some time, are still attempting to win it for the first time.

Political parties are also engaged in an epic game – the game of political power. **Political parties** are groups of like-minded politicians and political figures seeking, through working together, to *win elections*. There are many political parties in the United States, but only two have realistic chances of gaining any real power in national politics – the Republican Party (also known as the Grand Old Party or GOP) and the Democratic Party. Although the identities of these parties have changed drastically over time, these two political giants are in a constant struggle to win over the hearts and minds of the American public and, through the popular support of said citizens in the electoral process, elected office. In this chapter, I compare political parties and the interest groups that support them to professional hockey teams in the National Hockey League and their sponsors. First though, let me give a brief summary of how the game of hockey works for those of you who are unfamiliar with the sport.

Hockey as Played in the NHL

Equipment

The three most important pieces of equipment used in hockey are hockey sticks, pucks, and skates. Hockey sticks are long pieces of wood with a broad, curved blade on the bottom which is often covered with tape. Hockey sticks are used to corral and shoot the next piece of equipment of note – a hockey puck. Hockey sticks come in many lengths, and the blades on the end come in different shapes and widths. The length is usually determined by the height of the player while the style and width of the blade is usually determined by the player's position and personal preference. Forwards (or offensive players) and defensive players typically use sticks with curved blades on them while the goaltenders (or goalies) use sticks with flat blades so as to prevent hockey pucks from going into the goal net (Pure-Hockey 1, 1-4).

Hockey pucks are round, short, cylindrical pieces of black, vulcanized rubber measuring roughly 1 inch (25 mm) high and 3 inches (76 mm) across. The average hockey puck weighs in at a mere 6 ounces (170 g), but the puck is weightier than it seems when it whizzes down the ice rink. Many a hockey player has lost teeth when pucks are mis-aimed. Those 6-ounce pucks can do a lot of damage. In a typical NHL game, each puck is frozen before the game to keep it from bouncing on the ice and is emblazoned with the logo of the home team (Robertson, 38-39).

Another unique piece of equipment unique to this game is hockey skates (Robertson, 36). The boot on these skates is typically made of leather and nylon while the blade of the skate is made with metal. Hockey skates, unlike figure skates, have a rounded blade on the bottom which provides more precise turns and more physical control of one's body. Goalie skates are made slightly different from the skates worn by the other players. They tend to be stiffer and have less curvature on the blade. Typically in the NHL, hockey skates are black with white laces. Hockey players typically own several pairs of skates in case one set is damaged in some way.

Other important gear that hockey players wear consists of various types of protective equipment. Pads (and lots of them), helmets, arm and knee guards, jock straps, and face masks are all pieces of equipment typically used in NHL games. Some of the equipment is not mandatory; face masks are not required (though recommended) and neither are helmets – although those are coming closer to becoming required gear everyday with all of the concussions or 'upper body injuries' that hockey players seems to consistently sustain (Robertson, 38).

The goal net, the final piece of important equipment, is affixed to the goal line with

Notice the difference between the pads on the goaltender and the forward (an offensive player – one who tries to score goals). Also take a look at the skates the forward is wearing. These are much different from figure skates as the bottoms are curved instead of straight.

© Lorraine Swanson, 2014. Used under license from Shutterstock, Inc.

This is a hockey net. Notice the goal posts, crossbar, net tie bar, semicircular goal base, and netting.

flexible, neon green pegs. The goal itself is made, often, of PVC pipe. It rises 4 feet off the ground and the ends or 'posts' of the goal net are 6 feet apart. A piece of PVC pipe stretching atop the net from post to post is known as the crossbar. The top and back of the goal are covered in durable netting material and secured with a net 'tie bar' that attaches in the middle of the crossbar and the bottom of the back of the goal. A semicircular goal base stretches around the back of the bottom of the goal from goal post to goal post (Robertson, 16-17).

The Rink

NHL hockey is a game played by men on skates moving about on an oblong ice rink. A professional hockey rink is 200 feet (60.96 meters) long and 85 feet (25.91 meters) across. There are five lines painted onto the ice that are worthy of note. The first line that the players utilize is known as "center ice." It is painted exactly down the middle of the hockey rink and divides the rink in two. The next pair of lines is painted blue, and they divide the hockey rink roughly into three zones – two attacking zones on either end and a neutral zone in the middle. Each team controls one attacking zone of the rink; this is known as that team's defensive zone. The opposing team's defensive zone is the attacking zone of the opposition. The last two lines on the rink are painted near the end of the rink. It is a thin, red line that denotes, once the goal-net is properly placed, where the "goal line" is (Robertson, 16).

The rink is surrounded by wooden boards and plexi-glass windows with netting affixed to the glass and ceiling in the attacking zones. The boards can be useful in playing the puck or for 'checking', or body-slamming, opposing players. The boards are mostly white with a yellow stripe that stretches around the base of the rink. Oftentimes, team sponsors' logos will be painted on the boards as well (Robertson, 16).

Playing Hockey

Hockey is played in three 20-minute sections or 'periods' which are separated by 20-minute intermissions. Thus, play in a regulation hockey game is 60 minutes long. After each

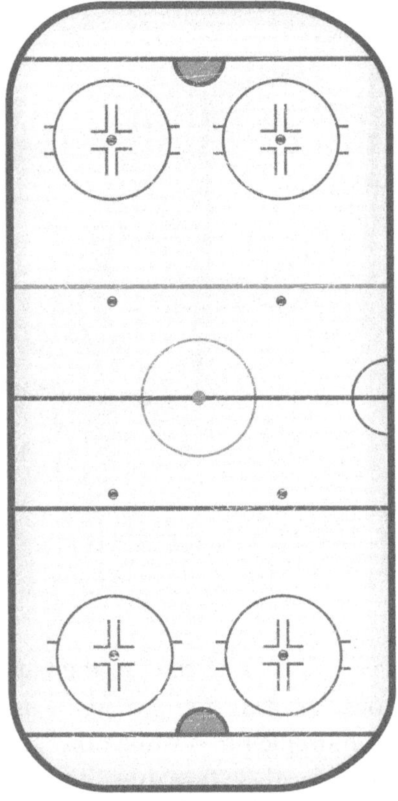

This is what a hockey rink looks like from above. Notice the center-ice line and the two goal lines on the far ends.

period, the teams swap offensive and defensive zones. The home team shoots at the same net during the first and third periods and uses the other net during the second period and vice versa. The away team uses their original net during the first and third period but use the other net during the second period. In between each period, the ice is cleaned by two Zamboni machines. In rare instances, games can go into overtime. If this occurs, the teams play for 5 minutes. If neither team scores a goal, the game goes into a shootout. Whoever ends up with the most goals (or points) the quickest is designated as the winning team (Robertson, 65).

During the three periods, the *forwards*, or offensive players, attempt to get the puck past the opposing team's goalie, over the goal line, and into the net. There are three forwards on the ice at a time, and these forwards tend to work together consistently on a 'shift' or 'line'. This enables these players to become familiar with each other's style and eccentricities so as to make goal-scoring easier. Generally speaking, each NHL team has three or four offensive lines (Robertson, 28-29).

Also on the ice for each team are two *defensemen*. Their job is to help their goalie protect the goal line and net from the opposing team's forwards. Defensemen can and have scored goals for their team, but this is the exception and not the norm. Defensemen, generally speaking, tend to be large, stocky guys so as to cover more space, to make the opposition's chances of getting the puck in the net less likely (Robertson, 28-29).

The last player on the ice is the *goalie*. It is his job to keep the puck from crossing the goal line and entering the net. The goalie has a glove which he employs to catch the puck. He also has a blocker pad that he uses to prohibit the puck from entering the net. His stick, as mentioned before, has a flat blade which inhibits pucks on the ice from making it into the goal. Generally speaking, each team has two goalies on hand at every game, but – unless he performs poorly – the team only uses one goalie per game (Robertson, 29).

He shoots, he scores!!!!

Hockey Teams and Their Sponsors: Political Parties and Interest Groups

Hockey is a sport that has garnered support over the years from many major cities in the United States – particularly in northern states where hockey is a sport that individuals can play on their very frozen backyard pond. The professionals who play this sport, however, are in it to win it – Lord Stanley's Cup. Similarly, political parties focus on winning their own 'game' by employing certain tactics and attracting voters to win elections.

Looking for Wins

Hockey teams in the National Hockey League attempt to win games so that, at the end of the season, they can compete in the playoffs to win the Stanley Cup. The road to the Cup is not an easy one. Some teams have won Lord Stanley's Cup multiple times while other teams are still striving for their first title. To win, teams have to make sacrifices, appease the fans, and gain sponsors so that the team can put itself in the best possible position to succeed. In the National Hockey League, winning is the name of the game, and the pursuit of a Stanley Cup title incites contests of titans that are hard-fought and dearly bought.

Similarly, **political parties** are groups of like-minded politicians and political figures who are bent on a quest of *getting their candidates elected.* Some are striving for congressional seats, others seek gubernatorial positions, and still others – the strongest candidates – seek the seat in the Oval Office, the presidency. Winning elections, like hockey teams' quest to secure a Stanley Cup championship, is a difficult, painful, nasty process which involves individuals compromising principles and slinging mud in the name of ensuring that their aspirations for an elected position are achieved (Maisel, 29-33).

Hockey teams compete to win games and ultimately, the Stanley Cup. Political parties run candidates in hopes of winning elections and political power.

Playing as a Team

In the NHL, the only hope that professional teams have of winning the Stanley Cup is that they successfully learn to play as a team. Professional teams bring together a number of extremely talented players. Unfortunately, sometimes those players are attempting to further their career and gain individual attention rather than working for the team's goal – winning the Stanley Cup. Bob Kirk, a sports writer and avid hockey fan, notes the top 25 players in the recent past who are the most desperate for attention; among their number are: Jeremy Roenick, Mike Modano, Chris Chelios, Dominick Hasek, Chris Pronger, Brett Hull, Brendan Shanahan, Gordie Howe, and others (Kirk, 1-9).

Back in the days of America's inception, George Washington warned against the formation of political parties and suggested that they would be a hindrance to good governance (Washington). His words seem to have proved all too true. The two major political parties, vying for power, are the perpetrators of political gridlock in Washington, D.C. President Obama has one agenda, and the opposition party has another – (seemingly) the exact opposite of the president's (Liberto, 1-2). Some contend that the Republican Party has valid reasons for opposing the president's agenda while others contend that the GOP is merely trying to keep Obama from getting what he wants.

Political parties, like hockey teams, perform best and get their candidates elected more often when they have a unified message. Doing so, however, is much harder than it seems. America's two major political parties, the Republicans and Democrats, are parties that appeal to very broad groups of people. Naturally, when millions of voices are heard and addressed, division can and does occur. Not only do political parties have problems solving political division caused by their incessant competition with each other; dissention within the political parties themselves is also becoming more pronounced – especially recently.

In the Republican Party, a new faction has emerged – the Tea Party; this group is a radical faction of the Republican Party that advocates for less government interference in the lives of individuals, lower taxes, the protection of religion, family, gun rights, and so on. The Tea Party, while representative of a modest number of Republicans is by no means a majority faction within the party. There are enough Tea Partiers in Congress, however, for them to stall or kill legislative propositions that are supported wholeheartedly by more ideologically moderate Republicans. In fact, some contend that Tea Partiers – and the GOP more broadly – were responsible for the lengthy government shutdown that occurred in October 2013; others notably have argued otherwise (Lewison, 1).

The Path to Victory Requires a Game Plan – a Platform to Stand On

The path to the playoffs requires each team to focus on a variety of things. First, teams need to ensure they have players who are skilled but that also, when working together, work well. Second, hockey teams need players who can score goals – lots of them. Teams dedicate a lot of funding toward recruiting and keeping players who have this essential skill. Third, teams spend lots of money finding and keeping good goalies. If scoring goals to win games is the most important thing in a hockey game, preventing the other team from scoring is the next most important thing. In short, in order for hockey teams to succeed and win the Stanley Cup, they have to find, train, and keep good forwards, defensemen, and goalies.

Similarly, political parties have to focus on a variety of issues in order to attract potential voters. The list of issues and potential solutions for those problems is known as a party's **platform** or agenda. Each political party has its own agenda, and over time, these agendas change. Typically, each party's agenda is officially laid out every four years at each party's respective convention which also witnesses the selection of each party's presidential nominee (Maisel, 91-95).

The agendas of each political party are similar in the views of what problems exist in society; their proposed solutions to these problems and the reasons behind them are what differentiate the two. For example: both the Republicans

In order to win Lord Stanley's Cup, hockey teams have to perfect their use of offense, defense, and goal-tending just as political parties have to learn to project a unified message.

and Democrats believe that abortion is a problem. The Republicans want to outlaw it so as to protect human life. The Democrats wish to allow abortion to remain legal, because they believe that a woman has the right to make decisions about her body and that the programs available for single mothers have had their funding significantly cut (Saad, 1-4). Another example: both parties believe that the level of taxes needs to be changed. The Republicans believe that taxes should be cut because the government wastes a lot of money and the money might be better spent by the individuals who actually earned it. The Democrats, conversely, believe taxes should be higher – particularly for high-income earners – because vital social programs, from their perspective, are being gradually de-funded, our roads and infrastructure are falling apart, and our debt is exponentially high (Hodge, 1).

Another thing worth mentioning is that political parties' platforms change strategically between elections. Sometimes to gain the support of voters, political parties have to reconsider their stances on issues and alter their platform. Some argue that to win in the 2014 midterm (or congressional) elections, the Republican Party's platform needs to change in order to ensure that certain demographic groups (women, minorities, and low-income earners) are not ostracized and discouraged from supporting the Republican Party. Some argue that only through changing their stances on issues that affect these voters does the Republican Party have any chance of remaining relevant in future national elections (Espinoza, 1-3).

A Two-Team Competition in a Sold Out Arena

A hockey game – any hockey game – is one where two teams compete to win but by extension, the number of wins and losses contribute to a team's chances of winning the Stanley Cup. So, while in a game, only two teams compete to win, other teams are competing as well. One team's win or loss has the potential to affect the likelihood of any other team to make it to the Stanley Cup Playoffs where the best teams face off in epic contests to determine which team will take home Lord Stanley's Cup.

In American politics, like in hockey games, only two major political parties (generally) square off to compete in elections. In America, the two major political parties we have now are the Republicans (the conservative party) and the Democrats (the liberal party). These parties, however, are the third set of two that has existed in our country's history. The first set of political parties included the Federalists and Anti-Federalists. The Federalists believed that the federal government should have far more power than state governments; conversely, the Anti-Federalists believed that the federal government had too much power and that it instead belonged in the hands of each respective state government (Berg-Anderson, 1-3). The next party system included the Jacksonian Democrats (formerly the Federalists) and the Whigs (formerly the Anti-Federalists). The Jacksonian Democrats were known for being the party of the everyday folk – a title they earned, at least partially, because of Andrew Jackson's attempts to

Two teams face off in a hockey game just as the two major parties (Republicans and Democrats) face off in elections.

make a meaningful connection with average folks (Berg-Anderson, 3-4). The Whigs, on the other hand, portrayed themselves as the party of industrial growth and economic development. They also became recognized as the party that detested and worked against the institution of slavery. Unfortunately though, the Whig presidents elected directly before the Civil War, Zachary Taylor and Millard Fillmore, were unable to prevent the growing division between states that was occurring because of the slavery debate (Berg-Anderson, 4). The final party system – the one we have now – includes the Republicans (formerly the Whigs) and the Democrats (formerly the Jacksonian Democrats). The Republicans of today are widely recognized as the party of big business, tradition, family values, and individual initiative and accountability. Like Jackson's Democrats, the Democrats of today are the party of the average people. They are also accredited with being the party that supports minorities, societal tolerance, the environment, animal rights, pacifism, and government interference in economic affairs (Berg-Anderson).

Strictly speaking, the Republican Party has had more presidential nominees elected than any other political party, followed closely by the Democrats. The Federalists and Anti-Federalists weren't around long enough to make any lasting track record, and the Whigs and Jacksonian Democrats weren't around much longer than them. So, one can make the argument that the Republicans have been the most successful party in presidential elections. This might be, at least partially, because the Republican Party is known as the party that maintains the status quo, and generally speaking, most people are afraid of change – especially when times are good. It could be that America's electorate and, by extension, the Electoral College seeks to maintain and preserve rather than progress and change (Whitney, 574-579).

Structure of the NHL and the Internal Structure of Political Parties

The National Hockey League is made up of 30 teams and is divided into two conferences – the Eastern and Western Conferences. To make the path to the Stanley Cup more interesting, however, the teams are further divided into divisions. In the Eastern Conference, there are eight teams in each division while in the Western Conference there are seven teams that compete in each division. This divvying out of the teams incites competition within each division and further, in each conference. Thus, the path to the Stanley Cup is ensured to be jam-packed with nail-biting drama that keeps hockey fans everywhere on the edge of their seats (NHL, 1).

Like the National Hockey League, America seems to be politically divided into two parties – or conferences – the Republican Party and the Democratic Party. Again, like the NHL, political scientists have denoted the three divisions of each political party – the party in the electorate, the party organization, and the party in government. These three divisions of each political party allow these giants to function successfully on a national, state, and local level.

Political parties are not singularly comprised of rich moguls seeking to get their paws on more power, influence, or funding. Each political party, in order to survive, must garner the support of average Joes like us. This is known as the **party in the electorate.** This is the group of loyal voters in every locality that will consistently, no matter which politician is running, vote along party lines (Maisel, 71-74). No lies – there are some voters who are so loyal to their party that they would vote for my dog if she showed up with the 'R' or

In order for things to change, average people like us have to express our wants and needs to the government. Here, supporters of health care reform publically express their desires in a peaceful demonstration.

'D' next to her name. These are the citizens who participate in grassroots organizations that attempt to bring political awareness to their peers – whether in their neighborhoods, schools, workplaces, churches, and other places of public interaction. These are the people who stuff envelopes that end up in your mailbox. They make the phone calls that advertise for candidates or encourage you to get to the polls. These folks, some argue, are the most dedicated party members out there, because without them, it is possible that the party they are affiliated with wouldn't garner the local support they need to win in national elections.

To be successful, political parties require the involvement of thousands of people, and many of them never run for public office. These competitive bodies in American politics are large, complicated **party organizations** whose sole goal is to get their candidates elected and to push their agenda (Maisel, 57-58). The folks involved in the party organization are party presidents (typically the party's last presidential nominee), secretaries, treasurers, campaign managers, donors, focus groups, individual volunteers, media supporters, and so on. Moreover, these personalities exist on national, state, and local levels. Political parties are not simple structures; they are complicated, large, and difficult organizations to manage, unite, and drive toward common goals.

The last division of political parties is known as the **party in government.** Once elected, this is the element of the party that pushes the party's agenda through the proposal, passage, and implementations of government policy (Maisel, 86-88). Partisans in Congress attempt to craft legislation that will best serve the party's interests. The president, as the head of his party, attempts to push the party's agenda insofar he is able through his presidential powers. Although most would not outwardly admit it, some contend that the Justices on the Supreme Court are politically inclined as well and serve the interests of their chosen political party as ardently as any representative or senator (Aron, 1-2). The party in government attempts to use its power, though the efforts of elected officials, to achieve goals and milestones set by the party organization which, at least at some level, is demanded by the party in the electorate.

The Redefinition of a Team and of a Party – Realignment

After the National Hockey League's season ends in June, each team takes a good look at itself in an attempt to determine what it can do to be more successful in the coming season. Sometimes, improvement requires trades, player releases, the firing and hiring of new management, the building of a new complex in which to play, and so on. Each year, the teams we see on the ice are different. Some differences from year to year are drastic while others are not. Nevertheless, a team's success rests, at least partially, on its ability to change and adapt. Successful teams have to make changes so that their players and facilities give the team the best possible chance of winning the Stanley Cup (Peceny, 1-3).

Political parties also, on occasion, undergo major changes – either in ideology or in the

© KamiGami, 2014. Used under license from Shutterstock, Inc.

The Republicans and Democrats – parties in government, propped up by the party organization, supported by the party in the electorate.

types of people who support them. Such a major change in the makeup or ideology of a political party is known as a **partisan realignment** (Levendusky, 121). One example of a partisan realignment occurred after the death of John F. Kennedy and the passage of the Civil Rights Act. Many Democrats (particularly in southern states) left the Democratic Party and became Republicans and vice versa; many Republicans, ashamed of their party's opposition of the Civil Rights Act of 1964, left the GOP and became Democrats. Thus, the Democrats are now associated as the party of racial equality whereas before, the Republicans held that claim (Connelly, 1-3).

Some contend that we are on the verge of another partisan realignment, but not because of a change in partisan identification but, rather, a change in ideology. Some contend that the number of people supporting the Republican Party in elections is getting so small that their chances of remaining relevant in national elections are becoming more remote. Some believe that to survive as a political party, the GOP will have to re-define itself by catering to groups that are, at least currently, part of the makeup of their opposition. Some of the groups that are frequently mentioned in this discussion are women, minorities, and homosexuals. The only thing, thus far, keeping the GOP from attracting these people is the Republican Party's unwillingness to forsake their own principles – an act I myself would find hard to complete. Some contend, however, that if the GOP continues to attempt to win elections without increasing their electoral support, the Democrats will consistently win and their agenda will dominate American politics because, put simply, there seem to be more Democrats out there than Republicans – at least for the moment (Espinoza, 1-3).

Successful Teams' Advantage over the Underdogs – Major Parties vs. Third Parties

The teams that win a lot – like the Montreal Canadiens, Toronto Maple Leafs, Detroit Red Wings, Chicago Blackhawks, and others – are able to secure things that less successful teams simply don't have access to. Most notably, these teams garner a lot of public support; thus, their fan bases are larger. Their reputation for success draws better players to the teams than poorer, less successful teams do. Finally, when a team has a large fan base, the organization – through the sale of merchandise, seats at the arena, concessions, and other such things – draws in massive amounts of money; this is a monetary feat that most small-market teams can never hope to accomplish.

The same advantages that successful NHL teams possess are also bonuses that major political parties (i.e., the Republicans and Democrats) are able to secure which third-parties (minor parties) are not. The most important advantage that major parties have is that large fan base or **party base.** These are the individuals who will consistently support the party and vote for their candidates. The parties that cater to a broader audience are able to secure for themselves a larger base, thus making their potential vote count higher and their chances of getting their candidates elected in local, state, and national elections greater than that of third parties that lack such support (Maisel, 23-25, 108).

Just as popular hockey teams garner more public support, money, and media attention than low-market teams, major political parties hold the same advantages over third parties.

Picking the Team to Beat and Candidate Electability

Every year, ESPN, *Sports Illustrated*, and other giants in the world of professional sports attempt to pick which team they think will win the Stanley Cup. They consider lots of different things including the dynamics of each team's front office, the teams' farm systems, the team itself, the support of each team's respective fan base, and so on. All of these factors are considered when choosing one's pick to win the Stanley Cup. When this choice is made – particularly if multiple sports organizations or personalities pick the same team, that team tends to gain more widespread public support, funding, and other nonmaterial benefits that can and does aid the 'chosen team' on their path to Lord Stanley's Cup.

The same is true for politicians. The goal of political parties is to choose candidates that are 'electable.' In general, political parties are reluctant to nominate candidates with a sketchy past. They tend to select candidates that are physically attractive as that is a quality that some voters consider. Parties consider the persuasiveness and eloquence of a potential candidate's oration skills as charismatic speakers tend to attract votes far more easily than dry, boring, repetitive folks do. Up until recently, men were the candidates of choice since women, up until the recent past, didn't run for national office. All kinds of things have the potential to affect a candidate's electability, and these factors are things that political parties consider long and hard months before a candidate is ever nominated or added to the ballot (Eligon, 1-2).

The Sponsors of the Game: The Interests of the American People

Many businesses sponsor NHL teams – and the League more broadly. These businesses do so in an attempt to bring in more customers and also, to encourage hockey fans, players, coaches, and refs to pass on their experience to friends and family. These businesses would be happy to see their chosen NHL team (if any) win the Stanley Cup, but that is *not* their main objective; their biggest priority is pushing their product.

There are a wide variety of businesses that support the NHL and have permission to advertise and/or sell their products at the games. Beer companies like Budweiser, hot-

Budweiser, a sponsor of St. Louis Blues Hockey, flaunts their most famous symbol – the Clydesdales pulling a beer cart with the Dalmatian riding along.

dog companies like Hunter, heating and cooling repair companies like Jerry Kelly (a local company in St. Louis), Rottler Pest Control (another St. Louis business), and many others have the right to advertise their products and, in some cases, have permission to solicit for business at NHL games.

In the realm of American politics, **interest groups** – groups of individuals who share a common political interest and an agenda to push that interest – are a lot like the businesses that sponsor NHL teams in the universe of the National Hockey League. Interest groups are one of the public's venues for participation. It is here that average Joes like you and I can have a say in issues we care about and also see results – an opportunity that gives the impression that, in this venue at least, that an individual's voice can and does matter. Unlike political parties, however, their goal is *not* to get candidates elected. Rather, it is to attempt to ensure that their issue is taken seriously by the government. That is the difference between interest groups and political parties. Interest groups, like sponsors, are bent on *or particular interest* while political parties are solely interested in *so that they can push the party's agenda as a powerful figure in government* (Nownes, 4-7).

Like the sponsors of NHL teams, there are many different types of interest groups. There are business groups – like the Motion Picture Association of America (MPAA) – the guys who rate movies for adult content. There are labor groups like the American Federation of Labor and Congress of Industrial Organizations (AFL-CIO), a labor union conglomerate that seeks to promote the interests of skilled workers and defend them when, and if, their employers become neglectful of their rights to fair wages, normal working hours, safe working conditions, and so on. There are environmentalist groups like the Environmental Protection Agency (EPA), a very, very powerful interest group that seeks to preserve the environment. There are animal rights groups like the Humane Society of the United States, an interest group that seeks to promote the interests of pets as well as other animals. The list of interest groups is endless. For virtually any issue or interest you can think of, there is likely an interest group that represents it.

Purpose of Sponsorship and Interest Groups

The sponsors of NHL teams, as stated before aren't as concerned with their team winning as they are of winning new customers. This, in short, is their purpose for sponsoring the hockey team. Even if the fans at the game or at home don't use the products that these sponsors advertise, there is a chance that they will tell their friends and families about the advertisement. One of my favorite advertisements that they play on TV during a St. Louis Blues game is the Budweiser ad that has the quote, "Great times are waiting. Grab some Buds" (Budweiser). Typically, the Blues announcer, Chris Kerber, will quote this ad as the puck is dropped to begin the hockey game.

Similarly, interest groups seek to feed information out to the public so that they might become more knowledgeable about the issues at hand and also, if they are unhappy with the way things are, that they might mobilize, become active, and attempt to change things from the way they are now to the way things ought to be. Interest groups also serve another vital purpose; during election years, they typically provide information on the candidates running for office – particularly related to their issue of concern but not always exclusively limited to that realm. This makes researching the candidates and becoming politically educated easier for the average citizen – although citizens should be wary of information handed out by these groups as it may be biased to sway them toward one candidate and away from others. Third, interest groups – being sources of a vast amount of information – are often called to present information before congressional committees or other government bodies so as to inform policymakers about the issues facing our country. Again, the potential for bias is there, but most politicians can spot bias a mile away – as most of them use propaganda, scare tactics, and the like to get themselves elected (Nownes, 40-48).

Interest Groups Are Great, But...

What a great deal!! Sponsors can sell their product, advertise their goods, and win new customers. Well, that sounds all fine and good, but it's not that simple. The biggest drawback of sponsoring an NHL team and advertising at games is that doing so is extremely expensive. Another potential negative is that there is a distinct chance that there may be no return for the financial investment that sponsors put into advertising at hockey games, on TV, or on the radio. Some small-market teams – particularly when the team historically performs poorly – draws very small crowds and has even smaller audiences on television and the radio. The less loyal a fan base is, the more likely that the sponsors of a hockey team – at least in that city – will fail to financially break even and gain a profit from their efforts. This is particularly true for sponsors whose goods or services are those that an individual would only need to use every once in a while – like a heating and cooling repair company (hopefully your furnace doesn't go out every year).

While interest groups can and do serve a vital role in American politics, there is a negative side to all of this as well. Most notably, most Americans believe that the politicians in Washington are more willing to listen to the voices of interest groups, PACs, and lobbying firms than to the voices of their own constituents. A **political action committee (PAC)** is a group where individuals in it pool monetary resources to donate to political candidates. Most PACs are tied to an interest group or a conglomerate of interest groups, but a handful of them are not. The most well-known PACs are the ones that are made up of corporations and other businesses and (typically) donate to Republican candidates (Nownes, 145-151). In 2010, the Supreme Court heard a case (referenced earlier – *Citizens United*) that enabled corporations to form PACs and donate unrestricted amounts of money to political campaigns. Assuredly, this decision further solidified the conviction of many Americans that their voices, efforts, and campaign donations were just a drop in the hat compared to the vast resources donated by these huge corporations; many Americans remain convinced that politicians' support is bought by interest groups and lobbying firms and that the less affluent American public is and always will be secondary in policy considerations.

A Sponsor's Potential Consumer: An Interest Group's Typical Member

Exactly what kinds of people buy into the ads that the sponsors of NHL teams put onto the air? Generally speaking, the individuals that buy into the advertisements directly are the people who typically consume the type of good or service being advertised. For example: beer drinkers are more likely to be captivated by a Budweiser ad than someone who does not typically consume alcohol. An individual who always gets a hot-dog at the hockey game would be more likely to get a hot-dog than someone else. Someone whose furnace has broken is more likely to call Jerry Kelly than someone whose furnace is functioning properly. These sponsors' ads are, generally speaking, geared toward an audience full of familiar faces – individuals that have, in the past, consumed their product, some on a regular basis.

Interest groups tend to attract certain groups of people as well. The most notable charac-

The typical interest group activist is usually affluent and possesses a college education. Therefore, we can infer that these college graduates are more likely to support an interest group than individuals who haven't graduated from college.

teristic of interest group members is that they tend to be more affluent than most Americans. That, from a certain perspective, makes perfect sense. An individual who has extra money to spend actually *has* extra cash to put toward issues that he or she cares about. Another typical characteristic about the members of interest groups is that they tend to be more educated than the average person. Again, this seems a logical conclusion one could make. The people who are interested in these issues first had to know that problems exist in the area of interest and also, they had to know that groups like the one they belong to exist so that the people – average people like you and me – can fight for our causes of choice and potentially make a difference in whatever interest we pursue (Nownes, 55-57).

Winning Customers and Pushing an Agenda

The businesses that sponsor NHL teams struggle, through various means, to recruit new customers and retain the ones they already have. To do so, these businesses spend millions of dollars on marketing their products. Some of this funding goes toward advertising on the boards of the rink, on TV, the radio, or even on billboards that are in close proximity to the hockey rink. These businesses are also constantly trying to improve the actual products themselves. Budweiser now includes a 'born-on-date' so that consumers can be reassured that their beer is fresh and tasty. Mountain Dew, another sponsor, has repeatedly changed the print on their cans and boxes to make the product look more attractive. Jerry Kelly even made a radio jingle – which is actually very catchy. All of these tactics are strategies that the sponsors of NHL teams employ in hopes of drawing in new customers and keeping the customers they have satisfied, excited, and loyal.

Interest groups have different strategies for pushing their 'product' or interests as well. One of the most common is their sharing information about their issue and agenda with the public (Nownes, 209-210). One of the most moving attempts at this, at least for me, is the Humane Society's TV ad which shows very sad looking dogs and cats in cages – some of which have clearly been abused by previous owners – and implores watchers to aid the Humane Society in helping these animals get a second chance at life. Though not the sole reason for my efforts, I argue that this ad, at least partially, encouraged me to rescue my beagle, Stormy, as opposed to getting a puppy from a breeder.

This beagle is a rescue from the Central Missouri Humane Society. Interest groups reach out to individuals to push their agenda and inform the public. In this case, an animal advocacy group attracted the attention of an animal lover and found this hound a home.

Interest groups also get their message out by lobbying politicians and providing them with campaign funding or other necessary resources for individuals in public office (Nownes, 89-138). You can be sure that Al Gore, a widely recognized advocate of protecting the environment, receives some of his campaign funds from the Environmental Protection Agency, Greenpeace, the Sierra Club, and other environmentalist interest groups. Similarly, you can be sure that President Obama receives a lot of campaign funds from women's rights advocacy groups as he is a proponent of a woman's right to contraception and abortion services.

Another strategy that interest groups can employ to get their agenda noticed and implemented is using the legal system to prosecute and convict people who violate laws that relate to their interest. A good example is *Humane Society of the United States vs. Hodel.* In this case, the Humane Society challenged some recent decisions of the Fish and Wildlife Service. Apparently, this organization was allowing hunting on protected lands – an act which the Humane Society alleged was unlawful (Humane Society of the United States, 1-5). Interest groups bring cases like this before the courts all the time in the hopes of pushing their agenda into the realm of law and legal precedent.

The last tool that interest groups utilize is to provide information regarding their interest

The goals of hockey teams compare to the aspirations of political parties. Similarly, the sponsors of hockey teams parallel interest groups.

to politicians as well as committees in Congress. By doing so, they can ensure that the politicians who make our laws have the facts regarding the issues on which they make decisions. For example: the AFL-CIO might appear before Congress to discuss the potential advantages and drawback of increasing or decreasing the manufacturing capacity of America in terms of the average skilled worker. As a general rule of thumb, politicians are keenly aware that all groups have a bias and that the 'facts' are sometimes buried in propaganda – a tactic that is no different from that which politicians use during their own campaigns to enhance their candidacy.

The NHL and Its Sponsors, Political Parties, and the Interest Groups That Support Them

The National Hockey League is a conglomerate of 30 teams that vie for the Big Prize – the Stanley Cup. Sponsors like Budweiser, Hunter, and others draw fans in as well as provide the funding necessary to acquire good players and therefore, a potentially successful hockey team. Political parties are groups of political personalities who seek to win elections while interest groups struggle to push their own agenda regarding their interest of choice. They attempt to influence politicians by aiding their campaigns, providing the government and the general public with information about their interest, and combatting legal obstacles that block the path of their own agendas.

Food For Thought

Political Parties

Why is winning elections so important? Is it possible for a political party to build a 'fan base' without winning elections? Do you think party unity is as important as political scientists argue; in other words, can a divided party establish dominance or maintain control in American politics? Which of the three aspects of party (electorate, organization, or government) do you think is the most important element of a political party?

Do you think partisan realignment is common or rare? Can you give an example of partisan realignment that has occurred in your lifetime? Do you think the Republican Party needs to remake itself or can it succeed the way it is? If the party requires alteration, what would you change and why? Does the Democratic Party require changes as well? What would you do to change the Democrats? Why is it that name change is automatically associated with ideological change? For example: most people associate the Republican Party with the end of slavery since Lincoln was Republican, but have trouble reconciling the GOP's current position regarding the equal treatment of minorities. Similarly, the Democratic Party used to be known as the party of racism and the Confederacy and yet today, they are the party that champions equal rights for a variety of people. The names of the parties have not changed, but their ideological tendencies have changed a great deal. Why?

Which do you think is more powerful: interest groups or the American electorate? When votes win elections, why is it that politicians seem to do what interest groups, PACs, and lobbyists want rather than what we want? Which interest groups out there do you or would you support? Do you think that interest groups provide factual information to the public, or do you think that the information that they provide is slanted to make their agenda seem more appealing? Do you think interest groups should have any say or 'standing' in the legal system? Is it possible to ensure that the individuals from interest groups that appear before Congress provide these lawmakers with factual information rather than political propaganda? If so, how can this be achieved?

President Snow, dictator of Panem – the former United States: "Let the Seventy Fourth Hunger Games begin! May the odds be ever in your favor."

At the beginning of the big presidential debate, the moderator exclaimed,

"May the odds be *ever* in your favor."

(Collins, 19).

Works Cited

Aron, Nan. "The Supreme Court: Just Politics By Other Means." *The Huffington Post: Politics. http://www.huffingtonpost.com/nan-aron/supreme-court-political-bias_b_1627458.html.* Posted on 06/26/2012.

Berg-Anderson, Richard. "A Brief History of American Major Parties." *TheGreenPapers.com. http://www.thegreenpapers.com/Hx/AmericanMajorParties.html.* 05/21/2001.

Budweiser. "Great times are waiting. Grab some Buds." Advertisement. http://www.budweiser.com/en/us/content/

epic-ads/video/commercial-epic-toast. Posted on Viewed on 12/2/2013.

Collins, Suzanne. *The Hunger Games.* New York: Scholastic Press, 2009.

Connelly, Joel. "The Sad, Sorry Republican Retreat From Civil Rights." *The Seattle PI. http://www.seattlepi.com//local/connelly/article/The-sad-sorry-Republican-retreat-from-civil-4757025.php.* Posted on 08/23/2013.

Eligon, John. "Finding Democrats to Run Where Republicans Win." *The New York Times. http://www.nytimes.com/2013/05/29/us/politics/democrats-weigh-electability-in-backing-candidates.html?_r=0.* Posted on 05/28/2013.

Espinoza, Chip. "Making the GOP Relevant – To Win Elections the Elephant Needs More Than a Makeover." *Fox News. http://www.foxnews.com/opinion/2013/04/04/making-gop-relevant-elephant-needs-more-than-makeover/.* Posted on 04/04/2013.

"Hockey Stick Glossary." Pure Hockey: We Are Hockey. http://www.purehockey.com/guidance-info/hockey-stick-sizing-guide-hockey-stick-sizes-pure-hockey. Last updated on 11/29/2013.

Hodge, Bob. "Democrats vs. Republicans on Taxes." *Money Matters. http://www.moneymatters360.com/index.php/democrats-vs-republican-on-taxes-21468/.* Posted on 02/24/2009.

"*Humane Society of the United States vs. Hodel.*" Animal Legal and Historical Center. http://www.animallaw.info/cases/causfd840f2d45.htm. Court decision handed down on 02/16/1988.

Kirk, Bob. "The 50 NHL Players, Past and Present, Most Desperate for Attention." *The Bleacher Report. http://bleacherreport.com/articles/1276457-the-50-nhl-players-past-and-present-most-desperate-for-attention/pa/ge/27.* Posted on 07/30/2012.

Levendusky, Matthew. *The Partisan Sort: How Liberals Became Democrats and How Conservatives Became Republicans.* Chicago: University of Chicago Press, 2009.

Lewison, Jed. "Tea Party Ringleader Admits that GOP Shut Down the Government For Nothing." *The Daily Kos. http://www.dailykos.com/story/2013/10/16/1247832/-Tea-party-ringleader-admits-the-GOP-shut-down-the-government-for-nothing#.* Posted on 10/16/2013.

Liberto, Jennifer. "Washington Gridlock Risks $7 Milk." *CNN News. http://money.cnn.com/2013/11/26/news/economy/milk-farm-bill/.* Posted on 11/26/2013.

Maisel, L. Sandy. *American Political Parties and Elections: A Very Short Introduction.* Oxford: Oxford University Press, 2007. (political parties in the United States)

Michaels, Robert. *Political Parties.* New York: Free Press, 1966. (ORGANIZATION)

National Hockey League. "Current Standings." *NHL.com. http://www.nhl.com/ice/standings.htm?navid=nav-stn-main#.* Last updated on 12/01/2013.

Nownes, Anthony J. *Interest Groups in American Politics: Pressure and Power.* New York: Routledge Publishing, 2013.

Peceny, Scott. "NHL Preview: The 10 Best Teams in Hockey." iSports-

Web – Sports in Perspective. http://isportsweb.com/2013/09/16/top-10-nhl-teams-2013-14-season/. Posted on 09/16/2013.

Robertson, Steve. *Ice Hockey Guide: Basic Rules.* Cupertino: My EBook Publishing House, 2013.

Saad, Lydia. "Republicans, Dems Abortion Views Become More Polarized." *Gallup Politics. http://www.gallup.com/poll/126374/republicans-dems-abortion-views-grow-polarized.aspx.* Posted on 04/08/2010.

Washington, George. Farewell Address. Posted in *The American Daily Advertiser.* http://www.ourdocuments.gov/doc.php?flash=true&doc=15. Included on 09/17/1796.

Whitney, David C. Edited by Robert Vaughn Whitney. *American Presidents: Biographies of the Chief Executives from George Washington to Barack Obama.* New York: Reader's Digest, 2012.

CHAPTER 10

The Hunger Games, Campaigns, and Elections: Beating the Odds That Are Never in Your Favor

Suzanne Collins, not long ago, wrote a post-apocalyptic trilogy about the country of Panem – formerly known as North America – before disaster, war, and insurrection swept across the thirteen (now twelve) Districts (or states) that are left. To prevent future insurrections, the Capital – the government of Panem – asserts and maintains its power through an epic annual reality TV show – The Hunger Games. The government of Panem mandates that a pair of tributes from each of the twelve Districts (one boy and one girl between the ages of 12 and 18) should be selected and sent to the Capital to compete in the annual Games – a competition which, over several weeks, is a fight to the death (Collins, 18).

Similarly, every four years in America, we as a nation are thrust into an epic drama as well – a journey that typically ends, like in *The Hunger Games*, one victor and many politicians who see their political futures 'die'. The parallels between this best-selling novel and the electoral process are uncanny; investigating their parallels makes the process easier to understand and relate to. Here we go and "may the odds be *ever* in your favor" (Collins, 19). First though, let's give those of you who are not familiar with *The Hunger Games* a brief synopsis of the book.

The Hunger Games

At the beginning of the book, we meet one of the two main characters of the book – Katniss Everdeen, a sixteen-year-old girl with brown hair arranged in braids. She lives in a dilapidated home with her younger sister, Primrose (known as Prim), and her mother, a woman who was constantly fighting the depression that had plagued her since her husband (and Katniss and Prim's father) was killed in a tragic mining accident. With her mother unable to adequately provide for the family, Katniss spends most of her time hunting (illegally) and gathering various plants to eat. Katniss and her family live in District 12 – the poorest of the twelve Districts in Panem. In District 12, survival is a daily struggle (Collins, 3-8).

Reaping Day

The story begins on Reaping Day, the day that the two tributes to participate in the Hunger Games are selected from each District. Katniss' chances of being selected are much higher than her sister Prim's; Katniss, in order to help provide for the family, had taken out tesserae. Each tessera provides the individual with a year's worth of food and supplies in exchange for the addition of one extra entry into the lottery of potential tributes. The more tesserae an individual takes out, the more likely it is that the individual will be selected as one of the District's tributes (Collins, 13).

Katniss and her family go to the Reaping ceremony, and unpredictably, Prim is chosen. In the hopes of saving her sister, Katniss volunteers as the female tribute and Prim is excused from the duty. The male tribute selected is Peeta Mellark, one of Katniss' former schoolmates and a young man whom she has a history with. When Katniss was younger and shortly after her father's mining accident, her family was starving, and it had become her custom to raid the trash cans of the wealthier citizens in the District. On a cold, rainy night, Peeta – the son of a baker – ventured outside and gave Katniss a loaf of bread despite his mother's violent reaction. In fact, Peeta's mother physically chastised him for this act of kindness, and for that, Katniss has never been able to forget him or shake off the feeling that she owes Peeta something; the fact that she would be competing against him – to the death – is almost more than she can stand (Collins, 25-33).

After the tribute selection, Katniss and Peeta are packed off on a bullet train headed toward the Capital; on board, they meet the only surviving Victor from District 12, Haymitch Abernathy. Haymitch is a severe alcoholic, but amidst the drunken babble, he informs Katniss and Peeta that he is to coach them and prepare them for their week in the Capital. Their time there would consist of nationally televised presentations and interviews – all of which would affect their likelihood to gain sponsors, individuals who had the power to send them needed food, medicine, or supplies which might enable them to survive the Hunger Games. The first and most important advice Haymitch gives the pair of tributes is how best to attract the aid of sponsors – help that might prove to be the difference between life and death inside the arena (Collins, 54-60).

Peeta Mellark (Josh Hutcherson): the male tribute from District 12

Katniss Everdeen (Jennifer Lawrence) – The Girl on Fire!

A Week in the Capital

The first thing that occurs when Katniss and Peeta arrive in the Capital is that both tributes are separated and given makeovers. Generally speaking, citizens in the Capital consider people from outlying Districts like Katniss' to be dirty and uncivilized. Katniss' and Peeta's makeovers are conducted by the stylist, Cinna – a new addition to the Games in this particular year. His costume designs are revolutionary, and they gain Katniss and Peeta instant support. Their clothing, when they turn or move, produces artificial flames. Katniss is thereafter referred to as 'Katniss Everdeen – the Girl on Fire" (Collins, 64-71).

Sixty seconds on the pedestal and the Hunger Games begin.

The next week is filled with training and politicking; each tribute gets a chance to perform in front of potential sponsors, and Katniss makes a positive impression. Peeta, however, wins the audience's heart when he reveals, in an interview, that he has loved Katniss for years. Katniss initially resents this, but later comes to grips with her own feelings of affection toward Peeta. She is unsure whether or not her feelings for Peeta are plutonic or romantic, but she is advised by Haymitch to play the audience and sponsors' sympathies and use the "lovebird card" to win sponsors and the favor of the audience. The interviews occur the night before the beginning of the Games; Katniss and Peeta spend some time during the night talking about their pasts and unintentionally solidify their bond even further (Collins, 138-147).

The Hunger Games

The Games begin with each tribute stationed on a black pedestal in the middle of a grassy plain with a tree line. The twenty-four tributes (two from each District) are situated in a circle around the Cornucopia, a horn-like structure where vital supplies are strewn about for tributes to seize. Instead of falling for the bait and pitting herself against the other tributes, Katniss runs into the forest area of the arena – the area where most of the action in the Games takes place. She runs for much of the next couple days and she approaches the border of the arena. The Chief Gamemaker, Seneca Crane, induces a forest fire that keeps Katniss from crossing the arena boundary, but in the process, her leg is badly burned. She flees, but right into danger as she, by chance, encounters a number of the other tributes; some are Career tributes who train from childhood to participate in the Games from Districts 1 and 2. Peeta is among them; it seems the Careers are keep-

A tracker jacker nest hangs near the limb where Katniss rests. Katniss is stung by a few of the genetically engineered wasps, but she successfully cuts the nest from the tree. While the tributes below face the fury of a hive full of angry tracker jackers, Katniss is able to escape.

ing him alive in the hopes of luring Katniss to them. They discover Katniss hiding in a tree and decide to wait her out. As she perches in the tree, she discovers that the wound on her leg has becoming infected and requires medical attention. At this point, her chances of winning the Games appear to be slim. Fortunately, a sponsor sends the needed medicinal salve and her leg heals. The morning after she receives the medicine, Katniss awakes, no nearer to escaping Peeta and the Career tributes, but she then sees Rue, a young girl from District 11 who alerts her to a massive tracker jacker nest just within her reach; tracker jackers are genetically engineered wasps which have lethal poison in their stingers. Katniss uses a machete knife to cut the nest from the tree limb, and a few of the Career tributes are killed. Only Peeta, Cato, and Clove – Careers from District 2, and Foxface – a stealthy tribute from District 5 – survive the tracker jackers (Collins, 148-191).

In an attempt to destroy the supplies the remaining Careers were hoarding, Katniss' ally, Rue, is killed. Upon Rue's request, Katniss sings to her as she dies, and out of respect, Katniss buries Rue and surrounds her in flowers that she picked herself. She decides that the next rational move is to seek out Peeta. Upon her journey to him, the Gamemakers change the rules to allow tributes from the same District to team up and jointly win the Games if they are the last tributes standing. Katniss searches for and finds a badly injured Peeta. He confesses his feelings for her, and – playing the game and the audience – Katniss reciprocates. The Gamemakers then announce a 'feast' – an event where each District could, if they dared, acquire some item that they desperately need. Knowing that Peeta's wounds, if left untreated, will kill him, Katniss assumes (correctly) that the desperately needed item is Peeta's medicine. Through the mercy of Thresh, the male tribute from District 11, Rue's District, Katniss is able to return to Peeta with the medicine needed to heal his injuries (Collins, 218-288).

At this stage of the Games, the only tributes left are Foxface (District 5), Cato and Clove

Medicine for Peeta and hope for District 12

(District 2), and Peeta and Katniss (District 12). The Gamemakers introduce genetically mutated hounds into the arena which kill Foxface and Clove. Peeta, Katniss, and Cato flee to the Cornucopia in the center of the arena for the supposed final showdown, and Cato is defeated by the pair. Katniss and Peeta, bruised and bleeding, are the last tributes standing. Despite an attempt of the Gamemakers to change the rules, Katniss and Peeta, through an act of defiance, are crowned the Victors of the Seventy-Fourth Hunger Games (Collins, 325-345).

Campaigns, Elections, and the Hunger Games

Suzanne Collins' *Hunger Games*, while a brutal book full of the immoralities typical of most dictatorships, supplies us with numerous facets that one could compare to campaigns and elections in the United States. Both the *Hunger Games* and the American electoral process share numerous similarities. Some of these are more obvious, and others take a bit of explaining. It is these parallels that are examined in the following pages.

Competition

As stated before, the Hunger Games is a competition that is held annually. Adolescent boys and girls (ages 12 to 18) are required to submit their names into a lottery; whoever is chosen serves as the female or male tribute for their own District. All of these tributes – twenty four in all – compete in the arena in a month-long battle to the death. The conditions in the arena are unknown to the tributes until the Games begin; the arena could be a grassy forested area, icy tundra, sizzling desert, or any other number of possibilities. The tributes have to survive in whatever conditions the area presents while, at the same time, combatting the other twenty-three tributes. The tributes compete within the arena until only one is left standing. He or she is crowned the Victor of the Hunger Games (Collins, 18-19).

In the American political 'arena', campaigns and elections are another type of competition, though definitely less brutal than the combat that occurs in *The Hunger Games.* In a political campaign, *political candidates compete to win public office through the electoral process.* Like in *The Hunger Games,* both major parties begin with a pool of candidates, but personal blunders, media attention, and public support narrow the competition down to one nominee for each party. These two square off in the General Election, and their political fate or 'life', if you will, is decided on Election Day.

Political campaigns can and have been every bit as messy as the Hunger Games. In 1968, Robert F. Kennedy ran for the presidency but was assassinated before he had the chance to be considered by the Electoral College (or the American electorate) on Election Day. Four presidents, after having secured victory, were assassinated during their terms of office (Lincoln, Garfield, McKinley, and John F. Kennedy). Politicians and the individuals who support (or oppose them) have splattered the history of the American presidency with the blood of past presidents who were not granted the grace of living out their terms of office (Oliver and Marion, 15-68, 113-131, 161-181).

Victors and Representation

To complete in the Hunger Games, I noted earlier that only one male and one female adolescent from each District could be chosen as tribute. However, I also noted that the chances of one being chosen increased with the number of tesserae that each respective individual takes out. So, although the choosing of tributes is random and absolute in one sense, one's chances of being selected are proportionally larger when the number of entries one has (because of tesserae) is larger (Collins, 13-14).

The Hunger Games and the American electoral system: an epic battle coming to a polling place near you.

In American politics, we have two kinds of representation and two different methods of allocating presidential electoral votes – the tallies that inevitably elect the president. The first form of representation and electoral allocation is known as the winner-take-all system. This is the system that most Americans are familiar with. Out of the 50 states, 48 states (Maine and Nebraska excluded) use the winner-take-all system in both representative and electoral scenarios. In a winner-take-all system, simply put, there is only one winner for each public office position. There is one winner that we send to Washington to represent us as there is one female and male individual that each District sends to the Games.

The other form of representation and electoral distribution is known as proportional representation. In this system, generally speaking, there are a number of people running for several elected positions – some are from one political party and some are from another. The percentage of the popular vote determines how many seats each party receives. For example: imagine that the state of Missouri has ten congressional seats open, and that the Democrats get 60% of the popular vote. In a proportional representation system, the Democrats would get six out of the ten seats (60%), and the Republicans would get four seats (40%).

In terms of the Electoral College, proportional representations work roughly the same way. Each candidate receives the number of electoral votes that corresponds with the percentage of the popular vote that they receive in that state. For example: Maine divvies out five electoral votes. Imagine that President Obama got 80% of the popular vote and Mitt Romney received 20%. President Obama would receive four out of the five electoral votes (80%) while Romney would get one vote (20%). In the Hunger Games, the more entries you have in the District lottery, the higher your chance of being chosen as tribute. With a proportional representation system, the higher your party's percentage of the popular vote, the more seats or electoral votes you or your party will receive.

The Districts

The country of Panem in *The Hunger Games* is divided into 12 Districts. District lines were drawn by the Capital to delineate different occupational trades as well as the average socioeconomic status in each District. Katniss' District 12 is an impoverished mining colony – the poorest District in Panem. Other Districts, like Rue's District 11, pursue other occupations such as agriculture, manufacturing, and so on. While better off economically than Katniss' District, Rue's District is still a center of appalling poverty (Collins, 4-6, 200-204).

Congressional districts in the United States are not organized so much by occupation or socioeconomic status, but rather, by political affiliation. Each congressional district has roughly 300,000 individuals living in it, but the population is constantly changing from district to district. Every ten years, a census is taken to see if the population has changed enough to merit redrawing the district lines – a process known as **redistricting.** Generally speaking, one political party is in charge and the other

A house like the one Katniss and her family lived in, in District 12 – a District immersed in poverty and hard labor.

is not. The political party with the power, in a lot of cases, tends to redraw district lines to ensure that their candidates will be elected in as many districts as possible. The attempt to redraw district lines to politically benefit one party over the other is known as **gerrymandering** (Engstrom, 191-206).

Let's look at a modern-day example. In 2010, the Census Bureau a census and, because the Republican Party was in power, district lines were redrawn in some states to benefit future GOP candidates. Some of the most noteworthy winners of elections in these districts are members of the Tea Party – an extreme fringe of the Republican Party. In 2013, a government shutdown and a debt crisis pitted the Tea Party against the more moderate wing of the Republican Party as the Republicans attempted to silence, or at least temper, the voice of the Tea Party in national politics. Some, particularly Democrats, are hoping that these Tea Party politicians will lose their seats in the 2014 congressional election, but others are hesitant to predict Democratic victories because of the supposed gerrymandering that was employed when congressional district lines were redrawn in 2010. Instead, they contend that it is more likely that some of the Tea Party candidates will be defeated by more moderate Republicans; these folks allege that the districts are gerrymandered too intricately to expect or predict the victory of Democrats, but one should expect to see a modest number of Tea Partiers packing their bags to head home after the 2014 elections are over (Caldwell, 1-3).

The Process

Each year during the Hunger Games, the same process is followed from the first day of the process – Reaping Day – until the new Victor is crowned at the end of the Games. It is a two-part process. The first part is the Reaping – the event where the two tributes from each District are chosen, brought to the Capital, presented to the sponsors and (through television) the citizens of Panem, individually interviewed by Caesar Flickerman (Collins, 124-130), trained by the surviving Victors from their Districts, and evaluated by potential sponsors. Once the Reaping and the week of media hype in the Capital is over, the second half of the process, the Hunger Games, commences; in the Games, the twenty-four tributes square off and eliminate each other until only one is left standing and is crowned the Victor.

The American election season is separated into two parts. The first elections are known as **primary elections** or **caucuses**. In this part of the electoral process, each political party selects a number of potential candidates and narrows them down to one. An important point to make here is that primaries and caucuses (though very alike in outcome) are different in terms of how each of these election styles are carried out. In a **primary election**, voters go to their polling place, receive a ballot and vote secretly in a booth – a process most people are familiar with. A **caucus**, however, is an entirely different animal. In a caucus, districts hold primary elections and then send representative delegates for the winning candidate to the state capital. In a building with a large room – generally a convention center or something similar, each candidate is positioned at different corners of the room and each respective delegate is directed toward the corner of the room where the candidate their district popularly supported is located (Jaime, 21-22).

In the general election, the two candidates left from the primaries – one from each party – square off in a three-month battle for the office in question. Advertising, debates, get-out-the-vote efforts, and lots of annoying phone calls comprise the three-month fight for each candidate's political career – political survival. General elections are generally heated affairs where each candidate attempts to dig up as much dirt on their opponent as possible to make their adversary appear as un-electable as possible (Maisel, 91-116).

Let the 'Games' Begin

Reaping Day is the beginning of the brutal affair that is known as the Hunger Games. Adolescents between 12 and 18 are dressed in their best garb, kissed by their families, and are brought before the Justice Building in their respective District to see which boy and girl will be selected out of the District's lottery to represent their District as tributes. There is no cheering, no laughing; there are canned speeches and propaganda films, and there is the Reaping itself. One boy and one girl are sent from their District to compete in the Hunger Games. Likely, neither will survive the affair (Collins, 15-20).

That's a pretty somber picture, but not unlike the views held by many Americans when the presidential campaign season actually begins – the Iowa Caucus and the New Hampshire Primary. For the next year, presidential hopefuls across the country bombard the public with advertisements, phone calls, doorbell rings, junk mail, and other such tools. These candidates will confront each other on every issue – from politics to personal character flaws, and most Americans, simply put, dread the beginning of the Big Show – just like the citizens of Panem shudder at the thought of what will occur on and after Reaping Day. It all begins though, in Iowa and New Hampshire.

The Iowa Caucus occurs first, typically in early March. The New Hampshire Prima-

Katniss and Peeta: the two tributes from District 12 selected on Reaping Day. Like them, presidential hopefuls begin their journey to the White House with the Iowa and New Hampshire primaries.

ry is held roughly a week afterward. These two events are seen as key indicators of who the potential presidential nominee from each party will be. Generally speaking, if one candidate wins both contests, that presidential hopeful tends to win his or her party's nomination. If each contest is won by a different candidate, the primary campaign season is typically messy – sometimes going down to the wire, even days before the next major event – the party conventions (Maisel, 91-95).

The Importance of 'Sponsors'

After having been chosen, the twenty-four tributes from all twelve Districts are transported to the Capital for a week of media exposure. The reason for this week-long stay in the Capital is two-fold. First, it provides footage for the Capital to broadcast to the citizens of Panem and allows for the development of fan favorites. Second, it enables the sponsors who have the ability to aid the tributes with resources in life or death situations the ability to determine who they will support and to what extent; this personal evaluation of the tributes continues during the Hunger Games competition as well.

In the story, Katniss, like all of the other tributes, has a chance to perform before the Gamemakers. The overall ratings of the Gamemakers are known for garnering the support of sponsors for some tributes and not others. After (seemingly) being ignored in her private session, Katniss boldly shoots an apple out of one of their hands with an arrow. Her mentors fear that she may have been too bold and discouraged any support whatsoever but finds out through a televised assessment of each tribute by the Gamemakers that Katniss is perceived to be the most likely tribute to win the Hunger Games and thus will likely have many willing sponsors to aid her in her journey to become the Victor (Collins, 86-108). During the Hunger Games themselves, Katniss appeals to her sponsors – and to Peeta's – by pretending to be romantically interested in him. Haymitch convinces the Gamemakers to pursue Peeta and Katniss' love story and offers Peeta and Katniss incentives for playing along with his plot; it pays huge dividends – particularly when Peeta and Katniss are both sick and hungry (Collins, 187-188, 244, 260-261, 297-302).

Just like sponsors enable the tributes in *The Hunger Games* to survive, **interest groups –** groups of individuals who work together to push a common political interest – provide political candidates with much needed funding and resources necessary to run a successful campaign. Certain interest groups are known for specific political parties. In general, businesses (small businesses and corporate groups), gun-rights groups, family or Christian groups, conservative political groups, banks or financial groups, agriculture groups, and so on are typically supporters of the Republican Party. Conversely, labor groups, environmental groups, civil rights groups, women's rights groups, animal rights groups, and so on are big supporters of the Democratic Party (Maisel and Berry, 519-532).

Some interest groups, particularly the large and powerful ones, have the propensity to significantly impact elections through their donation capabilities. It is hoped by these groups that, if elected, the politicians they support will, in turn, aid these interest groups in pushing their agenda – whether it be in the House of Representatives, the Senate, or in the White House. The goal of all interest groups is the same – to push their issues and their agenda regarding those issues (Maisel and Berry, 519-532).

Katniss and Peeta's love story captivates the audience of the Hunger Games and attracts the help of sponsors, just as presidential candidates try to gain the support of wealthy campaign donors.

Only the Strong Survive: The Beginning of the Games and Party Conventions

Katniss comments that she has sixty seconds to stand on the black pedestal – one like the other twenty three tributes perch atop – before she can begin her epic battle for survival. Once the minute is expired, she can either flee to safety or attempt to capture some vital resources strewn around the Cornucopia. She grabs a backpack and flees. In her absence, eleven of the twenty-four tributes meet their demise within the first two days. In the Hunger Games, only the strong survive the first few hours of the competition, and Katniss was one of the lucky ones (Collins, 148-153).

Katniss and the other tributes use their unique strengths to eliminate their competition just as the media use the blunders of candidates to help the public unofficially eliminate candidates from the presidential race. Katniss' strength is her accuracy with a bow. Most candidates' weaknesses are either what comes out of their mouths or what they do in their private lives.

Just as the 'weak' tributes are eliminated during the early stages of the Hunger Games competition, weak candidates are weeded out during the primary elections which leave only the best candidates to compete for their party's nomination at their respective party convention. At the party conventions, each party has two main objectives. First, they set their political agenda for the next four years. Second, they nominate a candidate for president. The nomination process is executed by **pledged delegates** and **unpledged delegates** or **'superdelegates'.** Pledged delegates are the individuals sent by each respective state to represent the popular vote determined by the state's primary or caucus. A very small group of these delegates, particularly for the Republican Party, are high-ranking party members or elected officials (sometimes known as PLEO). Superdelegates, strictly speaking, are high-ranking party officers or elected officials that have the ability to case votes so as to represent the will of the political party itself. The Republican Party's use of superdelegates is limited; in the event of a landslide, their nominations are typically not counted. The Democrats, conversely, widely use superdelegates in their nomination process. Most of these superdelegates are 'unpledged', meaning that – until the party convention – these individuals have not outwardly determined which candidate to nominate (*Boston Globe*).

Playing 'The Games' and the 'Game of Thrones'

The book by Suzanne Collins reaches its emotional peak as the Hunger Games commence.

The twenty-four tributes, quickly reduced to eleven, scramble, hide, and engage each other in a frantic effort to survive and be the one lucky enough to be crowned the Victor of the Seventy-Fourth Hunger Games. Our protagonist, Katniss, encounters a forest fire and a group of Career tributes from Districts 1 and 2. Only through the intervention of Rue (the tracker jacker nest) and Peeta (who lets her escape after the next had been destroyed) did Katniss survive. After Rue is killed, the Gamemakers change the rules to allow for the surviving tributes from the same District to work together to win the Games as a team. Katniss immediately begins to search for Peeta and, under Haymitch's instruction, plays the public's sympathies and pretends to be in love with Peeta. It appears to gain both of them sponsors and public support through the reality TV show which the Gamemakers shaped, under Haymitch's suggestion, to turn this year's Games into a love story. Ultimately, it is this epic romance which leads Katniss and Peeta to win the Victor's Crown (Collins, 148-345).

The final stretch of the presidential campaign season is the general election. In the final three months of the campaign trail, each party's presidential nominee squares off against the other in an epic battle for their political futures; it is a general rule of thumb that losing a presidential election is typically considered to be the end of a politician's political career. So, like the tributes whose lives end in the Hunger Games, failed presidential nominees see their political careers die as well.

During the general election, a number of things occur that are worthy of note. The first events that occur at the behest of each political party are a push to get people registered to vote. This is generally considered an effort to ensure that 'your' political party has more physical votes possible than the opposing party does. These events are known as voter registration drives. These efforts take place on college campuses, county courthouses, and other major public centers (Polsby and Wildvarsky, 22 and 24).

The next major events to occur are the three presidential debates as well as the vice-presidential debate. In these showdowns, the presidential (or vice-presidential) nominees square off and attempt to convey to average Americans why electing them would make America a better place; moreover, each candidate goes in-depth and discusses how they would go about getting us from where we are now to where the candidate says that we should be.

Some people contend that these debates are superficial attempts of candidates to promise as much as they can to as many people as they can – regardless to whether they can keep the promises they make in these events (Dickerson, 1-3); they might intend on keeping them, but oftentimes the attempt at doing so calls their sincerity and resolve into question (Bernstein, 1-2). The questions, many argue, are provided to the candidates beforehand and therefore have the chance to formulate answers that might make their intended audiences happy (Sides, 1-2). Others contend that presidential debates are the closest most Americans come to seeing the candidates up close and are the most intensive arena for receiving information about each candidate; thus these showdowns are necessary and beneficial (Schroeder, 1).

The final events to occur before the end-game of the presidential campaign, Election Day, are the get-out-the-vote efforts. These programs attempt to ensure that as many people make it to the polls as possible so as to make sure that as many people's voices are represented as possible. Assuredly, the political parties themselves push these efforts hoping to get more people who are likely to support their candidate to the polls than their opponents do, but regardless, the effort to ensure that as many people as possible exercise their right to vote is an effort that unmistakably makes the American presidential campaign process better and enables the will of the people to be represented more accurately (Green and Gerber, 1-11, 108-119).

The Role of the Media in the Arena and in the Electoral Process

As discussed before, the Hunger Games and all the strings that are attached create, among other things, a reality TV show, and viewership is required by all citizens of Panem (Collins, 18-23). Before the Games begin, the Gamemakers familiarize the citizens of Panem with the twenty-four tributes by presenting to the nation in an epic broadcast (69-72). They are able to enter into the personal lives of the tributes by learning more about them through the individual interviews held with the host of the Hunger Games, Caesar Flickerman (123-130). During the Games themselves by strategically placing cameras all over the arena, the Gamemakers are able to shape the Games also, the reality TV show which shapes public support for specific tributes. This is how the love story between Katniss and Peeta is shaped, and it is the media – the creator of the reality TV show – who is ultimately held responsible for the crowning of Katniss and Peeta as Victors (172-177, 244, 273-277, 344-345).

During the presidential campaign season, the media swings into gear and is always looking for the next major occurrence, blunder, or memorable moment created as only pol-

The Hunger Games, while being a lethal competition, is also a reality TV show. The American media play a large role in the race to the White House.

iticians can. Political blunders during the general election, whether executed by the presidential or vice presidential nominee, are extremely damaging – even if the actual blunder was fabricated. One of the most recent examples of the media shaping a nominee's persona was *Saturday Night Live*'s shaping of Sarah Palin as stupid and uninformed; this characterization might be totally incorrect, but the media's shaping of this persona ruined her chances – and John McCain's – of winning the White House (Jacobs, 1).

The media, conversely, is known for choosing and promoting a favorite candidate. Early in the 2008 presidential primary season, Barack Obama and Hillary Clinton faced off in the Democratic primaries. Until late in the summer – indeed, right before the party convention, there was no clear indication as to who would win the nomination. The media, however, had their own winner picked weeks in advance. The media pundits – both conservative and liberal – seemed to pick Obama as the favorite, and some argue that it was the media's favorable attitude toward the, at the time, young senator from Illinois that enabled him to secure his party's nomination for the presidency. Hillary, some contended, was at a disadvantage from the start simply because of her gender and her brusque personality, and media outlets seemed to indicate that to be true and portray Obama as a likable, knowledgeable man ripe for leadership (Bedard, 1-2).

Another thing the media plays a large role in is the development and production of political campaign ads. Particularly when advertisements were first shown on television, these ads were typically positive descriptions of what the candidate in question would do to help America and its people. More recently, however, campaign ads have turned nasty and are far more negative; instead of discussing what the candidate in question will do, ads today discuss the negative qualities and agenda of the candidate's opposition. Many Americans are frustrated with the level of negativity evident in current campaign ads, but evidence suggests that these appeals to the public are effective nevertheless (Brader, 27-29).

Playing to Your Strengths: Getting Out Your Voters, and *Moneyball*

In *The Hunger Games*, both Katniss and Peeta, during their training period, are advised to make good use of their strengths. Katniss was an archer of unparalleled ability, and Peeta's immense strength was a formidable weapon. Haymitch, however, contends that their greatest asset is, put simply, each other. After Peeta's interview with Caesar Flickerman which reveals Katniss as Peeta's love interest, Haymitch suggests to the pair that they use the 'star-crossed lovers' story to win the support of sponsors and the citizens of Panem (Collins, 88-147). Indeed, Katniss and Peeta's ability to see and use their strengths against their opposition enables them to win the Hunger Games and be crowned the Victors.

Unlike Katniss and Peeta, most politicians and the parties that nominate them have failed to adequately asses their electoral strengths – that is, until a book was written that changed

The media displayed many images like these of President Obama in 2008 during the campaign to win the White House – "Hope and Change" became his tagline and it stuck.

the political landscape of American elections – *Moneyball*. This book, written by Michael Lewis, describes the successful season of the 2003 Oakland Athletics despite massive payroll problems. Rather than looking for big-name players that are expensive, Bill James and his cohort of economic experts suggest that teams were approaching the game from the wrong angle. Ballgames, they argued, are won by scoring the most *runs*; therefore, it only makes sense that teams would search for players with high on-base percentages (percentage of the time they get on base) or high slugging percentages (total bases divided by total number of at-bats). By looking for players with those two skills, Billy Beane – the general manager of the Athletics – was able to acquire undervalued players and build a team that nearly won a championship. His revolutionary method of team-building through the analysis of sabermetrics changed the landscape of baseball forever (Lewis, 43-63).

Just as the philosophy that is laid out in *Moneyball* changed baseball forever, so too has the book changed the way political parties and presidential hopefuls approach elections (Randoll). If baseball games are won by getting the most *runs*, elections are won by getting the most *votes* – votes, in presidential elections, translate into *electoral votes*. Donald Green and Alan Gerber, two political scientists, have noted the parallels between the philosophy laid out in *Moneyball* to the tactics employed in elections since the success of the 2002 Athletics. They argue that, like in baseball, every individual has intrinsic value, every voter's vote has the potential to make a huge difference in the allotment of his or her state's electoral votes. The problem is, however, that political parties have not, up until recently, spent enough time finding the people who are likely to support them, haven't got them registered to vote, and if they are already registered, they haven't ensured that those people make it to the polls (Green and Gerber, 135-164). Since the release of *Moneyball*, presidential campaigns have demonstrated that doing these things ensures the political party and candidate who employ these methods a good chance of winning their election. In the 2004 election, Ken Mehlman took the principles of *Moneyball* to aid George W. Bush in his re-election bid – which he won (Mehlman, 1-4). In the 2008 election, David Axelrod did the same for President Obama (Axelrod, 1-5).

Since 2004, Nate Silver, a statistician, has made predictions regarding who would win what state's electoral votes based on which party best applied the principles of *Moneyball* in their campaigns by limiting potential 'losses' in voter turnout by finding potential voters and maximizing 'wins' by registering those voters and ensuring that they make it to the polls (Silver, 74-107). Let's put it this way: by making predictions based on a campaign's successful implementation of the principles of *Moneyball*, Silver has been far more correct than any pundit on television using exit polls has ever been. In fact, Silver was entirely correct in his 2012 Electoral College prediction. That takes some skill - or maybe just throwing around a baseball – the 'Moneyball' (Harding, 1). Just as Katniss and Peeta played to their strengths in the arena throughout the duration of the Hunger Games, by employing the philosophy of *Moneyball* to the electoral process, presidential candidates and political parties have learned to play to theirs by finding potential voters, registering them, and getting them to the polls.

Crowning the Victor

Near the end of the Hunger Games, the only tributes left are Peeta, Katniss, and Cato – a

Politicians playing 'Moneyball' – finding potential voters, getting them to register, and making sure they make it to the polls.

Career tribute from District 2. The Gamemakers introduce genetically engineered hounds or 'muttations' into the arena to chase all of the tributes together for an epic showdown, and their efforts are successful. The tributes congregate at the Cornucopia and Katniss and Peeta engage Cato. The tributes from District 12 prove strongest, however, and Cato is eliminated. Although the Gamemakers attempt to change the rules at the last minute to allow only one Victor to be crowned, Katniss and Peeta – through an act of defiance of the Capital, threatening to kill each other and leave the Games with no Victor – are crowned the Victors of the Seventy-Fourth Hunger Games (Collins, 325-345).

The end-game for the presidential election season is Election Day. This day is always on the first Tuesday following the first Monday in November every four years. On this day, citizens across the country go to the polls to cast their ballots for president and also for lesser offices, public **referenda** (bills that must be approved by popular vote), tax increases, and so on. Especially during presidential elections, the lines at the polls are typically long – especially after people start getting off from work (Smith, 1-3).

Millions of people flock to the polls on Election Day, but some do so unlawfully – or so some say. Voter fraud is an issue that has been a notable problem – especially recently. Some individuals show up at the polls and use someone else's identity to vote; some of these people are even alleged to be dead (Cergol, 1). Other voters suspected of fraud used someone else's voter ID card to enter the polls and cast ballots (Collins II, 1-3).

Another typical occurrence during polling hours on Election Day are statistical efforts to determine who is voting for who and why; these attempts to capture the public's vote before the ballots are counted are known as **exit polls.** On the way out of a polling place, voters are pulled aside by a pollster who asks them questions about who they voted for and why. Pollsters also collect demographic information on voters so as to determine what kinds of people are voting for each candidate (Best and Krveger, 18-21). Exit polls have produced mixed results; some years, they prove to be extremely accurate while in other years, they are less so (Best and Krveger, 17-18).

After the polls close in each state (except for Maine and Nebraska), the popular vote is determined and each respective state declares (informally) which candidates will receives their votes in the Electoral College's formal election of the president. In Maine and Nebraska, electoral votes are allocated based on the popular vote in each congressional district. The media plays a major role in informing the public which candidate will receive the electoral votes in each state. The formal vote of the Electoral College, however, does not occur on Election Night; it occurs on the Monday after the second Wednesday in December (NARA, 1-2).

The Hunger Games is a brutal contest of skills where only the strong survive. I believe the same can be said about the American electoral process. It is a contest of political giants; one goes to Washington and one goes home. Suzanne Collins' *Hunger Games* denotes the best and worst of human nature – our willingness to sacrifice for others but also our willingness to do unspeakable things in the name of survival. The electoral process does the same; men become lions and rip each other's reputation to shreds while also appealing to what's best about America – its people.

The American electoral process is a contest where America decides, with the mediation of the Electoral College, who will govern us, reassure us during times of turmoil, and guide us in times of uncertainty. Just as Katniss and Peeta are crowned the Victors of the Hunger Games by the Capital, the government of Panem, so too we – through the Electoral College – elect our Victor – the President of the United States. The next time election season comes round, don't forget to wish the candidates "a Happy Hunger Games. May the odds be *ever* in their favor!" (Collins, 19).

Food for Thought

The Hunger Games

The Hunger Games is a post-apocalyptic novel. Why do people seem to be so interested in this genre of literature? Do you believe that most dictatorships are as cruel as Panem's

The Victor of our 'Hunger Games' – the president. For those who seek to take the president's place, "May the odds be ever in their favor." (Collins, 19)

capital? Have governments of the past ever employed methods of political suppression this extreme? If you lived in Panem, would you stand up against such brutality or would you remain silent? Why do you think the citizens of Panem hold their silence? Do you think the fabricated relationship between Katniss and Peeta was an appropriate method for gaining the favor of their sponsors and the public? As fans of reality TV in general, do you think *The Hunger Games* would be entertaining as a TV show? What does that say about our society's desensitization regarding senseless murder and the pursuit of survival?

The Hunger Games and the Electoral Process

In your opinion, do we really have much of a choice as to who is nominated and elected president or who is elected to serve in Congress? Do you believe any average person can become president? Why or why not? Is this a political competition or a popularity contest? In your opinion, what is the most exciting part of the electoral process? Do you feel you have more of a say during the primary elections or during the general election?

Which form of representation/electoral voting do you prefer – winner-take-all or proportional? Which do you think is more democratic? Would proportional representation work in the United States? Why do some states employ proportional electoral apportionment while most of the others do not? Why do you think that the Founders found it necessary to implement the Electoral College rather than letting the president be chosen by popular vote? Do you think that the Founder's rationale was correct?

Do you think that congressional districts should be redrawn as often as they are? Should they be re-drawn by a neutral party rather than the political party that happens to be in power? Are there advantages and disadvantages to gerrymandering? Do you think some of the gridlock in Congress is, at least partially, due to the intricate level of the gerrymandering that is employed? What kind of electoral atmosphere do you think would exist in districts if gerrymandering did not occur? Would elections be more or less competitive? Would that be good or bad for American democracy?

Do you think the public should have more of a say as to which candidates are even considered in primary elections? Do you think the political banter that occurs during the primaries puts candidates at a disadvantage in the general election? Specifically, what types of candidates are more in danger of being negatively affected by primary elections? Do you think that politicians' images are shaped more during the primaries or during the general election?

A lot goes on during the general election in the public eye that isn't generally noticed in the primary elections; what are some examples of this? What do you pay attention to the most? Do you watch the presidential debates? What about the vice presidential debates? Do you think the candidates intend to keep the promises they make, or are these assertions simply hollow statements intended to win votes? What kinds of advertising do you feel is the most effective – the ads that tell you what the candidate intends to do for you or the ads that describe the negative attributes of a candidate's opponent? What do you think about the application of *Moneyball* to the electoral process? Do you think that such a theory will hold up over time or is it merely a coincidence that this strategy has been effective recently?

Do you think that the Electoral College is outdated and that the popular vote should elect the president? Should voting be electronic or is there an advantage to having paper ballots? Is there any value in exit polls? If you were asked to participate in an exit poll survey, would you do so? Do you watch presidential election returns? What do you think the candidates do as the election returns come in? At the end of the night, the loser is expected to call the 'victor' and concede the election. How soon is too soon? Do you think electing our president deserves all of this pomp and circumstance, or do the media overdo it? If you could change the electoral process in any way, what would you change and why?

The steps of the Capitol Building – where the Wearers of the Cloak of Invisibility reside when in session.

> The easiest way to win 'the Hunger Games'
>
> Is to put on that Cloak of Invisibility – Congress sure uses it well…

Works Cited

Axelrod, David. "Interview with Margaret Warner." *PBS NewsHour. http://www.pbs.org/newshour/vote2008/july-dec08/Axelrod_09-23.html.* Posted on 09/23/2008.

Bedard, Paul. "Media Sexism Doomed Hilary's 2008 Bid." *U.S. News. http://www.usnews.com/news/blogs/washington-whispers/2011/12/23/media-sexism-doomed-hillarys-2008-bid* . Posted 12/23/2011.

Bernstein, Jonathan. "Campaign Promises: What They Say Is How They Govern." *The Washington Monthly. http://www.washingtonmonthly.com/magazine/january_february_2012/features/campaign_promises034471.php?page=all* . Posted on 01/05/2013.

Best, Samuel J. and Brian S. Krveger. *Exit Polls: Surveying the American Electorate, 1927-2010.*

Brader, Ted. *Campaigning for Hearts and Minds: How Emotional Appeals in Political Ads Work.* Chicago: University of Chicago Press, 2006.

Caldwell, Leigh Ann. "When moderates fight back: GOP civil war could be brutal in 2014 elections." *CNN News. http://www.cnn.com/2013/11/06/politics/2014-republican-civil-war/* . Posted on 11/8/2013.

Cergol, Greg. "More Than 200 Dead People Shown To Have Voted in NY County Elections." *NBC News, New York. http://www.nbcnewyork.com/news/local/Dead-Voter-List-Long-Island-Nassau-County-Newsday-230030371.html* . Posted on 11/01/2013.

Collins (II), Christopher. "Voter Fraud, Illegal Activities Discovered in Several States." *The Examiner. http://www.examiner.com/article/voter-fraud-illegal-activities-reported-several-states.* Posted on 11/11/2012.

Collins, Suzanne. *The Hunger Games.* New York: Scholastic Press, 2009.

"Delegate Types Explained." *Boston Globe.* Posted 06/02/2008.

Dickerson, John. "Did President Obama Break His Health Care Promise?" *CBS News. http://www.cbsnews.com/news/did-president-obama-break-his-health-care-promise/* . Posted on 10/30/2013.

Engstrom, Erik J. *Partisan Gerrymandering and the Construction of American Democracy.* Ann Arbor: University of Michigan Press, 2013.

Green, Donald P. and Alan S. Gerber. *How to Increase Voter Turnout. Second Edition.* Washington, DC: The Brookings Institution, 2008.

Harding, Luke. "Numbers Nerd Nate Silver's Forecasts Prove All Right on Election Night." *The Guardian. http://www.theguardian.com/world/2012/nov/07/nate-silver-election-forecasts-right* . Posted on 11/07/2012.

Jacobs, Tom. "Was Sarah Palin's Image Hurt by Tina Fey? You Betcha!" *The Pacific Standard. http://www.psmag.com/politics/was-sarah-palins-image-hurt-by-tina-fey-you-betcha-40288/* . Posted on 03/08/2012

Jaime, Catherine McGrew. *Understanding Presidential Elections: The Constitution, Caucuses, Primaries, Electoral College, and More.* Madison: Creative Learning Connection, 2012.

Lewis, Michael. *Moneyball: The Art of Winning and Unfair Game.* New York: W. W. Norton & Company, 2004.

Maisel, L. Sandy. *American Political Parties and Elections: A Very Short Introduction.* Oxford: Oxford University Press, 2007.

Maisel, L. Sandy and Jeffrey M. Berry. *The Oxford Handbook of American Political Parties and Interest Groups.* Oxford: Oxford University Press, 2010.

Mehlman, Ken. Interview with Gwen Ifill. *PBS NewsHour.* http://www.pbs.org/newshour/bb/politics/july-dec05/mehlman_7-18.html. Posted on 07/18/2005.

Oliver, Willard and Nancy Marion. *Killing the President: Assassinations, Attempts, and Rumored Attempts on the U.S. Commander-in-Chief.* Santa Barbara: Praegar Books, 2010.

Polsby, Nelson W. and Aaron Wildvarsky. *Presidential Elections: Strategies and Structures of American Politics.* New York: Seven Bridges Press, 2000.

Randoll, Steve. Interview: *Moneyball* and Presidential Elections. 11/08/13.

Schoeder, Alan. "Not Perfect, but They Serve a Purpose." *The New York Times.* http://www.nytimes.com/roomfordebate/2012/10/02/a-better-approach-to-presidential-debates/criticisms-of-the-televised-debates-miss-the-point . Posted on 10/03/2012.

Sides, John. "Do Presidential Debates Really Matter?" *The Washington Monthy.* http://www.washingtonmonthly.com/magazine/septemberoctober_2012/ten_miles_square/do_presidential_debates_really039413.php?page=all . Posted on 09/05/2012.

Silver Nate. *The Signal and the Noise: Why So Many Predictions Fail, But Some Don't.* New York: Penguin Press, 2012.

Smith, Matt. "Long Lines but Few Snags in U.S. Elections." *CNN News. http://www.cnn.com/2012/11/06/politics/election-voting/* . Posted on 11/06/2012.

"What is the Electoral College?" *National Archives and Records Administration (NARA). http://www.archives.gov/federal-register/electoral-college/about.html.* NARA site last updated on 11/27/2013.

CHAPTER 11

The Elder Wand and the American Presidency: A Powerful Weapon for Those Who Win Its Allegiance

In the seventh installment of the Harry Potter series, *Harry Potter and the Deathly Hallows*, Harry, Ron, and Hermione (three characters that we met earlier in this book) come across a Wizarding fable in a book that was bequeathed to Hermione upon the death of Hogwarts' previous headmaster, Albus Dumbledore. The book, a collection of Wizarding fables, is entitled *The Tales of Beedle the Bard*. In the book is a story known as "The Tale of Three Brothers." As was mentioned before, it tells the story of three brothers who meet Death on a lonely road but who initially succeeded in evading him and are given prizes for having done so. The eldest brother, Antioch Peverell, receives the Elder Wand – the central object in this chapter. In the second chapter of this book, I argued that the Elder Wand and all of its characteristics can be used to understand the American presidency. In this chapter, I elaborate on that comparison to provide you with a deeper understanding of the institution that is the American presidency and all the trimmings that go along with it. First though, let's take a closer look at the fictional comparison, the Elder Wand, and the events that occur around and because of it.

The Elder Wand: In a Story, in Wizarding History, in Harry Potter's Present

The Elder Wand is perhaps the most discussed of the three Deathly Hallows as Rowling describes them in Beedle's "Tale of the Three Brothers" and also in the seventh installment of the Harry Potter Series, *Harry Potter and the Deathly Hallows*. The story in Beedle's book describes the Wand as immensely powerful, as a formidable weapon, and a tool worthy of someone who had done something that no one had yet done – conquered Death. Let us briefly delve deeper into the Elder Wand's history as described both in Beedle's tale and *Harry Potter and the Deathly Hallows*

"The Tale of Three Brothers"

The Elder Wand is described in the story as "a wand more powerful than any in existence, a wand that must always win duels for its owner," and "a wand worth of the man who had defeated Death" (Rowling BB, 88). The eldest brother and the original owner of the Elder Wand, Antioch Peverell, is described as "a combative man," and once he had possession of the Elder Wand, he sought out a wizard with whom he had quarreled. With the Elder Wand as his weapon, he could hardly lose and he left his murdered enemy's lifeless body dead upon the floor (Rowling BB, 89). The brother's combative nature enabled him to use the power of the Elder Wand to his own ends. It was his arrogance and stupidity, however, which caused his possession of the Elder Wand to become problematic.

Ultimately, one can argue that it was Antioch's possession of the Elder Wand that brought about his undoing. Soon after, in a bar nearby the place where he had murdered his erstwhile foe, the eldest brother bragged about the power the Elder Wand possessed and how the Wand made him invincible to any witch or wizard that stood in his way.

One of the bar's patrons overheard his boasting, and while Antioch lay asleep, the stranger stole the Wand and murdered the eldest brother. Ultimately, the power of the Elder Wand and Antioch's eagerness to boast about it cost him his life (Rowling BB, 88-89).

Harry Potter and the Deathly Hallows: History of the Wand and Its Owners

In Rowling's seventh installment of the Harry Potter series, Harry learns much concerning the Elder Wand. The first thing he learns is, of course, from Beedle's story, but he is then enlightened further by the man who was the first to expose them to the tale, Xenophilius Lovegood, their friend Luna's father. Xenophilius tells Harry that, contrary to popular belief, the Elder Wand is, in fact, real, and can be traced throughout Wizarding history. Xenophilius asserts that "the bloody trail of the Elder Wand is splattered across the pages of Wizarding history" (Rowling DH, 412).

Xenophilius also discusses how the Elder Wand has passed from owner to owner. He contends, as do many who study these matters, that the Elder Wand passes to a new owner upon the murder of the old possessor. Another authority on this subject, however, disagrees on this point. His name is Mr. Ollivander. Ollivander is known for making the finest magic wands in England (Rowling SS, 81-82) and is reputed to be one of the most knowledgeable wizards alive in the field of wandlore. Lord Voldemort, Harry's nemesis, sought Ollivander's knowledge and tortured him for information regarding the Elder Wand, its powers, and its whereabouts.

After a scenario where Harry indirectly rescues Ollivander from certain death at Malfoy Manor, the home of Harry's nemesis at school, Draco Malfoy, Ollivander tells Harry everything that he related to Voldemort. Ollivander tells Harry that he told Voldemort that the Wand passes from wizard to wizard upon the *defeat* of its previous owner. Voldemort interprets this to mean that *murdering* the Wand's previous owner is necessary in order for the Wand to be truly his, but Voldemort misunderstood what Ollivander said.

Mr. Ollivander – the wandmaker, the scholarly authority on the Elder Wand

When Harry saved Ollivander, he captured Draco Malfoy's wand. Harry asks Ollivander if he can safely use it, and Ollivander indicates that, yes – he can, because he sensed that Draco's wand had shifted its allegiance to Harry. Harry points out that Ollivander "speaks about wants as if they've got feelings" (Rowling DH, 493). Ollivander, throughout the series, insists that, "the wand chooses the wizard" (Rowling SS, 85). He contends that wands ally themselves with their owners and only upon their defeat will a wand's allegiance change; he does not agree with Xenophilius' assertion that murder is necessary to gain a wand's allegiance – only the *defeat* of its previous master (Rowling DH, 494-495).

The Elder Wand, in the history described in *Harry Potter and the Deathly Hallows*, denotes the five most recent owners of the Elder Wand. The first of these was Gregorovitch, a Bulgarian wandmaker and Ollivander's competition in the market of wand-making. According to Ollivander, it was rumored that Gregorovitch had captured and began replicating the qualities of the Elder Wand in the products he himself sold so as to become wealthy (Rowling DH, 498).

Harry deduces that the next owner of the Elder Wand, Gellert Grindelwald, had stolen the Wand from Gregorovitch (Rowling DH, 499) and sought to use it to bring the lower rungs of Wizarding society (half-blood wizards and other magical creatures like house elves) under a regime which only recognized 'pure blood wizards' as worthy of living (Rowling DH, 716). However, only one wizard stood in his way to prevent this autocratic,

Albus Dumbledore – taming the Wand to save others from it's allure

tyrannical regime, Albus Dumbledore, a man who had once been Grindelwald's best friend (Rowling DH, 716).

Dumbledore, unlike the other possessors of the Wand, decided that he was able to possess it in order to "tame it and use it, not for gain, but to save others from it" (Rowling DH, 720). He kept and used the Wand for the causes of Good for the greater part of his life, but was in the end, defeated by a man

Draco Malfoy, not Severus Snape, the wizard who defeated Dumbledore and won the allegiance of the Elder Wand

less than one-third of his age, Draco Malfoy. Upon being sent to kill Dumbledore, a task which he did not (and seemingly could not) perform, Malfoy Disarmed Dumbledore with the *Expelliarmus* spell; thus, Dumbledore was defeated and the Elder Wand's allegiance passed to a new bearer.

Malfoy, however, remained unaware that he had gained the allegiance of the most powerful wand in existence (Rowling DH, 742). Instead, the rumor went out through Voldemort's servants, the Death Eaters – who witnessed Dumbledore's murder, that Severus Snape, Hogwarts' Potion Master and Voldemort's most trusted servant, had killed Dumbledore. Voldemort then assumed that since Dumbledore was murdered by Snape, that the Elder Wand had given Snape its allegiance and only by murdering Snape could he, Voldemort, become the true master of the Elder Wand.

When Harry rescued Ollivander at Malfoy's mansion, Harry dueled Malfoy and won. This occurred after Dumbledore's murder, so, though no one knew it at the time, the Elder Wand had shifted its allegiance away from Draco Malfoy to Harry Potter – the boy-hero seeking to defeat Voldemort, the wizard seeking to obtain the Elder Wand so as to defeat Harry Potter. When Voldemort and Harry square off in a final duel at the end of *Deathly Hallows*, the Elder Wand's allegiance that Harry now possessed protected him from Voldemort's Killing Curse. The Elder Wand killed the wizard to whom it has not given its allegiance – Voldemort, and the threat of Voldemort and his tyrannical regime was ended (Rowling DH, 743-744).

At the end of the novel, Harry's knowledge of the Elder Wand was enough for him to want to put an end to the problems it has caused throughout Wizarding history and, most particularly, in his own lifetime. Harry decides to return the wand to its former home – Dumbledore's grave – and to let it stay there for eternity. Upon Harry's death (assuming that no one defeats him during his life's du-

Harry Potter, the last master of the Elder Wand – who gives it up to end the Wand's power

ration), the power of the Elder Wand will die and its threat will be gone forever. Despite Ron and Hermione's protests, Harry goes through with this plan after repairing the wand he had used his whole life – his wand made of holly with a core of a phoenix feather (Rowling DH, 748-749).

The Elder Wand and the American Presidency

The Elder Wand is, as noted before, the most powerful wand ever made. It is a formidable weapon that passes from hand to hand by defeating the Wand's previous owner, and upon defeat, the Wand shifts it allegiance to its new owner. The whereabouts of the Wand are traceable throughout Wizarding history. Finally, there is a history of succession – a list of whom, most recently, had the Elder Wand and why a changing of hands occurred.

All of these things are comparable to the American presidency. Just as the Elder Wand is the most powerful wand ever made, so too is the president of the United States one of the most powerful (if not *the* most powerful) person in the world. Just as there are countless stories of how wizards have obtained the power of the Elder Wand, there are also theories that attempt to identify how presidents gain their power. The Elder Wand, a formidable weapon, is comparable to the

United States Armed Forces over which the president has authority because of his role as Commander-in-Chief. Finally, Wizarding history and the final installment of the Harry Potter series illustrate for us a historical outline of the last five owners of the Elder Wand; so, too, is there a line of succession when a president dies, is assassinated, or is removed from office by some other means.

The Elder Wand and Presidential Power

"The Tale of Three Brothers" indicates that the Elder Wand, created by Death for the eldest of the three brothers was "a wand more powerful than any in existence, a wand that must always win duels for its owner. It is a wand worthy of one who had defeated Death" (Rowling BB, 88). Beedle, the author of the tale, is quick to note the *power* the Elder Wand possesses. He further notes that it is more powerful than any wand ever made before. I contend that the immense power of the Elder Wand is comparable to the power allotted to the president of the United States through his **expressed powers** – the powers given to the president by constitutional design and his **implied** or **inherent powers** – the powers the president has claimed for himself over time due to the vagueness of the Executive Clause.

The Oval Office: the seat of presidential power

Expressed Powers

The Elder Wand was *given* to the eldest brother, Antioch, by Death. Similarly, the president's expressed powers are *given* to him by the mandate expressed in the Constitution. The powers allotted to the president via the Constitution range from legislative powers to diplomatic powers, from judicial powers to political powers, and so on.

Legislative Powers

The president's most widely acknowledged powers allot him the ability to affect what legislation that has been passed by Congress becomes law. These are known as the president's **legislative powers.** These powers enable the president to approve or deny the passage of legislation that Congress writes and passes. If a president chooses to approve a bill, he will sign it. If the president chooses to deny a bill's passage – that is, **veto** the bill, which prevents the bill from becoming law – then typically the bill goes back to Congress along with reasons why the president denied its passage. The president can also use another tactic if the bill comes to the Oval Office at the end of a congressional session, namely, a **pocket veto.**

Traditionally speaking, bills that sit on a president's desk for ten days without a response by the president during a session of Congress automatically become law without the president's signature. For a pocket veto to occur, the bill must come to the president's desk and sit there for at least some period of time that Congress is *not* in session during those ten days. If that occurs, the president can use the pocket veto power. The only way Congress can prevent a pocket veto is to have a member of Congress stay behind to collect presidential vetoes – a tactic that has become more common over time.

Presidents seem to be more apt to use pocket vetoes when the bill they seek to kill is controversial. If the president were to sign it, he would upset roughly half of the population. If the president were to veto the bill, the other half of the American public would be up in arms. The pocket veto is a tool the president can use to minimize the amount of political damage that could result from the passage or rejection of controversial legislation that Congress passes.

Another tool presidents have used to shape legislation is something known as a **signing statement.** Unlike a **line-item veto**, a tool where the president selects parts of taxation or other monetary legislation that he will *not* enforce, a signing statement is where a president makes notes on signed laws about what parts of the law the president will put particular emphasis on or notes on constitutional limitations or directives regarding the new law. Some argue that presidents have used signing statements to modify the original intent of legislation (Shear, 1) – much like the line-item veto – but signing statements, at least currently, are still considered to be one of the tools available to presidents which enable them to shape policy.

Diplomatic Powers

The president, as the executive officer of the United States, is expected to meet with the leaders of foreign countries to discuss events going on across the globe and also to settle any grievances that might arise. The president has the power to make **executive agreements** – accords with foreign countries that assert that two or more nations will not enter a state of warfare. Executive agreements are eerily similar to treaties – the sole difference being that Congress must authorize a treaty while an executive agreement does not require congressional approval. Some of the agreements that the president enters into with foreign powers have nothing to do with warfare; instead, some of the discussions foreign leaders have deal with protecting the environment, international trade, the preservation of human dignity through the prevention of human rights violations, and so on. The interactions the president has, therefore, should not be assumed to be exclusively about whether or not to blow someone up. Often,

President George W. Bush meeting allies in Israel as America's chief diplomat

however, warfare relating to the United States or one of its allies is the topic of discussion.

Should treaties or executive agreements fail to prevent military conflict, the president is free to utilize his expressed powers as Commander-in-Chief and has the final say-so in any military action. The president can send troops into combat without congressional approval but can only keep them in action for 90 days without seeking the consent of Congress to continue the military campaign. Generally speaking, Congress typically supports the continuing of military action so as to prevent the troops in that region from becoming more vulnerable.

Influencing Economic Stability and Growth

Another expressed power that is allotted to the president is the power to influence the American economy. This is not directly addressed per se in the Constitution, but two other presidential responsibilities are. First, the president has to propose a budget; a president's willingness to spend or save arguably can have a tremendous impact on the American economy. Second, the president is required, after the first of the year, to present his views regarding America's current status and an agenda to Congress that hopefully Congress will aid in implementing over the coming years; we know this address as the Presidential State of the Union Address.

Both of these tools can be used to present the case for more spending, an act which typically increases our national debt or **deficit** or for more saving which could create an economic **surplus** – an excess of funds. Typically, another economic topic that presidents address in these two presentations is a plan for national taxation. If the economy is poor, presidents (especially Democrats) propose tax increases so as to raise more money to curb the national debt and fund programs that the government and the American public deem to be necessary (Jones, 1-3). In times where a surplus exists, presidents tend to propose tax cuts since the government appears to be taking in more money than the government needs to operate (Philips, 1-2).

An important thing to point out here is that while the president has the ability to make suggestions regarding the economy by proposing a budget or giving the annual State of the Union Address, the president's ability to directly affect the economy is extremely limited if not nonexistent. Many people seem to blame presidents for economic troubles that plague the country, but this is one area where blame seems to be misplaced (Cass, 1-4). The body with real influence over the economy is Congress and the Federal Reserve – our national bank which is, ironically, independent of government control.

Political Power

Another power given to the president is his political power. Traditionally speaking, the president of the United States also serves as the leader of his political party. President Obama, during the duration of his presidency, will continue to serve as the leader of the Democratic Party and will continue, in a real and noticeable manner, to shape the agenda of the Democratic Party. Also, the presidential nominee who lost in the previous election also serves as the leader of the other party. It is important to note, however, that the leader of the opposition party only serves as a ceremonial leader whereas the president plays an active role in shaping his party's agenda and working toward its policy objectives (Reiter, 1). The president also serves as a very real symbol of his party. If the president's performance is perceived to be good, the party is likely to be perceived in a positive manner. Conversely, if the president has a tough time keeping campaign promises, the party will likely suffer because of the president's perceived failure.

Executive Powers

The president, while an exceptionally powerful individual, is only one element of the Executive Branch. The president's Cabinet, the joint-chiefs of staff, much of the federal bureaucracy, and other influential bodies are considered to be elements of the Executive Branch. The president must learn to work with, take advice from, and compromise with these individuals and groups in order to be perceived as a successful president. This power of the president, ironically, amounts to the president admitting, perhaps indirectly, that there are some instances when advice and added support augment the position of power rather than limit it. Many presidents have failed to take advantage of their advisors' wisdom and have consequently been labeled as presidential failures for neglecting advice and making poor decisions.

The president works closely with a number of groups. One worth mentioning is the Office of the President; this bureaucratic agency is responsible for the implementation of the policies that the president signs into law and encompasses a wide array of other important elements of the bureaucracy including the Office of Management and Budget (OMB), the White House Office, the National Security Council, and the Council of Economic Advisors. These agencies not only help the president fulfill job obligations but also give direction to other government bodies regarding the implementation both of laws that are new but also laws that have been on the books for some time.

All of these powers are – either directly or indirectly – allotted to the president someplace within the Constitution. The president is expected to adhere to these specifications and operate within their parameters. Other powers, however, have been accrued by past presidents over time. Some of these powers fit into the other form of presidential powers – inherent powers.

Inherent Powers

While Death gave the eldest brother the Elder Wand in "The Tale of Three Brothers," every owner after him had *taken* the Wand – either by force or by defeat – from its previous owner. Similarly, while some powers that the president possesses are given through constitutional mandate, the president has taken and claimed other powers for himself over time. These are known as **implied** or **inherent powers.** The president, over time, has been able to garner more power through the application of a specific clause in the Constitution – the Executive or 'Take Care' Clause. This Clause states that the president must 'take care' to ensure that the laws are executed. Presidents, through the aid of the Supreme Court, have expanded presidential power by noting the vagueness of the scope of presidential power. Because presidents have used the Take Care Clause to claim more power for the office, we can conclude that presidential power, through a president's implied or inherent powers, have expanded over time.

One implied power that presidents have claimed for the office is the ability to write **executive orders** – presidential directives that carry the same weight as congressional bills that the president has signed into law. Some people consider executive orders to outside the application of the Take Care Clause, but the Supreme Court, at least as of yet, has allowed presidents to use executive orders in the recent and not so recent past. Some presidents use executive orders more than others, but they have been and likely will continue to be tools that presidents will use to shape the American political, social, and cultural landscape.

Another implied power that is widely debated among the American public is a president's right to **executive privilege** – the ability of a president to keep information discussed with close advisors secret from Congress and the courts. Presidents derive this power from the Founder's separation of powers concept; if the branches of government were intended to be, at least in part, separate, then certainly each branch of government has the right to withhold certain information from the others (Rozell, 21, 23). Some contend that executive privilege allows presidents to say and do things that the American public won't agree with and are unable to hold them accountable for (Napolitano, 1-2), but presidents seem more than willing to use this power nevertheless.

Sources of Presidential Power

In the Harry Potter series, numerous characters make arguments regarding how the Elder Wand passes from hand to hand. Mr. Ollivander teaches Harry the secret of wand transfer – "the wand chooses the wizard." To gain a wand's allegiance, you have to *earn* it either by defeating the previous owner or, in extreme circumstances, by killing the wand's current master. Xenophilius Lovegood contends that, while there are notable gaps in the Wand's whereabouts, the Wand appears in numerous places in Wizarding history – typically periods of turmoil, and one master of the Wand (typically a tyrant) loses the Wand to one who seeks to restore peace (just as Dumbledore won the Elder Wand from Grindelwald and intended its power to die with him). The same is true of the acquisition of presidential power. Some believe presidents must *earn* their power while others believe that the acquisition of presidential power is the product of historical circumstance.

Richard Neustadt: Power Through Persuasion

In his book *Presidential Power and the Modern Presidents*, Neustadt, like Ollivander, contends that presidential power and greatness is earned, not given. He contends that a great president will gain power through his ability to persuade the people around him to support his agenda. The book Neustadt wrote encompasses his theory of the acquisition of presidential power. His book addresses the modern presidents – those holding office from the time of Franklin Roosevelt to present (Neustadt, 3-9).

In his book, Neustadt concludes that presidents since the time of Franklin Roosevelt have had more to deal with in terms of negotiation than previous presidents. The expansion of the federal bureaucracy due to the creation of the New Deal greatly expanded the size of the executive branch and thus, presidents inherited a new group of people with which he has to contend in his policy battles. Not only do presidents have to convince the American public, both political parties (or a majority of their members), Congress, and the courts to

The power to persuade, the willingness to compromise, and one's reputation lead to the expansion of presidential power.

support his agenda – now he has to encourage the thousands of people working under him as fellow members of the executive branch to support his policy prerogatives. That is a tall order indeed. For a president to be truly great, Neustadt argues that a president has to garner support from most or all of these groups (Neustadt, 4-5).

Some of a president's ability to work with the folks in Washington depends on his "professional reputation" (Neustadt, 50-51). His professional reputation is essentially how the folks in Washington perceive the president on a professional level. Is he willing to compromise and work with both political parties? Are there some issues that the president is unwilling to compromise on? Are there issues that the president's position is firm? Is he reliable? Is he trustworthy? Is he 'presidential' or does he behave like most would argue that a president should act? All of these things go into the interpretation of a president's professional reputation. A positive reputation, argues Neustadt, makes it easier for the president to get his way; a poor professional reputation makes it more difficult for the president to get the folks in Washington to take him and his agenda seriously (Neustadt, 50-52).

Neustadt, while arguing that effective persuasion among political figures inside the government is important, puts a significant amount of emphasis on public support of the president or his 'prestige' (Neustadt, 73-74). By public prestige, I mean how the American people regard the president. Although the public's opinion of the president has no direct impact on policymaking, some believe that widespread support of a president constitutes a 'public mandate' – the American public's indirect assent to the president's proposed agenda (Leuchtenburg, 1-3).

Just as Ollivander argued that a wand's allegiance must be won for the wand in question to work properly, so too does Neustadt contend that a president must win the allegiance of a wide array of people to ensure that his agenda is taken seriously and implemented during his duration in office. While persuasion is definitely one important thing that shapes a president's success and perceived greatness, historical circumstance certainly plays a part as well.

The Power Presidents Make: History, Turmoil, and the Cycle of Political Regimes

Xenophilius Lovegood told Harry Potter that the Elder Wand was traceable throughout Wizarding history. Ollivander elaborated on that and notes that there were long gaps between time periods when the Wand surfaced but that the Elder Wand assuredly was a real object that had been passed down through the centuries by one master of the wand being defeated by the new owner. Similarly, one can argue that great presidents surface during times of historical, political, societal, or cultural distress. While other presidents fill the void that is the rest of history, great presidents are often most easily recognized by rectifying problems thrust upon America during traumatic periods of its history. This is essentially the argument that Stephen Skowronek makes in his book *The Politics*

Two conceptions of time: linear (secular) and cyclical (political)

Presidents Make: Leadership from John Adams to Bill Clinton. There are a number of things that make Skowronek's theory notable. The first is his two conceptions of concurrent time. The second is his defining of a **political cycle** or **political regime.** The third is his description of the presidents that build up and tear down these regimes and thus denote presidential greatness.

Conceptions of Time

In his book, Skowronek discusses two different conceptions of time. The first form of time is one that we would recognize as 'regular time'. This is where tomorrow follows today, next week follows this week, and next year follows this year. This form of time is *linear* and is constantly moving forward in a straight line. Skowronek calls this form of time **secular time** as its meaning is widely recognized among the public. In this book, we will refer to it, however, as *chronological time* as it moves forward like the clock does (Skowronek, 30, 55).

The other form of time discussed in Skowronek's book is one he invents himself. He calls it **political time** and argues that, unlike secular time, political time is *cyclical*; in other words, political time *repeats itself.* In each cycle of political time exists a phenomenon that Skowronek identifies as a **political cycle.** Here, we will refer to these cycles as *political regimes.* Political regimes are groups of presidents, generally spanning between 30 and 40 years, which share similar leadership techniques, ideological tendencies, or personality traits (Skowronek, 49-52, 55-58). Skowronek argues that, in each cycle of political time, three different kinds of presidents emerge: presidents of reconstruction, articulation, and disjunction. Rather than being dependent on the use of their own unique skills as Neustadt argues, Skowronek concludes that historical circumstance is more responsible for determining presidential power and greatness (Skowronek, 58).

Reconstruction, Articulation, and Disjunction

A **president of reconstruction,** according to Skowronek, is the president who builds up a new political regime and garners public and political support for it (36-39). Presidents like Thomas Jefferson, Andrew Jackson, Abraham Lincoln, and Franklin Roosevelt fit into this category (Skowronek, 62-85, 130-154, 198-227, 288-324). The next set of presidents, the **presidents of articulation**, mimic and build upon the ideas and attitudes set up by the presidents

I think Skowronek would agree with this - that the pages of American history are filled with the tales of men who insist upon repeating it.

of reconstruction (Skowronek, 41-43). Some presidents who fit into this category are James Monroe and Theodore Roosevelt (Skowronek, 86-109, 228-259). Finally, the last type of president that exists in a political regime is the **president of disjunction.** These presidents make the current political regime look bad and pave the way for the destruction of the current political regime and the rise of a new one (Skowronek, 39-41). Presidents who fit into this category are John Quincy Adams and Herbert Hoover (Skowronek, 110-127, 260-285).

Interestingly enough, it seems as if the 'great' presidents, the presidents of reconstruction, serve during a transitional period in history that moves away from turmoil and toward prosperity. Most Americans associate Andrew Jackson as the first accessible president – a man of the people. Most would associate Lincoln as the president that resolved the slavery and states' rights issues. Yet others label Franklin Roosevelt as the president that got us out of the Great Depression. All of these presidents are known for lifting America out of some sort of predicament that faced our nation during the time of their tenure in office. Skowronek's assertion that history plays a role in shaping the public's perception of presidential greatness appears, in a very real sense, to be exceptionally valid.

While Ollivander believed that the Elder Wand's allegiance had to be earned, Death mockingly gave the eldest brother the Elder Wand which, at least indirectly, suggests that power can be given. If you look at the two theories here that discuss the acquisition of presidential power, we see two views very similar to those described in *Harry Potter and the Deathly Hallows* and "The Tale of Three Brothers." One theorist, Neustadt, argues that presidential power and notoriety is earned through the power of persuasion, the garnering of public support, and the establishment of a well-known professional reputation. The other political scholar, Skowronek, argues that historical evolution hands certain presidents greater opportunities to become great – particularly those who serve during times of political upheaval. Presidents can either rise to the occasion during those times or risk the possibility of being forgotten.

The History of the Elder Wand and the Presidential Line of Succession

In *Harry Potter and the Deathly Hallows*, we are made aware of the last five owners of the Elder Wand and how the Wand changed hands. Gregorovitch, the wandmaker, lost the Wand to Gellert Grindelwald who stole it from his window-side nightstand. Grindelwald was defeated by Albus Dumbledore in an epic duel; the allegiance of the wand shifted then to Dumbledore. Dumbledore was Disarmed and defeated by Draco Malfoy; he became the Wand's new owner but remained unaware of it. Finally, Harry dueled and defeated Draco thus gaining the allegiance of the Elder Wand. *Deathly Hallows* indicates that if Harry Potter remains undefeated in his lifetime, that the power of the Elder Wand will end.

Just as there is a historical precedent in the Harry Potter series for the possession of the Elder Wand, so too is there precedent for who should assume the American presidency should the serving president die or become unable to carry out the duties. If a president dies, tradition (and the Presidential Succession Law of 1947) dictates that the vice president should assume the former president's duties. The line of succession continues and includes (in order) the Speaker of the House, the president pro tem in the Senate, the Secretary of State, the Secretary of the Treasury, the secretary of defense, the attorney general, and so on. All of these apply if the president *dies* in office. The link of succession, until the ratification of the Twenty-Fifth Amendment, was not so clear if the president lived but was unable to perform the duties.

When President Garfield was assassinated, he lived for two months before he finally died; during those two months, it was unclear who should be functioning as the acting president. The same was true at the end of Franklin Roosevelt's presidency; his ailments incapacitated him and appeared to inhibit his ability to govern as well. The Twenty-Fifth Amendment mandates that if a president believes himself incapable of fulfilling the duties, the president should notify Congress and the vice president would assume the president's duties until such a time (if any) that the president was healthy enough to carry out the duties.

Just as there is historical evidence that identifies a line of wizards who had possessed the Elder Wand, there is also a line of succession

The president of the United States: the true master of the Elder Wand...until it is won by his replacement.

for the office of the presidency, the human comparison to the esteemed magical object given to Antioch Peverell, the eldest brother in Beedle's tale. The power of both the Elder Wand and also the American presidency is a force to be reckoned with; some meet this power in the Oval Office while others encounter the president's power and massive presence on foreign soil. The president of the United States is the true master of the Elder Wand – until it is won by his replacement.

Food for Thought

Presidential Power

Is the presidency too powerful for its own good and for ours? What sort of reasons should a president have to veto a bill passed by Congress? Should the reasons be solely political or should there be some sort of concrete, pragmatic reasons to back presidential vetoes? If Congress knows that pocket vetoes are more likely to occur both in regards to controversial bills and happen at the end of congressional sessions, why does Congress typically save the controversial bills for last? What is the difference between a line-item veto and a signing statement, and what makes a line-item veto unconstitutional but a signing statement legal?

Why are executive agreements more common than treaties? Have treaties become obsolete or has the presidency been indirectly delegated this power by Congress? How influential is the president as Commander-in-Chief? How much say-so does the president have, do you think, over the military generals and commanders who spend their lives studying warfare? The president is our head of state as well as head of government; what kind of a person, do you think, should go abroad to speak for us? Should the president be stern or more diplomatic, or is there a happy medium to achieve in order to be an effective world leader?

Why do average Americans tend to blame the president for economic problems? If the president has essentially no active role in shaping America's economy, why does he even make propositions on how to fix or maintain it in his budget proposals and State of the Union Addresses? Do you think the economy is impacted much by government interference? If so, can the credit for proposals passed by Congress but proposed by the president that backfire be attributed solely to the president?

The president is considered to be the head of his political party. Do you think presidents actively play this role, or do political parties simply follow the lead of the president? Do you think presidents necessarily need to fill this role, or should they be more focused on governing? Why is it that the winner – the person who becomes president – has an active say-so in a political party's agenda whereas the loser of the presidential election – the leader of the opposition party – serves only a ceremonial role? Is it because this person is perceived to be a failure and thus his agenda is one that failed to resonate with Americans or is it something that can simply be attributed to tradition?

The president is only one element of the Executive Branch. The president must learn to work with, take advice from, and issue orders to the rest of this branch of government. What should the president's role be as head of the Executive Branch? Do you think presidents who work with the bureaucracy – an extension of the Executive Branch – are more successful than presidents who insist on having things done their way? With members of both political parties serving as bureaucratic agents, are cooperation and compromise necessary tools that successful presidents must possess?

While some powers are allotted the president via the Constitution, presidents have claimed powers over time due to the vagueness of the Executive Clause and, more specifically, the 'Take Care' Clause. Have these implied or inherent powers of the president been allowed to expand presidential power too far? How can future presidents and the Supreme Court determine how far to allow implied powers to expand? How can we ensure that future presidents don't use their implied powers to inhibit democracy but foster autocracy? Do you think the rise of autocratic rule through the use of a president's implied powers is a real threat? If so, what should be done to inhibit the further expansion of presidential power?

Sources of Presidential Power

Which do you think plays a larger role in a president's success, to date: his ability to get people to work with him or historical circumstance? Neustadt contends that as the federal government grows, so too does the need for a persuasive, cooperative, likable president. Do you think Neustadt is correct, or do you think he sets too much store in a president's personal skills and not enough in outside influences? Neustadt argues that the public's perception of the president has little real impact on policy; do you think he is correct, or do you think the president gains support for his agenda through a public mandate attained upon election?

Skowronek identifies two kinds of time: secular time (chronological time) and political time (cyclical time). Do you believe that history repeats itself as Skowronek argues or is repetition in history mere coincidence? Do you think, as Skowronek alleges, that groups of presidents have similar governing styles, agendas, ideological tendencies, or personal traits, or is he looking too hard at America's presidents? We have only had forty-four presidents; is that too few to start assessing patterns as Skowronek is trying to do? Skowronek describes the three types of presidents that exist in each cycle of political time – reconstruction, articulation, and disjuncture. Do you think there can be more than one president in each type per cycle of political time? If so, which type of president has manifested itself the most?

Presidential Succession

Why didn't the Founders deal with presidential succession in the original text of the Constitution? Why did it take our government so long to amend the Constitution to establish a plan for presidential succession? After the vice president, do you think a special election should be held to elect a new president or is the line of succession as it stands okay? Might there be major political implications if the Speaker of the House was to become president but belonged to the party that opposed that of the president? What would such a change do to the dynamic of American politics?

Who wants an unbeatable wand when you can bring the dead back to life?

Works Cited

Cass, Connie. "Many Voters Still Blame Bush for Bad Economy." *Yahoo News. http://news.yahoo.com/many-voters-still-blame-bush-bad-economy-005118068--election.html.* Posted on 11/06/2012.

Jones, Susan. "Obama Will Insist on Tax Hikes in Budget Deal." *CNN News. http://cnsnews.com/news/article/susan-jones/obama-will-insist-tax-hikes-budget-deal.* Posted on 10/17/13.

Leuchtenburg, William E. "The Power in a President's Mandate." *Yahoo! Canada News. http://ca.news.yahoo.com/power-presidents-mandate-142710304.html.* Posted on 10/16/2013.

Napolitano, Judge Andrew P. "President Obama, Attorney General Holder, and Executive Privilege." *Fox News. http://www.foxnews.com/opinion/2012/06/20/president-obama-attorney-general-holder-and-executive-privilege/.* Posted on 06/20/2012.

Neustadt, Richard E. *Presidential Power and the Modern Presidents.* New York: Macmillan Publishing Company, 1990.

Philips, Anne. "How the Clinton Surplus Led to the Bush Tax Cuts (Or, the Real Story You Might Not Be Hearing About the Fiscal Cliff)." *The Huffington Post: Business. http://www.huffingtonpost.com/anne-phillips/fiscal-cliff-bush-tax-cuts_b_2234324.html.* Posted on 12/10/2012.

Reiter, Howard L. "Power: President as Party Leader." *The Courant. http://articles.courant.com/2000-09-10/news/0009101184_1_party-system-president-as-party-leader-congress.* Posted on 09/10/2000.

Rowling, J. K. (BB). *The Tales of Beedle the Bard.* New York: Scholastic Books, 2008.

Rowling, J. K. (DH). *Harry Potter and the Deathly Hallows.* New York: Arthur A. Levine Books, 2007.

Rowling, J. K. (SS). *Harry Potter and the Sorcerer's Stone.* New York: Arthur A. Levine Books, 1997.

Rozell, Mark J. *Executive Privilege: Presidential Power, Secrecy, and Accountability (Studies in Government and Public Policy). 2nd Edition.* Lawrence: University Press of Kansas, 2010.

Shear, Michael D. "Obama Pledges Sparing Use of Signing Statements." *The Washington Post. http://www.washingtonpost.com/wp-dyn/content/article/2009/03/09/AR2009030902135.html.* Posted on 03/10/2009.

Skowronek, Stephen. *The Politics Presidents Make: Leadership from John Adams to Bill Clinton.* Cambridge: Bellknap Press, 1997.

CHAPTER 12

The Resurrection Stone and the Judicial Branch: Bringing the Dead Back to Life

How many of you have ever wished that you could have said something to or done something for to a loved one who has died? Which of you wouldn't give up something (in some cases, anything) to see or talk to someone you loved who is no longer with us? What about spending time with them, laughing with them, maybe even crying with them? I venture to say that, in almost every person's life, there's at least one person – if we could do things over again – that we would love to bring back from the dead so as to do one or many of these things.

In "The Tale of Three Brothers," the second brother, Cadmus Peverell, asks Death for the power to do just that – the ability to bring people back from the dead; Death assented, plucked a pebble from the riverbank nearby, gave it to the second brother, and told him that the stone would have the ability to recall people from the grave. Except that it didn't – not really. The stone, known as the Resurrection Stone, only brought back pale shadows of individuals who had died. Because they were not truly alive, the living were prevented from fully enjoying the company of those recalled from death, and this distorted reality was ultimately Cadmus Peverell's undoing.

The power of the Resurrection Stone, bringing people back from the dead – from a certain perspective – is what the Judicial Branch is charged to do. By considering the Constitution, the writings of the Founding Fathers, and **legal precedent** – decisions the Court

The Resurrection Stone – the ability to bring back the dead

have passed down since the inception of our country, the judicial system 'brings back the dead' with every decision they render. In this chapter, I investigate the comparisons between the Resurrection Stone and the Judicial Branch that exist both in relation to what we know about the Stone as described in "The Tale of Three Brothers" and also as it's discussed in *Harry Potter and the Deathly Hallows.*

The Resurrection Stone: Bringing the Dead Back to Life

We encounter the Resurrection Stone on a number of occasions in the Harry Potter series, but most of these occur in the seventh installment of the series – *Harry Potter and the Deathly Hallows.* The first important encounter is, of course, in "The Tale of Three Brothers" – where Harry learns about the potential existence of the Resurrection Stone. It is later on in *Harry Potter and the Deathly Hallows* that Harry discovers the Stone's whereabouts, what it does, and what Albus Dumbledore intended Harry to do with the Stone. All of these things will serve as important comparisons later in this chapter to some element of the Judicial Branch. First though, let's look at the Resurrection Stone as it's described in the "The Tale of Three Brothers" and in *Harry Potter and the Deathly Hallows.*

"The Tale of Three Brothers"

The first thing we discover in Beedle's tale is that the second brother, Cadmus, asked for the Resurrection Stone out of *arrogance* in an attempt to humiliate Death (Rowling BB, 89). By giving the Stone the power to negate death, Cadmus thought he was being given the ability to negate Death's power and influence. Death gave the second brother this ability through the Resurrection Stone nevertheless by selecting a stone from the riverbank and presenting it to him (Rowling BB, 89).

Cadmus Peverell took the Stone to his home and sought to recall a former sweetheart from the grave – a woman he had once hoped to marry. For the Stone to work, he had to *turn it over three times in his hand.* It was then that the second brother discovered that the Stone doesn't really bring the dead back to life as we know it; instead, what returns to the living world is more like an echo or a shadow of the dead person's image – more than ghost but less than a living being...which was what the second brother actually intended to bring back. Cadmus, upon recalling his sweetheart from death, assumed that she would be as she was when she lived, but he was sadly mistaken; the tale describes her as "sad and cold and separated from him as if by a veil." His inability to act and communicate with her in the ways that he used to ultimately drives him mad, and he commits suicide so as to join his sweetheart in the way he had actually intended – totally (Rowling BB, 91-92).

Harry Potter and the Deathly Hallows

In Rowling's seventh installment of the Harry Potter series, not only do we follow Harry Potter's quest to destroy Lord Voldemort's Horcruxes (magical objects in which Voldemort has encased part of his soul through numerous acts of murder), we also find out a great deal about Harry's parents and also, the headmaster of Hogwarts during Harry's tenure at school, Albus Dumbledore. We discover that events in Dumbledore's young life led to the death of his younger sister, Ariana, and his lifestyle since her death was, some would surely argue, a desperate attempt to try and make things right (Rowling DH, 714-718).

The Deathly Hallows – the thing that united Grindelwald and Dumbledore

In his younger years, Dumbledore befriended a foreign wizard who had come to visit one of his neighbors, Bathilda Bagshot, and his name was Gellert Grindelwald. Both Dumbledore and Grindelwald were considered to be exceptionally bright and destined to do great things. These two young men, however, had their own ideas of what greatness was. Amidst trying to whip up a following that would bring about the rule of Wizard-kind and the suppression of half-breeds and non-magical beings, Dumbledore and Grindelwald – above all – sought to find and unite the Deathly Hallows (Rowling DH, 716-717).

At the end of the book, Dumbledore gives Harry a firsthand account of the days of his youth and asserts that, despite his misgivings, he thought he recognized Grindewald's evil nature before the rest of the Wizarding world did. He believed Grindelwald wanted to use the Resurrection Stone to create an army of Inferi – dead bodies animated by a Dark wizard to do their bidding – to drive the Wizarding world into submission. Dumbledore, on the other hand, felt that he was responsible for his sister Ariana's death which was the end result of a duel that began with Grindelwald torturing Dumbledore's brother, Aberforth (Rowling DH, 566-567). Before Ariana's death, Dumbledore sought to use the Stone to bring his parents back and relieve himself of the responsibility of raising his sister. After her death, however, Dumbledore desperately sought to find and use the Stone to summon his family back so he could apologize for his mistakes and attempt to make amends (Rowling DH, 719-720).

Years after the duel that killed Dumbedore's sister, the headmaster of Hogwarts discovered one of Voldemort's Horcruxes hidden in the abandoned shack that had once housed his only living relatives – the Gaunts. The Horcrux Dumbledore found was a ring with a large black stone set in its center. Only later did Dumbledore recognize the stone as one of the items comprising the Deathly Hallows, for he noticed that the symbol of the Hallows had been etched into the Stone's surface. Dumbledore, imagining that he was about to see Ariana and his family, had attempted to use the Resurrection Stone and bring his family back to apologize. He, in his eagerness to use the Stone, forgot that the ring had been turned into a Horcrux by Voldemort and likely carried a terrible curse – which it did. The curse upon the ring was an immensely powerful one and while the curse was trapped in Dumbledore's hand by Hogwarts' long-time Potions Master, Severus Snape, he tells Dumbledore that the curse will ultimately kill him. After Snape's ministrations, Dumbledore uses a magical sword to partially crack the Stone, break the curse, and kill the piece of Voldemort's soul that had been trapped inside it. Dumbledore then sets the Stone aside and saves it so as to pass it onto Harry when Dumbledore died (Rowling DH, 719-720).

The Resurrection Stone encased in a family heirloom, a ring – one of Voldemort's Horcruxes

In his living will, Dumbledore bequeaths Harry the Resurrection Stone but had encased it inside the very first Snitch (a small, golden, flying ball) Harry captured in his first Quidditch match (quidditch is essentially soccer played while flying on broomsticks with three goals instead of one). Harry is given this Snitch by Rufus Scrimgeour, the Minister of Magic (like our president) who asks Harry to try and open it as he suspects that Dumbledore encased something inside it. Scrimgeour believes that if anything is hidden in the Snitch, only Harry will be able to retrieve it as Snitches have 'flesh memories'; since no one touches a Snitch before its use (its makers wear gloves) Snitches magically recognize the touch of the first person who captures it. Harry tries to open the Snitch for Scrimgeour, but nothing happens (Rowling DH, 126-128).

Dumbledore wills Harry the Stone – the ability to bring back the dead.

It is only later that Harry reminds his friends, Ron and Hermione, that the first Snitch he caught was the one that he caught in his mouth. Upon putting his lips to the outer shell of the Snitch, the words, "I open at the close," appear on the Snitch in Dumbledore's writing (Rowling DH, 133-134). It is only later that Harry realizes that 'the close' referred to on the Snitch is *his* close, the end of his own life. He discovers that, unmissed by Voldemort, on the night Voldemort had attempted to kill Harry as a baby (and failed), a part of Voldemort's soul had been blasted from what remained in his body and latched itself onto Harry. Harry had become, unintentionally, Voldemort's seventh Horcrux, and until the piece of Voldemort's soul that was trapped in Harry's body had been destroyed, Voldemort could not be killed as it was his Horcruxes which tethered Voldemort to life (Rowling DH, 698-704).

Harry, according to Dumbledore's wishes (and his own personal desire), takes the Stone with him as he travels toward the Forbidden Forest, a locale on the Hogwarts school grounds where he knows Voldemort is waiting for him to give himself up so as to prevent the murdering of his friends. Harry, like the second brother, turns the Stone over thrice in his hand and his parents and their two best friends, Sirius Black and Remus Lupin, appear before Harry and give him the encouragement he needs to enable his self-sacrifice. The shadows of his parents and their friends follow Harry to the site where Voldemort stands waiting. Harry drops the Stone due to the numbness he's feeling in his hands and successfully allows the part of Voldemort's soul inside him to be killed (Rowling DH, 698-704).

After Voldemort unsuccessfully attempts to kill Harry in the Forbidden Forest, the piece of Voldemort's soul inside Harry is destroyed and thus, when Harry confronts Voldemort a final time and Voldemort's Killing Curse backfires, Voldemort dies (Rowling DH, 724-744). After Voldemort's death, Harry visits the headmaster's office inside Hogwarts Castle. He reveals that he plans on leaving the Resurrection Stone in the Forbidden Forest, where he had left it so as to ensure that the power of the Deathly Hallows would be broken and the allure of the Resurrection Stone would vanish (Rowling DH, 748).

The Resurrection Stone and the Judicial Branch

The use, power, and whereabouts of the Resurrection Stone in the Harry Potter series, I argue, is comparable to the second branch of government we investigate in this book, the Judicial Branch. The method for using the Stone, the historical timeline of the Stone's whereabouts, and the criticisms and drawbacks of such a magical object are comparable to elements of the American judicial system. Let us first consider the thing at its barest bones – the Stone's ability to bring back the dead and the Judicial Branch's attempt to do the same.

Bringing Back the Dead

In "The Tale of Three Brothers," Death assured the second brother, Cadmus, that the Stone that he gave him would have the power to bring back the dead, but Cadmus discovered, to his dismay, that this assertion was not entirely true. Instead of bringing the dead back into the world of the living, the dead remained with the dead, at least in part, but returned to the living world as shadows or echoes of what they had been while they lived. This is not what the second brother had asked for, but it is what Death gave him.

The judicial branch's job is much like the function of the Resurrection Stone. The courts, like the Stone, are supposed to re-interpret the intentions of the Founding Fathers based on what's written in the Constitution, the writings of the Founders, and in legal precedent – previous judicial decisions that have been handed down over time. Like the Stone, however, it can be argued that the courts fail at accurately 'bringing back the dead'.

There are many different kinds of law that the Judicial Branch is expected to consider and render decisions upon. Perhaps the form of law most relevant in our discussion is constitutional law – the attempt of the Judicial Branch to interpret the meaning and content of the United States Constitution. The justices can and do use both the Constitution and the writings of our Founding Fathers to render decisions in these cases, but there is no real way to ensure that the decisions they render would be supported by the Founders of our country; in short, the Judicial Branch is essentially guessing at the Founders' intentions – there is no way to guarantee total accuracy in what the Founders meant (Chemerinsky, 15-27).

The Judicial Branch considers other areas of law as well. One of the most widely accepted forms of law that the courts address is known as **common law** – laws passed down by judges that are steeped high in tradition and the decisions already handed down by the courts (legal precedent). Generally speaking, legal precedent will hold true in most legal cases. In legal terms, this is known as ***stare decisis*** or "let the decision stand"; judges are supposed to consider decisions made in the past and see how similar or different the case they're considering is in terms of facts and substance. This will enable them to use the decisions of the past to rule on issues presented to the courts in the present. Legal precedent is, for the most part, the foundation on which most judges build their decisions (Hall and McGuire, 10-15).

The Judicial Branch and the Resurrection Stone – the power to bring the dead back to life

Two more forms of law that the Judicial Branch addresses are criminal law and civil law. The field of **criminal law** addresses offenses that are considered so damaging (either emotionally or physically) to members of society that it is charged with prosecuting and punishing its violators (Hall and McGuire, 289-290). **Civil law**, on the other hand, is the realm of law where judges address the disputes between two parties that are not considered to be criminal (Hall and McGuire, 290-291). Divorce court, family court, and corporate court, to name a few, are examples of a few of the arenas where civil law is addressed.

Another important thing to consider when addressing law is the federal and state implications therein. It is entirely possible for something to be legal in one state but not in another (Hall and McGuire, 66-67). Federal judicial law, however, can prevent or allow things from occurring across the country (Hall and McGuire, 126-127). For example: the United States Supreme Court decision *Roe v. Wade* made abortion prior to the period of viability legal across the United States; federal courts have the power to affect laws on a national scale whereas states only have the power to influence what goes on within their own boundaries. Conversely, the states of Colorado and Washington have made the recreational use of marijuana legal (for now), but these assertions of legality only apply within the borders of those two states (Linn, 1-4).

The different types of law that the courts make rulings on enable them to use past precedent to make rulings on the disputes of today. Some relate to the interpretation of the Constitution. Other decisions resolve disputes between victims and perpetrators of crimes. Yet others resolve petty disagreements between two parties. Still others make decisions that affect either individual states or the entire country. The decisions by the judges hearing these cases are similar to the function of the Resurrection Stone – bringing the dead back as close to life as possible.

Three Flips of the Hand: The Three Levels of the Justice System

"The Tale of Three Brothers" indicates that to use the Stone, the owner must flip the Stone over three times in his or her hand in order to 'resurrect' their individual of choice. Similarly, there are three levels to the American justice system that exist at both the state and federal level. For each 'turn of the hand', we will investigate a level of the justice system so as to better understand the process by which judicial decisions are handed down and enforced.

The Trial Courts

The first level of the justice system (and the first 'turning of the hand' in terms of the Resurrection Stone) is one found in a neighborhood near you; this level of the justice system is known as the district court or trial court level. This arena of the judiciary is where you would find jury trials, defendants, plaintiffs, and the verdicts of guilty or not guilty. District courts are typically known as the level of the justice system that have **original jurisdiction** – the right to hear a case first. Generally speaking, the Supreme Court and its subordinate appellate courts do not hear

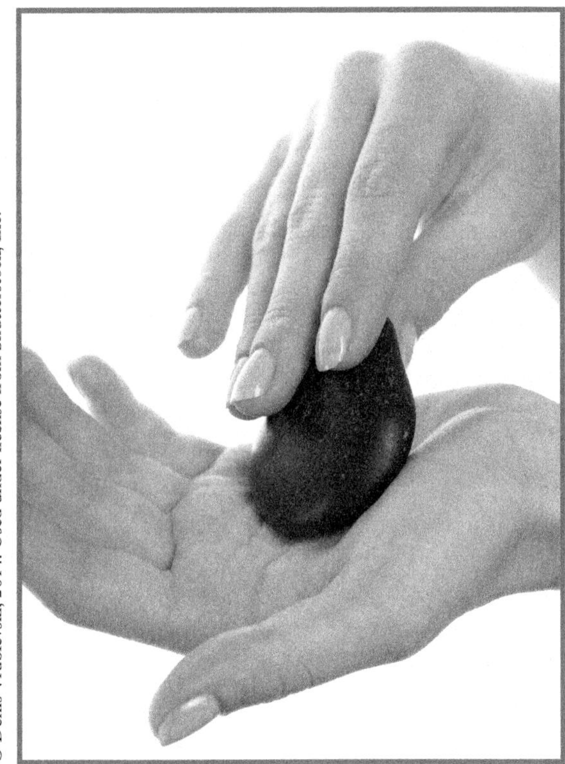

Three flips of the hand – three levels to the American justice system

cases until the trial courts have heard the cases first. District courts are also known as arenas of **general jurisdiction** – a level of the judiciary where any kind of case can be heard including criminal, civil, family, probate, or constitutional cases. The trial court level is also where the Fifth, Sixth, Seventh, and Eighth Amendments begin to hold sway as they are the Amendments dedicated to ensuring justice. All of these things occur at the trial court level. For this reason, the trial courts hear far more cases and render more verdicts than the other two levels of the judiciary. In the United States, there are 94 district courts and nearly 700 judges who sit and hear cases at this level.

The Appellate Courts

The second level of the federal justice system (and the second turning of the Resurrection Stone) is that of the appellate courts. Roughly 20% of trial court cases are heard by the appellate courts. At this level, judges hear cases based on specified issues. Different judges hear cases about different issues. Some judges specialize in capital cases (cases where the sentence handed down is the death penalty), international trade, copyright and patent laws, and so on. The U.S. Court of Appeals is a very issue-specific arena where judges become incredibly knowledgeable in the area of law in which they specialize. Most cases here, however, are attempts at preventing the death penalty from being carried out.

Other than the cases which the U.S. Supreme Court agrees to hear, all decisions at the appellate level are final. For this reason, most cases are heard by a three-judge panel. Some of these judges are retired who serve part-time; others have made appellate court cases their career path. Either way, there is an advantage for having more than one judge hear a case – the legal opinions of one judge might encourage the other two to change the way they rule on a case. With more than one judge presiding over a case, it is more likely that the intentions of the Founders – either in constitutional interpretation or the exacting of justice – will be more accurately represented.

The United States Supreme Court

The final level of the federal court system (and the last flip of the Stone) is the United States Supreme Court. Because it is the last place a case

District courts – the home of the jury trial

can be heard, it is known as **the court of last resort.** The Supreme Court handpicks the cases it hears. Each year, the Court hears roughly 100 cases and typically issues rulings on roughly 90 of them. This level of the court system is probably the most well-known as it has handed down numerous opinions that have changed America's social and political landscape. The Court has weighed in on numerous hot-button issues including race, gender, abortion, assisted suicide, the place of God in our society, health care reform, and so on. For better or worse, the Court has and likely will continue to play a role in America's ever-evolving political dialogue.

The Rightful Possessor of the Stone and the Selection of Federal Judges

In *Harry Potter and the Deathly Hallows*, three wizards find the Resurrection Stone in their possession and have the opportunity to use it; these wizards were Lord Voldemort, Albus Dumbledore, and Harry Potter. Each wizard sought the Stone and its powers for different reasons, and it is these reasons that allow us to identify the different personalities of the possessors. Finally, by considering the three wizards who possess the Stone in the book, we are able to identify which wizard possessed and used the Stone for the right reasons with innocent intent.

The first wizard to lay claim to the Stone in *Deathly Hallows* is Lord Voldemort. Voldemort, through much research, discovered one of the last surviving relics of Salazaar Slytherin's family – a large ring with a black stone set in its center – and traced it to the Gaunts, the only living descendants of Slytherin and also, Voldemort's only living relatives. Voldemort sought to capture the ring and turn it into another Horcrux – yet one more attempt to tether himself to life, and yet, despite his magical aptitude, he failed to recognize the Stone for what it was and therefore was unable to use the Stone as it was intended. Voldemort's ignorance prevented him from harnessing the power of one of the most formidable magical objects in existence (Rowling DH, 428-429, 719).

The next wizard to find and possess the Stone was Albus Dumbledore, the headmaster of Hogwarts. While searching for Voldemort's Horcruxes, he came across the ring in what remained of the Gaunt's shack. Dumbledore had found the item of the Deathly Hallows that he had coveted the most. He imagined himself apologizing ardently to his family and sought to use the Stone to make that wish come true while forgetting that Voldemort had transformed the ring into one of his Horcruxes and was bound to carry a terrible curse (Rowling DH, 719). The ring carried a fatal curse, but one that spreads over time; Dumbledore made it back to Hogwarts Castle and Severus Snape, the former Potions Masters, was able to trap the curse in one hand so as to slow the effects of the deadly curse (Rowling DH, 680-681). Dumbledore, like Voldemort, found to his sorrow that the attempt to use the Stone inappropriately without proper judiciousness prevented him from reaping the reward of one who had used the Stone for the right reasons at the right moment.

Dumbledore, recognizing his own folly and also that of Voldemort, sought to ensure that Harry Potter was the next possessor of the Stone, but he also wanted to ensure that, unlike himself, Harry would use the Stone at the right moment for the right purpose. He sealed the Stone into the very first Snitch Harry had ever captured and bewitched it to "open at the close" (Rowling DH, 134) – meaning, the end of Harry's life – when Harry would thrust himself in front of Voldemort so as to both remove one of Voldemort's links to life, the piece of Voldemort's soul that lived

Selecting federal judges – the possessors of the Resurrection Stone

inside Harry, and also enable Harry to use old magic; by dying for someone, he would magically protect all whom he died for from magical attack (Rowling DH, 708-709, 737-738).

Two of the wizards in *Deathly Hallows* sought the Stone and attempted to use it inappropriately while the other wizard, Harry Potter – through the mediation of Albus Dumbledore – used the Stone at the right moment and for the right reasons. The choice of when to use the Stone and for what reason is strikingly similar to the act of selecting of federal judges. Who should be chosen to serve and why? What should their ideological makeup look like? Where should they be from? What should they look like? All of these considerations are important ones in the act of selecting federal judges.

Federal judges are nominated by the president of the United States and confirmed by the United States Senate. Although the Constitution fails to mention what sort of qualifications candidates for federal judgeships must demonstrate before nomination or confirmation can occur, tradition dictates that federal judges must have a significant background in law. Nearly all federal judges were, at some time in their careers, lawyers and were proficient in at least one area of law. Federal judges at the district, appellate, and Supreme Court levels serve for life.

As of late, the act of nominating and confirming federal judges has become an ideological battle – particularly during the times when the ideological makeup of the president and the Senate are in opposition to one another. A judge's ideology is definitely one factor that presidents and the Senate consider during the nomination and confirmation process. Generally speaking, the ideology of the judges the president nominates matches his own. On only rare occasions, presidents can and have nominated judges whose ideological makeup differs from their own, but again this is exceptionally rare. It should also be noted that when this occurs, the judge that is nominated is typically not known for being an **ideologue** – a strict adherer to one ideology or another; put simply, if a judge's ideology doesn't mesh with the nominating president's, then the ideology espoused by the judge tends to be moderate rather than extreme in its perspective (Hall and McGuire, 145).

Another thing that those who select federal judges consider is the demographic makeup of the judges they select. Especially recently, presidents have attempted to select judges that represent America – not only on an ideological level but also on a racial, ethnic, educational, and gender level. President Obama has, so far, selected two Supreme Court justices during his tenure in the White House – Sonia Sotomayor and Elena Kagan, and both of these justices happen to be women. Up until the selection of Sandra Day O'Connor and Ruth Bader Ginsberg, the selection of women as federal judges was the exception and not the norm (Gutgold, 1-14). Recent presidents, like President Obama, seem interested in building courts that represent America – both on an ideological and a demographic level.

Finally, the last factor influencing the selection of federal judges is the political landscape in which these nominees are considered. There are certain periods of time when the Senate is controlled by the same political party as the president; during those periods of time, the confirmation of judges is fairly easy. There are other times, however, where the president's political party is the opposition party in the Senate; this often makes a president's chances of getting his judges confirmed an unlikely prospect. Still at other times, the partisan identification of the president and Senate conflict yet both entities find a way to compromise.

As usual, politics is a messy business in Washington, and it would be unreasonable for us to assume that politics fails to play a part in the selection and confirmation of federal judges. Just as the Resurrection Stone only truly aids the possessor who seeks to use it at the right time and for the right reasons, so too do the president and the Senate seek for potential nominees for federal judgeships that will take certain paths and will also be a visible representation of what America looks like.

When to Use the Stone: What Cases the Supreme Court Hears

Out of the three wizards who found and used the Stone – some in the way that it was intended and some not, Harry Potter was the one who used the Stone judiciously. Instead of using it for selfish reasons as Dumbledore and Voldemort did, Harry used the Stone to bring back his family and close friends so as to encourage him to complete the task on which Dumbledore had set him – the task of sacrificing himself so that others might live in a safer world. Dumbledore, in a vision, tells Harry one wizard in a million could use the Stone the way Harry did – that is, selflessly. His ability to do so correctly identified Harry as the true master of the Stone and the other Hallows as he used them not for his own gain but rather for the protection of others (Rowling DH, 720).

Just as Harry was the 'one wizard in a million' who could unite the Hallows, the Supreme Court hears only a few cases that are brought before it. Just as Voldemort and Dumbledore were unworthy of possessing and using the Stone, most cases are deemed unworthy of the Supreme Court's interest. Generally speaking, the cases the Supreme Court decides to hear either address an issue that is societally, culturally, or politically controversial or the case addresses some sort of ambiguity in the law. Cases the Court won't hear

Harry Potter, like the Judicial Branch, using the Stone (and choosing cases) in the right way

are **moot cases** – cases where the Court has made decisions on issues that require no more legal deliberation. The Court automatically throws those cases out and removes them from the list of potential cases. Another document the Court often receives is known as a ***certiorari petition*** – this is a legal petition to review a case that the Court has already ruled on. Roughly 7,000 of these are presented to the Court each year, but the high court only consents to hear around 100 of them and make decisions on even less.

The Chief Justice – the head of the Supreme Court – will compile a list of potential cases and pass it around to the eight other associate justices for them to amend and add to; this is known as a **discuss list.** The cases that end up on the final list are typically the ones heard by the Supreme Court. For a case to be heard by the Court, at least four of the nine justices have to be interested in hearing the case; this is known as the **rule of four.** In this way, the Court assures that roughly half of their number is actively interested in rendering a decision on the issue(s) in question.

Toward the Forbidden Forest and a Supreme Court Opinion

Harry's path to the Forbidden Forest was a long, winding one. To get to the Forest and use the Stone as Dumbledore intended, he first had to discover many things. Harry had to receive the Snitch that Dumbledore bequeathed to him in his will and had to discover the writing on the Snitch, "I Open at the close." (Rowling DH, 133-134). He had to discover the existence of the Deathly Hallows (Rowling DH, 409). Next, he had to deduce that Dumbledore had left him the Stone encased inside the Snitch (Rowling DH, 431). Then, Harry had to see that both Dumbledore and Voldemort's poor use of the Resurrection Stone backfired on both of them (Rowling DH, 680-681). Finally, Harry had to come to the realization that 'the close' was the end of his life, and that the Stone had been willed to him to make that final act easier. He was supposed to use the Stone to enable his final selfless act as opposed to selfishly calling loved ones back to allay his own grief (Rowling DH, 698).

Just as Harry's path to the Forbidden Forest and his own end followed a certain timeline, so too does decision making in the Supreme Court follow a certain order. The first part of the process is when the lawyers of each

The path to the Forbidden Forest: the process by which the Supreme Court makes judicial rulings

side of the argument being presented prepare **briefs;** these are the legal arguments that defend one side's desired court ruling. For example: say, the Court was hearing a case on making same-sex marriage legal on a federal level. Both attorneys would prepare legal briefs; one side would provide a legal defense for same-sex marriage while the other would mount a case against it. Sometimes, people with no **standing,** or any real stake, in the case will prepare their own arguments for or against the issue being put before the Court; these are known as ***amicus curiae*** **briefs** or "friend of the court" documents.

After the briefs are prepared and presented to the Court, each side makes its oral arguments. Both sides will present their case out loud before the Court and answer any questions the nine justices might have. Generally speaking, the Court's clerks enable the justices on the Court to be prepared with their questions by preparing **bench memos** – summaries of the arguments to be made by both sides and also potential questions the justices might see fit to pose to those making the arguments. At this point, everything from here on is done in secret. The nine Supreme Court justices consider the facts presented in the legal briefs and oral arguments in preparation for the conference meeting.

In the conference meeting, the nine justices bounce ideas off each other before they decide how they are going to vote in regards to the case in question. By talking to each other, they attempt to ensure that all legal arguments for or against a potential outcome are considered before a final decision regarding the case is made. There are three different models out there that explain how justices vote. First, there is the **legal model** which essentially argues that justices make their decisions based on legal precedent and their own interpretation of the Constitution and other legal writings (Wrightsman, 42-47). The second is the **attitudinal model** in which judges use their own political opinions or policy preferences to make decisions regarding the issue in question (Wrightsman, 20-22). The final model, the **strategic model** argues that justices consider not only their own policy preferences but also those of the other justices, the president, Congress, and the American people when making decisions; this model is the one that allows for justices to make decisions that might go against legal precedent but might also allow the Court to save face in scenarios where ruling against something will cause societal upheaval (Wrightsman, 25, 106-107).

Once the justices decide how they are going to vote, the Chief Justice assigns the writing of the assenting and dissenting opinions. The **assenting opinion** is the ruling of the majority or the 'winners' in the case. The assenting opinion writer may not agree with all of the facts that the other assenting justices do, and his or her reflection of that in the opinion writing has the potential to affect the overall decision handed down to the public. The **dissenting opinion** is the opinion of the minority or the 'losers'; the dissenting opinion can be very tame and simply disagree with the opinions expressed by the majority or it can be extremely condemning of the path the assenters chose.

The writing of these opinions is extremely important, for what is written in these opinions dictates whether or not laws stay on the books, what should be enforced, and what should be ignored. Judicial opinions can be written in one of two ways – narrowly or broadly. Narrow decisions are typically designed to impact only the persons with standing in the case; in other words, narrowly written opinions affect a very select group of people. Writing an opinion broadly, however, causes the Court's decision to apply to a broader audience – perhaps even every citizen in the United States. Broad opinion writing ensures that a large group of people will be impacted by the outcome of the Court's deliberations whereas narrow decisions have selective impacts in specified areas.

Hidden in the Snitch and the Checks on the Courts

In the beginning of *Deathly Hallows*, Harry Potter finds out that Dumbledore has bequeathed unto him the Snitch he caught in his first ever Quidditch match (Rowling DH, 133-134). He discovers that it will open and reveal its secret upon Harry's 'close', but until the end of the book, Harry is unsure what 'the close' is. Harry, upon deducing that the Resurrection Stone is hidden within the Snitch, desires to use it to see his parents whom he had never known but is prevented from doing so. Only on his way to the Forbidden Forest to be killed by Voldemort would the Snitch open for him and reveal the Stone; he then used the Stone in the way it was intended – to recall his family and friends from the grave to make it easier for him to seek his own (Rowling DH, 698-703).

Just as Harry was prevented from using the power of the Stone until the appropriate time and for the right reason presented itself, so too has the power of the Judicial Branch been limited by the other two branches of government. Both Congress and the president have powers that enable them to inhibit the ability of the Court to control law creation, interpretation, and enforcement in the United States. Some of these checks are more direct while others are sneakier and harder to constitutionally defend.

The President's Checks on the Judiciary

The president's most widely acclaimed check on the Courts is his ability to nominate candidates for federal judgeships. Ultimately, the man or woman who is confirmed by the Senate had the president's initial approval to begin with; obviously, if there is significant tension between the president and the Senate, the candidate who is

The power of the United State Supreme Court, like the Resurrection Stone, is hidden in the Snitch.

confirmed might be less appealing to the president than a nominee who more closely mirrors the president's ideology. Nevertheless, the president's ability to nominate candidates to the federal judiciary gives the president a significant amount of control in terms of what ideological framework the federal judiciary leans toward. Another method of checking the Courts available to the president is the power to pardon criminals. If the Court makes a ruling that the president doesn't approve of, the president can simply pardon the 'guilty' party and essentially nullify the decision that the Court handed down. The power of presidential pardons is not simply a tool used to give criminals a second chance; rather, it is an opportunity of the president to moderate judicial power.

Congress' Checks on the Courts

Like the president, Congress also has a number of tools in its chest that it can use to check the power of the judicial branch. First and foremost, the Senate has the power to confirm federal judges that the president nominates. No one sits on the federal judiciary without the Senate's approval. The duty to confirm federal judges ensures that the ideology of the courts is at least partially consistent with that of Congress. It is also the job of Congress to regulate the size of the federal judiciary; Congress therefore has the power to add or remove judges as it sees fit. In this way, Congress can attempt to ensure that the judiciary is stacked with judges that share the predominant ideology espoused by Congress.

Aside from confirming, adding, and removing judges, Congress employs other checks against the judicial branch. Although exceedingly rare, Congress has the power to impeach federal judges. As of yet, no Supreme Court justice has ever been both impeached and convicted, and only one – Samuel Chase – was impeached but was later acquitted. Impeachment can be used if Congress believes a federal judge has overstepped his Constitutional bounds or done something that is illegal. Generally speaking, however, the impeachment of federal judges is exceedingly rare, and the conviction of federal judges on the grounds of impeachment is rarer still.

The final tool Congress can utilize to check the judiciary is the ability to revise laws that the Supreme Court has struck down. If the Courts strike down part or all of a law passed by Congress, the law itself is null and void. If Congress rewrites the law with different language or with different elements and it successfully passes, the legislation becomes law and is enforceable until the Supreme Court considers and strikes down the new law. As the Supreme Court only hears an extremely limited number of cases each year, the likelihood of the new law being struck down is pretty unlikely. Just as Dumbledore 'checked' Harry's ability to use the Stone, so too do Congress and the president have the power to check the power of the Judicial Branch.

Using the Stone for the Wrong Reason and the Criticisms of the Supreme Court

In "The Tale of the Three Brothers" and in *Harry Potter and the Deathly Hallows*, we are introduced to various wizards who find the Resurrection Stone and use it; some use the Stone for selfish reasons but one does not. In both of these works, *Deathly Hallows* portrays Grindelwald's desire to use the Stone to create an army of the dead, Dumbledore wanting to call his family back to remove him from responsibility, and Voldemort's desire to use the Stone to store part of his soul as poor uses of the Hallow given to the second brother by Death. Harry Potter's use of the Stone, however, is depicted to be the appropriate use of the magical object; instead of using it for selfish reasons, Harry uses the Stone to give himself the courage to complete his mission of self-sacrifice, an act that is necessary if Voldemort is ever to be killed.

Just as Harry was the 'one man in a million' who could use the Stone as it should have been, some contend that the Supreme Court has a peculiar habit of overstepping its boundaries. One of the most notable criticisms of the Court is its tendency to employ **judicial activism** – the act of letting one's political ideology influence one's judicial rulings. Particularly on controversial issues, the Court is known for ruling on issues strictly along party lines. In 2012, the Court was accused of upholding the Affordable Care Act (Obamacare) for political reasons (Liptak, 1-2). Something worth considering is whether or not the ability to separate one's political ideology and interpretation of the Constitution is possible. In general, conservatives believe in a strict interpretation while liberals believe in a loose interpretation of the Constitution. Either way, it seems that one's ideological framework and constitutional interpretation go hand in hand. Assuredly, that might not always be the case, but it likely holds true the vast majority of the time.

Another criticism of the Court is its willingness to make rulings on a federal level what rightfully should be addressed by the states. Some contend that, especially recently, the Court has made decisions in a number of controversial cases which has made conservatives angry and wishing that the decisive power had, rather than being taken by the federal courts, been passed down for individual state courts to rule on (Weyrich, 1-2). Weyrich contends that many justices on the Court bristle at this accusation and believe that taking away the federal court's power simply because one is unhappy with the outcome does a disservice to democracy and inhibits the federal judiciary to fulfill the obligations set them by the Constitution – that is, the interpretation of laws on a federal level (Weyrich, 2).

A final criticism of the Court is its apparent unwillingness to protect certain individual rights. Some argue that the Court has sided with corporate interests, lobbyists, and other big-wigs in Washington and left the millions of Americans whose voices should be the movers and shakers in American politics by the wayside. Some contend that the 2010 Citizens United case did just that; the Court's decision permitted corporations to donate unrestricted amounts of money to political campaigns. While some people find this to be a non-issue, most folks believe that giving corporations this ability encourages elected officials to cater to the highest paying campaign donors, the corporations, rather than to the American people (Montopoli, 1-2).

From a riverbank, Death selected a stone, gave it to the second brother, and told him the stone would have the power to bring back the dead. So too do the courts through the process of constitutional interpretation.

Just as Beedle's "The Tale of Three Brothers" and Rowling's *Harry Potter and the Deathly Hallows* depict the paths of several wizards who found and used the Resurrection Stone to bring back the dead, so too has the judicial branch in the United States sought, over its many years, to 'bring back the dead' by re-examining the writings of the Founding Fathers in the attempt to see how the opinions of these men who lived so long ago apply to the world we live in today. While, at times, it seems as if the courts fail in this endeavor, it is also plausible to assert that the Court can and has been successful in many of its attempts to rightfully use the Stone given to the second brother in Beedle's tale.

FOOD FOR THOUGHT

Bringing Back the Dead

Do you think the judicial branch successfully 'brings back the dead' or are their attempts like the pale shadows of life that return when the Resurrection Stone is used? Why are there so many different areas of law? Which do you think is the most important? Is it possible to apply the Constitution to an issue that's not mentioned in it? If so, how? Give examples. Is it possible to overuse the Constitution in order to resolve modern-day issues? Is the

Constitution outdated and in need of revision or is it fine the way it is? Do you think that legal precedent should be subject to review and revision or should 'the decisions stand' as the ***stare decisis*** principle suggests?

Three Flips of the Hand and the Three Levels of the Judicial System

Why are there so many levels to the justice system? Do these levels increase or decrease the likelihood of justice being carried out? What, in your opinion, is a good definition of justice? At the trial level, juries hear and decide cases; do you think juries are impartial or do they have biases? The appellate level seems to have more judicial supervision since more than one judge sits on each case; does this increase or decrease the chances of justice being carried out? What are appellate courts looking for when they hear cases – missteps by trial attorneys, missing evidence, miscarriages of justice, or all of these? The Supreme Court is defined as the "court of last resort." Is this true of the supreme courts that exist at the state level? Should the Supreme Court be required to hear certain kinds of cases or is their 'hand picking' strategy okay?

Selecting Federal Judges

Why do ideological concerns plague judicial nominees? Are people in Congress really that afraid that the president picks someone just because their ideological frameworks are similar? Do you think presidents and the members of Congress strategically pick justices to make up the Supreme Court that 'look' like America? Should the representation of races, genders, and religions of the United States be a requirement when selecting federal judges, or should judges be confirmed or denied based on their legal expertise? Should Congress prevent the confirmation of federal judges solely based on the candidates' ideological matchup with the president, or should Congress be wary of one political party or ideology gaining too much power?

When to Use the Stone: What Cases the Supreme Court Chooses to Hear

Are any issues really 'moot' when society is always changing? Can't things be viewed and argued differently in different times? Should the Court hear cases simply because they're controversial? With over 200 years of law on the books, how can there be any kind of ambiguity left in the law for the Supreme Court to consider? Should the Court be willing to consider cases that have already been ruled on via **writs of *certiorari*** or should the Court deny reconsideration of cases that are similar to past ones? Why do four justices have to consent to hear a case? That's not even a majority. Shouldn't five or six justices be interested in hearing the cases? Does the 'Rule of 4' make it easier for the Chief Justice to determine who will write the Courts assenting and dissenting opinions?

Supreme Court Decision-Making Procedure

Why are both the legal briefs and oral arguments necessary when both essentially lay out the same arguments? Does the presence of written word make it easier for the justices on the Supreme Court to revisit facts presented during oral arguments? What do you think goes on in the conference? Is it simply justices bouncing ideas off one another, or are political deals made as well? Is it possible that the Chief Justice selects certain people to write opinions because he knows what they will write and knows how narrow or broad the opinion will be? Why does it seem that the cases we hear about on the news are broad and sweeping as opposed to narrow and applicably specific?

Hidden in the Snitch and the Checks on the Courts

As the only branch of government that is not popularly elected by the American people, should there be more checks on the judicial branch than the other two? Why or why not? Should the president be able to regularly pardon criminals in an effort to delegitimize the efforts of the Court to make and influence policy? How often do you think Congress rewrites legislation to essentially negate a Court ruling? Congress has the power to confirm federal judges and either expand or shrink the size of the federal judiciary. How much power does Congress have then to influence decisions made by the courts? Are there enough checks on the Judicial Branch? If not, what other checks should Congress or the president have over the Judicial Branch? Should judges be elected? Why or why not?

Criticisms of the Courts

Is the Court too political? Is it possible for justices to separate their ideology from their interpretation of the Constitution? Don't conservatives, in general, believe in a strict interpretation of the Constitution while liberals believe in a looser interpretation of the document? If that's the case, is it possible to exclude political preferences from judicial decision making? Do you think the United States Supreme Court oversteps its jurisdiction in making sweeping decisions on the federal level, or do you think that the Court should allow individual states less judicial power? Finally, do you think that the Court has become corrupt and caters to the important personalities in Washington rather than working for the American public? What does the Citizens United case demonstrate in terms of the Court's willingness to limit the political power of individuals? Is this 'just'?

Like the Resurrection Stone,
Dumbledore advised Harry in regards
to his Invisibility Cloak...

"Use it well..." (Rowling SS, 202)

Works Cited

Chemerinski, Erwin. *Constitutional Law: Principles and Policies.* 4th Edition. New York: Aspen Publishers, 2011.

Gutgold, Nichola D. *The Rhetoric of Supreme Court Women: For Obstacles to Options.* Lanham: Lexington Books, 2012.

Hall, Kermit L. and Kevin T. McGuire. *Institutions of American Democracy: The Judicial Branch.* New York: Oxford University Press, 2005.

Linn, Allison. "Colorado, Washington Approve Recreational Marijuana Use." *NBC Politics. http://nbcpolitics.nbcnews.com/_news/2012/11/06/14977250-colorado-washington-approve-recreational-marijuana-use?lite.* Posted on 11/06/2012.

Liptak, Adam. "Supreme Court Upholds Health Care Law, 5-4, in Victory for Obama." *The New York Times. http://www.nytimes.com/2012/06/29/us/supreme-court-lets-health-law-largely-stand.html?_r=0.* Posted on 06/28/2012.

Montopoli, Brian. "Supreme Court Doubles Down on 'Citizens United'." *CBS News. http://www.cbsnews.com/news/supreme-court-doubles-down-on-citizens-united/.* Posted on 06/25/2012.

Rowling, J. K. (BB). *The Tales of Beedle the Bard.* New York: Arthur A. Levine Books, 2008.

Rowling, J. K. (DH). *Harry Potter and the Deathly Hallows.* New York: Arthur A. Levine Books, 2007.

Rowling, J. K. (SS). *Harry Potter and the Sorcerer's Stone.* New York: Arthur A. Levine Books, 1997.

Weyrich, Paul M. "Criticism of Supreme Court Critics of the Supreme Court." *Accuracy in Media. http://www.aim.org/guest-column/criticism-of-supreme-court-critics-and-of-the-supreme-court/.* Posted on 03/23/2006.

The Cloak of Invisibility and the Legislative Branch: Transparency, Electability, and Trust

Upon Christmas Day during Harry Potter's first year at Hogwarts, he unexpectedly receives a number of Christmas gifts, and among them was a lumpy package wrapped in brown paper. Inside the packaging was a cloak unlike one that Harry had ever seen. It was an invisibility cloak which, predictably, made the wearer transparent. Included with the cloak was a note from the headmaster of Hogwarts which read, "Your father left this in my possession before he died. It is time that it was returned to you. Use it well" (Rowling SS, 201-202).

It was much later, early in Harry's adulthood, that he discovered that this was no ordinary cloak; it was the Cloak of Invisibility given to Ignotus Peverell by Death in Beedle's "The Tale of Three Brothers" (Rowling BB, 89). The Cloak was the last of three 'Hallows' that Death bestowed upon the three brothers in Beedle's tale, and it is the final Hallow that we explore in this book. I propose that the Cloak of Invisibility given to the third and youngest brother, Ignotus Peverell, is comparable to the final branch of government, the Legislative Branch. Both the unique abilities of the Cloak and also the uses to which Harry puts it are akin to important aspects of the United States Congress. Before we discuss those connections though, let us first investigate the Cloak as it is described and bestowed in Beedle's tale and also how Harry, the most recent owner of the Cloak, obtains and uses it throughout the Harry Potter series.

Harry receives his father's Cloak of Invisibility as his first Christmas gift at Hogwarts – the same Cloak that was given to Ignotus Peverell, the third brother, so long ago.

"The Tale of Three Brothers"

Ignotus Peverell is the last of the three brothers to be given a gift by Death in Beedle's tale. He had witnessed the gifts that Death had given to his brothers and saw Death's willingness to Ignotus, according to the story, is "the youngest, wisest, and most humble of the brothers" (Rowling BB, 89). He also feared that Death sought to ensnare himself and his brothers, so he asked for an object that would prevent Death from doing so. Therefore, Death "most unwillingly" gave his Cloak of Invisibility to Ignotus (Rowling BB, 89).

Ignotus Peverell receives Death's Cloak of Invisibility – a gift that will enable him to evade Death's clutches.

So far in the tale, we know very little about the Cloak but a good deal about Ignotus, the third brother. We are told that he was young but also wise and humble. We know that he saw through Death's attempts to 'reward' the brothers and foresaw that Death intended the gifts he gave the brothers to be their undoing. Thus, as the story notes, the youngest brother was wary of Death and his intentions. So, Ignotus asked for an object that would thwart Death's intent for both himself and his future family – descendants as well, so Death gave him an invisibility cloak of immense power. Death's unwillingness to fulfill this wish only makes sense as Death recognized that Ignotus had caught Death in his sinister plan but had no choice but to bestow upon him his desire – the ability to hide from Death. Ignotus got his wish in the Cloak of Invisibility.

The story goes on to show the demise of Ignotus' two brothers, Antioch and Cadmus. Death is unable, however, to find the third brother (Rowling BB, 92). It is only in his old age that Ignotus bequeaths his Cloak to his son and Ignotus allows himself to be led into the next life by Death; thus Ignotus, the third brother, and Death leave this life "as equals" (Rowling BB, 93). They were equals in the sense that neither outsmarted the other while neither could entirely defy the other. The Cloak of Invisibility, the Hallow that readers are 'supposed' to choose as the best (Rowling DH, 414), is also the most widely discussed in the Harry Potter series.

The Harry Potter Series

Harry Potter and the Sorcerer's Stone

In *Sorcerer's Stone*, Harry receives the Cloak of Invisibility as a Christmas gift from Albus

Dumbledore. Harry's father, James, had left his Cloak with Dumbledore so he could inspect it (Rowling DH, 720). Harry finds out in *Deathly Hallows* that Dumbledore suspected even then that the Cloak being passed from father, James, to his son, Harry, was none other than the Cloak given to Ignotus Peverell by Death so long ago (Rowling DH, 720). Upon inferring this truth, Dumbledore resolved to save the Cloak and give it to Harry when he was old enough to use it and understand what it was. Keeping with the tradition dictated in "The Tale of Three Brothers," Dumbledore ensures that the Cloak passes from father to son.

In *Sorcerer's Stone*, Harry's first use of the Cloak enables him to find an intriguing magical object, the Mirror of Erised which allows any that looks into it to see their heart's greatest desires; when Harry looks in the mirror, he sees the family he has never known as his parents were murdered by Lord Voldemort when he was a baby. Harry returns nightly to visit the mirror and, by extension, his parents, until Dumbledore reveals the use of the mirror and moves it to a new location (Rowling SS, 207-209, 213).

So, in the first installment of Rowling's series, Harry obtains the Cloak and he uses it both to *connect with people he cares about* and to *protect others from a dangerous enemy.*

Harry hurries along the corridors of Hogwarts Castle by night under his Cloak to see his parents which are shown to him by the Mirror of Erised.

Harry Potter and the Chamber of Secrets

The second installment of Rowling's series tells of Harry's attempts to save the students and teachers of Hogwarts from a monster hidden in a mythical chamber of the castle, the Chamber of Secrets – a chamber accessible only to the one known heir of Salazaar Slytherin, Lord Voldemort (Rowling CS, 151). In order to gain the information he needs to solve the mystery of the Chamber and Slytherin's heir, Harry uses his Cloak to sneak around the castle and its grounds (Rowling CS, 259). In *Chamber of Secrets*, Harry's use of the Cloak is to *gain information in order to make accurate deductions so that wise decisions can be made*.

Harry uses the Cloak to enjoy a snowy day in Hogsmeade with his friends.

Harry Potter and the Prisoner of Azkaban

Harry's use of the Cloak in the third installment of the Harry Potter series is pretty limited, but it is worth mentioning. In the third book, a mass murderer, Sirius Black, is allegedly hunting Harry down to kill him, and so he is prohibited from leaving Hogwarts Castle and visiting Hogsmeade – a small town students visit on weekends if their guardians give permission (Rowling PA, 46-47, 149-150). Harry, however, sneaks out of the castle using his Cloak so as to have some fun with his friends on a snowy day in Hogsmeade (Rowling PA, 275-281). In the third installment of the Harry Potter series, Harry uses the Cloak *for recreation and to connect with his closest friends, Ron and Hermione.*

Harry Potter and the Goblet of Fire

In the fourth installment of Rowling's best-selling saga, Hogwarts plays host to a magical competition between three schools – Hogwarts (in England), Beauxbatons (in France), and Durmstrang (in Bulgaria); the competition is very similar to a magical interpretation of the Olympics – one 'champion' from each school competes to win the competition – the Triwizard Tournament (Rowling GF, 186-192). In a freak accident where Harry is selected as a fourth champion to represent

Hogwarts (Rowling GF, 271), he finds himself an unwilling contender in the Triwizard Tournament (Rowling GF, 288-292).

Harry's friend Ron is extremely jealous and refuses to speak to Harry while Hermione is sympathetic with Harry's plight (Rowling GF, 289-290). Harry and Hermione plan a weekend together in Hogsmeade; afraid Ron will be there though, Harry brings his Cloak so as to hide from his angry friend (Rowling GF, 317-322). He, Harry, finds himself worried about the upcoming first task but thankfully is assisted by his friend, Hagrid. Although Hagrid is supposed to be impartial to the champions competing in the tournament, he summons Harry to the Forbidden Forest, a dangerous area on the Hogwarts school grounds, in hopes of giving him a hint in regards to the first competition in the tournament, but asks Harry to bring his Cloak for concealment. Harry does as Hagrid asks and discovers, under the Cloak, that his first task will be trying to survive an encounter with a dragon (Rowling GF, 322-328). In *Goblet of Fire*, Harry uses the Cloak both *to avoid encountering someone unwelcome* and to *gain information about the future.*

Harry Potter and the Order of the Phoenix

Harry uses the Cloak only once in the fifth installment of Rowling's series. Harry suspects that Lord Voldemort has captured and begun to torture his godfather and only 'family member', Sirius Black (Rowling OP, 726-731). He seeks to contact him at his home to make sure that he has indeed vacated the premises and been taken by Voldemort. To do so, he uses his Invisibility Cloak to sneak into the temporary office of the headmistress to contact Sirius or anyone else at his residence, Number Twelve Grimmauld Place (Rowling OP, 736-741). He finds out that Sirius is not home and sets out to rescue him – an attempt which fails. So, in this installment, *Harry uses the Cloak to conceal his agenda and his plan to bring it to fruition.*

Harry Potter and the Half-Blood Prince

In *Half-Blood Prince*, the first use of the Cloak is on the Hogwarts Express – the train that takes Hogwarts students to school. Earlier in the book, Harry saw Draco Malfoy and a number of Voldemort's supporters engaged in what looked like a ceremony of initiation, and Harry believes that Malfoy has been welcomed into Voldemort's fold as a Death Eater – one of Voldemort's followers (Rowling HBP, 122-130). Because of these suspicions, Harry uses the Cloak to spy on Malfoy while he talks to his friends hoping to have his theory confirmed (Rowling HBP, 147). Even under the Cloak, however, Malfoy detects Harry's presence. Once the train arrives at Hogwarts, Malfoy stuns Harry with a spell, breaks his nose by stomping on it, and covers him with the Invisibility Cloak – hoping that no one would find Harry before the train arrived back in London at King's Cross Station. Fortunately, however, Harry is rescued and makes it to Hogwarts (Rowling HBP, 152-157).

Upon the Hogwarts Express, Malfoy uses the Cloak to hide Harry and (hopefully) punish him for attempting to spy on him, and (hopefully) keep him from making it to school on time.

Harry's suspicions regarding Malfoy only become more pronounced as the book goes on; Harry discovers that Malfoy is spending large amounts of time in the Room of Requirement (Rowling HBP, 432) – a room that only appears when someone has true need of it and it opens and stands equipped for the seeker's needs. Harry also learns that Professor Snape knows about Malfoy's plan and offers to help him – an offer which Malfoy rejects (Rowling HBP, 521-526). Under the Cloak, Harry attempts to enter the Room to find and confront Malfoy a number of times with no success (Rowling HBP, 457-458, 463-465).

Another storyline in the book is the private lessons Dumbledore gives Harry detailing Voldemort's movements in the distant and recent past (Rowling HBP, 78-79). He demonstrates that Voldemort had seized (often through murder) a number of magical objects that were originally owned by the four founders of Hogwarts – Godric Gryffindor, Helga Hufflepuff, Rowena Ravenclaw, and Salazaar Slytherin. Dumbledore indicates that he's reasonably sure that Voldemort acquired an ornate locket that had been Slytherin's and a cup that had been Hufflepuff's (Rowling HBP, 433-438) and also a ring that had been passed down to Slytherin's descendants (Rowling HBP, 365-366). While it is clear that Dumbledore has suspicions as to why Voldemort wanted or needed these objects, he was not entirely sure, so he sets Harry the task of finding out.

By using the Cloak to get close to and to interrogate one of the professors who had been close to Tom Riddle (the young Voldemort) during his school days, Professor Horace Slughorn (a professor who has come out of retirement), Harry discovers that Voldemort had been using the magical objects he had collected to create Horcruxes – objects in which a Dark wizard encases part of their soul (Rowling HBP, 480-499). Dumbledore reveals that it was when Harry had presented him with Riddle's diary in *Chamber of Secrets* that he first suspected that Voldemort had made Horcruxes (Rowling HBP, 500); furthermore, it was something Harry had reported that Voldemort had said at the end of *Goblet of Fire* that he deduced that Voldemort had not made one but many of them – that he had gone "further than anybody" to take steps to ensure his immortality (Rowling HBP, 501).

The final use of the Cloak in the book occurs directly preceding and also at the time of Dumbledore's death – which ends up being a pre-planned arrangement (Rowling DH, 681-683). Harry and Dumbledore barely escape a cave where they had attempted to acquire one of Voldemort's Horcruxes. On Dumbledore's orders, Harry hides under the Cloak on the Astronomy Tower with a weakened Dumbledore and waits for Severus Snape to arrive, the man who can help relieve Dumbledore of the weakness he acquired from drinking a potion that magically prevented anyone from obtaining the Horcrux. Instead of helping Dumbledore, however, Harry sees Snape 'murder' Dumbledore by using the Killing Curse, *Avada Kedavra* (Rowling HBP, 595-596).

In *Half-Blood Prince*, the Cloak of Invisibility is used for a number of reasons by a few different people. First, it was used *against its owner in an attempt to discredit or harm him.* Second, the Cloak was used *to search for answers to problems facing Harry, his schoolmates, and his professors.* Third, the Cloak was used to *discover a significant, story-altering truth – the truth about Voldemort and his Horcruxes.* Finally, the Cloak is used to *conceal Harry's presence as he sees something he alone is meant to see.*

Harry Potter and the Deathly Hallows

In the final installment of the Harry Potter series, the Cloak of Invisibility is both discussed and used on several occasions. The first time the Cloak surfaces is when Harry, Ron, and Hermione use it to hide themselves from the detection of Voldemort's followers; these witches and wizards gain control of the Ministry of Magic, the Wizarding government, and a reward is offered for the whereabouts of Harry or his friends (Rowling DH, 162).

Next, Harry, Ron, and Hermione discover that the locket Horcrux that Harry and Dumbledore had failed to obtain in *Half-Blood Prince* is now owned by Dolores Umbridge, the headmistress who governed Hogwarts (if you want to call it that) at the end of *Order of the Phoenix* (Rowling DH, 222). She uses the locket to boost her pure-blood credentials, a characteristic that defines one's worth according to Voldemort's regime, and has risen high in its ranks (Rowling DH, 250, 261). Harry, Ron, and Hermione use the Cloak daily to visit the Ministry to reclaim the Horcrux – a plan that proves to be successful (Rowling DH, 227, 236-267).

While trying to determine how to destroy the locket Horcrux, the three friends travel across the English countryside and protect themselves and the locations where they stay with a number of powerful defensive spells. They use the Cloak to travel from place to place while hiding from Voldemort's supporters but also continue to search for Voldemort's Horcruxes. While they have cast protective spells over the places they reside, they use the Cloak when they travel as an extra precaution. Even after Ron temporarily leaves, Hermione and Harry continue to use the Cloak when mov-

In reading "The Tale of Three Brothers," Harry discovers that Ignotus Peverell received the Cloak of Invisibility – the Cloak that he now possesses – from Death.

ing from place to place (Rowling DH, 284, 290, 313, 320, 364).

The next encounter with the Cloak is in Xenophilius Lovegood's discussion regarding "The Tale of Three Brothers." Hermione reads the tale from the original version of *The Tales of Beedle the Bard* which had been bequeathed to her by Dumbledore (Rowling DH, 406-409). By hearing the tale in full, Harry learns about the existence of Death's Cloak of Invisibility that was given to Ignotus Peverell and deduces that his Cloak, the one his father had given him, might be the same magical object passed down to Ignotus' descendants in the story (Rowling DH, 411, 416-417, 430-431). While Hermione is extremely skeptical of that possibility, Harry ardently believes that he is correct in his deduction (Rowling DH, 431).

The Cloak comes up two more times but is used in both scenarios for concealment. The first occurrence is when Harry and his friends hide under the Cloak as they enter Hogsmeade, the small Wizarding village on the Hogwarts school grounds; they hide under the Cloak to enter the village undetected, a venture which turned out to be an epic fail. Only through the help of Dumbledore's brother Aberforth do they escape the encounter with Voldemort's Death Eaters unscathed (Rowling DH, 553-559).

The second scenario occurs after Harry, Ron, and Hermione had destroyed all but one of Voldemort's Horcruxes – his pet snake, Nagini. Voldemort is keeping her under magical protection as he now knows that Harry is hunting and destroying his Horcruxes; to kill Nagini though, Harry and his friends have to get close to it, so they hide under the Cloak in an attempt to do so (Rowling DH, 652). Unfortunately, Harry himself doesn't kill Nagini, but his friend, Neville does (Rowling DH, 733).

In *Deathly Hallows*, the Cloak is used for many unique purposes. It is used to *conceal Harry and his friends from Voldemort's Death Eaters – people who want to find and capture Harry so Voldemort can kill him.* Second, the Cloak is used *as a weapon in the war against Voldemort; they use it to hide themselves as they search for the locket Horcrux at the Ministry.* Next, the Cloak is used *as a security precaution as the three friends travel from hiding place to hiding place.* Next, *the truth about Harry's Cloak is revealed when Harry understands that the Cloak of Invisibility in Beedle's Tale is indeed his own.* Next, the Cloak is used *to avoid detection from the Death Eaters again.* Finally, the Cloak is used *to hide the presence of Harry as he attempts to get close enough to Voldemort's snake which happens to be the last remaining Horcrux.*

The Cloak of Invisibility and the Legislative Branch

The Cloak's power and uses are many and varied in the Harry Potter series, and the various powers and uses of the Cloak of Invisibility are comparable to the powers, duties, and activities of America's Legislative Branch. The powers of the Cloak and the Legislative Branch are not as straightforward as they may seem; rather, many of the activities of Congress are complicated, time consuming, and politically difficult. So too are the uses of Harry's Cloak – the one given to Ignotus Peverell by Death – more meaningful than they might initially appear.

The Wearers of the Cloak: Ignotus Peverell, James Potter, Harry Potter, and the United States Congress

In the Harry Potter series, we meet three owners of the Cloak of Invisibility. The first and original owner of the Cloak, Ignotus Peverell, acquired the magical object by evading Death's clutches in "The Tale of Three Brothers" as told by Beedle the Bard (Rowling BB, 89). The next owner was Harry's father, James. He lent the Cloak to Dumbledore to inspect, but before Dumbledore could give it back, James was murdered by Lord Voldemort (Rowling DH, 714-715). The final owner, of course, is Harry Potter – who receives the

The U.S. Capitol Building – where the Wearers of the Cloak govern

Cloak as a Christmas gift from Albus Dumbledore (Rowling SS, 202-203). These three wizards had the honor of owning and wearing one of Death's three Hallows.

The members of Congress, following the analogy, are the folks in our government who 'wear the Cloak'. Each house of Congress has different requirements in regards to which people are eligible to serve or 'wear the Cloak', and each chamber has its own rules regarding the duration of one's service. Being a senator, by tradition, is typically considered more prestigious than being a representative in the House (Hulse, 1-4); for this reason, the eligibility requirements for the Senate are more stringent than the requirements to become a member of the House of Representatives.

To become a member of the House of Representatives, candidates have to be at least 25 years old and have to have been a U.S. citizen for at least seven years. Senators, on the other hand, have to be at least 30 years old and must have been a U.S. citizen for at least nine years. Unlike the president, it is possible for immigrants to become representatives or senators; the president must be natural born (either on U.S. soil or to parents who are U.S. citizens). Generally speaking, representatives and senators have some public service background when they announce their candidacy for one of the two houses of the United States Congress. Some are lawyers while others have other professional backgrounds. Serving in the House, while not as respectable, is still considered to be a position worthy of recognition. Representatives in the House serve two-year terms while Senators serve six-year terms.

Both Houses function in entirely different ways. The House of Representatives is a very rigid chamber; rules, order, and set procedure are keynotes in this house of Congress. This is the congressional chamber that most moms would approve of – lots of 'please and thank you's'. Every act has a set procedure which, if violated, can lead to the embarrassment of certain members – typically, the individual who violates the established protocol. In the House, everyone has a set role and knows the boundaries of what they can and cannot do within it. Interactions between members are expected to be ultra-polite, civil, professional, and the manner in which these individuals interact is expected to be exceptionally formal. In the House of Representatives, order and the rule of established procedure reign.

The Senate, on the other hand, is a completely different ballgame. The Senate, though also a realm of professionalism, isn't held to the same high standards as the House of Representatives. Less leadership positions encourage fiercer and more personalized critiques of policy plans and, sometimes, of the individuals who propose such legislative changes. The Senate is the chamber of Congress famous for the prevention of votes through the use of **filibusters.** Literally, a senator wishing to enact a filibuster can pick up the phone book of Washington, D.C., or open his or her favorite book and read from it, or give a speech in support or opposition to a certain policy path, and so on; these filibusters are typically extended events as well. Senator Ted Cruz kept the Senate hanging for over 22 hours in a recent filibuster (FoxNews.com, 1). The way things are done in the House and Senate is as different as night and day in most respects.

Some individuals who 'wear the Cloak' are more noteworthy than others; specifically, I am referring to the leadership in both congressional chambers. The House, the more rigid, rules-oriented house naturally has more leadership positions than the more anarchical Senate. The House is governed by the **Speaker of the House** – an individual who is considered to be the mouthpiece of the majority party (the party in power). This individual has the ultimate say-so in regards to what bills are introduced, debated, and voted on; he or she can block any of those actions if it is perceived to threaten his or her political party or if it is suspected to be a poor policy path (whether politically, financially, or pragmatically) to pursue.

The next leadership positions in the House are the **majority and minority leaders.** These individuals are responsible for projecting their party's agenda and ensuring that the party's position on specified issues is widely known and understood – both by the party members in the congressional chamber in question and also by the American people. These individuals are often demonized by the media as being too rigid in their promotion of their party's agenda; to some, this is ironic because that is actually what their position requires of them.

The final positions of leadership in the House are the **majority** and **minority whips.** These individuals are essentially the party policemen. Their job is to ensure – especially in controversial and highly contested votes – that every member of their party votes along party lines. Some believe that the whips are responsible for personal threats to one's safety or career. The majority and minority whips are often perceived to be nasty, dangerous people – and with good reason some would say. The leadership in the House is supposed to ensure that the rigidity and the ardent dedications to rules and order notable in the House are maintained. The leadership in the Senate, on the other hand, seems to be less influential in enforcing rules and protocol.

Leadership in the Senate, unlike the House, appears to be less important. The leader of the Senate is the **president of the Senate** – who also happens to be the Vice-President of the United States. Other than being a ceremonial leader and an important figurehead, the president of the Senate has no political power except in the event of a tie-vote which he or she is required to break. The vast majority of the time, the President of the Senate is not required to attend Senate proceedings. This president attends occasionally to make a case for issues of great interest, but is not required to do much of anything; thus, the President of the Senate's political power is extremely limited.

The functioning leader of the Senate – the leader with the most real political power – is the **president pro temporae** (more commonly known as the president pro tem). The president pro tem, by tradition, is the most senior-ranking member of the majority party in the Senate. For example: suppose the Democrats control the Senate; the president pro tem would be the most senior-ranking Democrat. The president pro tem's role is very similar to that of the Speaker of the House. Because the Senate is, by nature, more anar-

The powers of the Cloak were specified by Death but expanded by the Wearers of the Cloak just as some powers are explicitly listed in the Constitution while others have been acquired over time.

chical, the ability of the president pro tem to control the goings on in the Senate is limited.

Finally, the last two leadership positions are again similar to positions held in the House – the **majority** and **minority leaders.** Like in the House, their job is to project the party's agenda and ensure that everyone – both in the Senate and across the country – know and understand what the proposed policy path of their respective political party is. All of these leadership positions were designed to enable both chambers of Congress to function in the way which the Founding Fathers intended. The wearers of the Cloak in the Harry Potter series and in the chambers of Congress ensure that the lawmaking process designed by the Founding Fathers is carried out appropriately – most of the time.

Powers of the Cloak and Congress

Just as the Cloak of Invisibility has certain powers, so too does the United States Congress. Some of the Cloak's powers are directly addressed in Beedle's tale while others require the owner's experimentation and imagination. Similarly, some congressional powers are explicitly stated in the Constitution; these are known as the **enumerated powers** of Congress. Other powers Congress has gained through the use of the Necessary and Proper

Clause; these are known as **implied powers** of Congress. The powers that Congress has accrued over time have enabled them to enhance their influence with the American people to rival that of the U.S. president and the courts. Congress, quite literally, is where the people's will is done – sometimes.

The Original Intent of the Cloak and the Enumerated Powers of Congress

The Cloak of Invisibility described in "The Tale of Three Brothers" indicates that the Cloak gives the wearer a specific power – the ability to become invisible so as to escape Death's clutches (Rowling BB, 89). That's all the Tale denotes in regards to the Cloak's power. The uses the Cloak is put to, however, suggest that the Cloak's gift of invisibility can be used for far more than Ignotus Peverell, the third brother, requested. Similarly, the United States Congress is guaranteed a number of powers directly by the United States Constitution while other powers have been claimed over time – the implied powers of Congress.

Congress has a number of powers explicitly noted in the Constitution. Most importantly, Congress is supposed to write and pass legislation which is to be reviewed by the president – the **legislative power** of Congress. The process by which a bill becomes a law is fairly complicated and one which takes a considerable amount of time – if it ever occurs; very often, bills don't survive to become laws. Generally speaking, political banter, indecision, and unpopularity among the American people are the most common reasons why bills fail to become laws or 'die'.

Unlike in the world of Harry Potter, pieces of legislation don't just appear out of midair. **Legislation starts off as an idea** which is proposed by the public and deemed important enough by a member of Congress to write a bill to change the law. Once the legislation is written, **it is then introduced formally on the 'floor' (or in front of everyone) in the House of Representatives.** This is to ensure that the members of the House know what types of legislation are being considered in each congressional session. Next, **the bill heads to its appropriate committee to be debated.** For example: a bill regulating the types of corn that famers can grow would go to the House Agriculture Committee. Many bills don't make it out of committee, however; some are too radical and others are controversial enough that no bi-partisan (cooperative) deal can be made regarding the policy intent of the bill. If the bill survives through a committee vote, **the bill is again brought to the House floor, debated, and voted on.** If the bill passes in the House, **it goes to the Senate, and the process essentially begins again – introduction on the Senate floor, debate in committee,** and finally **presentation, debate, and vote on the Senate floor.** If the *exact same bill that the House passed* also passes in the Senate, **the bill goes to the president's desk for approval.** If the Senate's bill is different than the one the House passed, **the bill goes back to the House to be re-evaluated, debated, and (hopefully) passed.** After the exact same bill is passed in both Houses, the president has the opportunity to sign the bill and make it law, veto the bill and deny its passage, or issue a signing statement – an attempt to put particular emphasis on the implementation on specific elements of the new law. While the process lined out here sounds simple and easy enough, I assure you the passage of a bill is a long, drawn out, nasty business – particularly if the bill is controversial.

The duty of Congress to propose and pass legislation is an important one but coincidentally isn't the only enumerated power delineated in the Constitution. Congressional duties are more extensive than just having legislative powers. It is also granted **judicial powers** which enable Congress to *establish the federal court system*, which serves as a model for most of the state governments, and also Congress has the power to *hold impeachment and conviction hearings for the president and federal judges*. Congress also has a number of **economic powers** which include *imposing taxes*, *establishing tariffs* (taxes on imported goods from overseas), *borrowing money from foreign countries*, *regulating commerce with foreign countries*, and *printing and coining money* (a power the Federal Reserve gained through congressional approval). The **national security** powers of Congress include *declaring war* (which is becoming exceedingly rare), *raising an army and enacting the Selective Service (the draft)*, *calling up National Guard assistance in the event of a disaster or national crisis*, *suppressing rebellions*, and *repelling enemy troops from reaching and invading the U.S. mainland or protected waterways*. Finally, the **administrative powers** of Congress include *establishing the procedure by which legal aliens are naturalized*, *establishing post offices and mail delivery services*, and *presiding as the government of Washington, D.C.*

Most of these enumerated powers never make it on the 5 o'clock news, but they are important nevertheless. The ability of Congress to protect us in times of war and national crisis enables most Americans to embrace a sense of normalcy and security that would likely be absent without congressional oversight. Their ability to impeach presidents and judges who knowingly overstep their constitutional boundaries prevent a national divergence from democracy and the rule of law into a quagmire of corruption and lawlessness. Their power to tax enables Congress to pay for the many services – both necessary and discretionary. Finally, their ability to regulate who comes into this country and how they

Members of Congress wear 'the Cloak' just as Ignotus Peverell and Harry Potter did. Some use it to become invisible or transparent while others use it to ensure re-election or to gain information that encourages good governance.

achieve entry (whether temporary or permanent) enables Congress the ability to regulate population growth, the allocation of jobs, the availability of resources, and the ownership of private property across the country. The enumerated powers of Congress are duties the Founding Fathers felt were necessary to ensure the safety and well-being of America and its citizens.

Uses of the Cloak and the Implied Powers of Congress

While "The Tale of Three Brothers" indicates that the Cloak of Invisibility was to be used to hide from Death so as to escape his clutches (and avoid the fate of the other two brothers), Harry found many other uses for the Christmas gift he received in his first year at Hogwarts. He uses the Cloak to make contact with people that he cares about in *Sorcerer's Stone* (Rowling SS, 202-203) and *Order of the Phoenix* (Rowling OP, 736-741). Harry hides under the Cloak to gain information in *Chamber of Secrets* (Rowling CS, 151), *Goblet of Fire* (Rowling GH, 322-328), and *Half-Blood Prince* (480-499). The Cloak is also used for recreation (Rowling PH, 275-281). All of these uses of the Cloak that Harry puts it to are comparable to one of the implied powers of Congress.

Harry's first use of the Cloak was to interact with people he desperately wanted to see, be with, and make proud – his parents (Rowling SS, 205-207). Later in the series, Harry seeks to determine if his godfather, Sirius Black, is in danger (Rowling OP, 736-741). In both of these incidents, Harry's desire to interact with people he cares about encourages him to use the Cloak to achieve that end. Similarly, one of the most important objectives of the members of Congress is to interact with their constituents. They achieve this objective through a number of mediums. First, members of Congress can send mail to their constituents; often this correspondence indicates recent policy proposals that the politician has submitted or sponsored recently or asks their constituents for feedback on their recent actions that they had taken on their behalf. For this reason, members of Congress have **franking** privileges – the ability to send mail without cost. They also participate in **town hall meetings** – organized meetings with one's constituents to discover what they care about and what these people are willing to do, on a local level, to make those desires come to fruition. Members of Congress can also preside as ceremonial leaders at major events; some of these events are solely political in nature while others are recreational (like throwing out the first pitch as a baseball game). All of these tools enable members of Congress to interact with their constituencies and determine what policy paths their people want them to pursue.

One of Harry's most common uses of the Cloak of Invisibility was to gain information (Rowling CS, 259; PA 274-281; GF 322-328; HBP 147, 521-526; DH 681-683); Congress also spends a lot of time attempting to achieve the same goal. One of the most notable implied powers of Congress is their oversight duties. By **oversight,** I mean their ability to investigate, scrutinize, and alter the way that the Executive and Judicial Branches imple-

Constituents attend town hall meetings to convey their policy preferences to their elected officials in Congress.

ment policies that Congress passes; often, the president and the bureaucracy implement policy in a way that is not in line with the original intent of congressional legislation. In response, Congress has a number of ways to execute their oversight capabilities. First, Congress has the power to hold hearings to investigate how laws are being implemented, to determine how the law impacts government functionality, and how the law is being received by the American public. Second, Congress holds confirmation hearings to approve or reject presidential appointees; in this way, Congress can indirectly affect how laws are implemented by controlling who the high-ranking individuals are who will implement the policies that Congress passes. Third, if a law seems to have been implemented incorrectly, Congress can enact investigations to see who is responsible (if anyone) for the discrepancy in proposed action versus the actual outcome of the law's implementation. Finally, Congress (particularly the House) has the power to control funding and therefore has the authority to ensure that our tax dollars are being allocated to agencies and organizations that appropriately implement the laws that Congress passes. All of these oversight capabilities ensure that Congress has the power to be certain that the laws that they pass are implemented in the way that they were intended.

In *Prisoner of Azkaban*, Harry uses the Cloak to engage in a bit of recreation – more specifically, to enter and enjoy the Wizarding village of Hogsmeade located near the Hogwarts school grounds; while there, Harry seeks to discover what a Wizarding village is like as Harry grew up with 'Muggles' – non-Wizarding people (Rowling PA, 275-281). Similarly, the members of Congress are allowed (and even encouraged) to take **junkets** – vacations that have a policy-oriented purpose; this is considered to be an investigative implied power that the members of Congress possess. For example: say a member of Congress is on the Agriculture Committee; he might travel to Jamaica looking at the growth of sugar cane but garner a fantastic vacation trip as well. Say another member of Congress serves on the Armed Services Committee; he or she might travel to Europe or Asia in the name of foreign relations but, while there, also engage in tourism. Junkets, while allowing members of Congress to gain information on certain topics or issues, enable these public servants to travel and experience the wonders of the world as a tourist as well.

Invisibility: Political Transparency Through Partisanship

Throughout the Harry Potter series, Harry uses the Cloak of Invisibility on regular occasion because it enables him to, obviously, become invisible. The ability to be *transparent* allows Harry to explore the Hogwarts school grounds (and other places besides) with impunity. The Cloak gives him the power to seek and find answers to problems, protect the people he cares about, and ultimately to combat and defeat the most evil Dark wizard of all time, Lord Voldemort.

Just as the Cloak enables Harry to become *invisible*, the strong partisan influence in Congress makes our government far more **transparent** or predictable (Cox and McCubbins, 34). Transparency in one's government is usually considered to be a positive attribute. In a representative government, we elect representatives to propose policies that we would support; partisanship makes it easier to ensure that your intended outcomes will more closely match the actual ones. If your congressional district elects a Republican candidate, one can be reasonably sure what kind of policies he or she will advocate and oppose; the same goes for districts that elect Democrats. Partisanship makes politicians predictable, and predictability and trust go hand in hand. If you know what others are thinking, it is far easier to react to them than to those who are erratic and random. Political parties can and do play a major role in congressional proceedings.

One of the first events in a new congressional session is the **party caucus** – a meeting of high-ranking party members where the party's agenda for the current congressional session is decided. The issues the party will and won't consider as viable policy proposals are discussed here as well as various methods to aid members who will be facing re-election in the near future (Cox and McCubbins, 22, 28). During the caucus, party leaders in each congressional chamber are appointed; this enables the party to establish an identifiable chain of command and a method of ideolog-

Partisanship in Congress enables this branch of government to be more transparent and predictable than the others.

Finally, political parties clearly play a major role when Congress votes on certain bills. Some proposals are widely supported while others stir a great deal of controversy. Typically, political parties encourage (some would even say force) their members to vote along party lines when it comes to controversial legislation whereas the partisan enforcement of its platform is less strict when widely supported bills are brought to vote. For example: in 2010 when the Patient Protection and Affordable Care Act (i.e., Obamacare) was passed, both the Republicans and Democrats spent weeks lobbying members of their party (with mixed success) to support the party's platform (Murray and Montgomery, 1-4). In the end, the majority party in both Houses, the Democrats, won the day, and Obamacare was approved by Congress and later, President Obama. Political parties are a major force in congressional politics, and it is important to understand how their influence on individual members of Congress shapes the way legislation is written, debated, and (sometimes) passed; all of these processes, like the Cloak of Invisibility, make Congress more transparent.

ical enforcement to be used during times of political controversy. The party caucus is an important aspect of how party politics influences congressional lawmaking.

The various committees in each congressional chamber are also arranged according to party and power; congressional committees, in a way, are the mirror image of their respective congressional chamber and the power structure within it. For instance: say 40% of House members are Democrats; typically speaking then, roughly 40% of each committee will be Democrats and the other 60% will be Republicans. In this way, the power structure of the congressional chamber in question is maintained and reinforced. Political parties therefore play a role at the committee level as well as on a grand scale in each house of Congress.

An important point to make here is the difference between *transparency* and *invisibility*. *Transparency*, as stated before, is the ability to 'see through' Congress – the ability to find out what they're up to, what they're ignoring and why, what scandals are plaguing Washington, and so on. A transparent government is one that we can trust because anything and everything about them and the way they govern is readily accessible. This is much truer for Congress than for the other two branches of government which have constitutional protections that protect their right to secrecy in some things. Out of the three branches of government, Congress is most worthy of the Cloak because it is this branch of government that is the most transparent – if we are willing to seek out the information that will enable us to 'see through' them.

Transparency should not be confused with invisibility or the inability to see something. I think many folks out there would argue that Congress, along with the other two branches of government, is more invisible than it is transparent. Most people simply don't take the time to find out what's going on, and the truth is that most everything that Congress does is readily accessible. One can subscribe to receive the daily transcripts of Congress. Information on each congressional member is available online; they all have websites that outline what they've done, what they're doing, and what their future agenda is. We can also access Congress' website and see who votes for what bills. If you pay attention to a particular official, you can probably figure out why they vote for what they do. Politically speaking, invisibility and transparency are entirely different concepts; it is partisanship that aids in making Congress more transparent than the other two branches of government.

Under the Cloak of Incumbency: Seeking and Maintaining an Information Base

Throughout the Harry Potter series, Harry uses the Cloak to gain information about things going on. In *Chamber of Secrets*, he uses the Cloak to find out the truth about the Heir of Slytherin. In *Goblet of Fire*, he uses it to find out what horrors he will be facing in the Triwizard Tournament. In *Half-Blood Prince*, Harry uses the Cloak to try and find out what Draco Malfoy was doing in the Room of Requirement. All of these uses of the Cloak involve Harry *seeking information*. Both his knowledge of Hogwarts Castle (through experience) and the power of his Cloak enable him to collect the information that he seeks.

Another important aspect of congressional politics is the important role of **incumbents** – politicians that, once elected, are consistently re-elected. Now, some could probably make the case that having the same people in Congress for decades is partially why we have the level of corruption that we do in Washington, but it is also defensible that keeping them there has its benefits as well. In his book, Keith Krehbiel investigates the value of incumbent politicians and the information they accrue over time; he concludes that the more time in office a member of Congress serves, the more likely it will be that he becomes proficient in a certain area of information (Krehbiel). For example: if a Senator serves on the Budget Committee for thirty or forty years, he is going to accrue knowledge from all the deliberations that occur during his tenure on the committee. He or she probably knows more about budget planning, pas-

Just as Harry uses the Cloak to gain information by sneaking around the Hogwarts school grounds, members of Congress also seek and retain enormous amounts of information during their tenure in office. For this reason, incumbency often proves to be positive as the information accrued over time is accessible both to other members of Congress and also the American public.

sage, and implementation than anyone else in that congressional chamber.

That knowledge in the field is invaluable to both fellow committee members and us, for if someone has dealt with the same issues for the greater part of their life, then it is likely that this person will be more capable of dealing with problems that might arise than someone who is newer to the fold. The same goes for most of the committees that are permanent; the members of Congress that serve for extended periods of time are also the men and women whose knowledge in their field has expanded. So while it may seem that **term limits** – limiting how long members of Congress can serve – are a good idea from one angle, the other suggests that term limits would also hinder the accruement of information and may lead to poorer policymaking and implementation.

The information that members of Congress accrue during their (sometimes lengthy) tenures in office both enables the politicians in Congress to make better laws – legislation built on solid knowledge – and also makes it easier for these individuals to make decisions with a solid knowledge of the recent past in their fields. Whether we like to admit it or not, there are benefits to keeping incumbents in office – namely the large amount of information that these men and women accrue over time.

Hiding Under the Cloak and the Electoral Connection

On a number of occasions in the Harry Potter series, Harry and his friends use the Cloak to conceal their movements. In *Sorcerer's Stone*, Harry hides under the Cloak to explore Hogwarts Castle and also to hide from Professor Snape. In *Prisoner of Azkaban*, Harry and Hermione hide under the Cloak so as to rescue Harry's godfather, Sirius Black. In *Order of the Phoenix*, Harry hides under the Cloak so as to sneak into the office of the headmistress and attempt to contact Sirius (whom Harry suspects has been captured by Voldemort). In *Half-Blood Prince* and *Deathly Hallows*, Harry uses the Cloak to conceal his presence from Voldemort's supporters – the Death Eaters. In all of these cases, the Cloak was used to *conceal Harry's mischief or potential failures* whereas Harry chooses not to use the Cloak *when he's doing something honorable.* Never does Harry confront his foes while hiding under Death's Cloak; he instead faces all of his enemies face to face.

Just as Harry uses the Cloak to hide from his enemies, members of Congress hide the skeletons in their closet as well as their stances on controversial issues to make themselves appear to be more electable.

Politicians, like Harry and his friends, often see the benefit of hiding under the Cloak – particularly during election season. A political scientist, David Mayhew, makes the argument that the main goal of the members of Congress is to get elected and re-elected. In order to do that, they employ a number of tactics to ensure that end result; namely, they engage in *advertising, credit claiming, and position-taking* (Mayhew, 73). All three of these tools enable them to maximize their chances of re-election.

The first tool, advertising, is the effort to get the public familiar with your name, image, and proposed agenda; not only do these individuals seek to garner name recognition, but they do their best to ensure that their image and agenda are perceived in a positive manner by the public (Mayhew, 49). Members of Congress often post signs across their district, run very active advertising campaigns, and make numerous public appearances in the hopes of garnering some name recognition and support from his or her electorate. By advertising, members of Congress attempt to ensure that when you get into the polling book, you don't see their name on the ballot and think, "Who's that?"

The next tactic members of Congress employ to gain support is *credit claiming*. This involves members of Congress taking credit for things that either benefits the entire country or their district specifically (Mayhew, 52-53). Say, a member of Congress agrees to support a bill with the condition that *x* amount of money has to be allocated via the bill to that particular member's congressional district or state. Most people refer to these additions to bills as **earmarks** or **pork**, and typically speaking, most people have negative opinions regarding such legislative additions despite their positive effects (usually) on their district or state. I think if you asked most people about their feelings on earmarks, they would oppose them in general but support the earmarks that benefit them; ironically, the same can be said about the members of Congress themselves – they like their own but detest everyone else's. Regardless of our opinion of earmarks, however, the members of Congress are ready and willing to take credit for the ones that benefit you – their constituents, and earmarks that greatly benefit one's constituency can really help increase one's chances of being re-elected.

The last tool that members of Congress can use, the one most relevant to the Harry Potter analogy, is *position-taking*; this is the effort of exposing one's position on political issues or, if it might have a negative effect in the election, hiding one's stance on certain issues (Mayhew, 61). For example: one would not take a position on an issue that might ostracize a large part of the electorate – even if their actual agenda might espouse that very policy path. A current example of position-taking involves immigration reform; some contend that today, many Republicans are beginning to support immigration reform and amnesty for undocumented immigrants so as to encourage Latinos to support them (Fox News Latino). Many members of Congress are willing to do whatever they have to in order to win votes, and therefore election or re-election, even if it means lying to their voters to achieve that goal.

Members of Congress, much like the wearers of the Cloak of Invisibility in the Harry Potter series, use the tools available to them to achieve their desired end – election and re-election. This often means hiding one's past and present political agenda while exposing the elements of one's character that might make that particular candidate more appealing and electable. Just as Harry used the Cloak at times to break rules and push boundaries, so too members of Congress use the methods available to them to ensure that their tenure in Congress will be extensive.

The Wise Brother and Two Congressional Leadership Styles

"The Tale of Three Brothers" indicates that Ignotus Peverell, the third brother, was also the youngest, humblest, and wisest of the brothers and that the gift he requested from Death would enable the third brother to evade him. The story also indicates that while the other two brothers fall victim to Death's cunning plan by playing to each brother's weakness, the third brother refused to take the bait. Ignotus didn't ask for what he *wanted* necessarily; instead, he asked for what he *needed* so that he could deny Death another victim.

I think that most people, when electing members of Congress, expect our elected officials to represent and vote according to how their constituency would vote; that is not always how it works out. In Congress, there are two leadership models that the members of Congress can choose to espouse. The first is

The third brother receives the Cloak of Invisibility from a reluctant Death so that he could evade him throughout his life. It might not have been what Ignotus wanted, but it was what he needed. Sometimes, the members of Congress have to decide whether what we want or what we need is the most rational policy path.

known as the **delegate model**; members of Congress that adhere to this model *espouse policy and vote on it exactly how his or her constituency would vote on it* (Russell, 1). The other model of leadership is known as the **trustee model**; members of Congress that follow this path vote based on what they think is best for their constituents – even if the people themselves had outwardly spoken against the policy paths that the representative or senator chooses to advocate (Russell, 1). Both of these models of representation are alive and well within both chambers of Congress, and both of these leadership types have their drawbacks and benefits.

Why would you want to elect someone who espouses the delegate model? I think most of us would say that we expect the people we elect *to do what we want them to do* and not to do their own thing; who knows what's better for us than ourselves? This perspective is like a double-edged sword. On the one hand, the people's will is done through the efforts of the delegate. On the other hand, we – the people – are capable of making poor decisions. Given that a sizable portion of the American electorate have no idea what's going on, some would say that electing a delegate could be dangerous in terms of what kind of policy would be proposed and passed. The truth is that the public doesn't have access to a lot of the information that the members of Congress do. For us to dictate policy without the information needed to make informed decisions, the election of a true delegate could inhibit good policy from being passed and could also promote the passage of poor legislation.

Why elect someone who operates under the trustee model of representation? Instead of listening to the people's will, the decision a trustee makes has the best interests of his constituency in mind – even if we – the people – don't see it that way. This is not to say that a trustee totally disregards the will of the people. Rather, these elected officials use all of the information available to them to make policy proposals and decisions while keeping the advice of their constituents in mind. I think most of us would agree that making rational, informed decisions with as much information available is a good way to approach policy formulation and implementation; it might, however, be perceived as unpopular. A good chunk of the American electorate already feels as if their vote and voice doesn't matter; some might even say that electing trustees only adds fuel to that fire. Despite the positives and negatives of each representation style, both are alive and well in America's Congress. Like the three brothers, one's ability to make decisions as one sees fit can enable individuals to be both humble and wise or arrogant and shortsighted.

The third brother in Beedle's tale was found worthy of Death's own Cloak of Invisibility. So too are certain individuals deemed worthy of congressional service. Just as Ignotus Peverell, the third brother, requested Death's Cloak of Invisibility in hopes of escaping, for a while, the fate of his two brothers (i.e., death), Congress too uses the powers allotted to them for various purposes. The effect of relatively strong political parties in Congress makes electing representatives and senators, based on party, simpler for voters and also makes the potential acts of these members

Congress, the legislative branch of government, wears the Cloak of Invisibility – the Hallow given to the third brother, Ignotus Peverell, by Death. As Dumbledore advised Harry, hopefully Congress is wise enough to use it well.

of Congress more predictable, since political parties seem to be slow to change. Harry Potter used his Cloak to seek out information to solve puzzles and save lives on a regular bases; similarly, one who 'wears the Cloak' in Congress for extended periods of time becomes privy to knowledge that would take a new politician years (even decades) to acquire and process. Under the Cloak, Harry hid from his enemies to protect himself and his role of hero in Rowling's series; members of Congress also hide failures and emphasize success in hopes of gaining re-election. Finally, Ignotus Peverell asked for what he needed to escape Death, and the American people petition their elected officials in Congress on a regular basis; depending on whether one's representative or senator embraces the delegate or trustee model of leadership, those requests might be taken seriously or dismissed as a poor policy path. Death's Cloak has been put to many uses by Ignotus Peverell and Harry Potter; I believe it's a reasonable conclusion that the members of Congress are rather fond of Invisibility Cloaks themselves.

Food for Thought

The Wearers of the Cloak

Is there a reason for the age requirements for each chamber? Does the age restriction indicate that U.S. senators need to be more mature than House representatives? Do you believe that the maturity level difference is noticeable in the Senate and House? Why is it that being a representative is considered to be less prestigious than being a senator when the House's structure and organization is more ordered than that of the Senate? Why can immigrants become representatives but not president? Do you think that if the Senate had more leadership positions, it would be more like the House? Why doesn't the Senate use majority and minority whips? Do you think that the whips are necessary in the House? Are things in both chambers too partisan in nature, or should political parties be stronger than they are now? Are there positives and negatives to formality as seen in the House? Is the anarchical nature of the Senate a bad thing? If you could serve in Congress, which chamber would you serve in and why?

Powers of the Cloak and Congress

Some of the enumerated powers of Congress are considered to be obsolete and have been replaced by traditional dictates. Do you think that congressional power is less than it should be or more than it should be? Do you believe that Congress has the right to claim for itself any implied powers? If so, which ones? Could Congress become too powerful through the claiming of implied powers? Do you think that Congress should have the right to impeach the president or should popular mandate remove the president from office? Congress is responsible for collection taxes; how does Congress decide how much to tax? How do they decide who should pay more and who should pay less?

Do you think members of Congress spend enough time communicating and interacting with their constituents, or do they spend too much time soliciting campaign funding from lobbyists, interest groups, and corporations? What kind of information can members of Congress garner through town hall meetings and written correspondence? Do you think junkets should be legal? Are they any different from business trips that ordinary citizens take? Do you believe that any real information is gained through these trips, or do you think that junkets are a politician's excuse for taking a vacation paid for by our tax dollars?

Partisanship in Congress and Transparency

Do you think there's a difference between transparency and invisibility? How does partisanship make Congress more transparent? Would you know a Republican or a Democrat when you saw one? Do you believe a person's party makes their political agenda easier to predict? Do you believe political parties in Congress are strong or weak? What do the media suggest in terms of the strength of political parties in Congress? Do you think the party caucuses at the beginning of each congressional term encourage political gridlock or support the building and maintenance of certain principles? Why are committees arranged in terms of party control? Why is it that while we are encouraged to vote our conscience at the polls that members of Congress are compelled, sometimes by force, to support the party's line on controversial legislation? Is it possible to be partisan and principled at the same time, or is it necessarily one or the other?

Seeking and Retaining Information: The Benefits of Incumbency

Would you rather see term limits imposed to limit corruption or keep things the way they are? Do you think the information that incumbents accrue over time is worth the corruption that getting them re-elected costs? Do you believe that information accruement is something that is undervalued among the American public, or do you think that the political corruption, a result of incumbency, outweighs the good gained through the gathering of information? If you were in Congress, why would you want to know as much about the legislation you're working on as possible? Would the information you gained be a positive ally or could it make you enemies as well?

Hiding Beneath the Cloak and the Members of Congress' Bids for Re-Election

Do you think that the goal of most members of Congress is to get elected and reelected? What are the benefits of advertising? If you were running for Congress, what kind of advertising techniques would you use to win people's votes? Would you employ negative advertising? Are there pros and cons for taking credit for a piece of legislation? What else might a member of Congress take credit for other than legislation? Is there a time to remain neutral on issues, or should members of Congress be required to report their positions on political issues? Why do some members of Congress refuse to report positions on certain issues?

The Wisdom of the Third Brother and Two Styles of Representation

Which representative style do you like better: the delegate or the trustee model? Do you think there are more delegates or trustees in Congress? Do you think that delegates could be perceived as pushovers? Could trustees be perceived as arrogant or unconcerned? Which representation style would produce better laws and more effective governance? Do you think that it is possible for a trustee to be as uninformed and as uninvolved as the constituents he represents? Do you think we would be better served with more delegates or trustees in Congress? What do you see more of nowadays: delegates or trustees? Is that trend likely to continue? Why?

Now that you've got the Cloak on,
The only thing you're missing in your ensemble

Is a good pair of shoes that'll take you from where you are to where you ought to be…

Works Cited

Cox, Gary W. and Mathew McCubbins. *Setting the Agenda: Responsible Party Governance in the House of Representatives.* New York: Cambridge University Press, 2005.

"Cruz Concludes All-Night Speech Against ObamaCare As Vote Looms." *Fox-News.com. http://www.foxnews.com/politics/2013/09/25/cruz-vows-to-speak-against-obamacare-until-unable-to-stand-as-vote-looms/.* Posted on 09/25/2013.

Hulse, Carl. "Despite Prestige, The U.S. Senate's Allure Seems to be Fading." *The New York Times. http://www.nytimes.com/2009/02/05/world/americas/05iht-05senate.19944656.html?_r=0.* Posted on 02/05/2009.

Krehbiel, Keith. *Information and Legislative Organization.* Ann Arbor: University of Michigan Press, 1992.

Mayhew, David R. *Congress: The Electoral Connection.* New Haven: Yale University Press, 1974.

Murray, Shaiglah and Lori Montgomery. "House Passes Health Care Reform Bill Without Republican Votes." *The Washington Post: Politics. http://www.washingtonpost.com/wp-dyn/content/article/2010/03/21/AR2010032100943.html.* Posted on 03/22/2010.

Rowling, J. K. (BB) *The Tales of Beedle the Bard.* New York: Arthur A. Levine Books, 2008.

Rowling, J. K. (CS) *Harry Potter and the Chamber of Secrets.* New York: Arthur A. Levine Books, 1999.

Rowling, J. K. (DH) *Harry Potter and the Deathly Hallows.* New York: Arthur A. Levine Books, 2007.

Rowling, J. K. (GF) *Harry Potter and the Goblet of Fire.* New York: Arthur A. Levine Books, 2000.

Rowling, J. K. (HBP) *Harry Potter and the Half-Blood Prince*. New York: Arthur A. Levine Books, 2005.

Rowling, J. K. (OP) *Harry Potter and the Order of the Phoenix*. New York: Arthur A. Levine Books, 2003.

Rowling, J. K. (PA) *Harry Potter and the Prisoner of Azkaban*. New York: Arthur A. Levine Books, 1999.

Rowling, J. K. (SS) *Harry Potter and the Sorcerer's Stone*. New York: Arthur A. Levine Books, 1998.

Russell, Matthew. "Trustee or Delegate: A Legitimate Question Facing Political Representation." *Student Research Briefing Series: Volume II, Issue II*. Medford: The Department of Political Science at Tufts University, 2012.

"U.S. House GOP to Introduce Shortly New Immigration Plan, Including Path to Legal Status." *Fox News Latino*. *http://latino.foxnews.com/latino/politics/2014/01/17/us-house-gop-to-introduce-in-days-new-immigration-bill-including-path-to-legal/.* Posted on 01/17/2014.

CHAPTER 14

There's No Place Like Home: *The Wizard of Oz* and American Domestic Policy

One of the most iconic American films of all time is *The Wizard of Oz* with Judy Garland playing the young, likable Dorothy Gale who lives on a farm with her Aunt Em (Auntie Em) and Uncle Henry on the Kansas prairie. Dorothy is swept away by a tornado and whisked away to the magical Land of Oz, a land initially described in a novel by L. Frank Baum. The 'no place like home' philosophy Dorothy ultimately embraces embodies the subject matter discussed in this chapter – one dedicated to American domestic policy – the political realities facing Americans here at home. There are so many facets of domestic policy, I can hardly claim to cover them all, but I will certainly address the most discussed topics of the day and how they relate to the land that Dorothy finds 'over the rainbow'.

Dorothy in her Ruby Slippers in the magical Land of Oz

The Wizard of Oz

The musical film *The Wizard of Oz* begins in black and white sepia tones with Dorothy, a young Kansas farm girl, running home with her dog, Toto, in an attempt to outrun her malevolent neighbor, Almira Gulch. Gulch had attempted to strike Toto with a rake as punishment for chasing her cat, but Toto retaliates and bites Gulch on the leg, and the 'witch' swears retribution. Dorothy returns home to her Aunt Em and Uncle Henry and tells them of her plight, but they see her problem as minor and instruct her not to worry. Dorothy then seeks out three of the farm hands for advice. The first one, Hunk, tells Dorothy that she's not thinking rationally about the problem with Miss Gulch – like she had no brains and gives her rational advice about how to proceed with the problem – keeping Toto away from Miss Gulch's place (Bolger and Garland). Next, Dorothy speaks to Hickory, but he ignores her and dismisses her problem like he had no heart (Haley and Garland). Finally, she speaks to Zeke, and he tells Dorothy that maybe a bit of courage would do her good (Lahr and Garland). Dorothy finds little comfort in the advice given her and frets about what Miss Gulch will do about Toto (Fleming).

Indeed, Miss Gulch arrives at Aunt Em's house and demands custody of the dog in order to see that he is destroyed. Dorothy is distraught, but Toto escapes Miss Gulch before she can turn him over to the authorities. Sure that Gulch will return in an attempt to recapture Toto, Dorothy and Toto pack their bags and run away from home. Shortly after Dorothy leaves, she and Toto meet Professor Marvel, a magician and fortuneteller. He deduces that Dorothy has run away from home and tricks her into believing that her Aunt Em is dying of a broken heart caused by Dorothy's sudden departure. Dorothy rushes home, but as she arrives, a massive storm blows up and a tornado begins ripping away the Kansas countryside. Unable to escape into the safety of a storm shelter, Dorothy retreats to her bedroom and is knocked unconscious when her window is blown out by the tornado's ferocious winds. Dorothy wakes up to her house being tossed about by the tornado and sees a number of the people she had met that day flying by in the tornado's winds (Fleming).

When the tornado finally drops Dorothy's house and it lands with a crash, Dorothy opens the door to discover the dazzling Land of Oz – the first part of a film ever depicted in Technicolor. Dorothy emerges and investigates her surroundings and is greeted by Glinda, the Witch of the North. She asks Dorothy, "Are you a good witch or a bad witch?" because the people of that land, the Munchkins, had summoned her and informed

A tornado whisks Dorothy off to the Land of Oz – a land Dorothy supposes is over the rainbow.

her that a 'new witch' had dropped a house on and killed the Wicked Witch of the East (Burke). Dorothy assures Glinda that she is not a witch but only a Kansas farm girl who wants to go home. The Munchkins thank Dorothy earnestly for destroying the Witch of the East and begin to celebrate, but their elation is short-lived (Fleming).

In a plume of fiery smoke, another witch appears, the green-faced Wicked Witch of the West, and she is greatly angered that Dorothy killed her sister, the Witch of the East. She seeks the powerful Ruby Slippers that her sister, the Witch of the East, had used to shape the world as she pleased, but Glinda magically transports the Slippers from the dead Witch's feet to Dorothy's feet. The Witch of the West threatens to destroy Dorothy and Toto, but Glinda reminds her that Dorothy had killed her sister with the house that still lay atop her sister's dead body. The Witch of the West departs with the threat of, "I'll get you, my pretty, and your little dog too!" (Hamilton). Glinda warns Dorothy to keep the Slippers on at all times else she will be vulnerable to the Wicked Witch's power (Fleming).

Dorothy arrives in Oz, makes some friends, and defies an enemy.

Dorothy is distraught that she cannot get home, but Glinda tells Dorothy to seek out the Wonderful Wizard of Oz who lives in the Emerald City far away and directs her, with all of the Munchkins to, "follow the yellow brick road' (Burke and the Munchkins). Dorothy then begins her adventure skipping down the yellow brick road and comes across a cornfield where a scarecrow is hanging on a pole. Incidentally, the scarecrow himself is covered in crows. He unexpectedly speaks to Dorothy and laments over his plight. He believes that the crows fail to take his 'scariness' seriously because he is not smart enough to scare them away; he believes if he had a brain in place of the straw that filled his head, he would be able to deal with the crows and protect his cornfield (Bolger). Dorothy invites him to travel with her to the Emerald City to meet the Wizard of Oz – one who might have the power to give him a brain (Fleming).

The two friends travel on and enter an apple orchard. They happen across a very rusty man

Emerald City – the home of the Wonderful Wizard of Oz

made entirely out of tin, with his oil can just out of reach. Upon oiling him up, Dorothy finds out that he had been rusted into the position in which Dorothy had found him for a long time. Being made entirely of tin, the Tin Man laments that the tinsmith who built him forgot to give him a heart, and he puts his great desire to share the feelings of humans like Dorothy into song. Again, Dorothy invites her new friend to join her on her trip to the Emerald City in hopes that the Wizard can give her friend a heart. Before departing the orchard, however, Dorothy and her friends are confronted by the Wicked Witch of the West; the Witch warns Scarecrow and Tin Man to leave Dorothy alone so that she can exact revenge, but, in spite of the Witch, the two friends swear to protect Dorothy on her journey to the Emerald City, the home of the Wizard (Fleming).

The final stretch of yellow-bricked road that lies before the Emerald City leads the three friends into a dark, damp, and frightening forest. Dorothy, Scarecrow, and Tin Man hear noises and attempt to flee, but their progress is stopped by a Lion who chases Toto; Dorothy catches the Lion and slaps him. Shockingly, the Lion cries out and admits that he is a coward. He believes that rather than being the King of the Forest, he is a laughingstock because of his cowardice and wishes he had the courage to assert his position of royalty (Lahr). Dorothy invites the Cowardly Lion to join her, Scarecrow, and Tin Man on their journey to the Emerald City (Fleming).

Finally, the friends emerge from the forest and find that the Emerald City is in sight. Towering above the forests in the center of the beautiful landscape, Dorothy and her friends believe that the magnificence of the Emerald City is indicative of the Wizard's power. Before they make it to the Emerald City, however, the Witch of the West casts a spell on the meadow of poppy flowers that blocks their path which causes anyone who walks amongst them fall into a deep, death-like sleep. The Cowardly Lion and Scarecrow tearfully implore anyone in earshot for help, and magically, Glinda lends a hand by causing a light snow to fall which breaks the Wicked Witch's spell and allows the friends to advance to the Gates of Emerald City. While initially refused admittance, Dorothy's possession of the Ruby Slippers enables Dorothy and her friends to gain admittance to the City to seek an audience with the Wonderful Wizard of Oz (Fleming).

As Dorothy arrives in Emerald City, so too does the Witch of the West who, with massive black plumes of smoke, instructs Dorothy to surrender. This frightens the citizens of Emerald City and they seek out the Wizard for advice; the Door Guard to the Wizard's audience chamber assures everyone that everything is fine and that the Wizard has everything in hand (Morgan). Dorothy and her friends approach the doorman and ask for an audience with the Wizard and demonstrate that Dorothy is the one the Witch is seeking to destroy. After initially being denied, the four friends are admitted to see the Wizard. After walking down a long hall to the Wizard's audience chamber, they find a room dominated by a terrifying image of the Wizard created by white smoke. He seems to know what each of the friends wants, but in order for the Wizard to answer their pleas, he commissions them to go on a Quest to retrieve the broomstick of the Wicked Witch of the West (Morgan). Scarecrow points out that they might have to kill her to successfully complete the Quest (Bolger), but nevertheless, the Wizard dismisses them, and the friends depart toward the Witch's castle (Fleming).

Before they arrive, the Witch dispatches her minions – the flying monkeys – to kidnap Dorothy and Toto – a task they complete successfully. The Witch attempts to remove Dorothy's Ruby Slippers but is tormented by shock at the mere touch of them; she then remembers that the Slippers won't come off until Dorothy dies. She locks Dorothy in a tower and gives her an hour to live. In that time, however, Scarecrow, Tin Man, and Cowardly Lion infiltrate the Witch's castle and successfully rescue Dorothy from the tower. The Witch, however, attempts to block their exit by dispatching her minions around the castle, and the four friends are captured. The Witch attempts to kill the first of Dorothy's friends, Scarecrow, by burning him, but when Dorothy tosses a pail of water onto her friend to save him, the Witch is caught full in the face with the liquid and melts. Thus, Dorothy kills the Witch of the West, and her

The four friends destroy the Witch of the West and take her broom back to the Wizard.

minions gladly hand over the broomstick that the Wizard ordered them to obtain.

The four friends return to Emerald City and present the broomstick of the Witch of the West to the Wizard. After being told to come back tomorrow so that the Wizard can give thought to the wishes of the four, Toto reveals a man behind a curtain who, while appearing to be a normal guy, admits being the Wizard of Oz. He confesses that he has no magical powers, but his knowledge of science convinced the citizens of Oz that he was a wizard; he had used their folly to become powerful but had secluded himself so that the truth would never be discovered.

He is, however, able to keep his promise to Dorothy's three friends. He reveals to Scarecrow that he is already intelligent and wise, but the Wizard gives him a college diploma to remind him of his wisdom and problem-solving skills. Second, he tells the Cowardly Lion that he possesses the courage that he believes he lacks but bestows upon him a medal of honor to symbolize the courage he possesses. Next, he informs the Tin Man that the human emotions he desires can be both a blessing and curse but gives him a heart-shaped testimonial to remind him of the human emotions he already had. The Wizard informs Dorothy that her problem, unfortunately, is unlike the dilemmas faced by her friends. He concludes

The Wizard departs in his hot-air balloon but Dorothy, while trying to recapture her dog Toto, misses her ride back to Kansas.

that the only way to get Dorothy back home is for him to take her himself. As a man from Kansas himself, he proposes to return to Kansas via a magnificent hot-air balloon – the same method of transport that brought the Wizard himself to Oz.

"There's no place like home." (Garland)

Dorothy and the Wizard prepare to leave Oz by balloon, but immediately prior to the balloon's launch, Toto sees a cat and leaps from Dorothy's arms to chase it. Though the Wizard attempts to slow the balloon's ascent, Dorothy is left behind as the Wizard in his balloon is lifted away. Dorothy's friends try to comfort her but she is inconsolable. Scarecrow, in his wisdom, sees Glinda approaching and suggests that she might be able to help Dorothy with her problem. Glinda reveals that the Ruby Slippers that had been on her feet have the power to take her home. After saying fearful goodbyes to her three friends, Scarecrow, Tin Man, and Cowardly Lion, she clicks her heels together three times while repeating, "There's no place like home" (Garland). The Slippers transport her home and she awakes in her bedroom with her family surrounding her (Fleming).

Dorothy sees the three farm-hands and recognizes the faces of Scarecrow, Tin Man, and Cowardly Lion. Professor Marvel stops by her shattered window, and Dorothy recognizes him as the Wizard. Miss Gulch, upon reflection, reminded her of the Wicked Witch of the West. Dorothy concludes, after her adventure in Oz (which may or may not have been a dream), that sometimes the things we want are not as far away as they might seem; perhaps searching what one has will reveal what one is actually searching for, her musing indicates. She swears never to 'leave' again and asserts that, indeed, "There is no place like home" (Garland). Dorothy embraces her family and her dog, Toto, and the film comes to a conclusion (Peterson).

The Wizard of Oz and American Domestic Policy

Dorothy's adventures in Oz are eerily representative of a number of realities facing millions of Americans here at home. The transition from the black and white background of Kansas to the Technicolor depiction of Oz represents changes in the environment that, some believe, require the assistance of the government to alter. Dorothy's arrival in a 'foreign land' –

Oz – is similar to the experience of the immigrants traveling (some illegally) to the United States, and her reception by the Munchkins and the Wicked Witch depict both sides of the immigration reform debate. The four friends (Scarecrow, Tin Man, Cowardly Lion, and Dorothy), the Wizard, and the Wicked Witch of the West compare to other issues facing our nation – some more controversial and some less so. The needs and desires of the four friends are comparable to the different forms of government programs available for citizens that make it easier or more affordable for them to make their dreams come true. The friends' journey down the yellow-brick road is indicative of the engagement required of citizens if they wish to see political, economic, and social change. The Ruby Slippers that Dorothy obtains is comparable to the potential each individual has and the initiative each needs to take to succeed. Finally, the encouragement and direction that Glinda and the Munchkins provide Dorothy with is comparable to the wisdom and enthusiasm that average citizens could be and should be willing to share with those around them. I think that you will find that Oz, the land of infinite possibilities, provides us with a mirror we can use to investigate the problems that face America today; it will also allow us to assess both where we are as a country and in what direction we should be headed.

Seek and Receive: Civic Engagement and Government Assistance

The Wizard of Oz relates the journey of four individuals on the way to the Emerald City to see the Wonderful Wizard of Oz. Dorothy, a farm girl from Kansas, *wants to go home.* Scarecrow, believing himself to be an inept protector of corn, *wants the intelligence necessary to scare the crows away from his cornfield.* Tin Man, while made entirely of tin, *wants a human heart so he can experience human emotions.* Cowardly Lion, the King of the Forest in all but deed, *wants a bit of courage so he can assert his position as forest royalty.* All four of these individuals desperately desire something, and they travel to Emerald City to implore the Wizard, the head of government, for aid (Peterson).

Instead of giving these individuals what they desire outright, the Wizard demands something in return – the broomstick of the Witch of the West. Facing great danger, the four friends attempt and succeed in obtaining it and the Wizard then consents to grant their requests. The way these requests are fulfilled, however, is not how Dorothy, Scarecrow, Tin Man, and Cowardly Lion expect. Three of these individuals (Scarecrow, Tin Man, and Cowardly Lion) discover that the power or trait they desire is already theirs but are given reminders of its presence – permanent fixes for temporal problems. Dorothy's plight, however, is more complicated and the Wizard takes more direct measures in an attempt to ensure that her needs are also met, though indirectly (Peterson).

Like the four friends, many people across America are plagued with innumerable problems and personal setbacks, and most of these individuals look to the government to help them overcome the obstacles they face throughout their lifetime. More often than not, citizens seek financial assistance to make it from job to job, to help pay for health care, and so on. To get what they want, however, individuals have to be well versed enough in government to know where to go for help and how to ask for it. If the help they seek doesn't exist, it's up to them (and other people like them) to demand that the government establish programs that address their needs. This is known as **civic engagement** – the interaction of a government with its citizens. In a democracy, citizens are expected to be active participants in government so that the needs of the people are adequately addressed by the people's representatives in Washington, D.C.

Dorothy and her friends sought the power and wisdom of the Wizard to solve their problems, and he addressed them as best he could. Similarly, just as citizens are expected to appeal to their government in their need, so too is the government responsible for addressing the needs demanded by the people. While the national state and local governments can and do use the imposition of new laws to address the needs of the people, there are other methods by which the government attempts to provide what its citizens need. Another method of addressing the needs of the people is through **direct provision;** this is a policy tool that enables a government, once having made laws, to hire people to carry them out. For example: most people want their mail delivered in a timely fashion; to fulfill this need, the government creates post offices and a mail system to ensure that this particular need of the people is met. Another policy tool that governments employ is the **cash transfer**; with this policy tool, governments (national, state, and local) allocate monies to individuals who need it. Cash transfer programs would include unemployment benefits, Pell grants to college students, and Social Security funds divvied out to senior citizens of a certain age. All of these programs enable the government to financially meet the needs of citizens who require assistance. A similar policy tool governments utilize is the lending of money through loans to individuals who require it; one type of loan that most of you are probably familiar with is

Unemployment benefits – one of many cash transfer programs utilized by the federal government

the college loan. The government offers students low-interest loans, depending on their eligibility, to enable them to pursue a degree in their desired career field; the large sums of money the government lends to students is often a risk that traditional financial institutions are unwilling to risk lending to people with no current means of repaying it.

Black and White to Technicolor: Environmental Change

Though unimportant to the plotline of the film, the dramatic shift from the black and white background of Kansas to the Technicolor relation of Oz was a breakthrough for the film industry. The dramatic shift in landscape from drab to color encouraged Hollywood to utilize the effects of color to a whole new level. Instead of focusing on the plotlines, Hollywood began to put more effort into costuming, set design, and special effects – all because of the introduction of color to the Hollywood film scene. The switch from black and white to color altered American film history forever (Baker, 1-4).

Just as the physical landscape of film changed through the invention of Technicolor filming techniques, so too has the natural environment of America been altered. Most of this rapid environmental change is attributed to mankind putting its (often dirty) imprint on a fragile planet. Environmental change is wreaking havoc on our natural surroundings and destroying the very little natural landscape left on our planet. Some believe that it is the government's responsibility to address these problems while others contend that environmental protection should be secondary to other pressing issues.

As Americans spread across the country, they both built things up and tore things down. One of the things they tore down was the large forests that spanned the country. Deforestation, while a problem of America's past, is still an issue today. With citizens moving out of urban areas into less populated areas, deforestation is again becoming a real problem.

Just as the 'environment' of film changed with the invention of Technicolor, some Americans believe it's our job to protect our natural environment like this beautiful forest.

The Environmental Protection Agency, along with other environmental groups, is stepping up to try to limit deforestation both through the planting of new trees and by lobbying for laws that limit the level of deforestation (Biello, 1-3).

Another man-made environmental hazard being discussed is the attainment of natural gas through the 'fracking' process. Fracking is the use of water and other chemicals to force natural gas to ascend to the surface so that it can be used. Unfortunately, the chemicals used in the fracking process are known to get into the groundwater and cause major health problems. Numerous types of cancers are attributed to human exposure to the chemicals used in the fracking process (Steingraber, 1-4). The presence of these illnesses in and around fracking zones suggests that perhaps the natural gas industry's assertions that fracking is safe might be worthy of further scrutiny.

One of the most notable environmental topics out there today is that of global warming or 'climate change.' This issue refers to an unnatural warming of the Earth that is being caused by too much pollution entering into the atmosphere and also, perhaps, a natural cycling of global temperatures. The pollution prevents the sun's rays from reflecting off of the Earth's surface and returning to space which accelerates warming on the Earth – one which some say could be disastrous for mankind and many other species spread across the planet. Some contend that the rapid uptick of severe storms, tornadoes, hurricanes, and the like can be attributed to climate change (Mason, 1).

Climate change is often blamed for the uptick in devastating storms, severe droughts, and rising temperatures.

Conversely, some argue that climate change is a bunch of nonsense – that it's something liberals have invented so as to suck more money into environmental protection programs. They argue that while some scientists support the premise of climate change, many others do not and conclude that the Earth's climate rotates in cycles; they contend that right now, Earth happens to be in a warming cycle (Montopoli, 1-2). Climate change has been a hot-button issue since the late 90s when Al Gore, Bill Clinton's vice-president, aided in the production of a film discussing climate change, *An Inconvenient Truth*. This issue will likely continue to stir emotions for many years to come – so long as the summers continue to get hotter, storms continue to become more destructive, and droughts continue to become more severe.

Environmental change, though one of many issues facing our country, is one that millions of people are concerned about. The rapid change in our natural landscape – some say for the worse – is a subject that has received a high level of scrutiny. Whether man or Earth's natural weather cycles are the culprits of this change, many expect the government to address these issues so as to minimize the negative outcomes associated with environmental decay. The goings on in our world – both natural and man-made – are forever altering our country's national landscape just as the addition of color, as seen first in *The Wizard of Oz*, has stirred the hearts and minds of millions of Americans as they watch their favorite stories come to life on the big screen.

Dorothy – A Stranger in a Foreign Land: Immigration Reform

When Aunt Em's house finally lands after being tossed about by the Kansas twister, Dorothy emerges out of the front door into a dazzling landscape – the Land of Oz. Upon arriving there, she is cordially welcomed by the Munchkins – the inhabitants of the region where she landed – and by Glinda, the 'good' witch. They inform her that she has removed the threat of the Witch of the East and celebrate their freedom is musical fashion. The Witch of the West, however, welcomes Dorothy in a much more sinister way. She is upset that her sister, the Witch of the East, was killed when Aunt Em's house landed on her; she is further infuriated when Glinda bestows the Ruby Slippers unto Dorothy and not to her. The Witch of the West plots revenge, and it is the interaction between Dorothy and the Witch of the West that becomes one of the main elements of the film's plot line.

In America, we have many millions of individuals – like Dorothy – that have come here from other countries. Some of them have followed the legal procedures to become legal residents (some even pursue citizenship) while others see fit to enter the country, live here, and work here illegally. Just as Dorothy met two different points of opinion in regards to her presence in Oz, so too have the millions of illegal immigrants met two different philosophies regarding their presence in America. The first philosophy argues that immigrants who have come here illegally have the right to be here and pursue their dreams. The second ideological perspective contends that these immigrants should have followed the established procedures for entering the country and should either be penalized or deported back to their country of origin.

Proponents of the first perspective argue that most immigrants who come here illegally are seeking either a better life or the financial ability to provide for their families who remain in their home country. For this reason, those who believe that these immigrants have the right to be here also believe in **amnesty** – the idea that illegal immigrants would be pardoned for ignoring current immigration laws and permitted to, over time, pursue permanent residency or citizenship for themselves and later, their families. President Obama and his administration have been outspoken in the pursuit of legislation that would grant amnesty to the millions of illegal immigrants currently residing in the United States (Gomez, 1-4).

Opponents of this policy path argue that it is ludicrous to reward people for breaking the law; many realize, however, that it is likely impossible to deport every illegal immigrant living in the country and see the benefit in some sort of path to residency. Rather than granting illegal immigrants amnesty outright, some contend that these illegal immigrants should have to pay some sort of fine but then be permitted to live here barring any sort of criminal activities – which would be grounds for immediate deportation. Thus, these individuals hope to make productive law-abiding citizens out of these folks who, at least initially, came here by criminal means. Early in 2013, the former presidential hopeful for the Republican Party, Mitt Romney, shifted his position to reflect these sentiments (Fox News Latino, 1-4).

This position is much different than the line Romney took during the 2013 presidential campaign. Romney, some say, espoused an extremist perspective on immigration reform (i.e., deportation or 'self-deportation') and alienated the Latino vote (Madison, 1-2). This is the polar opposite of the amnesty line and one that a sizable number of Americans support (Kane, 1-3). For many Americans, there are only two choices in terms of immigration reform – either to grant them amnesty or to deport them. It seems, however, that the issue is more complicated still, for many of these immigrants didn't come alone; many brought their children and some have given birth on U.S. soil which grants those children all the rights of citizenship, even though their parent(s) are not legal citizens.

Another conundrum is what to do with the thousands of children who came here illegally with their parents. Should they be allowed to pursue jobs and a college education? The DREAM Act argues that yes, they should be given this opportunity, because it is no fault of their own that their parents brought them here and they shouldn't be held back in the world because of their parents' (arguably) poor decision. This is a piece of legislation that has been debated for over a decade, but in 2014, Congress has selected it as one of the first pieces of legislation that they will consider (Cornfield, 1-2); it is possible that they are doing so because of the upcoming congressional elections in November. The plight of undocumented immigrants and their children is one which could yield one of two end results, and I contend that their conundrum is akin to Dorothy's unexpected trip to Oz; some supported and welcomed her, and others did not.

Many college students expect that attaining a college diploma will guarantee them employment. Unfortunately, the current economy proves this belief untrue in many cases.

If I Only Had A Brain: Investing in Intelligence and Career Potential

Scarecrow is the first character that Dorothy meets when traveling down the yellow-brick road on her way to see the Wizard, and she discovers that Scarecrow is upset because of his lack of the brains to deal with the crows infesting his cornfield. He believes that a brain will give him the intelligence to deal with the crows and properly fulfill his role as the guardian of the cornfield. The Wizard, understanding that Scarecrow already has a brain, gives him a diploma to represent his intellectual prowess (Peterson).

Like the Scarecrow, so many Americans attempt to seek intelligence by entering into and completing their education. While fifty years ago, a high school diploma could get you a job with a living wage, today that is no longer true (Bauknecht, 1). Instead, young people are almost forced to pursue higher education in order to make them competitive in the job market; even with a college diploma, however, finding a job (especially in a tough economy) can be really rough.

Many Americans complain that while the benefits of a college education are high, the costs are astronomical. Most people who attend college are stuck repaying student loans deep into their 40s – many who are unable to find a job in their field of study (Berman, 1-2). For this reason, many people across the country – and many politicians in Washington – are beginning to contemplate the possibility of pursuing education reform. There are two sides to this coin; the first is reforming K-12 programs while the other focuses on reforming higher education systems.

K-12 reform predominantly addresses the problem of substandard schools – most of which exist in inner-city areas. Numerous programs like **busing transfer programs** – transporting students from a poor school district to a successful one so as to increase their chances of success – have been tried numerous times, but the results of these programs are inconclusive at best; the effort and funds necessary to pursue busing programs often cripple the districts (Crouch, 1-4). On the other hand, parents from the successful districts tend to get upset about the possibility that the students being bused in will increase crime, drug use, and other problems; many parents have expressed that rather than busing students to different districts, the government should pursue programs to revitalize school districts that are failing (Killeen, 1). All of these concerns – both in support and opposition to these transfer programs – are valid ones and will likely continue to prove problematic until conclusive evidence of their success or failure is found.

Reforming K-12 programs across the country has proved to be a very messy, complicated business; if we want future students to succeed in obtaining a good education and a career in their desired field, inadequate K-12 programs need to be reformed in some way so as to ensure that all students, with effort, have a fair shot at success. If we choose not to invest in the education of the young people of tomorrow, we can hardly expect their success to exceed or match our own.

While K-12 programs across the country are proving to be problematic, many claim that higher education poses some serious challenges to America as well. For one thing, the cost of higher education is exorbitantly high; to

Earning a college diploma, like the adventures of the Scarecrow, is often more difficult than one initially thinks.

attend college, most students have to take out loans to make college affordable – if you want to call it that. According to the Institute of Education Sciences, the average tuition for one year of college in the United States is $13,600 (public) and $36,000 (private) (IES, 1-3). So, the total average cost for an undergraduate education at a public university or college is someplace around $60,000. I could be wrong, but that seems awfully expensive – especially when considering that so many graduates don't even end up working in their field of study.

The cost of higher education in general is a real problem, but it is particularly problematic for low-income earners. These folks find it difficult – if not impossible – to afford a college education, and in a job market that essentially requires a college degree for HR to even look at your resume, not attending college (or some variation of it) is, for most, simply out of the question. While numerous scholarships and government loans are available for low-income earners, evidence still shows that low-income earners enroll (and therefore graduate) in far smaller numbers than middle- or upper-class citizens (Farkas, 1-4). I'm not saying that money buys an education, but we can conclude that it definitely makes getting a good education easier. Without the ability to pay for or subsidize a college education, people have a much smaller chance of entering into the field of their choice – even if their background in the field exceeds that of other candidates who possess a college diploma or certificate from a technical school.

Whether it is the K-12 programs or America's institutions of higher education, I think most would agree that our education system needs to be reformed in some way. Some believe that local school districts (in the case of K-12 education) should take the lead while others believe that the national government should play a more active role. Either way, Americans across the country are traipsing down their 'yellow brick road' seeking a brain-full of knowledge – and a diploma to prove it.

If I Only Had a Heart: America's Evolving Health Care System

After departing the cornfield with Scarecrow, Dorothy and her friend encounter Tin Man, a woodsman who was nearly rusted solid in an apple orchard. With an oil can nearby, his medicine of sorts, he laments that the tinsmith who made him forgot to give him a heart. He wants a heart so that he can feel the depths of human emotions, so Dorothy invites him to go to Emerald City to see the Wizard. The Great and Powerful Oz concludes that although Tin Man already has the capability to express human emotions, he needs a heart (of sorts) to remind him that the emotions he desires are there to experience; to fulfill Tin Man's requests, the Wizard gives him a heart-shaped clock with a chain (Peterson).

In a very real sense, thousands of Americans out there are in desperate need of a real human heart, but due to high health care costs along with the limited number of heart donors, for some, the odds of getting a new heart, unlike Tin Man's, are almost nonexistent. America's health care system, to put it simply, is a hot mess. The two most well-known programs

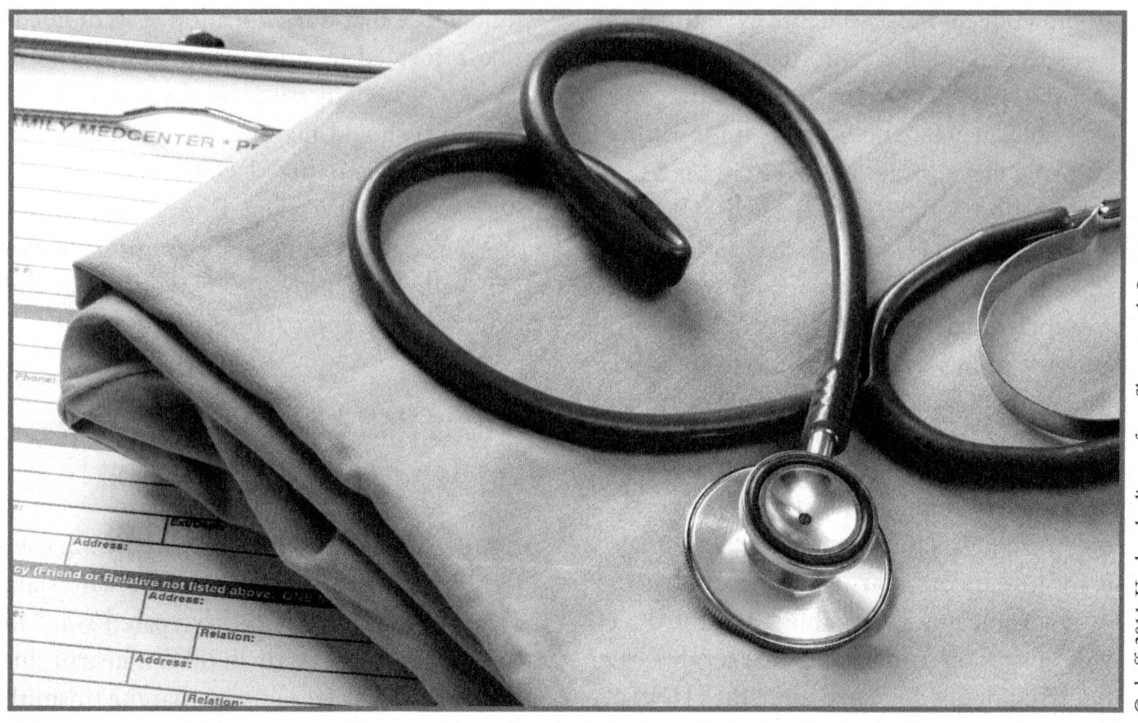

Just as Tin Man wanted a heart, so too do many Americans seek better health care; unfortunately, it often comes at a high cost.

out there which enable people to better afford health care – Medicare and Medicaid – are in big trouble. Because of this, President Obama (and many presidents before him) has pursued a massive health care overhaul. Obama's initiative, unlike those of previous presidents, survived – the Patient Protection and Affordable Care Act (i.e., Obamacare).

The first program, Medicare, was established to enable senior citizens, who have paid into the program all their lives through payroll taxes, better afford health care during the time of one's life where accessible and affordable health care is most important. Unfortunately, the program's funds are drying up due to an irregularly large population of senior citizens who are now using the system; most often, this group of seniors is referred to as the 'baby boomers'. Not only are there more people using the program, but the cost of health care is definitely on the rise. Joseph Newhouse, Professor of Health Care Policy and Management at Harvard University, argues that one reason costs are going up is the new medicines and procedures that modern innovation have been made available to patients nationwide; naturally, when things are new and relatively untested, the price tag of such procedures and medicines will be higher (Newhouse, 1). Both the increase in Medicare benefit recipients and the rise in costs due to inflation and innovation have put Medicare's future in doubt. Other programs in the health care field are feeling the heat as well.

healthcare.gov – the online tool where citizens can enroll in the health care exchanges mandated in the Patient Protection and Affordable Care Act

Another struggling health care program today is Medicaid – a social health care program designed to help low-income citizens of all ages across the United States who do not have the financial capability of affording health care. Medicare is the largest health care provider for low-income citizens in the United States. Individuals or families on this program are **means-tested** – meaning they must demonstrate their financial inability of paying for health care on their own before they can attain Medicaid coverage. This program, like Medicare, is financially struggling; since the financial crisis of 2008, more and more people have fallen into the 'low-income' category and thus qualify for this program's coverage (Goldstein, 1-3). With more people on the program with no additional funding, one can understand why the program's coffers are strained.

Perhaps the biggest news in American health care policy is the Patient Protection and Affordable Care Act (PPACA or Obamacare); it was signed into law on March 23, 2010. The PPACA is an attempt to entirely overhaul the health care system in the United States. It is predominantly created, like Medicaid, for low-income earners who find health insurance to be unaffordable but was also designed, over time, to lower health care costs across the country. While individuals still have the right to seek out private insurance, the PPACA created health care exchanges which are designed to enable citizens to search the different health care plans offered by the government and enroll if they so choose. It was not designed to change health care itself but rather the health insurance industry which is often blamed for the rising costs of health care (HHS.gov/HealthCare).

A number of provisions in the law guarantee young adults the ability to stay on their parents' health care plans until they turn 27. It also is supposed to prevent health insurance companies from denying individuals coverage who have pre-existing conditions. It ensures that most preventative care – like annual checkups, immunizations, and other essential medical care – is covered; some of these services are to be covered with no cost to the insured person. Most Americans consider these provisions of the PPACA to be positive changes (HHS.gov/HealthCare).

One change included in the PPACA is what most refer to as the 'individual mandate'; this requires all citizens 18 and over to have health insurance by 2014. A sizable number of Americans believe the individual mandate to be an invasion of privacy. They contend that individuals have the right to choose whether or not to buy health insurance; these argue that the government is overstepping its bounds when it forces its citizens to buy health insurance which, in some cases, they still cannot afford (Fox News).

Another controversial element of the PPACA is its coverage of contraceptive services. The bill requires all insurance policies to cover numerous methods of contraception as well as the morning-after pill. Many employers and religious groups have objected to this provision citing that contraceptive care goes against their religion, but the Obama administration, among others, contends that the choice to use contraceptives or the morning-after pill is one to be made by the individual and shouldn't be inhibited by one's employer. The issue is currently under scrutiny and is to be considered by the Supreme Court in 2014 (Mears, 1-3).

As I said before, America's health care industry is a hot mess. Millions of Americans need health care but cannot afford it – even with the new provisions included in the Patient Protection and Affordable Care Act. Medicare and Medicaid are on the verge of financial collapse. As usual though, millions of Americans across the country are heading to the 'Emerald City' and asking the Wizard for a heart – and other human appendages besides; we depend on the government to provide basic services, and some believe that health care is one of them.

If I Only Had the Nerve: Homeland Security

The last of the friends to join the crowd on the way to Emerald City is the Cowardly Lion, the King of the Forest who believes that he lacks the courage to do his duty. He laments being afraid of virtually everything, and so he joins Dorothy and company on their journey in hopes that the Wizard of Oz might give him some courage. After the Wizard sends them on the quest to retrieve the Witch's broomstick and Dorothy is captured, Cowardly Lion leads Scarecrow and Tin Man (dressed as the Witch's guards) into the Witch's castle to rescue Dorothy; the Lion

The medal of honor given to Cowardly Lion – a prize won by the folks brave enough to protect us and rescue us from potential domestic threats and those abroad

took action to get a certain reaction – namely, a successful rescue. For his bravery in dealing with the Witch, the Wizard bestows upon him a military medal of honor commemorating the courage he displayed – and actually had to begin with.

Just as Cowardly Lion sought to defend his home territory, the forest, and establish a position of power and reverent fear within it, so too does the government have a vested interest in promoting homeland security. Especially since the terrorist attacks of September 11, 2001, the federal government has taken steps to ensure the safety of the millions of Americans living here at home. Soon after 9/11, President Bush created the Department of Homeland Security (Washington Post) which was predominantly created to prevent future terrorist attacks on U.S. soil but also to force the number of government intelligence agencies to share information so as to limit the likelihood of future attacks due to the lack of communication.

Homeland security, however, is not just about preventing terrorist attacks; it also attempts to mitigate the damage and aid in the recovery efforts of disasters that happen across the country. When hurricanes slam into the U.S. mainland, earthquakes rattle dishes, or volcanoes erupt, it is the duty of the Homeland Security department to help the people who have to pick up the pieces after these disasters strike (Holthaus, 1-3). Granted, as the Department of Homeland Security is relatively new compared to other more established government departments, I think most would agree that it has done a pretty good job at fulfilling its obligations.

Despite its youth, the Department of Homeland Security has been home to its own set of scandals. Since 2010, the National Security Agency (NSA) was caught spying on American citizens' social networking pages, phone calls, and emails – in the name of national security. Unfortunately, most Americans perceive the surveillance of this government agency (and a wing of the Department of Homeland Security) to be a massive violation of our right to privacy as guaranteed us by the Fourth Amendment. Also, some contend that the 'innocent until proven guilty' standard was violated by these surveillance techniques

When disaster strikes, the Department of Homeland Security shifts into gear to help protect and save lives, homes, and businesses.

employed by the NSA (Risen, 1-2). The Department of Homeland Security, therefore, had to ensure that the agencies maintain a certain balance – one that both enables them to do their jobs but also keeps in mind the rights of the average American citizen.

Off to See the Wizard: Dorothy and the Citizen's Quest for Political Relevance

Dorothy, a simple farm girl from Kansas, finds herself swept away by a tornado to the Land of Oz. She discovers that the Land of Oz, in her eyes at least, is drastically different from Aunt Em's house in Kansas. She finds herself to be immersed in a land full of diversity and many interests vying for power – whether it is the Witches, the inhabitants of Oz, or the powerful people dictating policy in the Emerald City. All Dorothy wants is to go back where she came from, but Glinda informs her that her only hope is to seek out the Wonderful Wizard of Oz, and so Dorothy embarks on a journey to do just that (Peterson).

On her way to see the Wizard, she meets a number of characters who, like her, have needs and desires that they cannot attain on their own – or so they think. The four friends arrive in the Emerald City and successfully gain an audience with the Wizard. Instead of giving them what they want immediately, he demands a service of them – the retrieval of the broomstick of the Witch of the West. Once the friends successfully complete that task, the Wizard prepares to fulfill the friends' wishes. He finds, however, that three of them already possess the qualities they are seeking. Scarecrow has intelligence, Tin Man can feel and express human emotion, and the Cowardly Lion already possesses the courage he desires (Peterson).

Dorothy, however, has needs that cannot be met as the desires of the others are. Dorothy's desire to return home is something that the Wizard has to actively attend to; he himself, in order to fulfill her request, prepares to leave Oz and take her home via air balloon

– a venture that proves unsuccessful. Only Glinda's intervention enables Dorothy to discover how to get home – by using the Ruby Slippers (Peterson).

Dorothy, understandably, is supposed to be the character that we can most easily identify with. She, at least in this book, represents the average American and all the hopes and dreams they possess. Like many Americans, Dorothy looks to the Wizard – the power in government – to help her attain a basic need – to find her way home. Many Americans across the country also lack basic necessities like access to health care, a good education, housing, employment, and so on. Just as Dorothy seeks out the Wizard for help, so too is the government expected to step up and assist these people in getting back on their feet or, if they are incapable, providing them with basic necessities so as to ensure their survival in our society. Most people would call these programs **welfare** or **entitlement programs.** Simply put, there are far too many entitlement programs for me to discuss here, but I will address a few of them: social security, public housing projects, and food stamps.

Social Security is an entitlement program designed to aid seniors, low-income citizens, and severely disabled people along during times of need. The monies collected for Social Security via payroll taxes is then split up into two trust funds – one for seniors and low-income families and the other for disability assistance. For this reason, the program's financial stability has become more and more shaky. The program as initially created during Franklin Roosevelt's presidency was designed to aid low-income families, but benefits for the program have been extended over time while the population has also increased. One of the major reasons for the program's financial disparity, like Medicare, is the amount being paid into the program via payroll taxes is less than the amount being paid out of it in benefits (Burnett, 1-3). Despite the fact that social security is in financial trouble, it is an entitlement program that many Americans depend on.

Social Security, like Aunt Em's house (and Dorothy's home), provides individuals with comfort and security that the outside world often denies the folks who need it most.

Another program that thousands of Americans depend on is public housing projects. This program attempts to provide affordable housing for those who cannot afford a house or rent for an apartment. These building projects are typically owned by the government (either local or state) and thus can offer lower (and therefore, more affordable) monthly rates than most apartment complexes and are, in most cases, cheaper than a monthly house payment. The problem with public housing, however, is that it seems to draw a rather sour crowd. Many (but not all) public housing projects are riddled with drug deals, crime, and other unsavory activities; for this reason, most communities are reluctant to allow public housing projects to be pursued near them (Kirp, 1-3). Public housing projects, while being a blessing for those who utilize this government assistance, prove for some to be a real headache.

The last form of government assistance discussed here is food stamps. This form of government assistance has evolved a lot in the last few decades, but some contend that further changes are necessary. This program is meant to provide low-income or no-income Americans with basic sustenance. One of the most well-known food assistance programs is the Supplemental Nutrition Assistance Program (SNAP). It provides food and basic needs to low-income and no-income families; another well-known program that provides this form of government assistance is WIC (Women, Infants, and Children). WIC provides food and basic necessities to women who are pregnant, breastfeeding, or have children under age five.

Both of these programs have modernized in the last decade, but with modernization comes new ways of abusing the system. For both WIC and SNAP, the assistance recipients use a debit card to pay for the products they need; most of these cards allow people to get cash back – just like a normal debit card (Blaisdell, 1-2). Unfortunately, while both WIC and SNAP track what recipients purchase by tracking transactions made on the card, they are unable to track any transactions that are paid for in cash. It is likely that some recipients of these programs use the 'cash back' option to buy things that the government would not sanction. Despite this flaw, food assistance programs serve a vital purpose in aiding individuals who lack the means to provide these basic necessities to their families.

The Man Behind the Curtain: The Wizard and the President

Once Dorothy's house lands in Oz, she is approached by the Munchkins and also by Glinda who inform her that the only person with the power to return her to Kansas is the Wizard of Oz. As Dorothy travels along the yellow-brick road, she meets Scarecrow, Tin Man, and Cowardly Lion and convinces them that the Wizard might be able to help with their own ineptitudes. Once they arrive in Emerald City, however, they see the more political side of the Wizard. Once the friends successfully gain an audience with him, they present their pleas; instead of fulfilling their requests, however, he sends them on a Quest to (inevitably) destroy one of his political rivals, the Witch of the West. Once that is completed, the four friends return to Emerald City. Again, instead of receiving their reward, the Wizard instructs them to come back tomorrow so that he may consider how best to help them.

Mount Rushmore: a reminder that ordinary men like the Wizard of Oz, a simple man from Kansas, can attain greatness

Before they depart the Wizard's audience chamber, Dorothy's dog Toto discovers a man behind a curtain speaking into a microphone and working feverishly at a large machine. Dorothy and her friends confront the man and he confesses to being the Wizard of Oz – a man with no real magical powers at all. In fact he confesses to Dorothy that he is, "a very good man but a very bad Wizard" (Morgan). His wisdom, however, enables him to aid Scarecrow, Tin Man, and Cowardly Lion, but he is unsuccessful in aiding Dorothy in the disastrous air-balloon departure – though one could say that the balloon accident was Toto's fault and not the Wizard's (Morgan).

An important point to make about politics here in America is that it is a group effort. Just as the four friends travel to Emerald City to seek the Wizard's help, so too do many, many people aid in the formation, passage, and implementation of government policy. The inhabitants of Oz (namely Glinda and the Munchkins) convinced Dorothy that the Wizard was all-powerful and had the ability to solve any problem she and her friends might have; this proved not to be the case – not directly at least. Instead, the aid of others was necessary for Dorothy to see her wish come true.

This is a major point I want you to grasp. All too often, we hear on the news how something or other is either the president's fault or the president's success. Put simply, this point of view is very simplistic and often untrue. In a democracy like ours, millions of people take part in the legislative process – definitely Congress, the president, and the courts – but also the thousands and thousands of people working in the federal bureaucracy, the major political parties, and us – the American people. So just as Dorothy discovers that the Wizard possesses less power than rumor suggested, so too can we be sure that U.S. presidents are not nearly as powerful as the media portray them to be. Presidents cannot single-handedly write and pass laws and see to it that the laws are implemented in the way they want them to be. Presidents are incapable of forcing Congress to embrace their agenda. They aren't even granted the power to facilitate the moving and shaking in their own political party most of the time. Like the Wizard, presidents are only as powerful or weak as the people around them and can only accomplish the things that their moderate level of power permits them to pursue.

To be sure, presidents throughout the ages have used their rumored power to make campaign promises necessary to win votes. In nearly every presidential election, one candidate will promise to fix the economy in x number of years, or swear to reform the welfare system, the education system, Wall Street, or some such area in need. In general, these are promises that presidents cannot single-handedly keep on their own; they need the aid of Congress in passing and implementing laws that achieve these objectives, and they also need the support of the courts to allow the law to stay on the books. Presidents are by no means a Wizard; but neither was the man behind the curtain.

The Witch of the West: Green with Power Envy

Dorothy's only enemy in *The Wizard of Oz* is the Wicked Witch of the West, a wretched character with green skin and long, pointed nails. She is angry that Dorothy (indirectly) killed her sister, the Wicked Witch of the East. She is also upset because Dorothy has acquired her sister's Ruby Slippers – magical footwear with a hidden power. Glinda advises Dorothy to keep the Slippers on as the Witch's desire for them suggests that they are indeed magically powerful. Throughout Dorothy's journey to the Emerald City and beyond, the Witch seems to be right behind her, threatening her and her friends; the Witch hopes

The Wicked Witch of the West - Dorothy's greatest threat during her adventures in Oz

to bully Dorothy into giving up the Slippers, but that proves to be unsuccessful (Peterson).

The Witch eventually captures Dorothy and discovers by touching and being shocked by the Slippers (which remain lodged on Dorothy's feet) that the shoes won't come off so long as Dorothy lives. The Witch confines Dorothy to a tower in her castle and gives her an hour to live. Before the hour is up, however, Scarecrow, Tin Man, and Cowardly Lion rescue Dorothy and nearly escape the Witch's castle. The four friends are captured by the Witch and she attempts to kill Scarecrow by burning him to death, but Dorothy tosses a pail of water on him and accidentally causes the Witch to melt and die (Peterson).

The Witch of the West is a lot like the folks in Washington – lobbyists, large corporations, and so on – who attempt to control the policymaking process rather than letting it be dictated by the American people – the true seat of power in American government. So many voices seem to drown out those of the millions of Americans seeking a say in Washington politics. The inability to be heard often discourages citizens from getting involved and convinces them that nothing they have to say is going to be taken seriously; thankfully, this is not necessarily true.

One of the most recent events that re-enforces the impression that money runs the government was the Supreme Court's ruling in the *Citizens United* case. In this case, the Supreme Court ruled that corporations could donate unregulated amounts of money to any political campaign of their choice (Liptak, 1-3). Some people believe that such rulings reinforce the sentiment that the agendas of corporations will always outweigh the desires of the millions of financially restricted citizens across America – that money, for some, can buy happiness, influence, and power while everyone else is expected to accept both that their fate is to remain politically insignificant and their ideas, hopes, and dreams are irrelevant. We can only hope that the citizens of America are willing to take the steps to reclaim the power guaranteed the people by our form of government from those who, arguably, have usurped it or, in comparison, are willing to keep the Ruby Slippers, a noteworthy source of magical power, away from the Wicked Witch.

It's All About the Shoes: Taking the Initiative to Pursue the American Dream

Right after Dorothy arrives in Oz, she is presented with a pair of Ruby Slippers – footwear that had previously been owned by the Wicked Witch of the East. When the Witch of the West discovers that her sister has been killed, she immediately searches for the Slippers, but Glinda magically transports them to Dorothy's feet instead. Glinda advises Dorothy to "keep tight inside of them. They must be very powerful or she [the Witch] wouldn't want them so badly" (Burke). The Witch is infuriated when Dorothy refuses to give her the Slippers and plots revenge on her and pursues her for most of the story until, of course, Dorothy accidentally melts her (Peterson).

The Slippers become an integral part of the story when Dorothy's attempted departure

It's all about the shoes and the trip down the yellow-brick road: personal initiative and the individual journey of self-discovery

with the Wizard of Oz ends disastrously. Glinda appears and tells Dorothy that the Slippers had always possessed the power to take her back to Kansas; she simply had to understand their power – their ability to transport a person from one place to another. She ultimately uses the Ruby Slippers to transport her back home to Kansas and is reunited with her family.

From a certain point of view, we could say that the Ruby Slippers represent something very real in American political culture – personal initiative. Like the Slippers, it is a trait that most people have to have a desire to use; most find its use most appropriate after some sort of self-discovery occurs – as indeed happened to Dorothy during her trip down the yellow-brick road. Sadly, there are millions of people across this country that are brought up and, either directly or indirectly, taught that they will never amount to anything, have no potential, and wasting their time taking personal initiative in themselves or their dreams. I think Dorothy would disagree as her Slippers were the only thing that enabled her to get from where she was to where she wanted to be.

In the film, Dorothy had to wear the Slippers for most of the film to understand what she actually had on her feet – the key to attaining her dream of returning home to Kansas. Similarly, most people have to see for themselves what a bit of personal initiative can do for them before they totally commit to a lifestyle driven by it. This is not meant to suggest that people not taking initiative are lazy or unmotivated; instead, I prefer to think of these people, like Dorothy, as folks who have yet to realize how positive the outcomes of employing personal initiative can be. Or, they could be like Scarecrow, Tin Man, and Cowardly Lion – gifted individuals who are unable to see the beauty and potential in themselves and their dreams. A wise person once said to me that Dorothy and her Ruby Slippers are proof that the right pair of shoes can change a person's life. Perhaps that is also true for the rest of us as well – so long as we are willing to break the shoes in and use them, like Dorothy, to get from where we are to where we ought to be.

The Munchkins: Little People Have Big Voices

The first individuals Dorothy meets when arriving in Oz are the Munchkins, little people who had been governed by the Wicked Witch of the East. Unintentionally, Dorothy had released them from their slavery when her house landed on and killed the Witch. The Munchkins are a lively people and communicate their thanks to Dorothy in song – before the Witch of the West shows up. After Dorothy's enemy departs, the Munchkins attempt to help Dorothy begin her journey to the Emerald City with chants of, "Follow the yellow-brick road" (Munchkin choir). It was their encouragement and direction that set Dorothy on a path to Emerald City and ultimately, the fulfillment of her dreams.

The Munchkins are, like Dorothy, very similar to us; they are, quite literally, the little people. We believe – and you were taught – that in a representative democracy, the little people are the people with the power to make a difference in national politics. Unfortunately though, it seems that both in America and in Oz, more powerful people have taken control of the government. In Oz, the Witches and the Wizard control and subdue Oz's inhabitants while in America, corporations, lobbying firms, political parties, and many others besides seem to have far more power than you or I do.

The Munchkins' interaction with Dorothy provides us with a glimmer of hope, though. Instead of remaining neutral and attempting to hinder or dissuade Dorothy's journey to the Emerald City to ask for the Wizard's aid, they help her and attempt to direct her on the path she needs to take to get what she wants; Dorothy's path happens to take her down the yellow-brick road. If the 'little people' in *The Wizard of Oz* can aid Dorothy in her journey, why can't we, the little people in America, help each other, encourage each other, and teach each other about the importance of political involvement and activism? If more people were more interested in politics and concerned with what was going on around them, I think you would find America's citizens far less inactive; instead, I think we would find that the 'little people' can make a big difference.

The journey of Dorothy and her friends down the yellow-brick road in the Land of Oz, their desires and dreams, and their active role in attaining them is comparable to the many issues that face America here at home. From education to health care, from environmental policy to entitlement programs, America's agenda is booked for years to come. All we, as the little people, have to do is put on those Ruby Slippers and follow our dreams down the yellow brick road in search of that something that we desire that seems, like Dorothy's dreams, to be somewhere over the rainbow.

The yellow-brick road: the road on which to follow your dreams and believe in a better tomorrow.

Food for Thought

Civic Engagement

Why are so many Americans afraid or unwilling to be politically active? Are they afraid they won't see results from their own effort or do they just not care enough to do anything political? What would it take for you to become politically active? What are some political issues that you are concerned about? What should be done in regards to those issues? Do you believe that your voice would be heard if you tried to do anything political? If you attempted to be politically active, do you think your friends and family might as well? How much power does one person have to affect the world around them? Do you think that, if you tried hard enough, you could be the catalyst for big changes in this country? If so, what changes would you make first?

Immigration Reform

Which side are you on? Do you believe in amnesty or should those who broke the law by coming here be sent back where they came from? Is there a gray area when considering these two perspectives, or do you think that most people are either in support or opposition of immigration reform? Should children of undocumented workers be eligible for student loans as the DREAM Act argues or not?

Environmental Protection and Preservation

Do you believe that our natural environment is as fragile as the politicians in Washington say it is? Do you believe in climate change, or do you think that Earth's cycling temperatures are to blame for the recent changes in weather? What should we be protecting in terms of the environment? Should factories face stiffer regulations if it costs jobs, or should the livelihoods of people outweigh environmental concerns? How important, compared to other issues, is environmental protection? If it's really important, why are other issues less important and vice versa?

Education

Growing up, do you believe that you received a good education? What elements of your education were the best? The worst? What would be the first thing that you would change in the education system? Is education a right or a privilege? If you believe it's a right, why isn't a college education more affordable? If you believe it's a privilege, what other paths should those not financially able to attend college do in place of pursuing higher education? Should higher education be a venue for education, indoctrination, or both? Do you believe college professors are better educators or better indoctrinators? If you could change one element of your education, what would it be? What could the education system do to ensure more college graduates found jobs? What could potential employers do to indicate their employment needs to college grads or those nearing graduation?

The Health Care System

What, in your opinion, is the biggest problem with the health care industry? Who drives up costs, in your opinion – doctors or the health insurance companies? What can be done to fix the system? It seems that the problems with both Medicare and Medicaid is that too much money is going out and not enough is coming in; what can be done to resolve that problem? Was 'Obamacare' a good solution to our country's health care problem, or could we have done better? If you aren't a fan of Obamacare, what elements of it would you change? Do you think good health care is a right or a privilege? Defend your answer. Should everyone be required to have health insurance, or should purchasing health insurance be a personal choice? Should employers be required to provide insurance policies that cover contraceptives and, in some cases, abortion services, or should employers be able to opt out of those plans due to religious conflicts?

Homeland Security

Do you feel safe here in the United States? What makes you feel safe? What do you believe that our government could do to make us safer at home? Are we ready for the next terrorist attack? Is the government proactive enough to anticipate what the next threats might be, or are they too reactive in only fixing known vulnerabilities? Are we ready to deal with the next Hurricane Katrina or Superstorm Sandy, or have we yet to learn from our past mistakes in disaster recovery? Are you willing to give up certain personal liberties to be safer, or would you rather be freer in a world that's a bit more dangerous?

Government Assistance Programs

Do you believe that the majority of people receiving government assistance are using it in the right way, or do you believe that most people abuse the system? What can be done to limit the level of welfare abuse? Should government assistance recipients be drug tested before assistance is awarded? Is social security a program worth sustaining or should it be taken out of the government's hands and privatized? Should the government be responsible for protecting your future or should you? Social Security was initially designed to be a safety net – something to fall back on when times were tough, but now people live off of it as their only source of income. Is it possible that this is one reason why the social security trust funds are so depleted? How do you feel about public housing projects? Should the government be stepping in to ensure folks have a roof over their heads, or should people be able to do this stuff themselves? What about food subsidies for low-income or no-income families? How can these programs be reformed without hurting those that receive them (namely, the children of assistance recipients)?

Political Corruption

How corrupt do you believe the politicians in Washington are? Are all of them corrupt, or only some of them? Do you think your own representatives and senators are corrupt or just everyone else's? What is it about Washington politics that seems to encourage political corruption? How influential is money in this picture? What about the desire for greater power? Do you think political scandals are, more often than not, an attempt by one politician to oust another from a position of power, or are scandals self-induced problems?

Personal Initiative and Following One's Dreams

How motivated are you to achieve your personal goals? Do you think most people are as motivated as you, less motivated than you, or more motivated than you? What encourages you to follow your dreams, to work harder, and to risk more to get there? If you had been raised to believe that you had no potential and that your hopes and dreams would never come true, how would you live your life? How many people do you think this has happened to? How can the people who are motivated best aid the people who are not? Dorothy's trip down the yellow-brick road taught her the value of the Slippers she wore – the power to get from here to there. In your current situation, what is 'here' and what is 'there'? For America, where are we now and where should we be in the future? What can we do to get from Point A to Point B?

Encouraging Each Other's Political Potential

How seriously do your friends take your opinions? If you were to talk about political issues with them, would they dismiss the conversation, or would they become interested simply because you are interested? How influential do you believe your political opinions are in the grand scheme of things? Is it possible for one person to make a difference in his or her locality? State? Country? What would it take to encourage Americans to become more involved with the political process? Why does it seem that those who are uninvolved feel unimportant but those who are politically active feel that their efforts matter? Do you think, as with Dorothy, that's it's all about a little encouragement in the right direction?

We can take a trip down the
yellow-brick road
If you're willing to 'risk' it...

Works Cited

Baker, Lindsey. "Technicolor Fashion: The Wizard of Oz." *Colour Lovers. http://www.colourlovers.com/fashion/blog/2010/08/06/technicolor-fashion-the-wizard-of-oz.* Posted on 08/06/2010.

Bauknecht, Sara. "High School Isn't Enough for Job Market." *Pittsburgh Post-Gazette. http://www.post-gazette.com/education/2011/02/10/High-school-isn-t-enough-for-job-market/stories/201102100525.* Posted on 02/10/2011.

Berman, Jillian. "Underemployment Widespread Among College Graduates: Worst for Business Majors – An Analysis." *The Huffington Post: Business. http://www.huffingtonpost.com/2013/06/18/underemployment-payscale_n_3459887.html.* Posted on 01/10/2014.

Biello, David. "City Dwellers Drive Deforestation in 21st Century." *Scientific American. http://www.scientificamerican.com/article.cfm?id=city-dwellers-drive-21st-century-deforestation.* Posted on 02/08/2010.

Blaisdell, Elaine. "WIC Program Phases Out Vouchers for Debit Cards." *Cumberland Times News. http://www.times-news.com/local/x1267062943/WIC-program-phases-out-vouchers-for-debit-cards.* Posted on 11/18/2013.

Burnett, Bob. "What's Wrong With Social Security?" *The Huffington Post. http://www.huffingtonpost.com/bob-burnett/whats-wrong-with-social-s_b_3162372.html.* Posted on 04/26/2013.

Cornfield, Jerry. "State House Will Debate Dream Act on Opening Day." HeraldNet. *http://heraldnet.com/article/20140113/BLOG13/140119674/State-House-will-debate-Dream-Act-on-opening-day.* Posted on 01/13/2014.

Crouch, Elisa. "Normandy Says Transfer Law is Crippling District." *St. Louis Post Dispatch. http://www.stltoday.com/news/local/education/normandy-says-transfer-law-is-crippling-district/article_bb2bde66-afe1-5090-ae0a-7c457d6c80cc.html.* Posted on 11/12/2013.

Farkas, Karen. "Michelle Obama to Focus on Encouraging Low-Income Students to Attend College: Higher Education

Roundup." *Cleveland.com. http://www.cleveland.com/metro/index.ssf/2013/11/michelle_obama_will_focus_on_e.html.* Posted on 11/12/13.

Goldstein, Amy. "Medicaid Enrollment Rises Nationwide, Analysis Finds." *The Washington Post: Politics. http://www.washingtonpost.com/wp-dyn/content/article/2010/02/18/AR2010021805609.html.* Posted on 02/19/2010.

Gomez, Alan. "White House Immigration Plan Offers Path to Residency." *USA Today. http://www.usatoday.com/story/news/nation/2013/02/16/obama-immigration-bill/1925017/.* Posted on 02/17/2013.

Holthaus, Eric. "Department of Homeland Security Might Review Superstorm Sandy Warnings." *The Washington Post: Local. http://www.washingtonpost.com/blogs/capital-weather-gang/post/department-of-homeland-security-may-review-superstorm-sandy-warnings/2012/11/28/86fa3a94-398d-11e2-b01f-5f55b193f58f_blog.html.* Posted on 11/28/2012.

"Homeland Security Department." *The Washington Post: Politics. http://www.washingtonpost.com/politics/homeland-security-department/gIQALxPx4O_topic.html.* Site last updated on 01/11/2014.

"In About-Face, Mitt Romney Now Supports Legalizing Undocumented Immigrants." *Fox News Latino. http://latino.foxnews.com/latino/politics/2013/11/15/in-about-face-mitt-romney-says-undocumented-immigrants-should-have-path-to/.* Posted on 11/15/2013.

Kane, Tim. "Why 2014 Will Be the Year of Immigration Reform." *Fox News. http://www.foxnews.com/opinion/2014/01/03/why-2014-will-be-year-immigration-reform/.* Posted on 01/03/2014.

"Key Features of the Affordable Care Act." *HHS.gov/HealthCare. http://www.hhs.gov/healthcare/facts/timeline/index.html.* Site last updated on 01/10/2014.

Killeen, Kevin. "Normandy School District Chooses Accredited Francis Howell." *CBS St. Louis. http://stlouis.cbslocal.com/2013/07/03/normandy-school-district-chooses-accredited-francis-howell/.* Posted on 07/03/2013.

Kirp, David L. "Here Comes the Neighborhood." *The New York Times: Sunday Review. http://www.nytimes.com/2013/10/20/opinion/sunday/here-comes-the-neighborhood.html?_r=0.* Posted on 10/19/2013.

Liptak, Adam. "Justices 5-4 Reject Corporate Spending Limit." *The New York Times. http://www.nytimes.com/2010/01/22/us/politics/22scotus.html?pagewanted=all.* Posted 01/21/2010.

Madison, Lucy. "Romney on Immigration: I'm for 'self-deportation'." *CBS News. http://www.cbsnews.com/news/romney-on-immigration-im-for-self-deportation/.* Posted on 01/24/2013.

Mason, Rowena. "David Cameron 'Very Much Suspects' Climate Change is Behind Recent Storms." *The Guardian. http://www.theguardian.com/politics/2014/jan/08/cameron-suspects-climate-change-abnormal-storms.* Posted on 01/08/2014.

Mears, Bill. "U.S. Asks Court to Preserve Obamacare Contraception Mandate." *CNN News. http://www.cnn.com/2014/01/03/politics/supreme-court-obamacare/.* Posted on 01/03/2014.

Montopoli, Brian. "Rick Perry Suggests That Global Warming is a Hoax." *CBS News. http://www.cbsnews.com/news/rick-perry-suggests-global-warming-is-a-hoax/.* 08/17/2011.

Newhouse, Joseph. "What's Wrong With Medicare and How Can the Program Be Saved?" *Harvard University: Kennedy School of Government. http://www.hks.harvard.edu/news-events/news/articles/newhouse-interview.* Posted on 09/08/2008.

Risen, James. "N.S.A. Gathers Data on Social Connections of Citizens." *The New York Times. http://www.nytimes.com/2013/09/29/us/nsa-examines-social-networks-of-us-citizens.html?_r=0.* Posted on 09/28/2013.

Samuels, Bob. "Why All Public Higher Education Should Be Free." *The Huffington Post: College. http://www.huffingtonpost.com/bob-samuels/why-all-public-higher-edu_b_1099437.html.* Posted on 11/18/2011.

Steingraber, Sandra, Ph. D. "PA Public Health Assessment Finds Fracking Makes People Sick." *Eco Watch: Transforming Green. http://ecowatch.com/2013/08/27/finds-fracking-makes-people-sick/.* Posted on 08/27/2013.

"Supreme Court Upholds Individual Mandate, Obamacare Survives." Fox News. http://www.foxnews.com/politics/2012/06/28/supreme-court-upholds-individual-mandate-obamacare-survives/. Posted on 06/28/2012.

"Tuition Costs at Colleges and Universities." Institute of Education Sciences: Fast Facts. https://nces.ed.gov/fastfacts/display.asp?id=76. Site last updated on 01/10/2014.

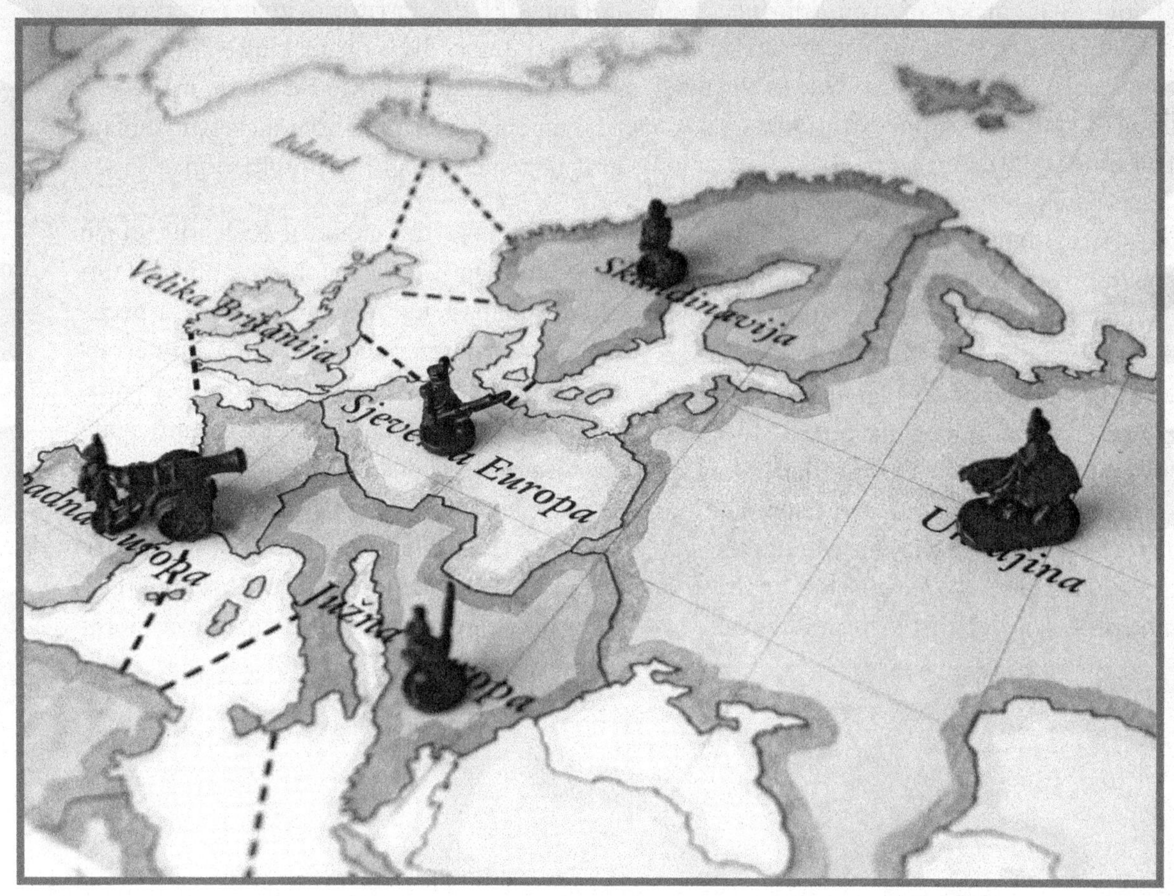

CHAPTER 15

A 'Risk' Worth Taking: The Board Game of Global Domination and America's Struggle to Win the Global Game of Thrones

I know that many of you, during your younger years, spent many a stormy day inside playing board games. One of the most famous (and most competitive) board games of all time is the game called Risk. The game is turn-based (players move clockwise as their turn arrives) and is played on a board that displays the rough depiction of a political map – which primarily shows territorial boundaries – of the world. The game encourages six teams to compete for 'global domination' or total control of the game board. Literally, true completion of this game (depending on how many players there are and how cautious the teams are) can take hours, sometimes even days – if the game is ever finished at all. The game of Risk is one that incorporates the randomness of the territories that one receives with strategic decision-making skills. The strategic decisions made throughout the rest of the game determine how successful a player is in achieving 'global domination.'

I contend that the game of Risk isn't much different than America's foreign policy strategies of the past and present. In some aspects, America's foreign policy can seem a bit erratic, even random at times. Other policy paths are clearly calculated and seek to anticipate the future decisions of other 'players' of the game – namely, foreign powers that seek to check or destabilize America's pre-eminence in the world. Like the game of Risk, the relations between countries are, whether we want

Just as players attempt to overtake the game board, so too do the countries in power seek to maintain it. Some of their strategies might seem random while others are clearly calculated.

to admit it or not, a struggle for dominance; some countries who have made it to the top have been benevolent leaders while others have discouraged support from other foreign powers. The same is true of the game of Risk. I think you'll find that American foreign policy, like the board game, is a 'risky' business.

The Game of Risk: Pieces and Process

Risk is one of the most well-known board games in which players employ calculated strategy and a bit of luck to enable them to succeed in dominating the game board. To win, players must be dedicated to their cause – even to the bitter end – willing to protect other players when strategy indicates that path of action is most appropriate, ambitious enough to go after territories (or countries) even though they seem impregnable, and wise enough to leave territories alone that clearly outmatch them. All of these characteristics are necessary – in their own measure – if one wants to win the game of Risk. This board game is a complicated one. Before we discuss the comparison between it and American foreign policy, let us first investigate how the game works.

The Pieces of the Game

In the game box, you will find a number of things. First, you will find a game board with a near-perfect rendition of a political map of the world. Next, you will find a deck of cards. Then, you will find six boxes with tiny pieces in them – some are square and some are oblong. Finally, you will find two sets of dice; three of the dice are white and three are red. All of these game pieces are integral to the game's beginning and conclusion.

The Board

On the game board, you will notice that all of the territories are divided into six continents (Antarctica is not included as that is considered to be international territory). At the bottom-right of the game board, you will see a box with the continent names and values next to them. This indicates how many extra armies you will receive – per turn – if you capture all the territories in that continent. Also on the game board are hashed lines from one continent to another. This indicates from which territories you may move from continent to continent; if continents are land-locked (do not require ocean travel), players are free to move between those continents at will.

The Deck of Cards

The deck of cards contains one card representing each territory as well as two 'wild cards'. As each player flips their cards over at the beginning of the game, they place three armies on each of the territories they were dealt. On each territory card is also a symbol – a knight, a cannon, or a soldier. When a player successfully captures a territory, he or she flips over one of their cards. Once you have three cards flipped that have either *the same symbol* or *three different symbols*, you receive five extra armies per turn. Two of the cards have no territories on them but instead have all three symbols printed on them. These are to be used as wild cards when attacking countries. Say you have two cards flipped that have soldiers on them; the wild card can be used as the third soldier and secure you five extra armies per turn. The deck of cards not only determines which player gets which territory but also aids players in gaining armies.

Each card in the deck either has a territory and a symbol (knight, cannon, or soldier) or is a wild card which has all three symbols depicted on it. The territory cards are important in determining which teams own which territories while the wild cards will aid teams in gaining a manpower advantage once they have attacked and captured enough territories.

The Six Boxes of Armies: The Teams

Strictly speaking, two to six players can engage in the game of Risk, but large groups can also play – provided that they divide into teams. In each of the six boxes are little cubes and oblong objects – all of the same color. The cubes represent one army while the oblong objects represent five armies. Because some of the territories on the game board are exceptionally small, sometimes it is necessary (in crowded spaces) to consolidate one's armies and trade in the cubes for the oblong objects (which henceforth I will refer to as submarines). If there are less than six players engaging in the game, I encourage people to either leave out the red box or the pink box as the colors, at a distance, appear to be very similar and the occupation of territories, when nestled together, can and has proved to be problematic.

The six teams that engage in game-play can be starkly different. Some teams are ultra-aggressive while others are super passive. Some teams openly attack weak territories while others leave them to fortify and make a valiant stand (often to the death). Some teams' strategies are unclear for most of the game while others are predictable to the point of absurdity. All of these teams interacting on the game board make for an intriguing dynamic – and lots of fun.

The Dice of the Attacker and Defender

In the box are two sets of dice; three are red and three are white. The red dice are known as the 'attacker dice' while the white ones are known as the 'defender dice'. People play this part of the game in many different ways – some of which veer starkly away from the

The red dice in the box – the dice of the Attacker

rule book. The method described henceforth is how I have always played it. When one player (or team) attacks another territory, that player has to declare how many dice he or she will roll. The same is true for the player defending the territory that is being attacked. Both sides roll the dice. The player with the highest number on a single di (the highest possible number is six) is the winner. Ties always go to the defender and thus, the attacker loses armies. If the attacker wins the roll, the defender *always* removes one army from the board. Conversely, if the attacker loses, he or she must remove the number of armies from the board equal to the number of dice rolled. For example: say the attacker rolls three dice and the defender rolls two dice. Say the defender rolls a six and a two. The highest number showing is a six, and the defender wins. Because the attacker rolled three dice, he or she has to remove three armies *from the attacking territory*.

All of these pieces in the game of Risk are important – both to the actual game-play but also to our comparisons to foreign policy which will be made shortly. The board divides the world into territories and continents – all for the taking. The deck of cards, when dealt out, determines who occupies each territory as well as who will have the manpower advantage once the players begin attacking and capturing territories. The dice determine how many armies players lose during attacks. While these elements of the game seem simple, actual game-play is a bit more complicated.

Playing the Game

The first task set to the players is to divvy out the six boxes of armies and to (if a large group is present) divide the group into teams. If I might speak from experience, I suggest putting at least one person on each team who has played the game before (if possible); this will ensure that, if anyone gets confused, there is at least one person on the team who understands what is going on and can explain it to his or her team members as the game moves along.

The next task it to shuffle and deal out the deck of cards. The dealer will pass out cards in a clockwise fashion until all the cards are dealt out; the cards need to be kept face-down by each team in a neat pile. When I play, there are usually six teams and therefore, always extra cards. I usually divvy those out by having the teams choose a number between 1 and 10, and the closest team (or teams if there is more than one extra card) receive the remaining cards. Once each team has their cards, they are to flip one card over at a time clockwise from the dealer; the team to the immediate left of the dealer goes first. The team will flip over their card which will reveal a territory or a wild card; if the card denotes a territory, that team needs to take three armies out of their box and place it within the territory's borders on the game board. Teams should move clockwise until the entire deck of cards has been flipped over. Once all of the cards have been flipped over, each team needs to take their cards, shuffle them, and put them in a pile face-down to be used later when attacking and capturing territories.

Next, each team needs to take 24 armies out of their box and divide them into eight piles of three. Each team (clockwise from the dealer) will place their three armies on any territory *that they own*. Teams can either place all three armies on one territory or they can spread them out. The point of this exercise is to fortify the territories the teams believe to be defendable while, in essence, abandoning those that seem to be doomed for defeat. For example: say a team has one territory in Africa – which happens to be dominated by another team. The lonely territory in Africa will likely be attacked so that the team occupying most of Africa can capture it and claim the continent and the extra armies that entails. Therefore, the team owning the 'lonely territory' would be wise to leave that territory alone and fortify territories that seem 'safer' or less prone to attack. Each team should place their armies in a clockwise fashion until all of the teams have placed all 24 of their armies.

Now, the fun begins. Each team, at the beginning (and for the duration) of game-play, takes three armies and places them on any of their territories. Then, that team has the ability to attack another territory. If they attack, the territory they attack must have fewer armies than their territory does; the territory they attack must also touch (either by land or the hashed lines across oceans) the territory from which the attacker is coming from. For example: say 'Western United States' wants to attack 'Central United States'; both of the territories touch so therefore, that attack is legal. For every territory that the attacker captures, that team gets to flip over one of their cards and potentially gain extra armies; if the attacker loses, that team does not flip over a card. Even if the attacker loses, however, that team can attack other territories until they decide to stop. At the end of each turn, the attacker can fortify their territories; this means that the attacker can rearrange their

Armies attack opposing territories so as to gain control over the entire game board.

troops in territories *that touch each other.* The attacker could not, say, send troops from Japan to England unless that team owned all the territories between those two points. The game progresses like this until one team takes over the entire board.

Although the instruction manual doesn't explicitly allow them, many teams playing the game end up organizing themselves into alliances. **Alliances** are agreements where countries (or, in this case, territories) agree to protect and defend each other. They can be widely beneficial for all parties or geared to benefit one of the included members of the alliance. The duration of alliances varies from very short to extremely lengthy. Ultimately though, any team wishing to win the game will have to abandon their alliance partners in the name of capturing those territories so as to take over the entire game board. Typically in a game where alliances play a part though, the game doesn't end with one team defeating the others. Instead, the other teams will oftentimes come to a mutual agreement not to attack each other. Thus a certain peace arises – albeit a fragile one.

Another action that can be taken in the game is for one team or alliance to punish another that seems overconfident or over-aggressive. Generally speaking, in a game of Risk involv-

Alliances are nations united in their resolve to defend each other from foreign powers. If one is attacked, all retaliate against the aggressor.

played on PCs across the country. Players log onto the internet and can compete against adversaries from across the globe – making the game even more realistic. The rules are the same as are the processes of playing. The only difference is that communication between players is limited to the chat function included in the game. The chat is viewable by all players in the game, so alliances (and mutual dislike) might not be as subtle in the online version as they are in the actual board game.

ing six teams, there is usually one that is far more aggressive and **risk-prone** (likes to take chances) than the others; it is generally this team that the other five groups seek to eliminate first so as to make the game environment less hostile and more open to the strategic development of the game. Being the gutsy, bold team is often one way to assure failure – especially if the other teams are much more **risk-averse** (very conservative in their attacks and hesitant to provoke retaliation).

Risk as a Computer Game – With the Same Mission

While Risk is traditionally played with an actual game board, cards, and other various game pieces, technological advancement has created Risk – the computer game. Now, the Game of Global Domination can be (and is)

The Game of Risk and American Foreign Policy

Risk, a board game where players attempt to 'take over the world', is one that has taken the world by storm. No pun intended, but the weather of the world is rather stormy as well. Countries combat each other all the time (both diplomatically and militarily) and thus attempt to achieve global dominance or **hegemony**. Rich countries seem to leech the resources out of poorer countries yet leave them to solve their own problems when times get tough. Ideological shifts occur across the globe; some countries approve and join in the ideological dance while others try to boogie to their own tune. Sometimes, countries try to solve problems on their own and other times, the countries of the world unite together to address mutual difficulties. All of these actions (and sometimes, deliberate inaction) occur in the realm of global politics. The United States, as a powerful country, has a lot more say in what goes on than most countries but has been unable to shape the international landscape in the way that it sees fit.

The Board Game of Global Domination: World Systems Theory

As stated before, the game of Risk is one where the goal is to occupy the entire game board or, put a bit differently, to take over the world. Some teams, based on the cards they are dealt, will have a far better chance of doing so as the territories they possess might be all clumped together or exist in strategically defensible locations. Conversely, there will be teams that really get the shaft. Their territories will be all spread out and, inevitably, next to the team with all of their territories clumped together. Territorial location on the game board as well as a team's overall makeup of their armies will determine whether or not occupation of the game board is likely or unlikely.

In the realm of international politics, there are countries, like in the game of Risk, who have a better chance of affecting global politics than others. One of the most widely recognized theories in political science that discusses this is World Systems Theory. It organizes the countries of the world into three groups: the **hegemon** (or boss country), the **semi-periphery** (the allies of the boss country), and the **periphery** (the enemies of the hegemon or countries that it has no material or military reason to defend) (Wallerstein, 55-66).

Putting this theory into perspective, I think most scholars would agree that, at least as of now, the United States is the country wielding hegemony over the rest of the world (White, 1-2). The United States is clearly one of the most respected countries in the world as many states seek our aid in times of disaster and request military intervention when foreign powers attack them. The nice thing about being the hegemon, generally speaking, is that nobody can boss that country around; what the hegemon says generally goes – unless the rest of the world collectively

The hegemon, no pun intended, has the world in its hands.

unites against the hegemon's intended plans. Hegemony is a privilege only granted to a few countries, but to whom much is given, much is also expected.

Countries that fill the role of the hegemon are often expected to do things that the countries in the semi-periphery and periphery cannot. Generally speaking, the hegemon is typically financially stable – at least, far more-so than the other countries in the world system. Therefore, the hegemon is often expected to bail out countries that fall on hard times or that are inundated by disasters (Revkin, 1-2). The hegemon is also expected to intervene in military conflicts that might not necessarily benefit it; some see the United States' intervention in Iraq in the early 2000s as an unnecessary conflict that only harmed the world's perception of America (Montopoli, 1-2). The general rule for the hegemonic country is thus: much will be required of those who are given much.

The role of the semi-periphery is essentially to be Robin to the hegemonic Batman country. They are expected to uphold the ideals and protect the interest of the hegemon – for a price. While the semi-peripheral countries tend to be military allies, they also tend to be economic trading partners, and this dual relationship often enables the semi-peripheral countries to maneuver the hegemon into making concessions (political, economic, or military) to them that would never be made to their adversaries in the periphery. More often than not, however, the relationship between the hegemon and semi-peripheral countries is extremely friendly. Only on rare occasion do any real squabbles rear their ugly head; fortunately, the relationship between these countries and their shared interests makes the seeking and finding of a compromise much easier.

The fate of the peripheral countries is not one that most of us living in a hegemonic country could ever relate to (and hopefully never have to). If the hegemon doesn't like your country or its politics, your country will likely be seen as a 'bad guy' for a good long time. The hegemon's projected dislike of peripheral countries can keep them from being included in trade agreements which make doing business internationally cheaper, hinder the ability of the peripheral country to find allies in times of conflict, and restrict the way the peripheral country runs its government; if the hegemon disapproves, that country can (though it might not always) pursue military action to remove the sitting government and prop up a government more to its liking. The indifference or outright dislike of the peripheral country, as projected by the hegemon, can inhibit the ability of the peripheral country to move forward in making the lives of its citizens more fulfilling and desirable. I can only imagine how the poorer peripheral countries feel when they seek aid from the hegemon or the semi-peripheral countries and are denied the basic necessities of life oftentimes because the richer, more powerful countries don't believe there is anything to gain from providing this (often) desperately needed aid.

This system including a hegemon, semi-peripheral countries, and peripheral countries is known as a world system and is also

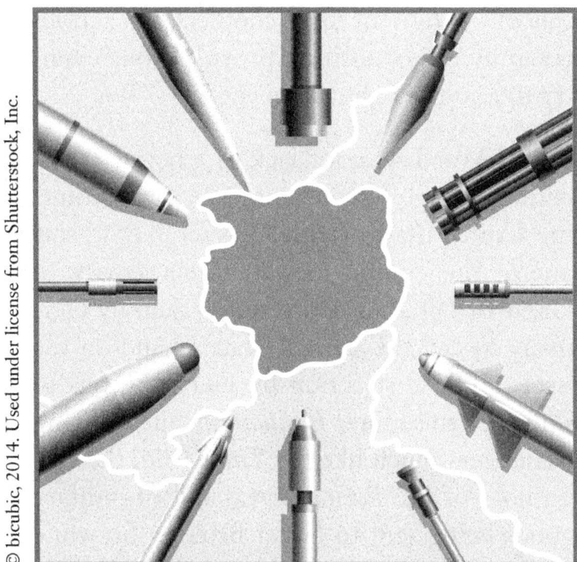

Just as some territories are more vulnerable than others, peripheral countries seem more prone to the ire of the hegemon and semi-periphery.

referred to as a **unipolar system** as there is only one hegemon. Another phenomenon can and has occurred where two hegemons compete for global power and the nations of the world divide between them. Each hegemon has its supporting semi-periphery and peripheral countries. This is known as a **bi-polar system** and it existed during the Cold War years. Both the United States and the U.S.S.R. (or Soviet Union) played the role of hegemon while Western Europe supported America, and Eastern Europe (west of Berlin, Germany) was the wingman of the Soviet Union. Finally, there can (and has been) many countries claiming global hegemony with their own supporting systems; this is known as a **multipolar system,** and it existed from the early 1800s until the end of World War II (Lundestad and Jakobsen, 1-3).

Just as a team's territorial position (both from a strategic and a 'big picture' standpoint) affects its quest to occupy the Risk game board, so too does a country's place in the world affect its citizens' chances of achieving success and happiness. The standard rule of thumb suggests that rich, powerful countries with rich, powerful allies are more capable of assuring happiness, safety, and order to their citizens than countries that are financially unstable and politically unpopular.

Strategies of the Game and the History of American Foreign Policy

There are many different strategies that are employed during a single game of Risk. Some teams employ the 'play it safe' method and attack other territories very rarely – if at all while instead choosing to fortify the territories they own. Other teams are very vocal as they play and threaten other teams when they threaten attack. Sometimes, a team's strategy will be very aggressive to start but will become more passive as the game goes on – typically because they lose so many armies. Other times, teams will see a potential problem area on the board and will attack prematurely – at least it might

The Cold War, the conflict between the United States and Soviet Union, was a tough pill to swallow for most Americans.

seem that way to the other teams – so as to prevent a larger problem from evolving later in the game. All of these strategies can and have aided teams in occupying the game board and achieving 'global domination.' So too has the United States employed many foreign policy strategies in its (comparatively) brief history.

Playing It Safe: American Isolationism

A lot of teams start off the game of Risk using what I call the 'play it safe' method. Oftentimes, teams are hesitant of attacking one another, because they fear that the victimized country will retaliate in turn. Other teams have territories that are so spread out that attacking other territories (rather than enabling that team to take over more of the board) makes it more likely that they will be eliminated quicker from the game. Also, some teams are made up of a group of wimps who really would rather watch than play; the 'play it safe' method is a method employed by teams who hope to simply maintain the **status quo** – the current situation. Minding one's own business is one way that teams seek to improve their chances in the game of Risk.

A similar strategy was employed by the United States from our nation's inception through the beginning of World War II – that of **isolationism.** Isolationism is the foreign policy strategy where countries attempt to remain uninvolved with the affairs of other countries; put simply, it's minding one's own business. This foreign policy strategy was relatively successful until the 20th century – particularly, I am referencing World Wars I and II. The United States made decent attempts to stay out of both of these conflicts, but actions taken by the opposition provoked our country to join the fight (Brinkley, 734-739).

World War I was, for lack of a better explanation, a huge European mess. At this time, the United States wanted desperately to stay out of the conflict despite their loyalty to Great Britain, but two actions taken by Germany forced the United States' hand on the issue. The first action by Germany was to sink the cruise liner *Lusitania*; while carrying passengers much like the *Titanic* did, the cargo hold of the *Lusitania* was full of military goods being sent to Great Britain. So while we were not totally innocent, sinking a cruise liner with innocent civilian passengers was perceived to be an act of war and worthy of action (Brinkley, 639). The sinking of the *Lusitania* was only the beginning, however. The real deal-breaker was the Zimmerman note.

The Zimmerman Note was a clearly malicious and militarily motivated telegram sent to the leaders of Mexico. The note promised the Mexican government that if they aided Germany in defeating the United States, the land that the United States had taken from Mexico would be returned to them. History indicates that the United States was less than pleased with the contents of the Zimmerman Note and the indentation of bombshells on German soil stand as proof of that. Although the United States valiantly attempted to stay out of World War I, it seemed that entrance into the war after these two actions by Germany was inevitable (Brinkley, 624).

America's hesitancy to enter World War II was much like the World War I scenario. The

United States was enveloped in a massive economic crisis (i.e., the Great Depression) and had no money to fund a massive war effort. The United States perceived the German threat (and the threat of Hitler) as something not worth risking further economic destabilization. Over time, however, then president Franklin Roosevelt saw the war as a tool to jump-start the American economy (Brinkley, 755). By engaging in the war effort, he put millions of people back to work producing war wares. He also united the country in giving them a common goal and identifying a common enemy – the Axis Powers (Germany, Italy, and Japan) (Brinkley, 756-758). Like most teams playing Risk at the start of gameplay, the United States was reluctant to get overly involved in international affairs. To put it simply, we had to learn how to play the game of world politics and won with flying colors – namely red, white, and blue. Our rise to global hegemony at the end of the Second World War, however, was short-lived, for a new kid on the block wanted a piece of our pie – the U.S.S.R. (or Soviet Union). The rise of a new challenger for global hegemony required the United States (and the Soviet Union in turn) to change their foreign policy strategy to one that discouraged their opponent from future challenges.

The sinking of the Lusitania (pictured) and the transmission of the Zimmerman note propelled the United States into World War I.

The Game of Threats: Deterrence and Containment

During game-play, teams are always goading each other and threatening rival teams. "If you attack me there, I'm gonna wipe you out here" or, "If you don't attack them there, I'm gonna attack your territory there." Phrases like this are heard about every two minutes – literally. Teams constantly threaten and blackmail each other into attacking a territory or refraining from attack to benefit their interests. It tends to be a very successful method of defense but is sometimes ineffective – depending on the nature of the opposing team. Some teams keep their word but others are lying or **bluffing.** One, in the game, however, needs to pay attention to the other teams and how they play. Teams need to note how aggressive other teams are, how often they keep their promises, and how willing they are to attack vulnerable territories. All of these things can change the dynamics of game-play and can critically change the overall game's outcome. If all teams act predictably, it is easier to move forward with a set strategy as the future actions of the other teams are more easily deciphered. Conversely, a game with one or two teams who act in an unpredictable way prevents other teams from being sure how the other teams will react and make a set strategy more difficult to formulate.

Nuclear war was perceived to be the worst possible outcome of the Cold War and neither side was willing to incur the costs associated with that decision – the massive loss of human life as well as the potential annihilation of life as we know it if an all-out nuclear war were to have occurred.

After the end of World War II, the United States and the Soviet Union began a titanic power struggle for global hegemony. One of the most visible reflections of this conflict was the nuclear **arms race** that ensued. An arms race is a competition between two countries in which both attempt to have the most technologically advanced weapons; in this instance, both sides developed nuclear armaments and threatened to wipe out the opposition with their new toys. Many Americans were terrified of this possibility and were afraid of the possibility of all-out nuclear war, but the possession of lethal nuclear weapons on both sides and the threat of their use kept both sides at bay; the nukes served, for both sides, as an unspoken threat. With the push of a button, one side could easily have annihilated the other, and that terrifying threat kept both sides from attacking the other. The use of a threat to *keep someone from doing something* is known as **deterrence.** This is one of the strategies employed by the United States at the beginning of the Cold War by means of the arms race (Zagare and Kilgour, 14).

Deterrence is a concept widely discussed in the field of political science, but the way deterrence is conceptualized has begun to evolve. Prior to the late 1990s and early 2000s, political scientists assumed that all-out conflict is not 'rational', meaning that the occurrence of all-out war is always the worst possible outcome (and in most cases, unacceptable) for any actor. Recently, however, many political scientists have changed their tune. Seeing as large-scale wars have occurred on numerous occasions throughout history, one cannot accept all-out war as irrational and the worst possible outcome when history indicates that numerous actors (state and non-state alike) have not seen it that way. The new theory of deterrence, perfect deterrence theory, accepts that war can be and has been a rational (and productive) outcome between both state and non-state actors (Zagare and Kilgour, 76). No pun intended, but in the game of threats, you either win or you die – at least, that's how most political scientists who study deterrence theory see it.

Another foreign policy strategy employed by the United States during the early days of the Cold War was that of **containment.** The United States' main objection of the Soviet Union was that the U.S.S.R. was a brutal communist dictatorship that willingly engaged in numerous crimes against humanity. The United States sought to keep the threat of communism from spreading to other areas of the world or to 'contain' it. The Korean and Vietnam Wars are both historically recognized as part of America's containment policy (Leebaert, 189-191).

Looking back at World Systems Theory, as the global hegemon, the United States by definition wants to maintain its hegemony. If we assume this to be true, it makes sense that they would try to inhibit the power accruement of the hegemonic challenger – the Soviet Union. Similarly, it also seems to logically follow that the easiest way to keep a challenger at bay is to ensure that they believe you to be more militarily formidable and also more willing to utilize your tools to subdue them if they were to make a move to gain hegemony. Deterrence and containment proved to be useful strategies for the United

States against their communist adversaries at the beginning of the Cold War.

Taming the Game Down: Détente

Oftentimes, teams playing Risk will be aggressive for a time but, after having lost most of their armies or being unable to gain any ground, will back off and refrain from attacking territories or, at the least, will attack less often and will sustain those attacks less aggressively. This allows for the formerly aggressive team to rebuild their armies and re-fortify the territories that they deem to be the most critical to their gameplay strategy. By cutting back on their attacks, they actually make themselves stronger.

The United States and the Soviet Union also came to the same conclusion. After roughly two decades of endless saber-rattling, both sides finally decided to chill out a bit. Both sides quit threatening each other and entered into trade agreements; this is most famous under the Nixon administration (Gaddis, 180-184). The lessening of tensions between the United States and the Soviet Union during the early 1970s is a foreign policy strategy most refer to as **détente.** Specifically, it spurred on the addition of China as a vital global trading partner as well as a mon-

The relationship between the United States and the People's Republic of China began while the strategy of détente was being employed.

etary lender. The détente policy enabled the United States to gain a much-needed break from the edge-of-your-seat tension that had dominated the nation for over twenty years, but détente wasn't to last. When Ronald Reagan became president, he had other ideas in regards to the Soviet Union and how their hegemonic aspirations should be dealt with.

Bigger Problems Are Never Better Problems: Pre-Emptive Foreign Policy

Oftentimes during a game of Risk, it will become apparent that one team is massing their armies in one or two territories so as to launch a massive attack. Most teams will, in turn, mass their armies in nearby territories and engage the potential aggressor in conflict before their power becomes too strong to control. In essence, teams try to remove small threats from the game board before they become major threats to global or 'board' security. Sometimes teams engaged in alliances will mass their armies in territories that they can't hope to hold so that their ally, who is more capable of dealing with the aggressor, can mount an attack (and hopefully defeat) the overly aggressive team. Eliminating powerful and aggressive teams from the board makes it easier for other teams to move closer to global dominance on the game board and also removes potentially huge hazards before they can rear their ugly faces.

Just as teams play Risk attempt to remove potentially threatening teams from the game board, the United States has also employed a foreign policy strategy that attempts to achieve a similar goal – **pre-emption.** This foreign policy strategy can be employed either diplomatically or militarily. Ronald Reagan chose the diplomatic approach and strongly pursued the proliferation (or disarmament) of nuclear weapons across the globe (Lettow, 142-147) through the Strategic Arms Reduction Talks (START); and during a period of rapid economic growth, significantly increased defense spending so as to encourage the Soviet Union to do so during a time where they were experiencing an economic crisis (Lettow, 147-158). Both of these acts were pre-emptive. Reducing the number of nuclear weapons spread across the globe made the prospect of nuclear war far less likely while the beefing up of United States' defense systems forced the hand of the Soviet Union and ultimately drove it to economic and political collapse (Lettow, 247).

Reagan wasn't the only president to employ pre-emption as a foreign policy strategy. The president that is most renowned for his pre-emptive foreign policy agenda is George W. Bush. After the terrorist attacks of 9/11 on the Twin Towers and the Pentagon, Bush sought to remove the influence and power bases of Al Qaeda, the terrorist network responsible for the assaults. Both the wars in Afghanistan and in Iraq are often labeled as pre-emptive wars (Warren, 8-16). Bush's intent was to remove the threat of Al Qaeda and also the countries that harbored and sympathized with the terrorist group.

The United States' employment of this foreign policy strategy was by no means popular, especially in the cases of Afghanistan and Iraq. Both countries abroad and also many citizens

George W. Bush is the president most often associated with the utilization of the foreign policy strategy of pre-emption – more specifically in his advocacy of the War in Iraq.

at home opposed the pre-emptive conflict in Iraq while some also disliked the Afghani war as well (Weisman, 1). The Bush Administration's entry and occupation of Iraq was perceived negatively on a number of levels. Some thought that Bush was trying to finish what his father had started in the Gulf War (Rampton and Stauber, 21-22, 105, 107). Others thought that Bush sought to secure Iraq's oil fields and thus give a boost to America's economy (Friedman, 1-2). Still others thought that America was trying to assert its dominance in a region where its presence seemed to be lackluster. Just as cautious teams will attempt to eliminate potential challengers on the Risk game board before real trouble arises, so too has the United States sought to address small problems abroad before they became larger conflicts via the strategy of pre-emption.

Just as the interaction between the six teams on the Risk game board can be complicated, interesting, infuriating, and satisfying, so too has America's foreign policy been an emotional rollercoaster. From fear to security, from trust to doubt, the United States government and its citizens have had a bumpy ride – especially of late. America's position as hegemon requires rapid adaptation to changes in the international landscape.

Potential End to the Game: Inter-Team Cooperation and International Organizations

While some games of Risk end with one person taking over the entire game board, many do not. I would argue that a majority of games ultimately see teams allying with one another. When large alliances form, rather than having an epic battle at the end which can go on for hours, oftentimes the major alliances will agree to end the game and therefore prevent the continuation of attacks. Sometimes, all six teams are included in the alliance structure while other times, individual teams might choose to forego the alliance option and choose to go it alone. They sometimes attempt to molest territories controlled by an alliance, but that decision almost always results in that team's annihilation.

The flag of the United Nations – the international organization that attempts to resolve international disputes and create lasting partnerships between countries

Just as the teams in a game of Risk can agree to end and prevent fighting, so too have many nations across the globe united together to form international organizations whose aims are to prevent war and aid each other in times of economic, social, or political upheaval. One of the most widely recognized international organizations was created with the ratification of the Treaty of Versailles at the end of World War I: the League of Nations. The League of Nations sought to rebuild Europe after the war and also ensure that Germany's war reparations (or penalties) were paid to the Allied Powers that had won the war. By and large, the League of Nations (without the United States' involvement) proved to be a very ineffective venue for international discussion; it was unable to prohibit Hitler's rise to power and his attempts to overtake Eastern (and later Western) Europe (Brinkley, 638-641, 730, 733).

The international organization that most people are probably familiar with is the United Nations. This organization was founded at the end of World War II, and this time the United States embraced membership in this group. In this way, one of the world's hegemonic countries was involved in international debates and could intervene if the need arose (Weiss and Urquhart, 6-10). Over time, however, other nations rose to power. After the collapse of the Soviet Union, Russia was granted admittance to the United Nations and while the Cold War was over, it became apparent that Russia and the United States were still formidable rivals. With **veto power** or the ability to immediately strike down international proposals or **resolutions** has essentially enabled both sides to thwart each other's attempts to make any significant gains in the international realm either economically or politically (Lowe and Roberts, 75, 502). The incessant bickering between both of these countries has caused many to label the United Nations, like the League of Nations, as an ineffective venue to address international disputes (Haya, 1-3).

Just as grand alliances playing Risk can punish teams that attempt to threaten their interests, so too can international organizations punish countries that threaten global security or violate international law. There are a number of methods that international organizations can employ, but perhaps the most noteworthy of these methods discussed regularly on the news is the imposition of **economic sanctions** on countries that refuse to follow the lead of the UN. Economic sanctions are penalties placed on a deviant country by an international organization. These penalties can make trading with the deviant country more difficult (if not impossible) or can inhibit the transaction of money or resources to and from the deviant country. For example: the United Nations is, at the moment, imposing economic sanctions on both Iran and North Korea for pursuing nuclear weapons programs – an act which the United Nations has forbidden; some contend that sanctions aren't enough, however, as both deviant countries are still attempting to develop nuclear armaments (Jenkins, 1-2). Economic sanctions are a tool that the United Nations employs to discourage certain countries from pursuing projects that the rest of the world perceives to be threatening or potentially damaging.

Looking Out for the Little Guy and Humanitarian Aid

In almost every game of Risk that I've ever played, there is always one team who gets the raw end of the deal. All of their territories are spread out and it poor locations for defense. Inevitably, the ultra-aggressive teams will attempt to take them out first in order to flip over cards and, once enough have been flipped that match, gain more armies per turn. Oftentimes though, other teams are shockingly protective of the weaker teams – especially if people have friends on other teams. In those instances, teams will often come to the defense of the weak team and enable them to build up their armies and have more of a shot in the game. The real kicker is that sometimes, the act of saving the weak team sacrifices the strategic positioning of the stronger teams. The desire, and sometimes need, to defend the weaker teams is a phenomenon often seen when playing a game of Risk that is shared between friends.

Just as teams come to each other's aid in the game of Risk, so too do powerful countries come to the aid of less stable countries during times of economic struggle, in the face of natural disasters, or in situations where the preservation of human dignity is in doubt. The aid lent to less well-off countries by countries that are much better off is known as **humanitarian aid.** As the global hegemon, the United States is expected to lead in these efforts and has done so on a regular basis in the recent past. After the devastating tsunami hit the countries in Southeast Asia after a devastating earthquake, the United States quickly stepped up and became the country that sent the most aid (both in terms of funding and manpower) to the region (CNN News, 1-2). In 2010, a massive earthquake shook the small island country of Haiti and again, the United States was quick to help out and quickly sent needed supplies and funding in Haiti's direction (Blackburn, 1-3). Disaster seems to strike on a regular basis across the globe, but the United States has made for itself a reputation that it is ready and willing to help with calamity strikes.

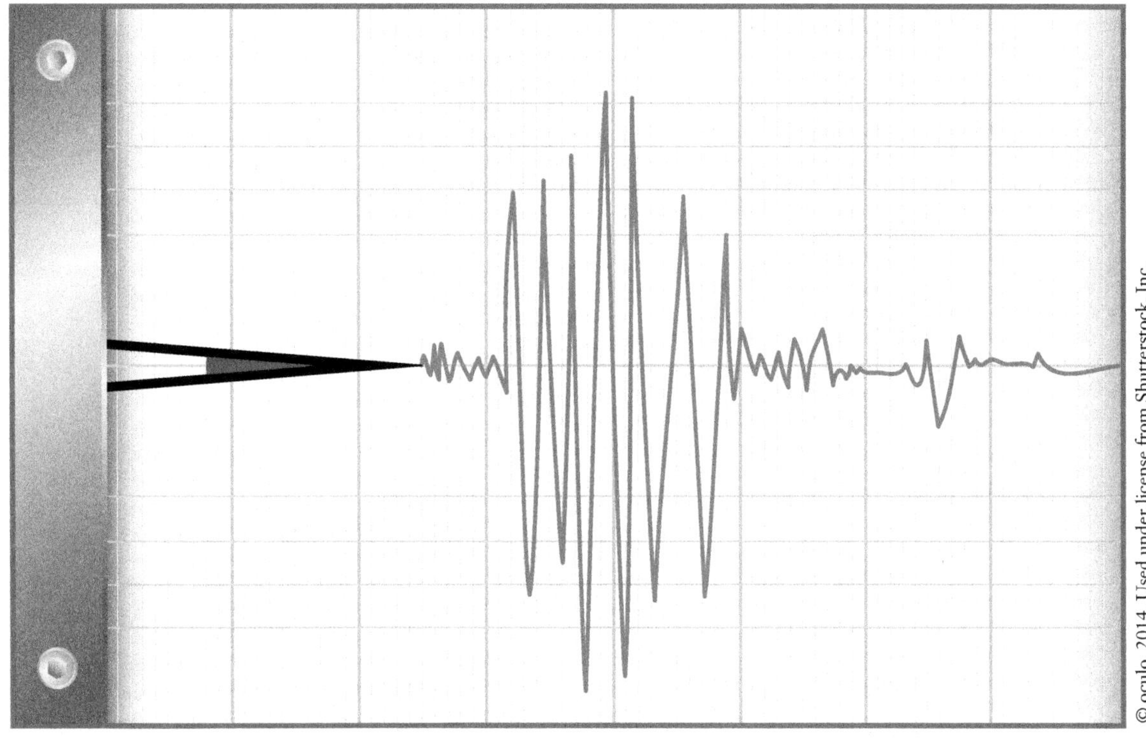

When earthquakes rock the land or tsunamis wipe out coastlands, the United States is one of the first countries to send humanitarian aid to the affected countries.

The United States is also well-recognized as a country that attempts to step in and intervene when foreign governments openly oppress some portion of their own population or another country's population. One of the earliest examples of the United States' intervention in human rights issues was the liberation of the Nazi concentration camps at the end of World War II. Like most humanitarian efforts, this was accomplished with the cooperation of other countries (namely, the United Kingdom and France); these countries, upon reclaiming territory held by the Nazis, released the prisoners of the various concentration camps, ensured that they had food, shelter, and clothing, and attempted to help them locate any surviving members of their families (Abzug). Injustices like that of the Nazi 'final solution' have reared their ugly head on a number of occasions, and the United States has attempted to do what it could to help put an end to the injustice and ensure that such atrocities are prevented from occurring again.

When playing the game of Risk, teams attempt to overtake the game board and achieve global dominance. Other teams attempt to thwart the attempts of opposing teams to achieve this goal. Through the use of strategy, threats, attacks, defense, and rescue, teams attempt to secure for themselves as much power and land as possible. I have contested here that

Just as the strongest teams attempt to attain and defend the most power and influence, the United States is engaged in an epic struggle to maintain global hegemony.

the overall goals of this board game are similar to America's foreign policy agenda. Through a bit of evolution in game-play, teams evolve from isolationists to global powers; so too has the United States moved out of the shadows into the position of global hegemony. In that position, it is expected to fulfill obligations that keep the world system in check. But it's not all fun and games; it's a rather risky business.

FOOD FOR THOUGHT

World Systems Theory

Do you think that World Systems Theory provides an accurate description of the global power structure, or do you think that the accruement and loss of power in global politics is more complicated? Do you think that the United States is a benevolent or selfish hegemon? Which country, if any, do you believe poses a threat to our hegemony? Do you think the United States cares about its semi-peripheral countries or do we simply use them to protect our interests? Why are some countries ignored while other countries aren't? Does the United States exclusively ally itself with countries it can 'get' something out of, or are we allies with some countries simply because we're altruistic? What would happen to the United States if another country replaced it as the global hegemon? Would it be annihilated or would it be welcomed as part of the new hegemon's semi-periphery?

History of American Foreign Policy

Do you think isolationism is an irrational foreign policy strategy? What are some potential positives and drawbacks of an isolationist strategy? Do you think isolationism is possible anymore? Does a global society like the one in which we live encourage or discourage isolationist tendencies? If we employed an isolationist strategy today, would be still be able to maintain our hegemony? What would be some good reasons to abandon an isolationist policy? Can you think of any other countries who seek to maintain an isolationist foreign policy strategy? How do you think they are received among the international community?

What is deterrence? Do you think that conflict can be a rational choice in a foreign policy strategy? What actors (state or non-state) might believe that war is a rational outcome? What could 'cost' more than war? Do you think the rules of deterrence change when nuclear weapons are thrown into consideration? How can one tell if an adversary is serious about a threat or is bluffing? Do you think deterrence was a good foreign strategy to employ against the Soviet Union or could we have pursued some other strategy that would have been more effective?

How effective was the United States' containment policy? Why would the United States want to contain the spread of communism even though it seemed apparent that communism was a flawed and tyrannical form of government? Did the United States attempt to contain communism at home as well as abroad? Can you give some examples of domestic containment policies? How were such policies received? What conflicts can you name that were fought in the name of the United States' containment policy?

What is détente? Was it a good foreign policy strategy to employ after utilizing deterrence and containment? What positives came out of the détente policy? Should we have continued to use détente or was Reagan's pre-emptive policies more effective in forcing the Soviet Union to collapse? Is détente a coward's policy or a strategy that a wise leader would employ? If we had continued to employ deterrence and containment, do you think that the United States and the Soviet Union would have eventually ended up in a nuclear conflict? I often refer to détente as the 'chill out' policy; was chilling out the most rational decision for the two rivals in the Cold War to make?

Pre-emption is the most recent foreign policy strategy employed by the United States. Is it a dangerous way to deal with international problems or is it rational? If a country is to employ a pre-emptive approach to international problems, what must they consider before attacking their noted adversary? Could a semi-peripheral country use a pre-emptive foreign policy strategy? If they could, how would that go down? If not, why would be a poor policy option? What about a peripheral state? Could pre-emptive strategies work out for them or no?

International Organizations

Both the League of Nations and the United Nations have proved to be rather ineffective in resolving international disputes. Are international organizations useless or do they serve any important purpose in our global society? Do you believe that the United Nations is flawed in some way? If so, can those flaws be successfully addressed, or are the UN's problems so disparate that they are unfixable? Do you think that the United Nations has aided in preventing wars? Have they aided in the distribution of humanitarian aid? Look up the funding that goes into the United Nations. Which country provides most of the funding the UN uses for humanitarian aid? Based on that information, what do we know about the other UN members? What can we assume?

Humanitarian Aid

Do you believe that the United States donates enough and does enough in terms of humanitarian aid? Do you think it tends to help countries in which it has a vested interest or does it tend to help countries irrespective of their value to the United States? Should the United States continue to fund humanitarian aid efforts during times of domestic economic crisis? Why or why not? Do you believe that we are more capable or aiding countries in need than other countries? Should other countries pitch in more to offset the costs of humanitarian aid efforts across the globe? If you were in charge of the distribution of funds for humanitarian aid for the United States, what area of the world do you feel would benefit most from our aid and in what form would you send the aid? Money? Food? Medical supplies? Educators?

The one similarity between bad foreign policy and Ebenezer Scrooge:

Those ghosts are gonna haunt you in your past, present, and future.

Works Cited

Abzug, Robert. H. *Inside the Vicious Heart: Americans and the Liberation of Nazi Concentration Camps.* New York: Oxford University Press, 1985.

Blackburn, Bradley. "U.S. Government and Aid Groups Rush Aid to Haiti." *ABC News. http://abcnews.go.com/WN/HaitiEarthquake/haiti-earthquake-obama-united-states-rushes-relief-aid/story?id=9552178.* Posted on 01/13/2010.

Friedman, Thomas. "A War for Oil?" *The New York Times. http://www.nytimes.com/2003/01/05/opinion/a-war-for-oil.html.* Posted on 01/05/2003.

Gaddis, John Lewis. *The Cold War: A History.* New York: Penguin Books, 2005.

Jenkins, Simon. "Whether It's North Korea or Iran, Sanctions Won't Work." *The Guardian. http://www.theguardian.com/commentisfree/2013/feb/13/west-loves-sanctions-not-much-dictators.* 02/12/2013.

Leebaert, Derek. *The Fifty Year Wound: How America's Cold War Victory Shapes Our World.* New York: Back Bay Books, 2002.

Lettow, Paul. *Ronald Reagan and His Quest to Abolish Nuclear Weapons.* New York: Random House Trade Paperbacks, 2005.

Lowe, Vaughan and Adam Roberts. *The United Nations Security Council and War.* New York: Oxford University Press, 2010.

Lundestad, Eirik and Tor G. Jakobsen. "A Unipolar World: Systems and Wars in Three Different Military Eras." *Popular Social Science: Bridging the Gap. http://www.popularsocialscience.com/2013/02/05/a-unipolar-world-systems-and-wars-in-three-different-military-eras/.* Posted on 02/05/2013.

Montopoli, Brian. "Poll: Most Americans Believe That the Iraq War Was a Mistake." *CBS News. http://www.cbsnews.com/news/poll-most-americans-say-iraq-war-was-a-mistake/.* Posted on 08/26/2010.

Rampton, Sheldon and John Stauber. *Weapons of Mass Destruction: The Uses of Propaganda in Bush's War in Iraq.* New York: Penguin Books, 2003.

Revkin, Andrew C. "From the Philippines to Haiti, Disaster Recovery is a Way of Life." *The New York Times. http://dotearth.blogs.nytimes.com/2013/11/11/from-the-philippines-to-haiti-disaster-recovery-is-a-way-of-life/?_php=true&_type=blogs&_r=0.* Posted on 11/11/2013.

"U.S. Ups Tsunami Aid from $35 Million to $350 Million." *CNN News. http://www.cnn.com/2004/US/12/31/us.aid/.* Posted on 12/31/2004.

Wallerstein, Immanuel. *World Systems Analysis: An Introduction.* Durham: Duke University Press, 2004.

Warren, Aiden. *Prevention, Pre-Emption, and the Nuclear Option: From Bush to Obama.* New York: Routledge, 2012.

Weisman, Steven R. "A Nation at War: A New Doctrine; Pre-Emption: An Idea With a Lineage Whose Time Has Come." *The New York Times. http://www.nytimes.com/2003/03/23/world/nation-war-new-doctrine-pre-emption-idea-with-lineage-whose-time-has-come.html?pagewanted=all&src=pm.* Posted on 03/23/2003.

Weiss, Thomas G. and Sir Brian Urquhart. *What's Wrong With the United Nations and How to Fix It.* Malden: Polity Press, 2012.

White, Thomas. "Why U.S. Hegemony is Here to Stay." *The Huffington Post. http://www.huffingtonpost.com/thomas-white/why-us-hegemony-is-here-t_b_4258264.html.* Posted on 11/12/2013.

Zagare, Frank C. and D. Marc Kilgour. *Perfect Deterrence.* New York: Cambridge University Press, 2000.

CHAPTER 16

TAKING CARE OF MARLEY'S UNFINISHED BUSINESS: *A CHRISTMAS CAROL* AND AMERICAN ECONOMIC POLICY

One of the most iconic pieces in classic literature is Charles Dickens' tale, *A Christmas Carol.* The story of the transformation of the miser, Ebenezer Scrooge, seven years after the death of his business partner, Jacob Marley, has been told and re-told ever since its publication in the mid-1800s. From the big-screen to TV musicals, Dickens' tale of Christmas 'spirit' has become one that is part of many families' Christmas traditions. I believe, however, that the story Dickens relates is one whose relevance spans far beyond the month of December. I contend that the journey of Scrooge from miserable miser to a man of repute is one recognizable in the history of American economic policy. Before we consider the connections between this famous holiday classic and America's economic development, however, let us first revisit the story that Dickens penned so long ago.

Charles Dickens' *A Christmas Carol*

"Marley was dead to begin with," is the first line of the iconic tale, and Dickens assures readers that if they don't believe that, the rest of the story is meaningless (Dickens, 5). Jacob Marley was Scrooge's business partner for many years but had died, seven years prior to the events in this tale, on Christmas Eve night. Seven years had gone by and while

Scrooge didn't "make merry at Christmas and couldn't afford to make idle people merry" (Dickens, 10).

Marley's partner, Ebenezer Scrooge, had been a miser before Marley passed, he had had seven years to become (if possible) even more socially detached and emotionless in the sight of human tragedy and struggle. "Oh, he was a tight-fisted hand at the grindstone, Scrooge! A squeezing, wrenching, grasping, scraping, clutching, covetous old sinner!" (Dickens, 8). Scrooge was a man of business, and the story makes it apparent that he was always out to take advantage of those who were less fortunate, for those were the people he made the most profit on.

The story begins seven years after old Marley's death on Christmas Eve. Scrooge is working in his counting house and is accompanied by his impoverished clerk, Bob Cratchit. Mr. Scrooge, being the miser that he is at the beginning of the tale, is hard on Cratchit and very nearly refuses to permit Cratchit to take the day off on Christmas Day. "A poor excuse to pick a man's pocket every twenty-fifth of December," Scrooge asserts (Dickens, 12), but ultimately Scrooge relents and Cratchit leaves the office happy to know that he'd be able to spend Christmas with his family (Dickens, 7-12). Before Cratchit leaves, however, Scrooge has unpleasant encounters with two other individuals.

The first gentleman to enter Scrooge's counting house is none other than his nephew, Fred. He wishes Scrooge a merry Christmas, and Scrooge responds with the all too familiar, "Bah! Humbug!" (Dickens, 7). Although his nephew is full of Christmas spirit, Scrooge wants nothing to do with him – or with Christmas. Scrooge dismisses the holiday as a commercial one partaken upon by those particularly who cannot afford the necessities that tradition required. He argued that every Christmas, men were "a year older but not an hour richer" (Dickens, 8). Scrooge's nephew makes a moving tribute in the name of Christmas and invites Scrooge to share Christmas dinner with him and his wife. Scrooge rudely declines and further decides to mock his nephew and his belief in love. With a heavy heart, Scrooge's nephew leaves the counting house with the impression that Scrooge thinks badly of him, his wife, and the holiday they were about to celebrate (Dickens, 7-9).

Scrooge's nephew, Fred, and his wife, Clara, upon Christmas Day

After Cratchit lets Fred out into the cold, two richly dressed gentlemen enter. They hand Scrooge their paperwork to demonstrate their legitimacy and implore Scrooge to donate some money to aid the poor in the name of Christmas. Scrooge questions the two men, "Are there no prisons?....Union workhouses?...Are the Treadmill and Poor Laws still in effect?" (Dickens, 10). The gentlemen assure Scrooge that, most unfortunately, that all was as it should be in those regards but they hardly provided holiday cheer to those worse off. Scrooge declines to donate money and suggests that his taxes which help to pay for the establishments he mentioned should be good enough for the poor. He goes as far to say that, if they'd rather die than go there, "...they'd better do it and decrease the surplus population" (Dickens, 10). Disgruntled, the men leave Scrooge's toxic presence to inquire of other, hopefully more generous, businessmen (Dickens, 10-11).

Before long, Scrooge locks and departs from his counting house to his mansion. Dickens' tale describes Scrooge's residence as cold, dark, and depressing (Dickens, 12). He approaches his front door and moves to open the door when he notices the knocker in the center of the door. Instead of its usual shape, the knocker's countenance is none other Scrooge's dead partner, Jacob Marley. Thoroughly frightened, Scrooge hurries into his residence and flees from the ghastly door-knocker. He retreats to his living quarters and searches them in fear that things are not as they should be. He finds everything to be in order and retreats to his bedroom and begins to eat a meager meal of cold gruel (Dickens, 12-15).

Marley's Ghost

That's when the front door-bell begins to ring. Soon thereafter, Scrooge hears the dragging of a great chain of heavy metal links up the stairs leading to his bedroom. Scrooge huddles in a high-backed chair, terrified, and is only further frightened when the Ghost of Jacob Marley walks through his bedroom door and advances in Scrooge's direction. Marley's Ghost approaches Scrooge and informs him who he is, as if Scrooge doesn't know, but Marley takes steps to ensure that Scrooge fully embraces the reality of the situation at hand – his reality and also his reason for coming. Marley informs Scrooge that he has come to save him from his own fate – being eternally chained and doomed to wander the earth to see all of the niceties of human emotion that he had failed to recognize and partake of during his life (Dickens, 16-19). Scrooge asserts that Marley was "a good man of business," but Marley, in a frightening voice thunders that, "mankind..., the common welfare..., charity, mercy, forbearance, and benevolence (were) his business" (Dickens, 18).

Marley informs Scrooge that he will be haunted by three spirits. If Scrooge takes to heart the messages the spirits teach, Marley asserts that Scrooge might escape the fate to which he was forever condemned. Though Scrooge is reluctant to accept Marley's ghostly help, his spectral friend informs him the day and time of the arrival of each ghost and leaves Scrooge's presence. After the Ghost of Marley leaves Scrooge, he reconsiders the encounter, largely dismisses it, and retires to bed (Dickens, 19-20).

The Ghost of Christmas Past

The first Ghost, the Ghost of Christmas Past, arrives the next day "when the bell tolls one" (Dickens, 21). The Ghost of Christmas Past appears almost angelic in dazzling, shimmering white robes and announces that it has come for Scrooge's well-being. By touching the Ghost's robe, he is transported back to the days of his childhood. While all of his schoolmates play in the snow on Christmas Day, Scrooge finds himself alone inside his old schoolhouse. He sees himself grow up alone and instead of nurturing relationships as all of his schoolmates do, he nurtures his mind by studying and reading. It is implied that Scrooge's father was a cruel, hard man which is why Scrooge spent so much time at the schoolhouse – even holidays. One day, his younger (and very beautiful) sister, Fan, comes to bring him home and promises that their father has come to his senses. Shortly after this meeting, we learn that Fan dies as a young woman and once again, Scrooge is left alone and assumedly friendless. The one person whom Scrooge had developed emotional attached to had been taken from him (Dickens, 24-28).

Next, the Ghost shows Scrooge as a young man apprenticed to a jolly man named Fezziwig. Although a strict master, Fezziwig is a jovial man who seeks to do right by his employees and the Ghost shows Scrooge the annual Christmas party that Fezziwig throws every year. Music, dancing, and mounds of food contribute to the joy of all in attendance. The Ghost points out how Fezziwig's gesture of generosity made being his apprentice tolerable – even enjoyable (Dickens, 28-31).

The Ghost then shows Scrooge a scene with his younger (but handsome) self with a beautiful young woman – Scrooge's old sweetheart, Belle. He notices that her eyes are glazed with tears. She tells Scrooge that, while she still loves him, she knows that he no longer loves her truly and would not, if he could do it again, choose her in a world with women who could bring far more to a marriage from a financial standpoint. She argues that Scrooge has changed from an honest businessman to a miser whose sole concern is the accumulation of wealth. Belle contends that his love for her has been replaced by his love of money and his insatiable desire to attain more of it. She breaks off their relationship and once again, Scrooge is left alone. After this devastating loss, it is implied that Scrooge swears off all human contact in order to prevent himself from being hurt again (Dickens, 32-33). The final scene shown to Scrooge by this Ghost is Belle as a middle-aged woman. She is married to a handsome man and has many children. Her husband mentions Scrooge and Belle falls silent, thus implying that she still has feelings for him. At this point, Scrooge has clearly had enough of the Ghost and extinguishes its light with an extinguisher cap. Scrooge finds himself back in his bed chambers, and again, he tries to sleep (Dickens, 32-35).

The Ghost of Christmas Present

The next night, at the stroke of one, Scrooge is awakened by the second ghost, the Ghost of Christmas Present. Instead of being a small creature like the first spirit who had visited him, the second spectre is gigantic. He (and

For a long while, the only thing Scrooge saw in the world was his sweetheart, Belle, but she comes to understand that, as time passed, Scrooge was blinded by his love and desire for money. She leaves Scrooge alone and hopes that he can live with himself and the choices he has made (Dickens, 33).

his presence) fills the whole room. He invites Scrooge in and introduces himself. Scrooge has never seen anyone like him, and this seems to perplex the Ghost as he has over eighteen hundred brothers and sisters. After Scrooge informs the Ghost that he is ready and willing to learn whatever lessons the Ghost wishes to impart, he is instructed to touch the Ghost's robe. When Scrooge had done so, both Scrooge and the Ghost are transported to a crowded street on Christmas morning. The people, while wishing passersby a merry Christmas, hustle and bustle to church or to their Christmas gatherings. Upon the many feasts they pass, the Ghost sprinkles some flavor upon them with his magical torch – but particularly on the poorer feasts, because as the Ghost notes, "they need it most" (Dickens 40-41).

Indeed, the Ghost seeks to emphasize the point and takes Scrooge to the home of his poor clerk, Bob Cratchit. Mrs. Cratchit and the children are aiding her in the preparations for Christmas dinner. Soon, Bob Cratchit and the couple's youngest son, Tiny Tim, enter the house. They had been at church and Tim, a cripple, thought it might do the churchgoers good to see him and to remember that Christ came to save poor cripples and broken men like him (Dickens, 43). The family sits down to Christmas dinner and Bob Cratchit proposes a toast to Mr. Scrooge. The rest of the family reluctantly answers the call; indeed, Mrs. Cratchit has a few choice words for Scrooge and his lack of human empathy but chooses to toast him all the same because it's Christmas. The cripple, Tiny Tim, however, responds as innocently as a child can, "God bless us, every one!" (Dickens, 45). Upon asking the Ghost if Tiny Tim will live, the Ghost predicts that if things don't change for Cratchit and his family, that Tiny Tim will die. The Ghost then proceeds to mock

Scrooge and cries, "But if he's going to die, he'd better do it and decrease the surplus population" – a self-defining quote from Scrooge earlier in the story (Dickens, 45-46). Scrooge can only shudder at his lack of vision while the Ghost leads on (41-47).

Tiny Tim – the youngest son of Bob Cratchit. Although crippled, Tim speaks with the innocence of a child.

The Ghost then takes Scrooge to the home of his nephew, Fred, and finds that the Christmas party that Scrooge had been invited to is in full force. The merry group is playing a game called 'yes and no'. Fred's friends and relatives are very merry indeed when they discover that the answer to the current query is Uncle Scrooge himself who is described in the clues as being "a disagreeable animal that growled sometimes that lived in London" (Dickens, 52-53). Scrooge is ashamed that his own extended family would mock him so but realizes that he had earned that ridicule through his cold and unfeeling actions (Dickens, 53).

The last vision that the Ghost of Christmas Present provides takes them both to a desperately impoverished area of London. Poor souls huddle by fires and fret about their futures, and the Ghost notes that these members of humanity are worthy of the same comforts as Scrooge because they all have to work hard to survive. At this point, Scrooge notices a number of feet sticking out of the bottom of the Ghost's robes. The Ghost pulls back his robes and reveals a pair of feral children – one boy and one girl. Desperately malnourished, Scrooge could see the despair and insatiable desire to Have in their eyes. The Ghost indicates that the two children represent two of humanity's greatest flaws. He asserts that, "The boy is Ignorance. The girl is Want" (Dickens, 54). The Ghost advises Scrooge to be wary of them as the traits they represent have led to the condemnation of many men. At this point, the Ghost of Christmas Present departs and leaves the old miser and leaves him waiting for the third and final spirit, the Ghost of Christmas Yet to Come (Dickens, 53-55).

The Ghost of Christmas Yet To Come

Scrooge finds himself in an eerie graveyard cloaked in fog and before him appears a gigantic spectre cloaked in black. Scrooge assures the spirit that he is willing to learn despite the fact that the Ghost's presence terrifies him. This Ghost first leads Scrooge to the money exchange where he did business and they encounter some of the gentlemen that Scrooge regularly did business with. They are discussing the death of one of their colleagues. None of them seem cut up about the affair but state that they would attend the funeral if lunch is served. The men depart and Scrooge is led down an alleyway by the Ghost and again the people are discussing the death of an elderly man; once again, the people seem almost jubilant that the man has died (Dickens, 57-59).

The Ghost of Christmas Yet To Come, shrouded in a billowing black robe, leads Scrooge around London to show him what might be if he fails to change his life.

Next, Scrooge is led to a shabby shop in which a man and two others are engaging in trade. Again, the discussion of an elderly man's death is the topic of conversation, but this encounter is far eerier as the objects the two visitors are selling appear to be identical to Scrooge's clothes, blankets, and bed clothes. Disgruntled, Scrooge is led to a dark, cold room with a large comfortable bed. On the bed is the body of a dead man, presumably, the man that has been the subject of the conversations he has been shown. Seeing the dead man on the bed thoroughly frightens Scrooge and he asks to leave and be shown gentle emotion connected with a death. The Ghost leads Scrooge from the room and suddenly they find themselves in front of a dilapidated shack (Dickens, 63-64).

It was the home of Bob Cratchit. Scrooge peers in the window and sees Mrs. Cratchit moving slowly in front of the cooking pot. She wipes a tear from her eye and can be heard crying. Her children rush to comfort her and they all comment that their father and husband, Bob, is past his usual time and how, with Tiny Tim upon his shoulders, that he had moved about at a rather brisk pace. Soon enough Bob Cratchit himself enters the house. He tells the somber family about the churchyard and how he had promised to visit his little son once a week; at this, Bob breaks down into sobs and laments the passing of Tiny Tim, but recognizes and embraces the love shown him by his family (Dickens, 65-67).

Lastly, Scrooge is taken back to the graveyard where his journey with the Ghost of Christmas Yet To Come had begun. They stand before a grave with a new gravestone where the inscription is covered by freshly fallen Christmas snow. Scrooge asks the Ghost who the dead man upon the bed was, and the Ghost points at the grave; he asks if the visions the Ghost has shown him are set in stone or alterable by a change in lifestyle. Again, the spectre points at the grave. Scrooge bends over

In this graveyard, Scrooge is forced to make a choice about what to do with his life.

and wipes the snow away to find his own name carved into the snow. Scrooge dissolves into racking sobs and collapses upon the snowy earth and promises to change his life, honor Christmas, and live its message throughout the year. When Scrooge comes to, he is no longer sprawled in the snow. He's at home in his own bed (Dickens, 68-69).

Scrooge's Transformation

All that he knew and loved about his old life lay before him strewn about his room, but most importantly, Scrooge realizes that he has been given a second chance and has the power to undo or offer penance for the many wrongs he has done. He opens his windows and discovers a bright, sunny day with a fresh blanket of snow upon the ground. As a young boy runs by, Scrooge inquires what day it is, and to his complete and utter delight, he discovers that it is Christmas Day and that he had the chance, today, to begin on his transformative journey. He asks the boy to go to the meat market, buy the prize turkey hanging in the window, and bring it to him – for a reward. In no time at all, the turkey has been delivered and sent to Bob Cratchit's house – anonymously (Dickens, 70-73).

Scrooge dresses and sets out into the glorious sunshine on Christmas morning but soon encounters the two men who had asked for the charitable donation that had been refused, mocked, and treated most shamefully. Scrooge apologizes and offers to donate an undisclosed (but clearly large) sum of money to their charity. At first the men believe Scrooge is joking but are eventually convinced that his intent is sincere. They agree to come and visit Scrooge and he departs to seek out his nephew Fred's home and hopes that despite the rude treatment that Fred had received, that he will be admitted to their Christmas party. Although shocked, Fred is ecstatic and Scrooge is welcomed into the fray and has a grand time with all of Fred's family and friends – including Fred's wife whom Scrooge had also previously insulted (Dickens, 73-74).

The next day, the day after Christmas, Scrooge gets to the office early and hopes to catch Bob Cratchit coming in late. He is not disappointed, for Cratchit is almost half an hour late for work. Scrooge greets him with his usual growling manner and instructs Cratchit to enter Scrooge's office. It is implied that Cratchit believes he is going to be fired. Quite the opposite occurs as Scrooge raises Cratchit's salary and offers to assist his family in whatever way he can. He gives Cratchit a purse of coins and instructs him to buy coal so they can discuss his family's affairs over a fire and a bowl of Christmas punch. Scrooge kept his word and his assistance prevents Tiny Tim from dying. Scrooge becomes a respected and reputable man in the town and is recognized for celebrating Christmas and embracing its message throughout the year. A night ago, on Christmas Eve, Scrooge was a miserable miser and the villain of Dickens' story. Today, upon Christmas Day, he is a changed man – and a hero (Dickens, 74-76).

A Christmas Carol and the History of American Economic Policy

On a number of levels, Dickens' *A Christmas Carol* is comparable to America's economic development and health. Scrooge's path from youth to adulthood is comparable to America's economic development from a capitalist society (as Adam Smith defined it) to a *laizzes-faire* system. The mediation of the three Ghosts of Christmas demonstrate how the labor movement in the United States shifted our economy to one that is regulated by

"Scrooge was better than his word. He did it all, and infinitely more. To Tiny Tim, who did NOT die, he became a second father. He became as good a friend, as good a master, as good a man as the good old city knew" (Dickens, 75).

the government. Scrooge's transformation at the end of the story indicates that America's economy is still changing and evolving and probably will continue to do so.

The Evolution of Ebenezer Scrooge and of America's Economy

Scrooge's journey from childhood to mature adulthood is comparable to America's economic development from a country dominated by agriculture to one that becomes entrenched in the Industrial Revolution and the embrace of *laizzes-faire* capitalism. From there, the labor movement encourages the government to become more involved in the regulation of businesses and the economy. Yet again, we have evolved away from manufacturing and toward a more service-oriented economy. All of these changes to America's economy also were experienced by the protagonist of Dickens' holiday tale.

Scrooge from Childhood to Adulthood: Growing Up and Economic Development

In Dickens' story, the Ghost of Christmas Past shows Scrooge his former self as a child. While the other children played together on the school grounds, Scrooge locked himself away inside the school house and persisted in working hard to make something of himself. The Ghost indicates that Scrooge followed this lifestyle choice until his sister, Fan, came to bring him home to a conciliatory father. The life that Scrooge led as a child was one that embraced hard work in hopes that one day, that work would be rewarded (Dickens, 23-27).

In its youth, America's economy was dominated by the agriculture sector. From the tobacco plants in Jamestown to the cotton fields in the Southern states to the corn and wheat fields in the plains states, America's agriculture sector was one that was (and still is, incidentally) envied by the rest of the world (Brinkley I, 37-38, 292-295, 278-279). While agriculture was the predominant economic driver at this point, the New England states embraced the early stages of industrialization (Brinkley I, 188-194). As the main vehicles for industrialization (manpower, factories, assembly lines, etc.) hadn't been embraced in the United States yet, it was agriculture that drove America's economy upward.

The development of an agriculture sector is typically considered to be the first step in any country's economic development. Sociologist Daniel Bell denotes the development of an agriculture sector as an integral building block on which most modern societies are built (Bell, 123-126). Countries that lack a strong agriculture sector in their economies are typically ones that develop at a less rapid pace when compared to powerful, highly developed countries like the United States (Bell, 124-126). For America to rise to its place as the global hegemon, it had to successfully develop a thriving economy, and it is America's agriculture sector that propelled it in the right direction.

Scrooge as a Man of Business: Industrialization and Its Repercussions

Once Scrooge finished with his schooling, the Ghost of Christmas Past indicates that

Scrooge, working under Fezziwig, became a man of business (Dickens, 28-29). He was apprenticed to Fezziwig for a time but then struck out on his own in hopes of developing his own successful business (Dickens, 32-33). The visions that the Ghost of Christmas Past shows Scrooge reminds him that he, in his youth, was not unfeeling and indifferent to human emotion; in fact, the Ghost suggests that Scrooge's change in demeanor might be attributed to the loss of his sister and sweetheart Belle. The Ghost implies that the devastation Scrooge feels in response to these two losses encouraged him to swear off and ignore all human emotion in order to prevent himself from being hurt again (Dickens, 33-35).

Just as Scrooge became a man of business, America's economy moved away from (but still held onto) its agricultural roots (Brinkley II, 467-470) and evolved into an economy dominated by the tools of industry. The Industrial Revolution had been in full swing in Europe during the mid-1800s but didn't find its way to the United States until the latter half of that century (Brinkley II, 500-502). At the same time, massive numbers of Europeans immigrated to the United States in hopes of finding a better life (Brinkley II, 503). The combination of those two phenomena made for a real adventure. With immigrants pouring into the country, the business tycoons had a seemingly endless supply of workers at their disposal. This reality discouraged these men

America's agricultural development and Scrooge's youth: growing up together

of business from putting protections in place that would have made for more stable and safe environments for their workers. Books like Upton Sinclair's *The Jungle* discuss the horrors of unregulated business in graphic detail; not only were conditions unsafe in most factories in this era, the food and drug production during this time period was unregulated and unsanitary (Sinclair). One of the most famous and deadliest workplace disasters of this era occurred at the Triangle Shirtwaist Factory. The factory was a sweatshop where women would arrive at work, were locked in until closing time, and were then released. One day, a fire started inside the factory, and the women inside had no way of escaping the flames save jumping out of the windows – to their death (Brinkley II, 591-592).

The Triangle Shirtwaist Company, much like this sweatshop, proved to be an unsafe working environment for the women working there.

Incidents like this and the one described in Sinclair's *The Jungle* impressed upon many people that businesses required regulation and workers required protection; most of the business tycoons of the day were reluctant to introduce such protections as it would have cut into their profits. Eventually though, workers began to organize and form collective groups or **labor unions** which served as a mediator between a company's workers and the owners of the business (Brinkley II, 592-593, 651-653). At first, labor unions had little impact on the practices of the businesses they sought to work with but gradually saw more success – particularly during the period of time between the late 1920s and the end of World War II (Brinkley II, 652, 711-713). Thus, the rigidity of the business community spurred on by rapid industrialization was ultimately brought into check through the mediation of labor unions and, in some instances, the federal government (Brinkley II, 488-496).

The New Scrooge: Okay, America – Now for Something Completely Different...

After Scrooge is visited by the Ghosts in Dickens' tale (Marley included), Scrooge swears that he will change his life, and according to the tale, he "is better than his word" (Dickens, 75). He dedicates much of his life to serving others as opposed to serving and considering only himself and his desires. He aids Bob Cratchit's family in escaping their poverty and prevents Cratchit's crippled son, Tim, from dying (Dickens, 75). Scrooge's drastic transformation from a man of business to a gentleman dedicated to service is partially why this story captivates so many – especially during the holiday season.

Daniel Bell argues that America has undergone a transformation much like the one experienced by Ebenezer Scrooge. While the United States' economy used to be dominated by manufacturing and the production of goods, it has shifted to something completely different. While manufacturing jobs still exist in the United States, the vast majority of the jobs out there are elements of the service sector. A country that moves beyond industrialization and production toward an economy dominated by service-oriented positions is what Bell identifies as a **post-industrial society** (Bell, 14-15). Some say that post-industrial societies are possible because of **globalization** – the gradual spread of national values, traditions, and goods across the globe. For example: McDonald's (a fast-food restaurant for those of you who've never heard of it) has its roots in the United States but has become so successful that it has spread to other parts of the world. Most European countries have them and so do some countries in Asia (James, 1-3). Another example: many of Hollywood's more notable films make their way across the ocean and are translated into other languages; many people abroad watch these films and find elements within them that they deem to be 'American' and embrace those features of supposed 'American culture' as part of their own identity (Kai, 1-3).

With more international relationships than ever, the United States can and has sent many of its factories overseas, most notably to Asian countries, and left the average American factory worker at a loss. Instead, Americans are encouraged to engage in the service or business sectors of the economy and abandon the manufacturing positions to workers overseas who will work longer hours for far less money and benefits; some argue that the move to utilize cheap labor abroad is essentially the application of laizzes-faire capitalism (and the wage inequality associated with it) on a global scale (Feenstra and Hanson, 240-245). The move from an industrial to a post-industrial society has propelled the United States away from an economy dominated by manufacturing and industrialization to one dominated by the service sector; similarly, Ebenezer Scrooge's experiences with the Ghosts in Dickens' tale encourage him to embrace a life of service and abandon his life as an indifferent, unfeeling man of business.

The Characters of *A Christmas Carol* and the Evolution of Economic Philosophy in America

Hopefully, you are beginning to see that Ebenezer Scrooge is an extremely complex fellow. His evolution from a bright young man to a miser yet again to a man reluctant but eventually willing to be transformed by his own past, present, and potential future makes Scrooge one of the most complicated heroes in classic literature. His transformation over time is eerily comparable to the change in economic philosophy that America has experienced to date. From moderate to extreme capitalism, from labor uprisings to the decline of American labor, from the presentation and rejection of a moderated, reformed capitalism to its eventual embrace, America's economic philosophical mindset has changed numerous times despite our relative youth as a country.

In his book *The Wealth of Nations*, Smith lays out a new economic philosophy that has been embraced by most of the countries across the globe – capitalism.

Scrooge and Smith: The Beginnings of the Men of Business

As shown by the Ghost of Christmas Past, Scrooge was apprenticed to a jovial, elderly businessman named Fezziwig. While in business to make money, the Ghost is quick to demonstrate to Scrooge that his focus was not solely profits; the Ghost shows Scrooge Fezziwig's annual Christmas party, an arena where Fezziwig spares no expense in his attempts to make his employees feel valued and appreciated (Dickens, 28-31). For Fezziwig, seeking profits was a worthy goal, but people – both the ones he served *and* those who served under him – were more important than the profits they put into his pocket.

The same can be said of an economic philosopher – the man credited with the philosophy of **modern capitalism**, Adam Smith. Modern capitalism is an economic system which encourages the production and sale of goods and services in the expectation that the producer will make profits off the goods and services that he or she successfully sells in the market. Smith argued that the development of a consumerist or capitalist economy would enable individuals to produce goods and services that were previously unavailable and garner the producer profits while at the same time fulfilling an imperative societal need – that is, for individuals to develop their own sense of self-identity (Smith, 543-549). Smith believed that economies are self-regulating; capitalist economies should cycle between periods of prosperity and turmoil thus keeping the number and types of businesses in check; Smith refers to this natural shifting of the economy as "the invisible hand" (Smith, 572).

While Smith believed in a self-regulating economy rather than one that is strictly regulated by the government, Smith believed that moderation by the producers was imperative to the success of this kind of economic system. He discouraged the poor treatment of workers and also overly low wages; he contends that the better workers are treated and the more they are paid (within reason), the more productive these employees will be. Smith admits that the regulation of free enterprise might be necessary to keep the system from getting out of hand (Smith 170); put simply, Smith recognized the tendency to be greedy and self-centered as the darker side of humanity and admits that certain protections might need to be put in place to prevent some people from abusing the economic system (Smith, 170-172). Smith's economic philosophy spread across Europe, particularly during the Industrial Revolution of the late 1700s and early 1800s and began to significantly affect the American economy after the resolution of the Civil War (Brinkley II, 483-490). Unfortunately however, the 'capitalists' who employed Smith's philosophy ignored the need for moderation and embraced an extreme interpretation of Smith's capitalism – ***laizzes-faire* capitalism** – one that discouraged all government regulation of the economy – an act that proves to be one difficult to rectify.

Marley and Marx: The Business of Mankind Should Be Mankind

The first spectral scene in *A Christmas Carol* occurs when the Ghost of Scrooge's dead partner, Jacob Marley, returns from the grave to visit Scrooge and warn him about his impending fate and how he can escape it if he is willing to positively change his life. Marley appears to Scrooge and laments the time he wasted in their counting house that could have been spent bettering the lives of the people around him. "Mankind was my business," Marley thunders at Scrooge, "The common welfare...., charity, mercy, forbearance, and benevolence were all my business" (Dickens, 18). Marley's rejection of these principles left him "captive bound and double-ironed" (Dickens, 18) and eternally condemned to see what he could have done but chose not to do to improve mankind's lot in the world. Marley warns Scrooge that failing to heed his message and change his life would leave Scrooge in far worse a situation than he, Marley, was condemned to for eternity (Dickens, 18-20). Marley offers Scrooge a bit of hope, however, and informs him that he will be haunted by three spirits who, if Scrooge would allow them, could aid Scrooge in moving his life in the right direction – away from greed and indifference and toward empathy and service (Dickens, 19-20).

Adam Smith was the philosopher who spoke in favor of the development of a capitalist society in his iconic book, *The Wealth of Nations*; his counterpart viciously attacked its shortfalls and even suggested that capitalism itself needed to be destroyed. The philosopher who projected that view was a German economic and political philosopher, Karl Marx. Marx lived during the worst years of the Industrial Revolution in Europe and found the massive disparity between rich and poor to be intolerable (Marx, 494, 497). Marx argued that the money and power that exists in a capitalist system is only shared by a few while the masses (or the **proletariat)** who produce the products and fill the coffers of the capitalists (or the **bourgeoisie**) live in misery on the bottom rungs of the economic ladder (Marx, 799, 855). Marx further contends that while the bourgeoisie continually get richer, the proletariat continues to sink deeper into poverty but also becomes more politically active because of that reality (Marx, 69-72). Marx believed that the massive disparity of incomes between rich and poor would become so inhumane that eventually the masses being oppressed by the capitalists would take steps to remove their oppressors and would assume control of the means of production. From there, the masses would work collectively and one would "produce according to his ability and receive according to his need"; Marx defined this new economic system a **socialist** system (Marx, 468-469).

Karl Marx – the founder of modern socialism

Marx's philosophy, like Smith's, has been investigated and interpreted over and over again by the generations who came after him; like Smith's capitalism, it's had its fair share of criticism. Smith's capitalism is often accused of being unfair and biased toward the ultra-rich (Toyama, 1-3). Marx's socialism is often accused of being endlessly ineffective as the lack of individual benefits to partaking in the system tends to stifle the initiative of the citizens living in collectivist societies (Perry, 1-3). Socialism is also accused of being insufferably ruthless when translated into a political system where the government controls the means of production; this is known as a **command economy** (Brinkley II, 778-785). One final negative in communism's camp was that the United States was engaged in a titanic fifty-year power struggle for global hegemony; we know this as the Cold War (Brinkley II, 907). All of these criticisms have been leveled against Marx's theory and the system that came into existence because of his writings. Like Marley's Ghost, Marx believed in the intrinsic value of humanity and the need to protect and defend the rights of those whom society traditionally exploits or overlooks.

The Ghosts of Christmas and America's Labor Movement: Didn't See It Coming

After Marley's Ghost departs from Scrooge's presence, Scrooge is visited by three other spirits: the Ghost of Christmas Past, the Ghost of Christmas Present, and the Ghost of

Christmas Yet To Come. The three Ghosts, rather than informing Scrooge that redemption is possible, attempt to impress upon Scrooge how his redemption can be achieved. The Ghost of Christmas Past attempted to demonstrate how the lack of human empathy turned Scrooge into the unfeeling miserable creature he had become (Dickens, 21-35). The Ghost of Christmas Present attempted to demonstrate how Scrooge's present decisions impact the people around him (Dickens, 36-55). Finally, the Ghost of Christmas Yet To Come seeks to impress upon Scrooge what might happen if he fails to learn the lessons the Ghosts sought to impart upon him (Dickens, 56-69). The Ghosts of Christmas play the role of mediator between Scrooge and the grave so that, as Marley implied, Scrooge might escape his fate.

Labor unions go on strike to defend the rights of workers everywhere.

If Karl Marx could travel into his future (and our present), I think he would be surprised to learn that the proletariat never arose to overthrow their capitalist oppressors. Something completely different occurred; instead of overthrowing the capitalists, America's overworked, underpaid, and undervalued workers organized and formed labor unions which, like the Ghosts, became the mediator between the workers and the capitalists. The establishment of labor unions during the Progressive Era (the early 1900s) was initially perceived by the capitalists of the day as an attempt to inhibit their ability to be profitable. The Pullman Strike was one such event and ultimately, the Pullman railcar company ultimately sought government intervention in the strike and the National Guard was called in to end it (Brinkley II, 494-495). Despite the initial backlash, however, labor organizations across the country continued to go on **strike** – an act where workers walk off the job – in hopes of garnering better pay and safer working conditions for the workers whom they represented.

The true heyday of America's labor movement was in the midst of the most significant economic crisis in American history – the Great Depression. During this time, millions of Americans were out of work and the people who managed to hold onto their jobs wanted to ensure that their jobs were stable. For this reason, the labor movement in America became far more militant; the Great Depression encouraged the formation of some of the most militant labor organizations in existence: the United Auto Workers (UAW), the American Federation of Labor (AFL), and the Congress of Industrial Organizations (CIO) (Brinkley II, 710-713). Other such labor organizations formed during this time which incidentally encouraged Franklin Roosevelt and the federal government to take an interest in workers' rights as well. Under Roosevelt's administration, restrictions on the ability of labor organizations to fight for their people were lifted; this change ultimately enabled labor groups to fight for some of the things workers today take for granted like the 40-hour workweek, workman's compensation, and the minimum wage rate (Brinkley II, 711).

Just as the Ghosts in Dickens' tale all departed from Scrooge's presence (some voluntarily and some less so), I think that many Americans would argue that the presence and influence of American labor organizations is declining and the key reason for this is the new 'right to work' legislation being passed in states across the country. Contrary to the label, 'right to work' laws don't guarantee individuals the right to a job nor does the absence of such laws indicate that individuals have a smaller chance of being employed. Instead, these new pieces of legislation are intended specifically to weaken the power of labor unions both in terms of their effectiveness and in regard to their ability to represent the workers under their wing. In 'right to work' states, labor organizations cannot mandate that union employees pay union dues; thus, many non-union members are able to benefit from the union's efforts without actually being a union member. This is known as a **free-rider problem**, and it is a huge setback for unions attempting to operate in states that have embraced these new laws. On the opposite side of the coin, 'right to work' legislation has caused labor organizations to lose most of their mediation powers – their ability to lobby for fair wages and safe working conditions. Currently, nearly half of the fifty states have adopted 'right to work' laws and have thus dealt organized labor a difficult hand to play with (Davey, 1-3). 'Right to work' legislation has not only inhibited the ability of labor unions to protect the workers they represent but also left the average worker in a far more vulnerable position than they would be if this legislation weren't on the books.

Scrooge's Transformation, America's Reformed Capitalism, and Keynesian Economics

At the end of Dickens' story, we know that Scrooge's interactions with the Ghosts encouraged him to change his life. He makes amends with his clerk Bob Cratchit, reconciles with his nephew Fred, and apologizes to the businessmen raising funds for their charity. All in all, Scrooge swears off his lifestyle as a greedy miser and dedicates his life to one of service and selflessness (Dickens, 70-76). For most of his life, Scrooge was (and had been remembered as) a miserable, greedy character who was out to get ahead by trampling the rest of humanity underfoot, but the intervention of Marley's Ghost and also the Ghosts of Christmas forced Scrooge to reflect on his past behavior but also to embrace the reform which ultimately saves him from the fate of his dead partner.

Just as Scrooge chose to embrace self-reformation, America's economy has been significantly altered from its position during the Industrial Revolution. Through the intervention of American labor organizations and the federal government, America's economy can no longer claim to be unrestrainedly capitalist but neither can it claim to be in line with Marx's ideology. Instead, the economy of the United States falls somewhere in the middle; most economists refer to economies like that espoused by the United States as a **mixed economy.** A mixed economy employs notable government regulation while at the same time limiting the ability of outside forces to significantly interfere with the means of production. Thus, the capitalists are happy because they can still pursue profits and economic success while the workers are content because there are protections in place for them if business owners choose to overstep their boundaries.

Some refer to America's economy as **reformed capitalism**. Assuredly, America's economy is much more akin to the system espoused by Smith rather than Marx, but we cannot say that Marx's economic and political philosophy played no part in the evolution of America's economy – especially since the days of the Industrial Revolution and Progressive Era. Rather, we can say that instead of the workers embracing the proletarian revolution that Marx believed to be inevitable, the United States instead chose to reform capitalism rather than rebel against it (Hindery Jr., 1-3).

In Dickens' story, it says that some who noticed Scrooge's transformation scoffed at him but also that he permitted them to do so (Dickens, 75). Similarly, many Americans seem to be unable or unwilling to accept that it isn't necessary for the United States to espouse one economic philosophy or the other but can instead embrace elements of both Smith's and Marx's works. Many Americans contend that we are moving away from capitalism and toward socialism – particularly since the election of President Obama (Harper, 1), but others disagree and argue that the deregulation of businesses (both small and large) is moving us back in the direction of unregulated capitalism (Dionne Jr., 1-4). Whichever way we're moving, it is certain that the effects of that move will be felt both by those wielding power and by those seeking to attain it. Scrooge's transformative journey in *A Christmas Carol* and his interactions with his ghostly counterparts provide us with a window from which we ourselves can revisit the transformation of America's economy through the evolution of economic philosophy.

While Scrooge's transformation from miser to gentleman was relatively quick, economic change occurs much more slowly. One of the most recognized methods for economic regulation was proposed by an English economist, John Maynard Keynes. In his book *The General Theory of Employment, Interest, and Money*, Keynes argues that in certain economic climates, governments should take certain actions to maintain a certain level of economic

Through increased spending and stimulus packages, President Obama attempted to apply the principles of Keynesian economics to revive America's economy.

stability (Keynes, 250-251). During periods of prolonged economic prosperity (an **economic boom**), Keynes recognizes that it is likely that governments will be taking in more money in taxes than they are spending; this is known as an economic **surplus** (Keynes, 213-215). For this reason, Keynes argues that during periods of economic growth, governments should raise taxes and invest the extra funds (rather than spending them) to have set aside for use periods of economic decline or **recessions** to create jobs and thus stimulate the economy back in a positive direction (Keynes, 286-288). Conversely, during an economic **depression**, a prolonged economic recession, Keynes advises governments to increase spending rather than cut it and take the risk of spending more than it is taking in; this is known as **deficit spending** (Keynes, 128-130). More spending, Keynes argues, should aid the government in stimulating the economy and put the country in a situation where raising taxes and decreasing spending would again be plausible (Keynes, 309).

The ideas of John Maynard Keynes have been embraced by many of America's politicians including our sitting president, Barack Obama. After having been elected in 2008, President Obama – like his predecessor, George W. Bush – had to decide how to approach the economic recession the United States was then immersed in. Obama embraced Keynes' proposals regarding economic recessions and significantly increased spending and, at the same time, cut taxes for middle-class Americans. Keynes' economic upswing did eventually occur but not at the rate that most Americans (and the president) expected (Ferrara, 1-3).

Keynesian economics is not the only philosophy to be used in America's recent past. Perhaps one of the most familiar economic theories was proposed and applied by our former president, Ronald Reagan. His **supply-side economics** or **'trickle-down' economics** suggests that taxes for the rich should be cut and the regulation of businesses and corporations should be scaled back so as to encourage the '1%' to pass on their wealth to the rest of America through the creation of jobs and the redistribution of wealth through wage increases. Essentially, Reagan believed that putting the political and economic power in the hands of individuals who actually have the money to significantly alter the economic landscape would enable a poor economy to recover more quickly (Harper, 1-4). Fortunately for Reagan, many economists give his theory of economics a significant bit of credit for turning the American economy around during his presidency (Harper, 2).

George W. Bush attempted to apply the principles of supply-side economics after the collapse of the American economy which occurred partially as a reaction to the terrorist attacks of September 11 but found that this philosophy worked far less effectively than it did for Reagan. Instead of the wealthy suppliers passing down their wealth to those below them on the socioeconomic ladder, Bush and the rest of the country quickly discovered that these folks were just as quick to save their money as everyone else. For this reason, some contend that Bush's application of supply-side economics was a failure (Williams, 1-2).

The Fate of Tiny Tim and America's Economic Health Checkup

One of the most iconic characters in *A Christmas Carol* is Bob Cratchit's crippled and sickly son, Tiny Tim. Despite his infirmities, he clings to and celebrates life and everyone in it. His heart-tugging exclamation of "God bless us, every one!" is one that most readers of classic literature are familiar with (Dickens, 45). Tim's continued existence in Dickens' tale, it seems, is exclusively up to Scrooge. The Ghost of Christmas Present argues that unless Scrooge's treatment of Bob Cratchit and his family improves, Tiny Tim will die (Dickens, 45). So, in effect, Tiny Tim's health is determinant upon Scrooge's willingness to change his life and therefore by extension, the lives of the people around him.

Just as Tiny Tim's health becomes indicative of Scrooge's emotional and spiritual health, there are indicators out there that allow individuals to measure, grade, and track America's economic health. Some measure America's annual on-site productivity. Others measure the purchasing power of the American dollar. Yet others compare the United States to other countries and how happy our citizens are versus the rest of the world. All of these measures enable us to get an idea of how healthy or sick our economy is and also what economic problems might be making life in America more difficult than it has to be.

The first and most regularly talked about measure for economic health is the **GDP** or

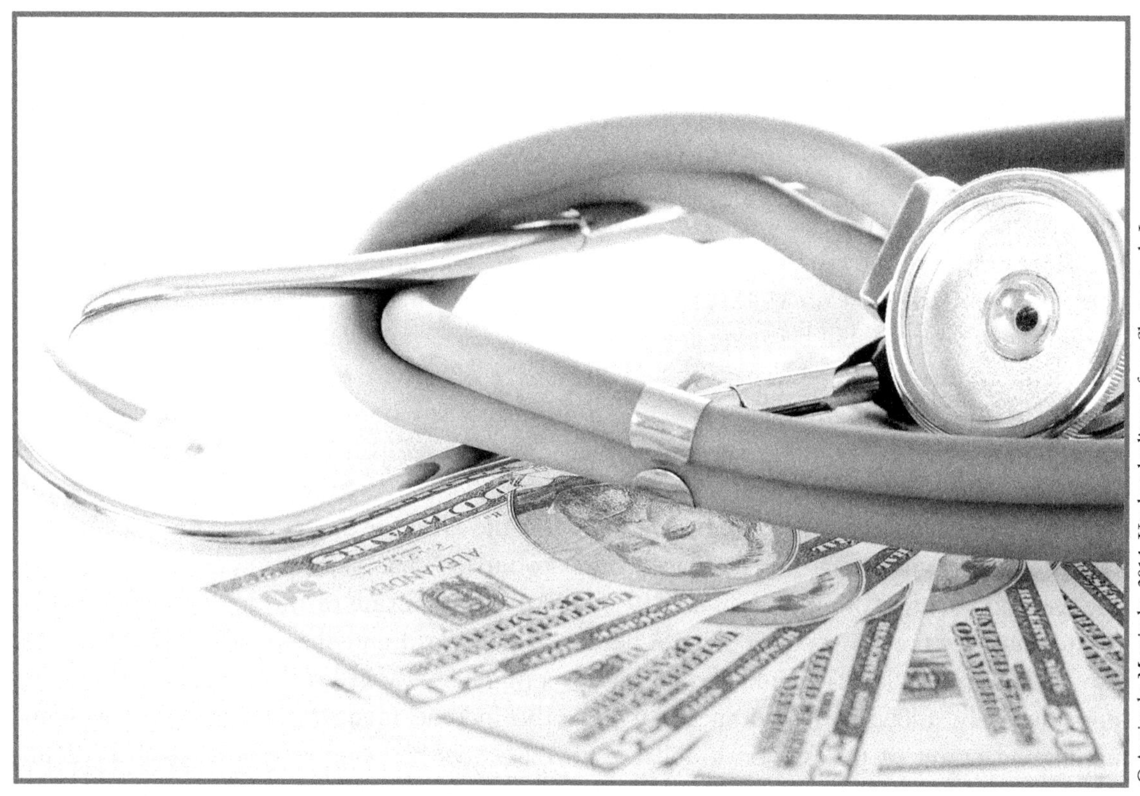

Preventing Tiny Tim's death: promoting economic health

gross domestic product. GDP measures the total amount of goods and services produced within a country's borders in a given year; it is often considered to be a measure of a country's standard of living. The inherent problem with this measure, however, is that a significant amount of goods and services produced by American companies are produced in factories on foreign soil; because most of these goods and services are produced outside the United States, America's GDP fails to reflect the production of these products. The relocation and production of American goods on foreign soil is known as **outsourcing** and has become increasingly popular since the 1990s; outsourcing makes it easier to produce more goods at a cheaper price, because foreign countries often have few (if any) labor regulations and can pay wages far below America's minimum wage requirements (Hartung, 1-2). Because goods and services produced through outsourcing are not considered in a country's GDP, one could argue that a country's GDP has the potential to underestimate economic growth – the United States included.

Another measure of economic health investigates the purchasing power of America's currency – the dollar. This measure is known as the **CPI** or the **consumer price index.** This measure tracks the rate of **inflation** – the rise in prices for a good or service over a specified amount of time – on a set basket of consumer goods set by the Bureau of Labor Statistics. For example: say you go to the grocery store and buy some routine vittles (milk, eggs, bread, meat, etc.) for $20 but in two weeks, you go back and discover that those same groceries are more expensive and cost $25. The value of these products have gone up while the purchasing power of your $20 bill has gone down as it no longer enables you to buy what you bought before; in this scenario, the rate of inflation is said to have increased. The CPI investigates a variety of different types of goods and services over time and investigates how the purchasing power of Americans increases or decreases with the rise and fall of inflation. A higher CPI indicates that the purchasing power of the American dollar has gone down and inflation has gone up; conversely, a lower CPI indicates that the purchasing power of the American dollar has increased and inflation has gone down. Inflation has traditionally been a problem in the United States as of late, so it should be no surprise that America's CPI historically increases gradually over time; thus, inflation can also be said to be steadily but gradually increasing as well (Bureau of Labor Statistics, 1).

The last measure of economic health to be considered here is the **human development index (HDI).** This measure attempts to capture social and economic development within a country or, put another way, a country's standard of living as compared to other countries; this measure has been adjusted to account for income inequality present in different countries so as to make the index more accurate. Unlike the GDP and CPI, however, this measure considers more than mere economics; it captures social impacts of economic woe. If a country's economy is developed but provides a rudimentary standard of living for its citizens, it is possible for the HDI for that country to be lower than countries that share similar circumstances. America has one of the highest HDI ratings in the world and shares close company with a number of Western European democracies; the income inequality present in the United States has kept it from being the highest ranked country included in the HDI for

The CPI considers the value of a set basket of products to determine if inflation has gone up or down.

some time (Portero, 1-2). The HDI provides countries with a comparative measure of one country's standard of living versus others.

The Old and New Scrooge and Trade Policy: Protectionism vs. Free Trade Approaches

The Ghost of Christmas Past presents Scrooge with two visions that depict Scrooge losing two people who were important to him. The first person Scrooge loses is his younger sister, Fan – the only member of her family truly devoted to him (Dickens, 28). Next, we see Scrooge's sweetheart, Belle, leave him so he can more ardently pursue his career in business – an event that devastates Scrooge (Dickens, 32-33). In both instances, Scrooge's choice to become emotionally attached to these individuals ended up backfiring on him, and his actions and interactions after these losses implies that Scrooge intentionally distances himself from emotional attachment so as to ensure that he doesn't get hurt in the future. The intervention of Marley's Ghost and the three Ghosts of Christmas help to show Scrooge the benefits of such interactions. They demonstrate to Scrooge exactly what he is missing by intentionally ostracizing himself from humanity; ultimately, the visits of the Ghosts encourage Scrooge to open his heart again to his fellow man.

In *A Christmas Carol*, we encounter Scrooge in two capacities. The first image of Scrooge we are presented with is the Scrooge who has intentionally distanced himself from human emotion and empathy. This Scrooge is one who has abandoned humanity and all emotions associated with human interaction so as to protect himself from feeling the pain he knew twice in his past. Scrooge the Protectionist is the one we encounter and travel with during most of the duration of Dickens' tale. The other Scrooge, the more emotionally open Scrooge, is met after he discovers that the Ghosts who visited him have given him a second chance; the end of Dickens' tale depicts Scrooge as a benevolent, well-intentioned, and reformed individual who is ready and willing to re-engage in the world of human emotion.

Just as Scrooge embraces two perspectives on the exposure of his own emotions, so too are there two different methods countries can employ to protect or promote their own economic interests in the realm of international trade. The first method that countries typically employ is known as **protectionism** – a method for restricting trade with other countries so as to protect that country's own economic interests. This can be done by issuing **tariffs** - taxes placed on goods entering the country from a foreign country, **import quotas** – numerical limitations on how much of a foreign product can enter a country's borders, and other regulations that promote home-grown businesses and limits the access of goods from other countries. Countries typically employ protectionist policies as they begin to develop their economies but gradually open up trade with other countries as the country's economy becomes stronger (Fletcher, 1-5).

The alternative to protectionism is the application of **free trade policies.** Countries

The 'made-in-America' principle is one method of promoting protectionist policies and discouraging the import and purchase of foreign products.

that embrace free trade policies are reluctant to impose tariffs or other protections that might discourage other countries from engaging in trade with them. Free trade policies are known for bringing countries together and encouraging international competition whereas protectionist policies are meant to inhibit both of those activities. Generally speaking, industrialized and post-industrial societies tend to espouse free trade policies and avoid protectionist ones while developing countries tend to gravitate toward policies that are often labeled as protectionist. International trade agreements between countries also have the propensity to lead to the creation of military alliances as well; we can infer therefore that the freer a country's trade policies become, the more allies that the country in question will attain (Emanuel, 1-2). The United States is known for its advocacy of free trade policies but, in retrospect, had a stronger economy when employing protectionist policies (Fletcher, 3-4). Despite this assertion, America has moved away from protectionist policies and has become the global poster-child of free trade policies. Just as we are presented with Scrooge's two alter-egos in Dickens' story, America and other industrialized countries also experience a transformation in terms of international political economy. Countries develop their economies by employing protectionist policies but once these countries' economies are sufficiently developed, they move away from protectionist policies and toward free trade and international cooperation and competition.

Charles Dickens' *A Christmas Carol* tells the story of Ebenezer Scrooge – a miserable miser whose life is transformed by the visits of yuletide spirits. Similarly, the economy of the United States has undergone drastic changes since its inception. America has moved away from an agrarian economy to one that most political scientists identify as a post-industrial one. Its economy has been shaped by various proprietors of economic thought, altered by historical circumstance, and improved through the shift away from protectionist trade policies to ones that embrace free trade. America's economic development – both practically and philosophically – is comparable to the miserable miser who, until a few choice meetings with holly, jolly spirits with perspective, had dedicated his life to being a man of business instead of attending to the business of mankind.

Food for Thought

Economic Development

Why does economic development almost always seem to begin in the cornfields? Why is agriculture so important to a growing economy? Must the development of an agricultural sector occur before the rise of industrialization? Why is industrialization key to a developing economy? Are there any drawbacks to industrialization as part of the economic development process? Does industrialization fix or create more societal ills? Can these ills be completely rectified or are some of the problems of industrialization simply permanent parts of life that most societies accept? What, in your opinion, does a post-industrial society do? If, in a post-industrial society, most of the jobs are not in manufacturing or production, do you think that unemployment is higher in a post-industrial society or should the economy evolve and encourage the creation of different types of jobs? Post-industrial societies are noted for their large service sectors; name some service-oriented jobs that are available in a post-industrial society. Is a post-industrial society inherently 'better' or 'worse' than a society in the midst of industrialization?

Economic Philosophy

Adam Smith, the founder of modern capitalism, seemed to recognize the need for moderation with his own theory and perceived that mankind could take it to an extreme – as indeed happened during the Industrial Revolutions in Europe and the United States. Since Smith encouraged the government to be *minimally* involved in the maintenance of economic health, did the individuals who embraced capitalism employ its principles incorrectly or did they intentionally radicalize Smith's theory for their own benefit? Is capitalism an 'evil' economic philosophy or does it simply make use of of the darker traits of humanity?

Karl Marx's philosophy was essentially a critique of the unfettered capitalism that existed during the Industrial Revolution in Europe. Why did Marx believe that capitalism was evil? Were there more poor people (or proletarians) than capitalists? Why didn't the proletariat organize sooner than they did? Why did Marx believe that the proletariat would *forcibly remove* the capitalists from power instead of finding a more moderated solution? Do you believe that the formal organization of labor unions is a socialist idea? If you think so, then wasn't Marx at least partially right? Did labor unions give employees some say and some control over the means of production? Is the political and social revolution predicted by Marx necessary to move society in a more humane direction?

Labor unions serve as the mediator between the owners of the means of production (the capitalists) and their workers. Why would the capitalists have initially rejected the demands of organized labor? What ultimately changed their tune in that regard? Does the government have a place in shaping labor policy? Is there such a thing as too much work? What constitutes a safe work environment? What do you think about the new 'right to work' legislation? Is it bad or beneficial for the average American worker? Are labor unions as necessary now as they were in the 1920s and 1930s? If so, what can be done to protect their existence in the light of the 'right to work' movement? In terms of the progress labor unions have made for the average worker, is the 'right to work' movement a step forward in that endeavor or a step backwards?

John Maynard Keynes proposed a theory of government intervention in the economy to keep its effect minimized during recessions and depressions. Why would a government ever spend more money than it takes in? Is there any time where this is a good plan? What would Keynes say? Why would a government raise taxes during a time where people have less money to pay in taxes? Does Keynes' theory stretch people's billfolds at the wrong times or is his theory practical? During an economic boom, why is cutting taxes and spending a good idea? Typically speaking, do you spend more money when you have more of it or less? Do you think President Obama's application of Keynesian economics has been a successful venture or a failure?

Ronald Reagan's 'supply-side' economics places the power to alter the economy in the hands of those who own the means of production (the capitalists). Do you think that, in general, capitalists typically follow Reagan's philosophical direction and create jobs and raise wages during times of economic distress, or do they instead keep the extra cash from such endeavors for themselves? Did Reagan's application of this philosophy work out for him because the historical and economic atmosphere played into his hands, or is supply-side economics a valid economic philosophical framework? What about George W. Bush's application? Why did the application of supply-side economics backfire on Bush but not on Reagan?

Economic Health

Why does the GDP only include the goods and services produced within a country's borders when so many American companies have outsourced their production to foreign countries? Because of this fact, is the GDP an appropriate measure of economic growth? Do we need a new economic indicator that takes both domestic and foreign incomes into account? Should there be an economic indicator that takes into consideration America's spending as well? Since we live in a post-industrial society, do you think the GDP is dominated by the goods produced or the services that are rendered within America's borders? Is the GDP a better measure for an industrializing country, a post-industrial society, both, or neither?

The CPI attempts to capture a country's change in inflation. You often hear about people complaining about how bad inflation is. Compared to other countries, how bad is our rate of inflation, really? Do you think inflation naturally increases or decreases over time? If inflation is occurring, is the American dollar's purchasing power growing or falling? What if deflation is occurring? Is inflation a sign of economic health or ill? Are there any advantages to inflation? Deflation? Why would we want the American dollar to be strong? Why would we want a weak dollar?

The HDI measures the standard of living in the United States as compared to countries that are similar to us. In your opinion, is the standard of living in the United States higher or lower than it is in other countries? Are there any areas where we as a country could improve? The HDI statistic was altered to account for income inequality. How much of that do you believe exists in the United States? Is there a major disparity between rich and poor here? Is that good, bad, or just how it is? Should we be working to close the wage gap, or is that something that the economy should naturally regulate?

Trade Policy: Protectionism vs. Free Trade

Are protectionist economic policies patriotic? What about free trade policies? Why would a country want to employ protectionist policies in the era of a global marketplace? Are protectionist policies necessary to form economies that can cope with global competition, or is protectionism simply a method of assuring economic stability? Why would a country move away from protectionism and embrace free trade policies? Do you think that countries that employ protectionist policies have more or fewer allies than countries that embrace free trade policies? Do embracing free trade policies make a country more vulnerable or more untouchable? Are there industrialized or post-industrial countries out there that still employ protectionist trade policies? If so, name them and what policies they have in place.

As one story ends, another Story begins
It's not 'safe' like most stories are.
Once you open your heart to the Story's message
You will never be the same
You can never go back.

Works Cited

Bell, Daniel. *The Coming of Post-Industrial Society: A Venture in Social Forecasting.* New York: Basic Books, 1976.

Brinkley, Alan. (I). *American History: A Survey. Volume 1: to 1877.* New York: McGraw Hill Higher Education, 2003.

Brinkley, Alan. (II). *American History: A Survey. Volume 2: Since 1865.* New York: McGraw Hill Higher Education, 2003.

"Consumer Price Index." Bureau of Labor Statistics. http://www.bls.gov/cpi/#news. Posted on 01/16/2014.

Davey, Monica. "Right to Work Bills Face Uncertain Future in an Election Year." *The New York Times. http://www.nytimes.com/2012/03/21/us/right-to-work-bills-face-uncertain-future.html?pagewanted=all&_r=0.* Posted on 03/20/2012.

Dickens, Charles. *The Christmas Books of Charles Dickens.* Ann Arbor: Tally Hall Press, 1996.

Dionne Jr., E. J. "Capitalism's Reality Check." *The Washington Post. http://www.washingtonpost.com/wp-dyn/content/article/2008/07/10/AR2008071002264.html.* Posted on 07/11/2008.

Emanuel, Mike. "Allies Jump as Washington's Free Trade Delay Continues." *Fox News. http://www.foxnews.com/politics/2011/08/16/allies-jump-as-washington-free-trade-delay-continues/.* Posted on 08/16/2011.

Feenstra, Robert C. and Gordon H. Hanson. "Globalization, Outsourcing, and Wage Inequality." *American Economic Review.* 86. 2. (1996). Pages 240-245.

Ferrara, Peter. "President Obama's Predictable Budget: More Spending, More Tax Increases." *Forbes Magazine. http://www.forbes.com/sites/peterferrara/2013/04/19/president-obamas-predictable-budget-more-spending-more-tax-increases/.* Posted on 04/19/2013.

Fletcher, Ian. "America Was Founded as a Protectionist Nation." *Huffington Post: Politics. http://www.huffingtonpost.com/ian-fletcher/america-was-founded-as-a_b_713521.html.* Posted 09/11/2010.

Harper, David. "Understanding Supply-Side Economics." *Investopedia. http://www.investopedia.com/articles/05/011805.asp.* Posted on 11/04/2013.

Harper, Jennifer. "Poll: Obama Policy 'Will Move' US 'Toward Socialism.' " *The Washington Times. http://www.washingtontimes.com/blog/watercooler/2012/dec/17/poll-obama-policy-will-move-us-toward-socialism/.* Posted on 12/17/2012.

Hartung, Adam. "Outsourcing – Right or Wrong? 9 Key Questions." *Forbes Magazine. http://www.forbes.com/sites/adamhartung/2010/09/30/outsourcing-right-or-wrong-9-key-questions/.* Posted on 09/30/2010.

Hindery Jr., Leo. "Senator McCain, Regulated Capitalism Is Not Socialism." *The Huffington Post. http://www.huffingtonpost.com/leo-hindery-jr/senator-mccain-regulated_b_139736.html.* Posted on 10/31/2008.

James, Randy. "A Brief History of McDonald's Abroad." *Time Magazine. http://content.time.com/time/world/article/0,8599,1932839,00.html.* Posted on 10/28/2009.

Kai, Zhou. "How American Movies Share Their Values." *Watching America. http://watchingamerica.com/News/168163/how-american-movies-spread-their-values/.* Posted on 07/25/2012.

Keynes, John Maynard. *The General Theory of Employment, Interest, and Money.* New York: Harvest Books, 1965.

Perry, Mark J. "Why Socialism Failed: Collectivism is Based on Faulty Principles." *The Freeman. http://www.fee.org/the_freeman/detail/why-socialism-failed#axzz2tRIFwn1E.* Posted on 06/01/1995.

Portero, Ashley. "Income Inequality Lowers U.S. Rank in U.N. Human Development Index." *International Business Times. http://www.ibtimes.com/income-inequality-lowers-us-rank-un-human-development-index-364430.* Posted on 11/02/2011.

Sinclair, Upton. *The Jungle.* New York: Penguin Books, 2006.

Smith, Adam. *The Wealth of Nations.* New York: Bantam Books, 1776.

Toyama, Kentaro. "Income Inequality Around the World is a Failure of Capitalism." *The Atlantic. http://www.theatlantic.com/business/archive/2011/05/income-inequality-around-the-world-is-a-failure-of-capitalism/238837/.* Posted on 05/13/2011.

Williams, Byron. "Supply Side Economics Sounds Good But Doesn't Work." *The Huffington Post: Politics. http://www.huffingtonpost.com/byron-williams/supply-side-taxes_b_1872005.html.* Posted on 09/13/2012.

EPILOGUE

The NeverEnding Story Has a New Hero

Many of you are attending college and are encouraged by your professors to purchase different books and absorb the information within them. This is particularly true in your English composition and literature classes. I have demonstrated here, in this book, how fantasy worlds and arenas of competition compare to the very real world in which we live. There is one final Story, however, that I would like you to consider.

This Story, however, is not like the ones you've read before. Those are 'safe' books (Hill); when you are done with them, you can go back to being whatever it was that you were when you began reading the book – a college student, a mom or dad, a professor – whatever. There is nothing in most fictional books that compels the reader to be anything more than a neutral bystander. The Story I'm about to share is different. Some might say that it's dangerous in a way, because it encourages you to become a major character in its plotline and forces you to decide what your role in the Story should be.

The NeverEnding Story

A young boy, Bastian, is misunderstood by his father and bullied by his classmates. His only refuge is his large collection of books, but even these begin to bore him as he's read them all many times. Bastian retreats to the local bookstore and searches the piles of books for something new, something exciting to read. He notices the bookshop owner, Carl Conrad Coreander, reading a book – *The NeverEnding Story*. Coreander warns Bastian that the book he's reading isn't like other books. Other books are 'safe' because they're only stories – the kind of tales that are perused by those who seek to remain neutral bystanders; Coreander tells Bastian that *The NeverEnding Story* is different and far more dangerous than other books. He explains that *The NeverEnding Story* is not a 'safe' book; it forces the reader to become an important part of the tale. Intrigued, Bastian takes the book while Coreander isn't looking and leaves a note promising to return it when he's done. Instead of going home, Bastian hides in the school attic and begins to read Coreander's book. Little does he know that by reading the book, he will become entangled in its storyline and discover himself to be more important than he could have possibly imagined (Petersen).

In the Story, Bastian enters the realm of Fantasia – a mythical, fantasy land like none you have ever dreamed of – but a land in grave peril nonetheless. Bastian witnesses a number of Fantasia's residents traveling to the Ivory Tower to seek the help of the Childlike Empress in defending Fantasia against 'the Nothing' – a mysterious, powerful darkness that has both begun to inundate and destroy Fantasia and also claim the Empress' health. In a weakened state, she summons and dispatches a boy-hero, Atreyu, to combat and defeat the Nothing else Fantasia be totally destroyed. As the Story progresses, Bastian notices that the boy Atreyu greatly resembles himself in both appearance and personality. The Empress gives Atreyu a mythical amulet, the AURYN, to protect him on his Quest to defeat the Nothing (Petersen).

Becoming part of *The NeverEnding Story* simply requires you to keep turning the pages – to have the courage to do something about the Nothing.

Through many dangerous adventures and the help of the luckdragon, Falkor, Atreyu reaches the Southern Oracle – a being that is thought to have the wisdom to aid Atreyu in his Quest to subdue the ever-growing power of the Nothing. The Oracle reveals that only the re-naming of the Empress by a human child can eliminate the power of the Nothing and save Fantasia. He also discovers that the human child that can save the Empress exists outside the boundaries of Fantasia. Just as Atreyu receives the message, however, the Nothing consumes the Southern Oracle, and Atreyu is forced to flee. As Atreyu desperately searches for a human child to re-name the Empress, the Nothing is never far behind; it consumes people, towns, rivers, oceans – everything in its path. All are powerless against its mysterious influence; even Atreyu himself begins to despair and wonders whether his attempts to defeat the Nothing are in vain (Petersen).

Before Atreyu is able to return to the Ivory Tower to pass on the knowledge he has acquired to the Empress, he is confronted by G'Mork, an evil wolf who has been stalking Atreyu throughout his journeys. G'Mork reveals that Fantasia, rather than being a fictional place, is the realm of human fantasy which has no boundaries. As a self-avowed servant of evil, G'Mork informs Atreyu that the Nothing is a destructive force in Fantasia that reflects humanity's emerging ignorance in the Real World; it encourages people to abandon their hopes and forget their dreams. Therefore, as humanity's ignorance and despair increases in the Real World, the Nothing consumes and destroys more of Fantasia. Before G'Mork can kill Atreyu and assure Fantasia's demise, the boy-hero stabs him and leaves the Nothing's greatest servant dead upon the ground (Petersen).

With G'Mork's revelations in mind, Atreyu returns to the Ivory Tower. The Empress is overjoyed, because Atreyu has unknowingly succeeded in bringing a human child into the Story – Bastian himself. Bastian is confused and refuses to believe that his presence can be felt by the characters in the Story, but the Empress reveals that by reading the book, he himself became part of the Story by taking part in Atreyu's adventures, joys, and sorrows. She tells Bastian that the only thing that can save Fantasia from the Nothing is his willingness to use the knowledge he has gained by reading *The NeverEnding Story*. He must believe that Fantasia can be saved and the power of the Nothing can be subdued. At the last moment, Bastian saves the Empress by re-naming her 'Moonchild'; Fantasia, however, isn't as lucky (Petersen).

Through the efforts of Bastian – one little boy – the glory of Fantasia is restored. You as an American citizen also possess that power – the ability to remake, rebuild, and renew America as you see fit. You are far more powerful than you realize and much more important than you know.

In a darkened room, the Empress appears before Bastian and hands him a grain of gleaming golden sand – the last remaining remnant of Fantasia. She tells Bastian that by making a wish and using his imagination, the glory of Fantasia – the realm of mankind's hopes and dreams – could be renewed. Bastian closes his eyes and makes a wish, and the land of Fantasia is re-created as it was before the Nothing came. Through Bastian's wish, the land of Fantasia is saved by the power of his imagination and his willingness to believe in the impossible (Petersen).

Our Part in the NeverEnding Story

What if I told you that Bastian, the boy reading the Story, and each of you reading this book have more in common than you think. Both of you have been led to believe that you are insignificant, unimportant, and incapable of making a definable difference. I am sure that, at least before reading this book, some of you believed it. I hope that reading this book – my book – has led you to question what most people have been trying to tell you about your power to interact with and shape America's Story. You, as a citizen of this country, have an incredible amount of power at your disposal, and I assure you that the citizens who are bold enough to think they can change the world, save it, remake it, preserve it, and protect it are the ones who succeed in doing so.

You, like Bastian, are an imperative element of our Story – America's NeverEnding Story. The days of being a neutral bystander, an objective observer, are long over. This book is **not** a 'safe book', because your role doesn't end when you shut the cover – at least, it shouldn't and I hope it doesn't. You have the power and the knowledge to address anything in the realm of American politics that is thrown your way. Unfortunately, most of America's inhabitants (citizens and otherwise) cannot say the same. They, like most of Fantasia, are drowning in the ignorance and indifference that is tolerated – some might even say encouraged – by so many Americans today. Only people like you who choose to

The blank pages of America's Story are being written by you; it is up to you to decide how wonderful and glorious our Fantasia will become.

embrace the knowledge that they have acquired and are willing to spread it have any chance of preserving this great nation of ours. We only have to be brave and bold enough to play our part in the Story well.

You are the hero in America's Story - our NeverEnding Story. Together, let us attempt to do something about the Nothing. Let us encourage our fellow citizens to have faith in their hopes and to pursue their dreams. Through these efforts, the glory of America – our Fantasia – can be restored.

America's Storybook is still open and there are many blank pages waiting to be written on by us – the authors of America's NeverEnding Story. That Story will continue on with or without you, but the likelihood of America's continued success is assured so long as you continue to inscribe our Story onto its pages. Be mindful of how your role in the Story – or your choice to remove yourself from that role – could have epic consequences for our country. All you have to decide is whether or not you are going to close the book on your fellow citizens (and on yourself) or whether you will keep reading, writing, and interacting with America's Story. Are you, like Bastian, willing to do something to combat the Nothing? The choice is entirely yours, but I suggest that you continue to interact with America's Story – our NeverEnding Story. With you playing the role of the hero, the Story is just now getting good and we are that much closer to doing something about the Nothing.

(Hopefully not)
The End

Works Cited

The NeverEnding Story (Die unendliche Geschischte). Dir. Wolfgang Petersen. Perf. Barrett Oliver (Bastian), Thomas Hill (Carl Conrad Coreander), Noah Hathaway (Atreyu), and Tami Stronach (The Childlike Empress). Warner Brothers Pictures, 1984.

The Declaration of Independence

IN CONGRESS, July 4, 1776.

The unanimous Declaration of the thirteen united States of America,

When in the Course of human events, it becomes necessary for one people to dissolve the political bands which have connected them with another, and to assume among the powers of the earth, the separate and equal station to which the Laws of Nature and of Nature's God entitle them, a decent respect to the opinions of mankind requires that they should declare the causes which impel them to the separation.

We hold these truths to be self-evident, that all men are created equal, that they are endowed by their Creator with certain unalienable Rights, that among these are Life, Liberty and the pursuit of Happiness.--That to secure these rights, Governments are instituted among Men, deriving their just powers from the consent of the governed, --That whenever any Form of Government becomes destructive of these ends, it is the Right of the People to alter or to abolish it, and to institute new Government, laying its foundation on such principles and organizing its powers in such form, as to them shall seem most likely to affect their Safety and Happiness. Prudence, indeed, will dictate that Governments long established should not be changed for light and transient causes; and accordingly all experience hath shown, that mankind are more disposed to suffer, while evils are sufferable, than to right themselves by abolishing the forms to which they are accustomed. But when a long train of abuses and usurpations, pursuing invariably the same Object evinces a design to reduce them under absolute Despotism, it is their right, it is their duty, to throw off such Government, and to provide new Guards for their future security.--Such has been the patient sufferance of these Colonies; and such is now the necessity which constrains them to alter their former Systems of Government. The history of the present King of Great Britain is a history of repeated injuries and usurpations, all having in direct object the establishment of an absolute Tyranny over these States. To prove this, let Facts be submitted to a candid world.

He has refused his Assent to Laws, the most wholesome and necessary for the public good.

He has forbidden his Governors to pass Laws of immediate and pressing importance, unless suspended in their operation till his Assent should be obtained; and when so suspended, he has utterly neglected to attend to them.

He has refused to pass other Laws for the accommodation of large districts of people, unless those people would relinquish the right of Representation in the Legislature, a right inestimable to them and formidable to tyrants only.

He has called together legislative bodies at places unusual, uncomfortable, and distant from the depository of their public Records, for the sole purpose of fatiguing them into compliance with his measures.

He has dissolved Representative Houses repeatedly, for opposing with manly firmness his invasions on the rights of the people.

He has refused for a long time, after such dissolutions, to cause others to be elected; whereby the Legislative powers, incapable of Annihilation, have returned to the People at large for their exercise; the State remaining in the meantime exposed to all the dangers of invasion from without, and convulsions within.

He has endeavored to prevent the population of these States; for that purpose obstructing the Laws for Naturalization of Foreigners; refusing to pass others to encourage their migrations hither, and raising the conditions of new Appropriations of Lands.

He has obstructed the Administration of Justice, by refusing his Assent to Laws for establishing Judiciary powers.

He has made Judges dependent on his Will alone, for the tenure of their offices, and the amount and payment of their salaries.

He has erected a multitude of New Offices, and sent hither swarms of Officers to harass our people, and eat out their substance.

He has kept among us, in times of peace, Standing Armies without the Consent of our legislatures.

He has affected to render the Military independent of and superior to the Civil power.

He has combined with others to subject us to a jurisdiction foreign to our constitution, and unacknowledged by our laws; giving his Assent to their Acts of pretended Legislation:

For Quartering large bodies of armed troops among us:

For protecting them, by a mock Trial, from punishment for any Murders which they should commit on the Inhabitants of these States:

For cutting off our Trade with all parts of the world:

For imposing Taxes on us without our Consent:

For depriving us in many cases, of the benefits of Trial by Jury:

For transporting us beyond Seas to be tried for pretended offences

For abolishing the free System of English Laws in a neighboring Province, establishing therein an Arbitrary government, and enlarging its Boundaries so as to render it at once an example and fit instrument for introducing the same absolute rule into these Colonies:

For taking away our Charters, abolishing our most valuable Laws, and altering fundamentally the Forms of our Governments:

For suspending our own Legislatures, and declaring themselves invested with power to legislate for us in all cases whatsoever.

He has abdicated Government here, by declaring us out of his Protection and waging War against us.

He has plundered our seas, ravaged our Coasts, burnt our towns, and destroyed the lives of our people.

He is at this time transporting large Armies of foreign Mercenaries to complete the works of death, desolation and tyranny, already begun with circumstances of Cruelty & perfidy scarcely paralleled in the most barbarous ages, and totally unworthy the Head of a civilized nation.

He has constrained our fellow Citizens taken Captive on the high Seas to bear Arms against their Country, to become the executioners of their friends and Brethren, or to fall themselves by their Hands.

He has excited domestic insurrections amongst us, and has endeavored to bring on the inhabitants of our frontiers, the merciless Indian Savages, whose known rule of warfare, is an undistinguished destruction of all ages, sexes and conditions.

In every stage of these Oppressions We have Petitioned for Redress in the most humble terms: Our repeated Petitions have been answered only by repeated injury. A Prince whose character is thus marked by every act which may define a Tyrant, is unfit to be the ruler of a free people.

Nor have We been wanting in attentions to our British brethren. We have warned them from time to time of attempts by their legislature to extend an unwarrantable jurisdiction over us. We have reminded them of the circumstances of our emigration and settlement here. We have appealed to their native justice and magnanimity, and we have conjured them by the ties of our common kindred to disavow these usurpations, which, would inevitably interrupt our connections and correspondence. They too have been deaf to the voice of justice and of consanguinity. We must, therefore, acquiesce in the necessity, which denounces our Separation, and hold them, as we hold the rest of mankind, Enemies in War, in Peace Friends.

We, therefore, the Representatives of the united States of America, in General Congress, Assembled, appealing to the Supreme Judge of the world for the rectitude of our intentions, do, in the Name, and by Authority of the good People of these Colonies, solemnly publish and declare, That these United Colonies are, and of Right ought to be Free and Independent States; that they are Absolved from all Allegiance to the British Crown, and that all political connection between them and the State of Great Britain, is and ought to be totally dissolved; and that as Free and Independent States, they have full Power to levy War, conclude Peace, contract Alliances, establish Commerce, and to do all other Acts and Things which Independent States may of right do. And for the support of this Declaration, with a firm reliance on the protection of divine Providence, we mutually pledge to each other our Lives, our Fortunes and our sacred Honor.

Georgia:
Button Gwinnett
Lyman Hall
George Walton

North Carolina:
William Hooper
Joseph Hewes
John Penn

South Carolina:
Edward Rutledge

Thomas Heyward, Jr.
Thomas Lynch, Jr.
Arthur Middleton

Massachusetts:
John Hancock
Samuel Adams
John Adams
Robert Treat Paine
Elbridge Gerry

Maryland:
Samuel Chase
William Paca
Thomas Stone
Charles Carroll of Carrollton

Virginia:
George Wythe
Richard Henry Lee
Thomas Jefferson
Benjamin Harrison
Thomas Nelson, Jr.
Francis Lightfoot Lee
Carter Braxton

Pennsylvania:
Robert Morris
Benjamin Rush
Benjamin Franklin
John Morton
George Clymer
James Smith
George Taylor
James Wilson
George Ross

Delaware:
Caesar Rodney
George Read
Thomas McKean

New York:
William Floyd
Philip Livingston
Francis Lewis
Lewis Morris

New Jersey:
Richard Stockton
John Witherspoon
Francis Hopkinson
John Hart
Abraham Clark

New Hampshire:
Josiah Bartlett
Matthew Thornton
William Whipple

Rhode Island:
Stephen Hopkins
William Ellery

Connecticut:
Roger Sherman
Samuel Huntington
William Williams
Oliver Wolcott

Text for the Declaration of Independence provided by the National Archives http://www.archives.gov/exhibits/charters/declaration_transcript.html

The United States Constitution

The Constitution of the United States

We the People of the United States, in Order to form a more perfect Union, establish Justice, insure domestic Tranquility, provide for the common defense, promote the general Welfare, and secure the Blessings of Liberty to ourselves and our Posterity, do ordain and establish this Constitution for the United States of America.

Article. I.

Section. 1.

All legislative Powers herein granted shall be vested in a Congress of the United States, which shall consist of a Senate and House of Representatives.

Section. 2.

The House of Representatives shall be composed of Members chosen every second Year by the People of the several States, and the Electors in each State shall have the Qualifications requisite for Electors of the most numerous Branch of the State Legislature.

No Person shall be a Representative who shall not have attained to the Age of twenty five Years, and been seven Years a Citizen of the United States, and who shall not, when elected, be an Inhabitant of that State in which he shall be chosen.

Representatives and direct Taxes shall be apportioned among the several States which may be included within this Union, according to their respective Numbers, which shall be determined by adding to the whole Number of free Persons, including those bound to Service for a Term of Years, and excluding Indians not taxed, three fifths of all other Persons. The actual Enumeration shall be made within three Years after the first Meeting of the Congress of the United States, and within every subsequent Term of ten Years, in such Manner as they shall by Law direct. The Number of Representatives shall not exceed one for every thirty Thousand, but each State shall have at Least one Representative; and until such enumeration shall be made, the State of New Hampshire shall be entitled to choose three, Massachusetts eight, Rhode-Island and Providence Plantations one, Connecticut five, New-York six, New Jersey four, Pennsylvania eight, Delaware one, Maryland six, Virginia ten, North Carolina five, South Carolina five, and Georgia three.

When vacancies happen in the Representation from any State, the Executive Authority thereof shall issue Writs of Election to fill such Vacancies.

The House of Representatives shall choose their Speaker and other Officers; and shall have the sole Power of Impeachment.

Section. 3.

The Senate of the United States shall be composed of two Senators from each State, chosen by the Legislature thereof for six Years; and each Senator shall have one Vote.

Immediately after they shall be assembled in Consequence of the first Election, they shall be divided as equally as may be into three Classes. The Seats of the Senators of the first Class shall be vacated at the Expiration of the second Year, of the second Class at the Expiration of the fourth Year, and of the third Class at the Expiration of the sixth Year, so that one third may be chosen every second Year; and if Vacancies happen by Resignation, or otherwise, during the Recess of the Legislature of any State, the Executive thereof may make temporary Appointments until the next Meeting of the Legislature, which shall then fill such Vacancies.

No Person shall be a Senator who shall not have attained to the Age of thirty Years, and been nine Years a Citizen of the United States, and who shall not, when elected, be an Inhabitant of that State for which he shall be chosen.

The Vice President of the United States shall be President of the Senate, but shall have no Vote, unless they be equally divided.

The Senate shall choose their other Officers, and also a President pro tempore, in the Absence of the Vice President, or when he shall exercise the Office of President of the United States.

The Senate shall have the sole Power to try all Impeachments. When sitting for that Purpose, they shall be on Oath or Affirmation. When the President of the United States is tried, the Chief Justice shall preside: And no Person shall be convicted without the Concurrence of two thirds of the Members present.

Judgment in Cases of Impeachment shall not extend further than to removal from Office, and disqualification to hold and enjoy any Office of honor, Trust or Profit under the United States: but the Party convicted shall nevertheless be liable and subject to Indictment, Trial, Judgment and Punishment, according to Law.

Section. 4.

The Times, Places and Manner of holding Elections for Senators and Representatives, shall be prescribed in each State by the Legislature thereof; but the Congress may at any time by Law make or alter such Regulations, except as to the Places of choosing Senators.

The Congress shall assemble at least once in every Year, and such Meeting shall be on the first Monday in December, unless they shall by Law appoint a different Day.

Section. 5.

Each House shall be the Judge of the Elections, Returns and Qualifications of its own Members, and a Majority of each shall constitute a Quorum to do Business; but a smaller Number may adjourn from day to day, and may be authorized to compel the Attendance of absent Members, in such Manner, and under such Penalties as each House may provide.

Each House may determine the Rules of its Proceedings, punish its Members for disorderly Behavior, and, with the Concurrence of two thirds, expel a Member.

Each House shall keep a Journal of its Proceedings, and from time to time publish the same, excepting such Parts as may in their Judgment require Secrecy; and the Yeas and Nays of the Members of either House on any question shall, at the Desire of one fifth of those Present, be entered on the Journal.

Neither House, during the Session of Congress, shall, without the Consent of the other, adjourn for more than three days, nor to any other Place than that in which the two Houses shall be sitting.

Section. 6.

The Senators and Representatives shall receive a Compensation for their Services, to be ascertained by Law, and paid out of the Treasury of the United States. They shall in all Cases, except Treason, Felony and Breach of the Peace, be privileged from Arrest during their Attendance at the Session of their respective Houses, and in going to and returning from the same; and for any Speech or Debate in either House, they shall not be questioned in any other Place.

No Senator or Representative shall, during the Time for which he was elected, be appointed to any civil Office under the Authority of the United States, which shall have been created, or the Emoluments whereof shall have been increased during such time; and no Person holding any Office under the United States, shall be a Member of either House during his Continuance in Office.

Section. 7.

All Bills for raising Revenue shall originate in the House of Representatives; but the Senate may propose or concur with Amendments as on other Bills.

Every Bill which shall have passed the House of Representatives and the Senate, shall, before it become a Law, be presented to the President of the United States: If he approve he shall sign it, but if not he shall return it, with his Objections to that House in which it shall have originated, who shall enter the Objections at large on their Journal, and proceed to reconsider it. If after such Reconsideration two thirds of that House shall agree to pass the Bill, it shall be sent, together with the Objections, to the other House, by which it shall likewise be reconsidered, and if approved by two thirds of that House, it shall become a Law. But in all such Cases the Votes of both Houses shall be determined by yeas and Nays, and the Names of the Persons voting for and against the Bill shall be entered on the Journal of each House respectively. If any Bill shall not be returned by the President within ten Days (Sundays excepted) after it shall have been presented to him, the Same shall be a Law, in like Manner as if he had signed it, unless the Congress by their Adjournment prevent its Return, in which Case it shall not be a Law.

Every Order, Resolution, or Vote to which the Concurrence of the Senate and House of Representatives may be necessary (except on a question of Adjournment) shall be presented to the President of the United States; and before the Same shall take Effect, shall be approved by him, or being disapproved by him, shall be repassed by two thirds of the Senate and House of Representatives, according to the Rules and Limitations prescribed in the Case of a Bill.

Section. 8.

The Congress shall have Power To lay and collect Taxes, Duties, Imposts and Excises, to pay the Debts and provide for the common Defense and general Welfare of the United States; but all Duties, Imposts and Excises shall be uniform throughout the United States;

To borrow Money on the credit of the United States;

To regulate Commerce with foreign Nations, and among the several States, and with the Indian Tribes;

To establish an uniform Rule of Naturalization, and uniform Laws on the subject of Bankruptcies throughout the United States;

To coin Money, regulate the Value thereof, and of foreign Coin, and fix the Standard of Weights and Measures;

To provide for the Punishment of counterfeiting the Securities and current Coin of the United States;

To establish Post Offices and post Roads;

To promote the Progress of Science and useful Arts, by securing for limited Times to Authors and Inventors the exclusive Right to their respective Writings and Discoveries;

To constitute Tribunals inferior to the supreme Court;

To define and punish Piracies and Felonies committed on the high Seas, and Offences against the Law of Nations;

To declare War, grant Letters of Marque and Reprisal, and make Rules concerning Captures on Land and Water;

To raise and support Armies, but no Appropriation of Money to that Use shall be for a longer Term than two Years;

To provide and maintain a Navy;

To make Rules for the Government and Regulation of the land and naval Forces;

To provide for calling forth the Militia to execute the Laws of the Union, suppress Insurrections and repel Invasions;

To provide for organizing, arming, and disciplining, the Militia, and for governing such Part of them as may be employed in the Service of the United States, reserving to the States respectively, the Appointment of the Officers, and the Authority of training the Militia according to the discipline prescribed by Congress;

To exercise exclusive Legislation in all Cases whatsoever, over such District (not exceeding ten Miles square) as may, by Cession of particular States, and the Acceptance of Congress, become the Seat of the Government of the United States, and to exercise like Authority over all Places purchased by the Consent of the Legislature of the State in which the Same shall be, for the Erection of Forts, Magazines, Arsenals, dock-Yards, and other needful Buildings;--And

To make all Laws which shall be necessary and proper for carrying into Execution the foregoing Powers, and all other Powers vested by this Constitution in the Government of the United States, or in any Department or Officer thereof.

Section. 9.

The Migration or Importation of such Persons as any of the States now existing shall think proper to admit, shall not be prohibited by the Congress prior to the Year one thousand eight hundred and eight, but a Tax or duty may be imposed on such Importation, not exceeding ten dollars for each Person.

The Privilege of the Writ of Habeas Corpus shall not be suspended, unless when in Cases of Rebellion or Invasion the public Safety may require it.

No Bill of Attainder or ex post facto Law shall be passed.

No Capitation, or other direct, Tax shall be laid, unless in Proportion to the Census or enumeration herein before directed to be taken.

No Tax or Duty shall be laid on Articles exported from any State.

No Preference shall be given by any Regulation of Commerce or Revenue to the Ports of one State over those of another; nor shall Vessels bound to, or from, one State, be obliged to enter, clear, or pay Duties in another.

No Money shall be drawn from the Treasury, but in Consequence of Appropriations made by Law; and a regular Statement and Account of the Receipts and Expenditures of all public Money shall be published from time to time.

No Title of Nobility shall be granted by the United States: And no Person holding any Office of Profit or Trust under them, shall, without the Consent of the Congress, accept of any present, Emolument, Office, or Title, of any kind whatever, from any King, Prince, or foreign State.

Section. 10.

No State shall enter into any Treaty, Alliance, or Confederation; grant Letters of Marque and Reprisal; coin Money; emit Bills of Credit; make any Thing but gold and silver Coin a Tender in Payment of Debts; pass any Bill of Attainder, ex post facto Law, or Law impairing the Obligation of Contracts, or grant any Title of Nobility.

No State shall, without the Consent of the Congress, lay any Imposts or Duties on Imports or Exports, except what may be absolutely necessary for executing it's inspection Laws: and the net Produce of all Duties and Imposts, laid by any State on Imports or Exports, shall be for the Use of the Treasury of the United States; and all such Laws shall be subject to the Revision and Control of the Congress.

No State shall, without the Consent of Congress, lay any Duty of Tonnage, keep Troops, or Ships of War in time of Peace, enter into any Agreement or Compact with another State, or with a foreign Power, or engage in War, unless actually invaded, or in such imminent Danger as will not admit of delay.

Article. II.

Section. 1.

The executive Power shall be vested in a President of the United States of America. He shall hold his Office during the Term of four Years, and, together with the Vice President, chosen for the same Term, be elected, as follows:

Each State shall appoint, in such Manner as the Legislature thereof may direct, a Number of Electors, equal to the whole Number of Senators and Representatives to which the State may be entitled in the Congress: but no Senator or Representative, or Person holding an Office of Trust or Profit under the United States, shall be appointed an Elector.

The Electors shall meet in their respective States, and vote by Ballot for two Persons, of whom one at least shall not be an Inhabitant of the same State with themselves. And they shall make a List of all the Persons voted for, and of the Number of Votes for each; which List they shall sign and certify, and transmit sealed to the Seat of the Government of the United States, directed to the President of the Senate. The President of the Senate shall, in the Presence of the Senate and House of Representatives, open all the Certificates, and the Votes shall then be counted. The Person having the greatest Number of Votes shall be the President, if such Number be a Majority of the whole Number of Electors appointed; and if there be more than one who have such Majority, and have an equal Number of Votes, then the House of Representatives shall immediately choose by Ballot one of them for President; and if no Person have a Majority, then from the five highest on the List the said House shall in like Manner choose the President. But in choosing the President, the Votes shall be taken by States, the Representation from each State having one Vote; A quorum for this purpose shall consist of a Member or Members from two thirds of the States, and a Majority of all the States shall be necessary to a Choice. In every Case, after the Choice of the President, the Person having the greatest Number of Votes of the Electors shall be the Vice President. But if there should remain two or more who have equal Votes, the Senate shall choose from them by Ballot the Vice President.

The Congress may determine the Time of choosing the Electors, and the Day on which they shall give their Votes; which Day shall be the same throughout the United States.

No Person except a natural born Citizen, or a Citizen of the United States, at the time of the Adoption of this Constitution, shall be eligible to the Office of President; neither shall any Person be eligible to that Office who shall not have attained to the Age of thirty five Years, and been fourteen Years a Resident within the United States.

In Case of the Removal of the President from Office, or of his Death, Resignation, or Inability to discharge the Powers and Duties of the said Office, the Same shall devolve on the Vice President, and the Congress may by Law provide for the Case of Removal, Death, Resignation or Inability, both of the President and Vice President, declaring what Officer shall then act as President, and such Officer shall act accordingly, until the Disability be removed, or a President shall be elected.

The President shall, at stated Times, receive for his Services, a Compensation, which shall neither be increased nor diminished during the Period for which he shall have been elected, and he shall not receive within that Period any other Emolument from the United States, or any of them.

Before he enter on the Execution of his Office, he shall take the following Oath or Affirmation:--"I do solemnly swear (or affirm) that I will faithfully execute the Office of President of the United States, and will to the best of my Ability, preserve, protect and defend the Constitution of the United States."

Section. 2.

The President shall be Commander in Chief of the Army and Navy of the United States, and of the Militia of the several States, when called into the actual Service of the United States; he may require the Opinion, in writing, of the principal Officer in each of the executive Departments, upon any Subject relating to the Duties of their respective Offices, and he shall have Power to grant Reprieves and Pardons for Offences against the United States, except in Cases of Impeachment.

He shall have Power, by and with the Advice and Consent of the Senate, to make Treaties, provided two thirds of the Senators present concur; and he shall nominate, and by and with the Advice and Consent of the Senate, shall appoint Ambassadors, other public Ministers and Consuls, Judges of the supreme Court, and all other Officers of the United States, whose Appointments are not herein otherwise provided for, and which shall be established by Law: but the Congress may by Law vest the Appointment of such inferior Officers, as they think proper, in the President alone, in the Courts of Law, or in the Heads of Departments.

The President shall have Power to fill up all Vacancies that may happen during the Recess of the Senate, by granting Commissions which shall expire at the End of their next Session.

Section. 3.

He shall from time to time give to the Congress Information of the State of the Union, and recommend to their Consideration such Measures as he shall judge necessary and expedient; he may, on extraordinary Occasions, convene both Houses, or either of them, and in Case of Disagreement between them, with Respect to the Time of Adjournment, he may adjourn them to such Time as he shall think proper; he shall receive Ambassadors and other public Ministers; he shall take Care that the Laws be faithfully executed, and shall Commission all the Officers of the United States.

Section. 4.

The President, Vice President and all civil Officers of the United States, shall be removed from Office on Impeachment for, and Conviction of, Treason, Bribery, or other high Crimes and Misdemeanors.

Article III.

Section. 1.

The judicial Power of the United States shall be vested in one supreme Court, and in such inferior Courts as the Congress may from time to time ordain and establish. The Judges, both of the supreme and inferior Courts, shall hold their Offices during good Behavior, and shall, at stated Times, receive for their Services a Compensation, which shall not be diminished during their Continuance in Office.

Section. 2.

The judicial Power shall extend to all Cases, in Law and Equity, arising under this Constitution, the Laws of the United States, and Treaties made, or which shall be made, under their Authority;--to all Cases affecting Ambassadors, other public Ministers and Consuls;--to all Cases of admiralty and maritime Jurisdiction;--to Controversies to which the United States shall be a Party;--to Controversies between two or more States;-- between a State and Citizens of another State,--between Citizens of different States,--between Citizens of the same State claiming Lands under Grants of different States, and between a State, or the Citizens thereof, and foreign States, Citizens or Subjects.

In all Cases affecting Ambassadors, other public Ministers and Consuls, and those in which a State shall be Party, the supreme Court shall have original Jurisdiction. In all the other Cases before mentioned, the supreme Court shall have appellate Jurisdiction, both as to Law and Fact, with such Exceptions, and under such Regulations as the Congress shall make.

The Trial of all Crimes, except in Cases of Impeachment, shall be by Jury; and such Trial shall be held in the State where the said Crimes shall have been committed; but when not committed within any State, the Trial shall be at such Place or Places as the Congress may by Law have directed.

Section. 3.

Treason against the United States, shall consist only in levying War against them, or in adhering to their Enemies, giving them Aid and Comfort. No Person shall be convicted of Treason unless on the Testimony of two Witnesses to the same overt Act, or on Confession in open Court.

The Congress shall have Power to declare the Punishment of Treason, but no Attainder of Treason shall work Corruption of Blood, or Forfeiture except during the Life of the Person attainted.

Article. IV.

Section. 1.

Full Faith and Credit shall be given in each State to the public Acts, Records, and judicial Proceedings of every other State. And the Congress may by general Laws prescribe the Manner in which such Acts, Records and Proceedings shall be proved, and the Effect thereof.

Section. 2.

The Citizens of each State shall be entitled to all Privileges and Immunities of Citizens in the several States.

A Person charged in any State with Treason, Felony, or other Crime, who shall flee from Justice, and be found in another State, shall on Demand of the executive Authority of the State from which he fled, be delivered up, to be removed to the State having Jurisdiction of the Crime.

No Person held to Service or Labor in one State, under the Laws thereof, escaping into another, shall, in Consequence of any Law or Regulation therein, be discharged from such Service or Labor, but shall be delivered up on Claim of the Party to whom such Service or Labor may be due.

Section. 3.

New States may be admitted by the Congress into this Union; but no new State shall be formed or erected within the Jurisdiction of any other State; nor any State be formed by the Junction of two or more States, or Parts of States, without the Consent of the Legislatures of the States concerned as well as of the Congress.

The Congress shall have Power to dispose of and make all needful Rules and Regulations respecting the Territory or other Property belonging to the United States; and nothing in this Constitution shall be so construed as to Prejudice any Claims of the United States, or of any particular State.

Section. 4.

The United States shall guarantee to every State in this Union a Republican Form of Government, and shall protect each of them against Invasion; and on Application of the Legislature, or of the Executive (when the Legislature cannot be convened), against domestic Violence.

Article. V.

The Congress, whenever two thirds of both Houses shall deem it necessary, shall propose Amendments to this Constitution, or, on the Application of the Legislatures of two thirds of the several States, shall call a Convention for proposing Amendments, which, in either Case, shall be valid to all Intents and Purposes, as Part of this Constitution, when ratified by the Legislatures of three fourths of the several States, or by Conventions in three fourths thereof, as the one or the other Mode of Ratification may be proposed by the Congress; Provided that no Amendment which may be made prior to the Year One thousand eight hundred and eight shall in any Manner affect the first and fourth Clauses in the Ninth Section of the first Article; and that no State, without its Consent, shall be deprived of its equal Suffrage in the Senate.

Article. VI.

All Debts contracted and Engagements entered into, before the Adoption of this Constitution, shall be as valid against the United States under this Constitution, as under the Confederation.

This Constitution, and the Laws of the United States which shall be made in Pursuance thereof; and all Treaties made, or which shall be made, under the Authority of the United States, shall be the supreme Law of the Land; and the Judges in every State shall be bound thereby, any Thing in the Constitution or Laws of any State to the Contrary notwithstanding.

The Senators and Representatives before mentioned, and the Members of the several State Legislatures, and all executive and judicial Officers, both of the United States and of the several States, shall be bound by Oath or Affirmation, to support this Constitution; but no religious Test shall ever be required as a Qualification to any Office or public Trust under the United States.

Article. VII.

The Ratification of the Conventions of nine States, shall be sufficient for the Establishment of this Constitution between the States so ratifying the Same.

The Word, "the," being interlined between the seventh and eighth Lines of the first Page, the Word "Thirty" being partly written on an Erasure in the fifteenth Line of the first Page, The Words "is tried" being interlined between the thirty second and thirty third Lines of the first Page and the Word "the" being interlined between the forty third and forty fourth Lines of the second Page.

Attest William Jackson Secretary

done in Convention by the Unanimous Consent of the States present the Seventeenth Day of September in the Year of our Lord one thousand seven hundred and Eighty seven and of the Independence of the United States of America the Twelfth In witness whereof We have hereunto subscribed our Names,

G°. Washington
President and deputy from Virginia

Delaware
Geo: Read
Gunning Bedford jun
John Dickinson
Richard Bassett
Jaco: Broom

Maryland
James McHenry
Dan of St Thos. Jenifer
Danl. Carroll

Virginia
John Blair
James Madison Jr.

North Carolina
Wm. Blount
Richd. Dobbs Spaight
Hu Williamson

South Carolina
J. Rutledge
Charles Cotesworth Pinckney
Charles Pinckney
Pierce Butler

Georgia
William Few
Abr Baldwin

New Hampshire
John Langdon
Nicholas Gilman

Massachusetts
Nathaniel Gorham
Rufus King

Connecticut
Wm. Saml. Johnson
Roger Sherman

New York
Alexander Hamilton

New Jersey
Wil: Livingston
David Brearley
Wm. Paterson
Jona: Dayton

Pennsylvania
B Franklin
Thomas Mifflin
Robt. Morris
Geo. Clymer
Thos. FitzSimons
Jared Ingersoll
James Wilson
Gouv Morris

Text for the United States Constitution provided by the National Archives
http://www.archives.gov/exhibits/charters/constitution_transcript.html

Index

C

D

E

F

G

H

I

N

O

P

T

U

V

W

Z

CPSIA information can be obtained
at www.ICGtesting.com
Printed in the USA
LVOW02s1303171216
517346LV00006B/1/P